EFFECTIVE
FLOWERING SHRUBS

MICHAEL HAWORTH-BOOTH, F.L.S.

EFFECTIVE FLOWERING SHRUBS

NEW REVISED EDITION

With forty-seven plates in
colour photography by the author

COLLINS
ST JAMES'S PLACE, LONDON

FIRST EDITION: 1951
SECOND EDITION: 1958
THIRD EDITION: 1962
FOURTH EDITION: 1970
FIFTH EDITION 1972

ISBN 0 00 214037 3
PRINTED IN GREAT BRITAIN
COLLINS CLEAR-TYPE PRESS: LONDON AND GLASGOW

TO MY WIFE
AND CHIEF COLLABORATOR

CONTENTS

7

CONTENTS

COLOUR PLATES

9

FOREWORD

THROUGHOUT this book I am out for flowers—large, bold, beautiful flowers, equal to, or surpassing, those borne by herbs, bulbs, annuals, orchids or anything else. I have no use for dowdy shrubs. These wretched things are so commonly put forward that a large section of the gardening public takes it as a matter of course that shrubs are inferior in flower to other kinds of plants.

One even hears the expression 'shrubs or flowers' and, no doubt arising from this mistaken attitude of mind, there is even a tendency to make out that Roses are not flowering shrubs, presumably because no one can deny their superlative flowers.

I hold that the finest, most effective, gardenable flowers are borne by flowering shrubs and, in the following pages, I shall do my best to prove it.

FOREWORD TO 1970 EDITION

IN my foreword to earlier editions I affirmed that I was out for flowers —large, bold, beautiful flowers—and had no use for dowdy shrubs. This objective holds good for this, our fourth, edition.

Gardening has continued to change as it reacts to changed conditions. It is now almost impossible to have paid gardeners maintaining the garden—or even regularly mowing lawns. I believe that this situation has really done gardening more good than anything. For gardening should be a pleasure. Fancy paying somebody else to ride your horse, sail your boat, play your tennis or use your skis!

As I have explained before (*The Flowering Shrub Garden Today*), after the war I had to invent a new kind of gardening that is fun to do all the time, drudgery is out. The new system works very well and the success of the Close Boskage shrub bed is plain for all to see who visit our Demonstration garden, now over 20 years old and open daily.

We must remember, however, that it is only closely planted flowering evergreen shrubs that look after their own ground effectively and that lawns are not labour-saving as they require weekly attention all summer; whereas Close Boskage beds, once established, can be left for six months at a time.

Indeed, I believe that lawns are overdone in this country. From the practical angle they are often an unusable greasy mess half the year, and from the artistic angle they are not necessarily better looking than areas of fine, specially selected gravel interspersed with both grouped and solitary evergreen flowering bushes forming an attractive garden landscape freed from the plainness enforced by convenient mowability. This type of garden is both beautiful and truly labour-saving, and in consequence is growing rapidly in popularity. The installation of the gravel is less costly than the grass, as the topsoil off the area can often be either sold or exchanged for sterile subsoil or hoggin, and only the spaces to be planted are left fertile. In twenty years the maintenance of our gravelled places has been negligible, and it is delightful to see how, after a shower, every little pebble shines clean and smooth as though a dozen gardeners had raked and cleaned it. In comparison stone paving is both ugly and dangerous.

This is, of course, "avant-garde gardening"; all unknowing, many still struggle with herbaceous borders relentlessly invaded by couch, ground elder and bindweed; mow grass weekly, snipping blind corners by hand, edging verges and weed-killing between frightened-looking wispy shrubs with alarming chemicals. Sadder still, one hears such nonsense as: "It's disgraceful! they haven't *dug* their gardens this year"; as though perpetual drudgery were essential to proper gardening. Let there be no mistake; there is nothing to prevent a garden being designed so that, after a year or two's nursing the newly planted shrubs along, there is no tedious work at all, only pleasant tending and minor tidying. If lawns are insisted on, this makes an extra weekly summer chore that must be contracted out or done by the owners.

Questions asked by visitors are interesting. "I suppose you have to cut the shrubs back to prevent their killing one another?"

The answer is no. A cut-back bush is an ugly, unnatural bush. I allow room for each to develop its natural size. Only a very few rampers are likely to kill any other shrub—Hypericum 'Hidcote' is an example. Most shrubs thrive as an interlaced community—particularly Lithospermum 'Grace Ward', Evergreen Azaleas and Heaths. For successful Close Boskage all shrubs interlace with their neighbours. All the sky is utilised by leaves, all the earth is utilised by roots, and so Nature is satisfied and the gardener works in harmony with her.

MICHAEL HAWORTH-BOOTH

Farall Nurseries
Roundhurst
Nr. Haslemere
Surrey

INTRODUCTION

THE phase of gardening which dominated the early part of this century was that of the botanist-gardener who was interested in growing the largest possible number of species. This arose from the amazing wealth of new plant material which poured in at that time from the Orient and many other parts of the world. Later, this flow waned, and, having grown and observed the new plants, we became able to take stock of their value. Selection, breeding and hybridisation then began. The assessment of the relative value of the selected forms and hybrids followed. Now, most gardeners are interested in the study of the cultivation and the arrangement of the finer products of this previous work, so that the best possible use may be made of this splendid plant material so as to form a satisfying garden.

The works of the late Alfred Rehder, the late Adolf Engler and Mr. L. H. Bailey, between them, cover the whole field of the species. The particulars given in such works of a species of flowering shrub of outstanding value can only be very brief, as all the other species of the genus are equally dealt with. The selected garden varieties and the hybrids, which are far the most important plants from the gardener's point of view, can only receive a short mention. In this book the purpose is to record and to give all possible information concerning only the most effective species for garden decoration and their hybrids and garden varieties. Hence its title.

Personal likes and dislikes as regards plants vary widely, so I have laid down a specification of what, in my opinion, constitutes an effective flowering shrub for the garden. Thus the basis of evaluation can be transferred from the realm of personal fancy into that of fact. The facts, only, can decide whether or not the plant measures up to the prescribed standard. A flowering shrub is taken to be effective if it fulfils the following conditions:—

1. It must be a good garden plant, able to grow healthfully and vigorously under conditions of soil and climate possible in a large proportion of British gardens.
2. The flowering must be of such vividness, profusion and good presentation as to colour the bush or pattern the whole with blossom for a reasonably long period.

3. The habit of growth must be such as to make the plant a decora-
    tive feature of the garden at all times of the year.

A plant fulfilling these conditions in an outstanding manner is
described as first class. There are, of course, minor complications. I
hold that the flower beauty of the garden should continue in uninterrupted sequence from spring to autumn and there are therefore periods
when the selection is more limited than at others. Under such circumstances the best plants available are given the benefit of the doubt.

The order in which the plants are described is, as nearly as possible,
in the sequence of their flowering. Thus the species are grouped by their
fellowship of blooming together rather than because they share certain
botanical characteristics.

Accuracy is so essential that I have sought it to the best of my ability.
In particular the colours of the flowers are described by the colour
names used in the Horticultural Colour Chart whenever possible.
These hues are distinguished by capitals and, when available, the number of the tint or shade of the hue, according to the Chart, is also given
in brackets. By reason of the clarity and accuracy that it brings to colour
evaluation I consider the Chart to be one of the most valuable achieve-
ments in horticulture today. The vagueness and chaos previously
reigning in these matters made many colour descriptions quite useless.

In addition to the absolute accuracy obtainable, the Chart has
clarified colour problems for many gardeners in another way. It has
enabled them to visualise the colours as a circle in which every hue has
its ordained place.

Starting at a point on the circumference with pure yellow this hue
passes through orange and becomes more and more suffused with red
until pure red is reached. Red in turn becomes progressively more and
more tinted with blue until, passing through purple and violet, we
arrive at pure blue. Blue, in turn, is gradually tinged with yellow until,
passing through green, we finally return to the pure yellow from which
we started. After using the Chart for some time a sort of "absolute
pitch" is attained which enables the gardener to state the exact colour
of any flower that he sees. A second volume has now been added to the
Colour Chart which shows abnormally deep shades and also hues to
which black has been added. In my view this makes matters too complicated for the average gardener and my hope that the Colour Chart
would come into common use has received a setback. Actually I have
found no flower which cannot be quite sufficiently accurately charted
by the use of Vol. I, except certain very dark Roses whose petals are

suffused with black. Such flowers and also those of slightly greyed hues would seem to me to be amply described by the addition of the words " deep " or " very deep " to the hue, and those of the second type by the addition of the words "dull " or " very dull ".

To my sorrow, a completely different new Chart with a new set of names and numbers now makes all the previous work a waste of time.

The plant names used in this work are those adjudged to be correct by the late Alfred Rehder according to the second edition (1947) of his great work " Manual of Cultivated Trees and Shrubs ". In cases where another name is commonly used in catalogues, etc. I have placed this in brackets alongside. By rights†, the specific names of hybrid races should carry the multiplication sign—e.g. *Ceanothus* × *delilianus* ' Gloire de Versailles '. I have, however, omitted this sign in the interests of readability and, instead, have stated that the plant is a hybrid.

Distinctions bestowed by the Royal Horticultural Society are significant as they give useful information on the quality of the plant and the date that it came to the notice of gardeners. Of the first importance among these, to the ordinary gardener, is the Award of Garden Merit, written A.G.M. This signifies a plant of outstanding excellence for general garden use, having been tried out at the Society's gardens. There is also the First-Class Certificate issued after trial at the Society's gardens. This is written F.C.C.* and shows that the variety is an improvement on its predecessors and the standard varieties. It does not indicate suitability for all garden conditions but that it is one of the best under suitable conditions. Next comes the Award of Merit after Trial, written *A.M. This is a slightly less high distinction similarly granted. In addition there is the First-Class Certificate, written F.C.C., given to a plant or piece of one exhibited at one of the Society's shows to the appropriate Committee. This indicates a fine decorative plant eminent among its fellows, but does not necessarily indicate that it is a good garden plant everywhere. The Award of Merit, written A.M., is a similar but slightly lesser distinction.‡

As far as possible botanical terms are either eliminated, or explained on the spot if they are so useful that their employment is thought desirable. Examples of really helpful words that save much explanation

† *R.H.S. Journal*, Vol. LXX, pt. 6, p. 180 (1945).
‡ For an interesting account revealing the highly competitive nature of Rhododendron Trials, see "The Trials of Hardy Rhododendron and Azalea Hybrids", by N. K. Gould, *The Rhododendron Year-Book*, 1946, R.H.S.

are those describing the way the flowers are assembled on the plant. For instance:—

CORYMB—A short and broad domed cluster whose outer flowers open first and which has the flower stalklets springing from various points on the main stalk. Common example, *Hydrangea macrophylla*.

CYME —A broad, domed or flat-topped flower cluster whose central flowers open first. Common example, *Viburnum Carlesii*.

RACEME—An unbranched, elongated assembly of stalked flowers, whose terminal members open last. Common example, *Wisteria floribunda*.

PANICLE—A branching raceme in which the terminal flowers open last so that the growing point may extend while the basal flowers are opening. Common example, Lilac.

The shapes of leaves are fairly straightforward. Oblong just means oblong with the corners rounded off. Elliptic means of the evenly curved shape of an ellipse. Ovate means shaped like the outline of an egg with the leafstalk at the big end. Obovate is the same but the stalk comes at the small end. Lanceolate is shaped like the head of a lance with the leafstalk at the blunt end. Oblanceolate is the same but the stalk is at the narrow end. Orbicular means circular in outline.

The terms for leaf-tips are a little more complicated. Acute means tapering evenly to a point, the sides of the leaf being convex or nearly straight. Acuminate is the term used when the point is so drawn-out and pronounced that the tapered sides are concave in outline so that the point looks longer.

There are innumerable other terms, but their use is so rarely required in this book that there is no need for me to use them, but a few are so convenient and exact that they are worth explaining.

A clone means one of a group of individuals resulting from vegetative (as from cuttings, layers, buds or grafts) and not seed propagation, from one individual plant and therefore identical to it.

A " miff " is a plant that, although appearing healthful, suddenly dies for no evident reason. A " mimp " is one that neither flourishes nor dies outright. Reginald Farrer invented these words some years ago and they are so useful that gardeners have used them ever since.

The " type " form of a plant is the original type first discovered and named. Usually it is the original wild species, but in some cases, where the plant comes from far countries whose inhabitants have been gardeners since time immemorial, the " type " is a garden form.

The illustrations are from my own colour photographs, mostly taken of actual growing shrubs. Such photographs are a more difficult matter than studio pictures as the photographer must cope with wind and cloud and rain. I think, however, that they give a more truthful picture of a plant's natural habit and the presentation of its flowers than can be got from pieces arranged in the studio. The colourings will be found to be correct on reference to the Horticultural Colour Chart.

In the preparation of this work I am much indebted to the officers of the Royal Horticultural Society for their kindly assistance at all times, both at Vincent Square and at Wisley; and in particular to Mr. Patrick M. Synge, editor of the *R.H.S. Journal*, and to Mr. W. T. Stearn, of the British Museum; also to the late Alfred Rehder for his invaluable " Manual of Cultivated Trees and Shrubs " and for his personal kindness in sending me an advance copy of parts of his new work, " The Bibliograghy of Cultivated Trees and Shrubs."

Acknowledgment is made in the text to the numerous other works referred to, as cited.

CHAPTER I

GARDENING
WITH FLOWERING SHRUBS

LAYOUT

WITH flowering shrubs a naturalistic layout is best. Rectangular beds and straight lines do not take advantage of the natural, year-round symmetry and beauty of the plantings possible with shrubs. Island-like curving shapes are much more pleasing.

Laborious tasks such as weeding are eliminated to a great extent by mulching, which is also essential to the health and growth of the shrubs.

Hoeing is avoided, as it destroys the feeding roots of many kinds and also the self-sown seedlings which are an added pleasure and often of considerable value.

A favourite general principle in design today is to provide a lawned glade stretching away as far as possible in a curving line with informal beds of shrubs at the sides. There are often two irregular lines of these: those nearer to the viewpoint having, mostly, lower-growing subjects and those at the back the taller species. Small flowering trees are set as specimens in the turf, so that they afford some shade to the occupants of the beds. Such a scene, in the natural style, is more pleasing to our eyes, surfeited by the straight lines and artificial enclosures of the ever-increasing towns, than more formal arrangements.

There are one or two new types of planting arrangement which I have found singularly satisfactory from both the cultural and the æsthetic points of view. They are mentioned in the chapters on species and varieties but perhaps require a little further explanation.

I have given much further study and practical experiment to the principle of having the garden landscape evenly decorated with flowers from spring right through the summer to autumn, and have worked out a simple method, which I call the 1, 2, 3, 4 system, that enables anyone to put this into practice without any difficulty at all.

Four main displays of flower are required to cover the season: number one in the period approximating to April or early spring;

19

number two in May, or late spring; number three at midsummer; and number four in late summer, which embraces July and August. Now it will be evident that if we cut down the representation of any particular period there will be a slump in flowers at that time, with perhaps a corresponding extra flush at some other period. Thus we must plant one quarter of the total shrubs available so that they flower at each of the four periods.

Next comes arrangement and I find that the most attractive garden landscape is made when the flowerers of periods 1, 2, 3 and 4 are perfectly interspersed singly. Thus Rose (period 3) neighbours Hydrangea (period 4) on one side and a Deciduous Azalea (period 2) on the other and has, say, Evergreen Azalea (period 1) in front. This system of planting took shape, in fact, by trial and error in constantly improving the sequence of flower display in my demonstration garden, which now provides a living example constantly on view to visitors at all times. The quantity of flower showing is regularly noted every week in the Journal and, curiously enough, quite soon after the principle started in operation the peak of flower was July 1st in one year, and, correction having been made, on August 8th the next and June 10th the next. Subsidiary factors affecting the selection of the shrubs are height and habit of growth, which suggest central or outside positions in the beds so that the growth starts on the verges with low types like Lithospermum, Helianthemums, Heaths and dwarf Genistas, grows higher with Evergreen Azaleas and higher still with the taller Roses and Hydrangeas, rising to the central tallest with *Genista virgata*, *Cornus kousa* and the larger Rhododendrons.

This grading of heights facilitated still closer planting to give more concentrated flower coupled with less maintenance work in weeding. For with the coverage of shrub branches and the annually renewed mulch of freshly fallen leaves weeds have little chance. Thus was evolved another useful system—that of planting deliberately so closely that the interspersed shrubs wove themselves into one another so that each bed formed one embroidered mound of varied foliage and flower. This I call the Close Boskage system. It has proved remarkably stable and almost self-maintaining, whilst the growth of the shrubs, which protect one another rather than compete, has been better than when they are isolated to bear the full force of the wind and have their roots in cold, unprotected ground.

The short chapter indexes which precede the descriptions of the shrubs flowering at each period are intended to help in the selection of suitable shrub material to realise these objectives on either type of soil.

FLOWER COLOUR ARRANGEMENTS

There are various schools of thought in these matters. Some gardeners are interested only in the botanical side of gardening and even use the adjective "mere" in connection with flower colour. Others admit an interest in colour, but are sometimes so encumbered with plants that they find indispensable in spite of their flowers being of a purplish-pink colour, that they must label as "difficult to place" any having flowers of pure and vivid colourings. Another large section of gardeners, among whose ranks may be numbered many of the most experienced and highly skilled, find a fascination in exploiting the rich, pure and beautiful flower colours now available to us. They hold that the only colour which is difficult to place in the garden is a muddy, pale, purplish pink. As this hue is the least effective in the garden landscape the simple course of doing without it provides an easy remedy.

In the body of the work, flowers of pure and vivid colourings are specially recommended. Readers will have their own views on their favourite colour harmonies.

The colour that prevents our enjoying the full value of vivid and pure colours is purplish pink. Unfortunately almost a majority of flowers in northern Europe affect this colour. If the gardener is sufficiently determined he can, however, cut it out altogether and I have no doubt that this is really the right course. Pure reds, yellows, oranges, blues, violets and purples can then be enjoyed without fear of clashes and the effect is far finer in every way.

Only bees like the Magenta colours—reddish purples or purplish pinks ranging from Solferino Purple and, going bluer all the time, through Magenta itself, Fuchsine Pink, Fuchsia Purple, Rhodamine Purple, Peony Purple and Mallow Purple to Cyclamen Purple. Next, and still going bluer all the time, we reach Orchid Purple—the colour of *Hydrangea villosa*, and the Scots Heath *Erica cinerea*, and this is just bearable, as is Petunia Purple—the colour of a bad *Rhododendron ponticum*. Then we reach Mauve and Imperial Purple which are followed by the Violets and all these are enjoyable. Anything less red than violet is blue and almost everybody loves a blue flower.

For the benefit of those without the Horticultural Colour Chart it may be worth while to describe the pink and red colours in their sequence. If we go redder from Solferino Purple all the way, we first find Rose Bengal, a slightly purplish pink, like that of the common Rhododendron 'Cynthia'; then Phlox Pink which is a rather better pink than cake-icing, and is the colour of Azalea 'Hinomayo'; then Tyrian Rose, the charming colour of the pink part of Dicentra or

"Bleeding Heart"; Rose Madder, which I would call rose pink; Neyron Rose, a warmer, better pink, and then Crimson—the colour of *Malus purpurea* and the best red Hydrangeas. Carmine comes next—the colour of *Tropæolum speciosum*; Turkey Red is, near enough, just a deeper shade of the same hue. Then comes that lovely hue Carmine Rose, the colour of Rose 'Picture'. Now we reach Geranium Lake; we are, of course, going more orange all the time, and this is the colour of the best red Camellias and "Japonica" (in particular *Chænomeles superba Simonii*). Scarlet is now reached and Signal Red is, near enough, a deeper shade of it. Getting still more orange, Vermilion follows, and this is the colour of the finest deciduous Azaleas. Azalea Pink is a slightly warmer and paler hue and is commoner for these Azaleas. Mandarin Red is an exquisite colour only attained by the Pomegranate flower, a few choice Azaleas and *Chænomeles* 'Knap Hill Scarlet'. Shrimp Red is really a soft orange only attained, so far as I know, by one or two Rhododendrons such as 'Fabia' in some forms. Thus we arrive at Poppy Red which speaks for itself and Capsicum Red which is attained by the Embothriums and *Leonotis Leonurus*. Fire Red is nearly orange and some forms of *Azalea Kæmpferi* can equal its paler tints. In a few more gradations of hues seldom found in the flowers of shrubs we come to Orange which is favoured by the Azaleas 'Farall Flamingo' and 'Emil Liebig'.

To be brief with the Yellows, we may start at the green end of the arc with Sulphur Yellow where we shall find *Rhododendron Keiskei*. Getting warmer in tone the next is Primrose Yellow which explains itself and then Dresden Yellow which gives us several Rhododendron species and some of the Potentillas. A little warmer is Canary Yellow with *Mahonia japonica*, *Senecio laxifolius*, Mimosa and Laburnum. Then comes Empire Yellow, the soft hue of *Cytisus præcox*, and Aureolin the colour of Spanish Broom, Forsythias and the tall Genistas. Lemon Yellow is now reached with *Rosa Ecæ* and *Hypericum calcynum*, and Straw Yellow—the colour of the common Yellow Azalea. Buttercup Yellow colours *Hypericum patulum Forrestii*, Gorse and *Kerria japonica*. The warmer Indian Yellow and Chinese Yellow are exemplified by a few choice Azalea varieties. Saffron Yellow and Maize Yellow begin to approach a soft orange and Rhododendron 'Goldsworth Orange' shows the latter hue. Cadmium Orange is now reached and Azalea 'Anthony Koster' and the buds of *Berberis stenophylla coccinea* give us this colouring. True Apricot follows but no shrub flower quite equals it and Tangerine Orange has only *Buddleia globosa* to offer us. Orpiment Orange is the colour of *Berberis Darwinii* and it is just one hue redder than the peel of the average orange.

SOILS

With flowering shrubs, garden soils may first be divided into two different types which each support quite a different flora. These are limy (or alkaline) soils and acid soils.

Naturally limy soils, or those that have been made limy by applications of artificial lime, although favourable for herbs and vegetables, will only grow a limited selection of flowering shrubs. Those that will tolerate such soils are always so described in the body of the work and I have been careful to include a large selection of these.

Acid soils are, fortunately, found in nature over the greater part of the British Isles, particularly in well wooded areas. All kinds of flowering shrubs will grow well in acid soils mulched with fallen leaves and bracken. So-called lime-loving plants will grow to perfection even in very acid soils if given a general fertiliser occasionally.

In gardens, such soils have often been made alkaline by applications of artificial lime. This is very disadvantageous for flowering shrubs. Iron starvation, and other shortages caused, prevent the growth of Rhododendrons, Azaleas, Camellias, Pieris, most Heaths, Eucryphias, Embothriums and many other genera. Apples and Roses can be grown, but often less well than in neutral or acid soils. The acidity of soil is measured by a scale called the pH scale. Between pH 5 and pH 6 the acidity is ideal; pH 7 is neutral and any pH figure over this must be classed as limy. Plants behave as though pH 6.50 was neutral.

Both types of soil may be again divided into sandy soils and clay soils. Sandy soils are warm and pleasant to work and to live upon. If moist enough, all flowering shrubs, *including Roses,* grow well on sandy soils which are also acid. Clay soils need much humus added, such as peat, leafmould or bracken, to keep them open, fertile and easily worked. Care must also be taken to provide drainage. If a bed is deeply dug in clay soil the undug soil surrounding it and below it forms a utensil from which water cannot escape. Shrub roots thus waterlogged soon die and this is a very common cause of the failure of Roses. Drainage must be provided and this can be a troublesome business on bowl-shaped or, even, level sites. Where drainage is available, acid clay soils grow most flowering shrubs quite well but, being colder, some kinds fail.

Mellowness is an important requirement of soil fertility. It means that the soil is so homogeneous—or completely mixed and blended—that there are no lumps of different character and colouring. Often a layer of dark topsoil overlies a pale, sterile subsoil. The layers must not be jumbled into a mixture of lumps of the two kinds. They must be kept separate with care, even though, as in bastard trenching, both layers may be loosened up and some humus may be incorporated with the lower layer. If, in this process, some admixture takes place it is necessary to fork the bed over, perhaps several times, until mellowness is achieved.

Sour soils are those which are so tightly packed or waterlogged that the soil atmosphere is driven out. The soil life, composed of teeming organisms essential to fertility, therefore cannot exist. Without them and without air, the roots of the shrubs or other plants cannot grow. The remedy is to break up such soil thoroughly and to mix in humus —not lime.

In great gardening countries abroad it is almost standard practice to improve acidity with top dressings of aluminium sulphate or flowers of sulphur—a good handful per plant (*Know Your Trees and Shrubs*, R. E. and C. R. Harrison, Howard Timmins, Cape Town).

CULTIVATION

Farmyard manure is not necessary, or even desirable for flowering shrubs. Enrichment of the soil is best achieved by annually mulching the surface with a layer of fallen leaves or bracken fronds. Owing to the fear that these may blow about the garden, and ignorance of the correct method of applying the mulch so that this does not occur, the mistake is often made of allowing the leaves to rot elsewhere first. In consequence their feeding value is largely lost. The composted, spent material is admirable as a rooting medium for seedings, etc. but, like used tea-leaves, lacks strength.

Fallen leaves may either be collected, or secured by arrangement with Local Authorities whose lorries collect enormous quantities from roadsides in wooded districts. To mulch a bed, take a full, tight double handful of the fallen leaves, which must be wet, and plant them firmly, just as they are, on the surface of the ground at one end of the bed. Do not spread them out or loosen them at all; keep them tightly pressed together. Place the next and subsequent, tight, double handfuls closely up against the first and so carpet the bed evenly until the far end is reached. Then take a light garden fork and pat down any loose places until all is firm and even. Lastly, if the site is very much exposed to wind, a scattering of ordinary yellow building-sand may be put on over all. No gale will disturb a mulch thus applied although blackbirds may painstakingly pull it out, in places, occasionally in the most annoying manner.

So long as no soil is put over the leaves few weeds appear through such a covering and if any do succeed they are so loosely anchored that a mere tweak dislodges them.

Cultivation of the ground after planting, by hoeing, etc. is not desirable and is rendered unnecessary by the mulch. Helianthemums and Halimiums are the only shrubs that I know that do not react spectacularly to the mulching system. Such small subjects may be given chopped bracken instead of leaves, however, with good results.

Bracken, cut in June before its rich contents descend to the rhizomes (fleshy roots) below for storage, is a remarkably powerful stimulant to rooting and contains many valuable plant foods in readily available form, particularly potash which many shrubs cannot assimilate in its crude state from the soil (see Mr. Colin Brooke, *R.H.S. Journal*, LXXVI, pt. 1, p. 26, (1951.) It is, however, much less discouraging to weeds than leaves are and therefore less labour-saving. If it is available, the best way to use it is to lay the fronds on the bed before applying the fallen leaves. All advantages are then secured. On the other hand when a bed is already planted with small subjects it will be found best to cut up the bracken first, either with a spade or a chaff-cutter.

The only cultivation required under the mulch system is a light and very shallow forking of the surface of those parts of the bed that are not occupied by surface roots when the soil has become rather bare just before the next mulching. This is best done by using a ladies'-size fork with one hand, with a jab-twist motion. The mulch should be renewed as often as is necessary to keep a layer of leaves from four to six inches deep over the surface at all times—particularly under Rhododendrons, Azaleas, Eucryphias and Camellias. But the mulch should be kept just clear of the stems, as if it gets piled up around them they may become soft and unhealthy.

The feeding properties of the mulch are not the only benefits. Moisture is retained so that the soil of beds thus covered after the autumn rains will remain moist all through even the driest summer. Furthermore, frost is prevented from damaging the roots and the young, emerging shoots of the shrubs, and planting can often be carried out in winter in unfrosted ground by merely moving the mulch to one side.

GARDEN CLIMATE

This subject is so important and so widely misunderstood that I offer no apology for devoting considerable space to it.

The climates reigning in the British Isles are extraordinarily varied. In America the climatic zones have been plotted very exactly and it will astonish many to find that a given zone will often cover, as a slender band, a range of longitude from 60 degrees to 33 degrees north†. Such zones have not yet been exactly plotted for Britain, so far as I know, but I think the zone extending from Kent through Sussex including south Surrey and all the southern and western coastal counties right up to the north of Scotland would be found to form the most favourable. Next would probably come a zone including those parts of the eastern counties that are close to the seaboard and also the more elevated parts of many southern but not coastal counties. Finally, the coldest zone would include the midlands and extend northward covering the remaining areas.

These zones would, however, only provide a rough guide because so many other factors operate. Katabatics, tree canopy, soil consistency and aspect can all exert a potent influence on garden climate.

The most powerful factor is air drainage or katabatics. The word comes from the Greek, meaning "to afford a means of descent". Cold air is heavy, and, provided that there is an uninterrupted downward path available, flows, like oil, slowly away downhill. Thus an elevated site with such facilities will remain unaffected by early autumn or late spring frosts. In the depths of winter the cold air is so widespread that the elevated site is submerged and quite as cold as anywhere else. At last, as the days lengthen and the quantity of cold air grows steadily less, the time comes when the high site re-emerges above the frost-line. For some while later, recurring frosts may still fill the undrained depressions below. Once spring is well begun, however, there is seldom sufficient volume of cold air to affect the high, air-drained site again.

Thus a site with good katabatic facilities has a remarkably favourable garden climate. The gardener cannot create such a climate in a low site, but many elevated gardens whose cold-air drainage is blocked can have their climate almost miraculously improved by removing the blockage. This is the only purpose for which I would even recommend the employment of a bulldozer if this were economically practicable. As I have said, the degree of cold reached in the depths of winter is no less on the katabatically favourable site. Thus shrubs which die, no matter how well ripened and prepared, when a certain degree of cold is reached are little assisted. On the other hand, the great majority of the more valuable sorts are those whose chief setbacks are due merely to untimely frosts, and these are able to grow with full vigour when given good air drainage. So decisive are these effects that gardens may be found in all parts of these islands whose climate is as favourable as those of places in the far southwest.

Another powerful factor is the existence of a tree-branch canopy.

† Dr. Rehder's "Manual of Cultivated Trees and Shrubs".

Land protected by such a canopy does not readily freeze. Thus wood-land, where the canopy is complete, does not provide cold to flow down into a hollow below it. This explains the good climate often enjoyed by woodland dells and even, though to a lesser degree, bare hollows below densely wooded heights. The gardener whose garden climate cannot be assisted by katabatics can yet take advantage of the facilities of the canopy system. To do this, admittedly, he may have to wait thirty years to grow the friendly oaks or other deep-rooting, benign trees required, or he may be able to remove his plantings into the shelter of an available wood.

It is the plants that tell us most about the garden climate. I call it "A1" if *Leptospermum scoparium* and *Cornus capitata* flourish. An "A2" garden climate can flower *Hydrangea macrophylla* and *Paulownia tomentosa* every year and *Eucryphia nymansensis* is undamaged. In a "B1" climate *Hydrangea macrophylla* vars. will fail except against the house walls, *Senecio laxifolius* is usually badly frosted and most Cistus are unreliable. A "B2" means trouble with Hydrangeas and Ceanothus even against the house walls, Escallonias won't grow and Hebes are cut to the ground every winter. A "C" climate won't permit Fuchsias of any kind and Choisyas and even Hardy Hybrid Rhododendrons are damaged and lose their flower buds while Evergreen Azaleas are ruined by late frosts in most years. This is a generalisation, for the factors affecting the microclimate are so potent that a garden may have all these climates in different parts.

INSTALLATION OR PLANTING

No factor in the life of an individual shrub is more important than the care and skill with which it is first planted out. If this is not well done its vigour and well-being are permanently affected. There is a time in the life of the young plant when a burst of energy is available and the best results are achieved when this is expended to produce new growth in the permanent position. This is the reason why the purchase of small, young plants is advisable in the case of the many species that are not what we call "good movers". With good movers, such as Rhododen-drons, the plant is so little affected by transplanting that youth is less important.

Briefly, good planting that ensures a favourable start includes the following requirements:—healthy plant material having latent vigour; carefully prepared soil conditions to suit the subject; exact placing of the plant as regards depth in the soil; well-arranged spreading of the root system so that anchorage will be secure and the main roots so spaced as to enable their rootlets and fibres to exploit a large area of soil; and, lastly, such firmness of the surrounding soil that close contact with the roots is ensured whilst such extreme density as to promote sourness is avoided.

Let us now set out in detail the requirements summarised above. The importance of good plant material has already been partly explained. Sometimes one has to deal with gnarled old plants that have been cut back and moved too often. Their energy is low; they have lost heart, so to speak. Provided that the plant is of a species that can safely be pruned, a drastic cutting-back the moment growth starts will often induce new shoots from the base that will soon form a vigorous new bush. Species that do not submit well to pruning may be planted partly on their sides and have the old growths carefully pegged down. This usually has the same result and, as a plant always tends to keep an exactly proper balance between the size of its roots and its stems, is often, in any case, more advantageous. (See p. 31.)

The type of soil required for the various species is described along with them in the seasonal notes on the different kinds. As one cannot easily change an alkaline soil into an acid one the gardener having such a soil must limit himself to the species described as supporting this kind of soil. An acid soil of good quality will grow both lime-tolerating and acid soil plants equally well. Indeed, I have yet to find a case of lime starvation with any shrub or tree of any kind growing on mulched ground. There are, however, species which insist particularly on free and rapid drainage, such as a chalk soil often affords, and these, although they will usually grow to perfection in well-drained sandy, acid soils, may fail in acid clays where waterlogging sometimes occurs.

As regards the best time of year to plant shrubs, there is no date between the tenth of October and the tenth of April that cannot be either almost fatal to re-establishment—or the most propitious moment of the whole year. It depends simply on the condition of the soil and the care taken to keep the roots moist and covered. The ideal is crumbly-moist, floury soil and a continuous light drizzle.

The exact stationing of the plant in the soil as regards depth is very important. If too shallow, the roots, unless heavily mulched, are exposed to air and frost. If too deep, the surface roots cannot get the air they require and consequently do not function properly; worse still, the basal buds cannot burst out into new shoots to renew the branch system, as many kinds require to do. Mark the point carefully, then, where stem becomes root, and station this exactly at soil level. Note that Rhododendron and Azalea roots are thus shown to require a position on the surface and accordingly cover them only with mulching material—not heavy, suffocating soil. Leaves should not be buried.

The roots must, further, be carefully spread out, individually, if they are bare, so that they radiate outwards and downwards from the centre. Friable soil is made firm about them as planting proceeds. At all times gentleness should be practised. The plant is out of its element, like a fish out of water or a drowning man, until it is re-established and able to resume its vital processes. Finally, one should make sure that the plant is really firm in the ground by gentle squeezing of the soil with the foot all round, and then apply a protective mulch at once in the manner already described.

STAKING

If the bush has a large top and the site is exposed to the wind, or if the subject is a young standard tree, staking may be necessary to prevent wind-rocking. A strong stake of suitable size is given a sharp, tapered point, and, a hole for it having been gently made with a pointed crow-bar, it may be inserted in the hole and hammered in until tight. Then a tie is made by threading a two-foot length of iron wire through a one-foot length of old rubber hose, or proportionately larger or smaller as required. A discarded nylon stocking also makes a good tie.

It is really much better to plant small " feathered " trees and not to stake them at all. They fight their way upright as the wild trees do, for their roots are often wrenched and broken by the wind so that the tree is stimulated to grow more of them and in the end it becomes firm. Severe gales with ice and snow will break and ruin many trees no matter how well staked or long established.

TRANSPLANTING

For transplanting a tree or shrub from one part of the garden to another, late autumn or early spring are the best times to choose if the subject is large or known to be of a kind likely to suffer by moving. A trench should be taken out in a circle just beyond the spread of the roots. Soil may be gently teased from these and the trench will then have to be cleared of soil again. Deciduous sorts that move well—such as Cherries and Maples—may have all the soil gradually removed. Specimens as large as a strong man may just carry, with bare roots, seldom suffer even a check if care and gentleness have been used. Evergreens, essentially, and Hydrangeas advantageously, and all fibrous-rooted subjects small enough to handle in this way, should have a ball of soil left enclosing the main root system. Large evergreens such as Rhododendrons and Camellias will require burlap to wrap up the large root-ball that it is essential to preserve, also cords to hold the burlap in position and ropes looped and thrust under the ball to provide a sufficient grip to haul them out of the ground. In such cases the stem must never be pulled at and gentleness, as always, is essential. Very large plants on sloping sites may be slid out on planks into their new positions remarkably easily. So long as the initial work is not scamped, and provided that the roots are intact within their surrounding ball of soil, there is no limit to the size of the plants that may be moved with safety. It is purely a mechanical problem. Gardeners in both Japan and America move even larger specimens than we do in Britain.

As for smaller specimens, we commonly move Azaleas and Hydrangeas of considerable size when in full bloom in the nurseries but, such is the care taken in securing the root system entire within the surrounding ball of soil, that the plants do not flag for an instant. In all such cases immediate replanting is, of course, essential.

PLANTING DISTANCES

When planting a bed, it is helpful to use two kinds of shrubs—permanent plants and temporary plants. This enables the planter to plan his ultimate effect without disadvantageous deference to immediate results and yet secure a good showing to decorate the waiting period. The permanent plants are first put in at such distances apart as will suit their ultimate development. Then the temporary plants are put in, closely filling the spaces between them. These temporary plants may be of sorts that are of little value and whose destruction later will not be regretted; they may be short-lived plants that will probably eliminate themselves automatically; or again they may be valuable plants of species that can be moved easily at any time. Common Broom seedlings and Heathers are examples of the first sort; annuals, Tree Lupins, Cistus and Ceanothus are examples of the second, and evergreen Azaleas of the third. It is essential, however, that they should be shrubs —not herbaceous plants. This is because not only do herbaceous plants spread so as to swamp the permanent shrubs but, in removing the herbs later, dangerous ground-disturbance is unavoidable in order to eliminate their persisting roots. With most shrubs, one good chop just below ground level puts paid to them and their roots may safely be left to rot and enrich the soil. This latter function is performed by leguminous plants with unusual efficiency.

PLANT LABELS

All the pure species should, perhaps, be labelled, and if they are rare it is even very desirable. But if the labels are lost there is no insurmountable difficulty in replacing them. With superior forms and garden varieties, it is quite a different matter. For every hundred persons who can determine the identity of a pure species there may be only one who can name a garden variety. Thus a permanent label is specially necessary. Metal labels inscribed with acid, or impressed, are very durable and probably unsurpassed for this purpose. A tongue of the metal or a piece of lead wire is generally used to attach them securely to the central stem. Our white plastic nursery labels last for four or five years.

Owing to the fact that the labels are attached to the growing plants no fears need be entertained that they will show up too prominently in the garden scene. Indeed, the difficulty is, often, how to find them among the masses of foliage.

PRUNING AND PEGGING-DOWN

Pruning is important in the shaping of young trees. Branches competing with the leader have to be shortened back to a branchlet, or a U-shaped double leader will cause danger. Later in life the tree is liable to split at the base of the U with disastrous results.

In general I would deprecate any but obviously necessary pruning, when an old or straggling branch cries out for removal. Apart from the exceptions, pruning should not, in my opinion, be looked upon as a *necessary routine* in growing flowering shrubs. If they are properly grown and arranged they do not need it. On the other hand with species that do not resent hard pruning a starved, gnarled specimen making poor growth may be first carefully fed and then, when growth starts, cut down with the object of growing a new bush up from the roots. If the plant is grafted or budded, care must of course be taken to make certain that the cutting process is done well above the initiation of the scion (or portion of the superior form).

In almost all cases with shrubs, though not of course, trees, the virtues of pegging-down should be carefully considered. In my view this is often much more effective than pruning. A plant always tends to keep an exact balance between its root system and its top. If we remove a portion of the top there is a corresponding slowing down of root growth. But if we bend down a branch and fix it to the ground with a peg or a large stone there is no such severe check. The sap is slightly obstructed by the bend and new shoots not only appear from that point but also, almost magically, from the base. Many other great advantages are gained by pegging-down young shrubs when first planting them. They are held firm against wind damage without troublesome stakes, layers are facilitated, the form and habit of the bush is made perfect at once, being fixed so that every branch is decoratively disposed, and the vulnerable stem is protected from frost and sun.

Among the subjects benefiting most spectacularly from this treatment are Rhododendrons, Azaleas, both evergreen and summer-clad, *Senecio laxifolius*, Rose species, large specimen Hydrangeas, Cistus, etc. Convenient pegs perfectly shaped for the purpose are provided by inverting Bamboo stems. *Sinarundinaria nitida* supplies these for the evergreen Azaleas and Cistus, *Pseudosasa japonica* for medium-sized shrubs and *S. fastuosa* for the larger sorts. When the projecting tops of the pegs are cut off above the hooks with the secateurs the bush appears to be naturally of perfect habit and form. By the time the pegs rot, the branches have become fixed in the proper positions and the phenomenal growth induced from the centre makes of the whole a verdant mound of healthful foliage.

BIRD DAMAGE

This is an increasingly serious problem, for with the wholesale elimination of the rough hedgerows, spinneys and coppices that they inhabited, our wild birds have either died out or had to learn to live in our gardens.

The effects of this have made many species highly unpopular. The bullfinch has become a pest of the most destructive kind for, bereft of hedgerow thorns and Crabs, its natural food is now the flowerbuds of our Cherries, Forsythias and Chænomeles and also the seeds in the berries of our Firethorns. The tits tear apart the flowers of the early red Rhododendrons to drink their nectar more conveniently. The blackbirds scatter the mulch off the beds unto the lawn and go all out for fruit in season and the sparrows and chaffinches snip off the primroses and crocuses as fast as they open. As a bird lover I forgive the minor nuisances but have to destroy the bullfinch whenever possible.

Black nylon netting is a useful protection that will save many bushes in all but very severe weather provided that it is thoroughly checked several times in the season. Black cotton and metal scarers are now quite ineffective. What is really wanted is an Act of Parliament to protect kestrels and sparrowhawks at all times of year. It is the lack of natural dangers of this kind that has made the small birds overbold and unmanageable.

CHAPTER II

PROPAGATION

CUTTINGS

ONE of the simplest methods of propagation for the amateur is by means of cuttings of half-ripe shoots of the year, from two to six inches long taken with a "heel" of old wood and placed in the sand box or under a bell-glass. When the branchlet is broken off the branch, the "heel" naturally comes away with it in most cases. It is a good plan to trim the base smooth with a sharp knife or razor blade so that any ragged point is removed and to *cut* off the lower leaves. If these are pulled off it may damage the stem. The cutting is then ready for insertion.

The sand-box is just a strong box about 14 to 18 inches deep, for choice, and about 18 inches wide by two feet long. Drainage holes are bored in the bottom and covered with a layer of crocks on which is next placed a layer of sifted leafmould or chopped bracken about an inch deep, then a layer of a mixture of equal parts of peat and sharp river sand about six inches deep and over all a layer of about half an inch of finer sand. " Building Sand " is poison to plants; actually, results quite as good may often be had by merely putting six inches or so of " rabbit sand ", from outside any new rabbit hole in a sandy spot, into the box. More important is the sheet of glass that is required to cover the box. As often as not, half a dozen odd pieces are used like a jigsaw puzzle held down with stones and bits of wood. When any local builder's yard would supply a pane cut to exactly the right size to make a snug fit for about eighteen pence I think it is worth while to save time and bother by getting a piece of glass cut for each box. Several of these boxes are needed so that there is always room to put in any cuttings that one may receive, at once.

The best method of insertion requires a smooth stick a little thicker than the cutting and about a foot long, and this is best kept handy by the box. The cutting is measured against the stick and the hand is slid down to register the top of the lower two-thirds of the cutting that will be buried. Without moving the hand from the stick this is plunged into the sand, at a slight angle, and the cutting when inserted in the hole will be at the right depth. The sand is then firmed round the cutting by a deep prod and twist with the stick, taking the most particular care that the base of the sprig is tightly surrounded on all sides and at the bottom, and the glass is then replaced.

The sand in the box is kept moist and the box stands in the sun where it keeps warm while the deep sides prevent the sun from wilting the leaves of the cuttings. In hot weather a piece of mutton-cloth to provide extra shade is held over the glass by a few drawing pins; better still, a frame of hessian or burlap, supported on sticks, may be suspended two or three feet *above* the glass.

The sand-frame is really only a larger and more carefully arranged and convenient model of this simple appliance. It is more suitable when large quantities of one kind, such as Hydrangeas or Evergreen Azaleas are required. In sharply drained ground the soil inside the frame is best excavated about eight inches deep and replaced with peat and sand mixture up to ground level again. To save labour, we use portable frames and lift them off, leaving the cuttings growing on, *in situ*, feeding them with liquid fertiliser as necessary. The frames are then reset as before in new positions for the next season's cuttings.

Glass bell-cloches are probably the most useful and effective of all propagating mediums for the amateur, (if unobtainable large glass jampots provide a useful makeshift) and sandy beds can be made up in both sunny and shady situations for them. Camellias, for example, strike best in shade, and softer cuttings of many kinds root more quickly when more warm and moist. The cloche cuttings usually keep sufficiently moist without artificial watering owing to the natural moisture of the soil, but mutton-cloth skirts, easily contrived by merely tying one end of this tubular-woven material round the knob of the cloche, are needed on hot days. Too much shading retards rooting, so it is advisable to shade no more than is absolutely necessary to prevent wilting, and in my experience results are notably better when the shading material is suspended high above the cloches.

For certain species that root easily from hard-wood cuttings a north wall-foot is one of the most valuable and labour-saving of all propagating mediums for the amateur. By merely digging out the soil and replacing it with sharp river sand and sifted leafmould we have an excellent propagating bed. Roses, *Kerria japonica*, Cistus, Fuchsias, Hydrangeas, Ceanothus, *Genista hispanica*, *G. tinctoria* and other species are easily rooted from autumn cuttings of firm wood in such a situation and, at a pinch, can be left to grow-on until the following autumn when they may be lifted and set out at once in their permanent situations. In these days, gardens both large and small have to help to pay their way, or at the least save some money having to be spent on replacements and additions, and a few rows of well-grown cuttings of some choice speciality of the garden will go far to achieve this.

SEEDS

The results of seed sowing are slower than those from cuttings in many instances and only in the case of isolated pure species or controlled pollination are the seedlings certain to be of value. But the possible reward of really interesting and even of highly exciting results makes it very well worth while.

This opens up the whole vast problem of plant breeding which is too complex a subject to deal with here. But briefly, it may be said that the objective is, first of all, to prevent the parent flower being pollinated by its own pollen or by chance, and, secondly, to effect pollination with the desired male parent.

There are wonderful possibilities in the creation of valuable new flowering shrub varieties at the present time. Many new crosses between species suggest themselves but perhaps the most generally rewarding are crosses between a species not previously used and a superior garden hybrid variety. Chænomeles, Hibiscus, Halimiums, Hydrangeas, Hebes, Cistuses, Loniceras and Viburnums bristle with exciting possible new crosses. One should however, I think, have a definite improvement in mind especially that of remedying the chief defect of the garden shrub concerned. For example in the foregoing list we should seek neater Chænomeles, earlier and less purplish Hibiscuses, more variously coloured Halimiums, dwarfer and oranger Hydrangeas, bolder Hebes, longer-flowering Cistuses, brighter Honeysuckles and smaller and more compact Viburnums rather than draw a bow at a venture to see what turns up. In this way the humblest amateur may well make history in the development of his favourite plant.

Where there are special requirements, further details of seed propagation are given in the body of the work under species headings.

GRAFTING AND BUDDING

Grafting and budding are more complicated, but some species such as Cherries, Crabs, Rowans and Hawthorns are fairly easily budded by the amateur and the following account of propagating Cherries can, with minor modifications, serve as a model for many kinds.

As a preliminary it is advisable to line-out young seedlings of the Gean (*Prunus avium*) or whatever stock is to be used, in early autumn when they are from about six to eight inches high. They will add a foot or more to their height during the following summer and be ready for budding in mid to late July.

The "wood" used for budding is taken from shoots of the current year, the good buds being located about the middle of the firm "wood". When cutting out the bud, the tip of the shoot is held towards the operator and the cut commenced on the further side of the bud which is removed by a clean slicing motion with a razor blade or sharp knife. The leaf is then cut off, leaving just under half an inch of its stalk in position. Next, the sliver of wood is removed from inside by a gentle pull. Sometimes a tiny piece remains in the centre. This fragment, which is said to perform the function of feeding the leaf, may also be taken away, great care being taken not to damage the delicate centre of the actual bud which will be seen as a tiny indentation surrounded by a little ridge. If moisture is seen to be glistening on the exposed surface of the inner bark the bud should be discarded as being too sappy, probably from wood too near the tip. If, on the other hand, when removing the sliver of wood the heart of the bud comes away as well, leaving a pin-head hole, it means that the wood is too hard, having probably been taken from a portion of the shoot too near the main stem.

A cross cut, at an angle of about forty-five degrees is now made with the knife in the stem of the stock, care being taken not to let the cut go deeper than the actual bark. Then, similarly, a downward vertical cut is made in the bark from the centre of the first cut forming a letter T with the top bar askew. With an ivory blade the bark is next gently lifted on either side of the vertical cut and the bud, on its strip of bark, lightly pushed down as far as it will go inside the slit. This strip of bark will now project above the cross cut, and should be cut off so that it fits snugly in below it. Now, a suitable length of raffia is taken and, starting at the bottom, just below the cut, carefully wound round stock and bud in such a manner as to draw the edges of the vertical cut together round the bud and its strip of bark, both below and above, care being taken not to cover the actual bud. Finally the raffia is tied in a reef knot at the top.

It is well to bear in mind that the success of the operation depends on the nascent life in the bud being preserved in spite of its undergoing a major operation without medical amenities. Consequently speed and cleanliness are essential and the exposed surfaces should never be touched with the hands. As it happens, the leaf-stalk forms a useful handle for the bud and this should be used exclusively. When bud-wood has to be sent long distances, the leaves should be snipped off and the cut ends of the shoots should be sealed with wax, and drying out further prevented by the use of damp packing material.

The knife must be specially ground and sharpened to a razor-like keenness; furthermore it must be absolutely clean and free from any decayed vegetable matter, however microscopic, for this might contain fungus spores.

The bud will remain dormant until spring and no further action need be taken until October, when it will be necessary to cut back the stock to about six inches above the bud.

In January, it will be advisable to cut off some grafting wood from those varieties which it is desired to propagate, so as to be in a position to graft any stock whose buds, as evidenced by their not having cast their leaf stalks, have died. These shoots should be of the last year's growth. They should be heeled in, that is to say, have the lower third portion buried in the ground, preferably under a north wall or in a shady spot free from drip. The reason for this procedure is that, in grafting, it is necessary to have the sap in the stock in a more forward state than that of the scion and by this method the ratio should be about right for this operation to be performed in March.

Having all materials in readiness for grafting, the first operation, that of beheading the stock about three inches from ground-level, can be performed. The cut is made horizontally, leaving a clean level surface. Next the scion is selected from the firm middle wood of the shoot. The large end of this is sliced off on one side, leaving the bark undamaged on the other. Assuming that the stock is about twice the thickness of a pencil in diameter, the cut thus made for this purpose would be about two inches or so in length. This length is then measured against the stump of the stock and a similar, opposite, portion of the stock cut away in such a manner that, when the two exposed surfaces are placed together, stock and scion appear as one shoot with the junction almost invisible. Upon the exactitude of this junction, throughout its length, much of the success of the operation depends. Having satisfied himself that this is as perfect as possible the operator then makes the last cut. This is an upward incision, at an angle of forty-five degrees, made in the scion at the point where the bark begins, on the shaved-off side. The cut should penetrate to slightly less than one-third the diameter of the scion. An opposite incision, that is to say one in a downward direction, is then made in the top of the stock in such a position that the little tongue of wood formed in the scion will fit into it, thus assisting in holding the graft firm. Stock and scion having been fitted together in this manner they can now be tied in position with raffia.

The method of tying the graft is slightly different to that employed in budding. The tie is started at the bottom and wound up in a rapid open spiral to the top, then the raffia is wound closely and firmly round, down to the bottom again, where it is made fast by a tuck similar to that used in splicing.

It now only remains to apply the grafting wax in such a manner as to exclude the air completely from the join, and the exposed surface of the top of the stock and of the scion where the tip of the graft was cut off. In order to be able to remove the wax easily and safely later on, in late spring, it is best to keep the non-grafted side clean and free from wax. Then it will only be necessary to cut the raffia to clear the stem by a gentle pull when it becomes evident, by the growth of the shoot, that the necessary callus has been formed.

When spring is well advanced there are few greater pleasures in gardening than watching the first growth of the buds and grafts. These must, however, be carefully tied and staked, or some incompetent bird, misjudging the strength of the union, will break off the precious shoot by alighting heavily upon it. The bud-shoots will require to be tied to the snag left on the budded stocks with successive raffia ties. They usually end up with about three ties, roughly four or five inches apart.

The grafted plants will require to have a stake for each scion firmly stuck in so that they can be secured similarly. The rate of growth, whether from tiny bud or insignificant twig is such as to appear at first sight quite unbelievable, provided caterpillars are kept away, and gives ample reward for all the trouble taken.

Finally, in late autumn when the little trees are in a dormant state, the "snagging" is done. This merely consists in cutting off the last snag of the stock to which the budded plants have been tied. A close upward slanting cut is made and the wound at once painted over with gas-tar. The young plants are now known as "maidens" and can be planted out in their permanent positions if desired, though they may well be allowed another season's growth in the Nursery.

In the foregoing description I have avoided technical terms and complications as far as possible in the hope of encouraging amateurs to try a few buds or grafts for their own amusement. In case it all sounds too serious and complicated may I say that I have, at times, committed most of the worst faults and used the wrong systems altogether and still had highly interesting and sometimes even surprisingly successful results? The fact is that Cherries, Rowans and Crabs lend themselves particularly to this method of propagation.

LAYERING

To layer a shrub, select a low branch which will conveniently touch the ground at a point about a foot from its tip. Scoop out a hole about six inches across and nine inches deep. Very gently and tenderly bend the branch into the hole so that it assumes a U shape with six inches of the tip emerging. Then fill the hole with sand and black mould mixture and make firm. For slender branches the hole may be narrower, as the bend needs to be as abrupt as is possible without breakage. The sap-flow of the branch is interrupted by the sharp bend and thus in the course of the following season roots are put out to keep the tip alive. In the following autumn, having made certain that the tip is now well rooted, the branch may be cut off where it emerges from the ground on the parent plant's side.

Sometimes the layer requires another growing season to make sufficient roots and in all cases of doubt it is wise to leave the layer in position after cutting the main branch. After the further season's growth *in situ* it should be well able to support the move.

The gardener should always *try* to propagate choice shrubs even if he can only apply the most rough and ready methods. Gardening history is full of amazing happy surprises in successful results. To give a few instances, a rare and precious Magnolia, destroyed by a storm, was preserved for posterity by one of the torn branches being firmly stuck into the ground although the species is usually hopeless as regards propagation from cuttings; one of the finest of the new Camellias was obtained merely by pressing the seed into the ground near the parent plant; a bundle of prunings of a fabulously costly Tree Peony was stuck into a heap of leafmould and all rooted admirably.

PESTS

The best appliance to kill insects is a puffer-pack or one of the new dust guns. It is too difficult to keep liquid sprayers in order and too troublesome to mix the noisome chemicals. The dust gun is always ready loaded with Derris and Pyrethrum which are harmless to anything but an insect. The ascending cloud of powder disposes of aphis, caterpillars, frog-hoppers and weevils by merely turning the handle. Slugs are killed with " Meta " baits and mice with " Warfarin ". Fungoid pests are more difficult to deal with. No really effective chemical control is yet possible against *Botrytis cinerea*. No new fungicide is better than freshly made Bordeaux Mixture but such more easily applied dusts as Copper, Sulphur and proprietary mixtures are almost as good if used often enough. (British Insecticide and Fungicide Conference, Brighton, 1961.)

CHAPTER III

EARLY SPRING AND APRIL

*Means that the plant tolerates limy soil.

41

EARLY SPRING AND APRIL

IN this time of early spring an ample selection of beautiful shrubs comes into flower, but restraint in their planting must be advised in gardens whose bad air-drainage, arising from low-lying or " cul-de-sac " positions, makes frequent spring frosts likely. A later and therefore more reliable effect is to be preferred in such places.

The choice available includes both shrubs of the highest quality and, unfortunately, cost, such as the Magnolias of the *stellata* and *denudata* sections, Camellias, Tree Pæonies, etc., and also a great number of the more inexpensive kinds.

Except for Camellias, Evergreen Azaleas, dwarf Rhododendrons and flowering trees, it is wise to keep the early flowerers to the less prominent positions, as most of them have a comparatively short season of bloom compared with those that flower later. On the other hand, the flowering evergreens mentioned as exceptions have such all-time value in the garden landscape that they may advantageously form the furniture of even the most prominent beds.

One of the earliest effective pictures of the season is made by the blooming of the flowering trees of Plum, Magnolia, Cherry, Peach and Almond. Many small shrubs flower at the same time, but the background scene of naked trees and sere old grass frequently spoils their effect. The blossoming trees have often blue sky and white cloud or, best of all perhaps, dark Pines to frame them.

The problem is to find room for these very early flowerers where they will not obtrude too much in the summer scene when out of flower. The flowering Cherries are perhaps the most effective and therefore the most to be recommended to serve also the useful role of giving light shade to some of the beds. They are more beautiful in form than the others merely as trees when out of flower and give us a second effect in autumn, when their leaves turn to fine shades of red and yellow. They should be planted well outside the beds.

Gardens with limy soils have a wide choice of fine shrubs flowering this month; notable among these are the " Japonicas " (Chænomeles), Berberis, Spiræas, Forsythias, Crabs and Cherries, Lilacs and Viburnums. With these the thoughtful gardener can contrive vivid and beautiful flower effects without recourse to those purplish-pink hues which prohibit the enjoyment of all pure and clean colours.

43

Among the **Plums** the best known are the varieties of *Prunus cerasifera*, the Cherry Plum or Mirabelle. *P. c. atropurpurea* (A.G.M. 1928), often known as *P. Pissardii*, is the commonest. Named by the German gardener Hermann Jaeger in 1881, it was said to have been first sent to France by M. Pissard, gardener to the Shah of Persia, in 1880. It forms a rounded, dense tree about 20 feet high. The delightful white, or less bold pinkish-white, blossoms appear in March or early April as the red young leaves start to open. Unfortunately, the flowering is often sparse owing to the evil work of bullfinches or to an insufficiently open position, and the leaves turn later to a dark, heavy colour. The sudden blob of sullen maroon in the garden landscape is anything but attractive in summer.

An interesting new form with pink flowers—*P. c.* var. *Lindsayæ*, was brought from Persia by Miss Lindsay and received an A.M. at the R.H.S. Show in February 1948. Also shown was the variety *P. c. Purpusii* with dark red, yellow and pinkish-coloured leaves.

A fine variety of *P. c. atropurpurea* is that clonally propagated as *Woodii*. The flowers are bolder, more shapely and long-lasting and of a blush-pink colour.

Particularly decorative is *P. cerasifera nigra*. In this variety the bolder flowers are very profuse and of a vivid pink exquisite on bullfinch-free suburban lawns.

The "type", *P. cerasifera*, is a native of the Caucasus and West Asia and has normal green leaves and white blossom of a slightly greenish cast and is quite attractive. It is sometimes used as a hedge, but close clipping, of course, prevents its flowering properly and, if not clipped, it is certain to get bare at the base in time.

Prunus blireiana (A.G.M. 1928) is a hybrid between *P. c. atropurpurea* and the Japanese Apricot, *P. Mume*. It has a purplish-red foliage similar to the first-mentioned parent but the flowers are large, semi-double and clear pink in colour and make it a very showy little tree in blossom. *Prunus blireiana Moseri* is rather similar but decidedly less effective.

It is a pity that *P. Mume* is not generally satisfactory in Britain. It is one of the most dearly loved trees in Japan where its white or pink blossom often bursts from the bare boughs while snow is still on the ground. Over here, it usually flowers rather sparingly except after unusually hot summers. Possibly an aged plant in poor soil might flower more effectively. It was reported to be free-flowering at Mr. J. C. Williams' famous garden at Caerhays in the West Country, and well-flowered branches were exhibited by Messrs. Hillier in 1948, so it should be worth trying in the South wherever Bullfinches are scarce.

Before we leave the Plums, mention must be made of the double-flowered form of our native Sloe, *P. spinosa* var. *plena* (A.M. 1950)

This is a most attractive, dense little bush that does well in even the most exposed positions. According to J. W. Bean ("Trees and Shrubs Hardy in the British Isles", Vol. II, p. 253) it seems first to have appeared spontaneously at Tarascon. It is specially worth noting for gardens whose limy soil precludes the growing of many choicer early flowering shrubs.

Another ultra-hardy shrub that is capable of giving a good account of itself anywhere may be mentioned here.

Mahonia Aquifolium (A.G.M. 1930) is one of the old standbys that one cannot leave out. Though it lacks the bold, arresting architecture of the winter-flowering *M. japonica* and *M. nepaulensis*, it is such a useful, ultra-hardy, evergreen ground-coverer, so free with its fragrant Canary Yellow racemes in April or earlier, and so accommodating, whether the soil be limy or acid, that it finds a place in almost every garden.

It is particularly valuable on an alkaline (or limy) soil, where fewer flowering evergreens are available to furnish the ground with an ever-green covert from which the stronger-growing deciduous shrubs may emerge. A little extra feeding may be necessary in such cases, but the difference in the winter attractiveness of the garden scene is so great that it is worth quite a lot of trouble. In fact I would go so far as to say that on such soils the larger number of deciduous shrubs that have to be grown make it necessary to carpet the ground with such evergreen carpeters as *M. Aquifolium*, Periwinkles, etc. if the winter appearance of the garden is not to be highly bleak and depressing. In autumn many of the Mahonia's leaves turn red or purple and thus add to the season-able décor of the garden.

M. Aquifolium can be increased by dividing up and replanting old plants and by seed which often gives hybrids where other species are also grown. Sometimes a fungus (*Puccinia mirabilissima*)† attacks the plant with a rust disease which has a disastrous effect.

There are a number of varieties:—

M. A. magnifica, a tall form up to eight feet high and very decorative indeed.

M. A. Moseri, a low growing bushy form with particularly richly coloured autumn foliage. Regrettably difficult to propagate, it is one of the rarer and more beautiful evergreen shrubs for foliage effect.

M. A. undulata, a tall form with crenulated foliage, very free-flowering.

† The late Mr. L. de Rothschild, R.H.S. Conference, " Ornamental Flowering Trees and Shrubs ", 1938.

Two allied species, *M. nervosa* and *M. repens* are rather rare, they are foot-high miniatures of *M. Aquifolium* in appearance and so restrained that they are even suitable for small rock gardens.

M. japonica, cultivated in Japan, is a striking evergreen of perhaps eight or ten feet, with foot-long spiny, pinnate evergreen leaves and drooping racemes of fragrant yellow flowers in February. It is reasonably hardy. It is a shrub of all-the-year-round decorative value as a foliage shrub of the highest order. Shrubs of this class are seldom given full value in modern plantings, boldly displayed as specimens near important paved areas where they give character and atmosphere to the composition. The winter leaves are often vividly tinted with red and yellow.

M. Bealei, a related species from China with upright, shorter, less fragrant panicles, is often considered to be hardier, if slightly less decorative in flower and less freely branching.

M. B. var. *hyemalis* is by some considered a superior form of the last-named, by others a form of *M. japonica*. When seedlings are grown from either type they appear with all sorts of inflorescences.† The important point is that, whether they are forms or species, certain superior individuals of fine flower and habit are clonally propagated by specialist nurserymen and, quite rightly, they charge more for these more troublesome items than for more seedling forms.

The queer "dragon-leaf" foliage and winter-flowering habit make the Mahonias look out-of-place in the well-planned flowering shrub bed. They demand specimen or "solitaire" positions. Then one enjoys rather than resents the alien look. Their verdure relieves admirably, for example, those grim black asphalt yards that are too often seen.

These Mahonias are not particular as to soil, moderately limy ones being quite acceptable. Some shelter from the worst of the winter winds is desirable to give a chance for the untimely flowers to expand. Propagation is not easy for the amateur without heated propagating frames, but if seed is ripened it should be sown with care in small pots as these plants suffer severely in moving.

The **Periwinkles,** without being vividly effective at a distance are useful, hardy, easy-going, low, evergreens with delightful, if often rather sparse and shy flowers that are prepared to make the most of any rough bank that we care to give them. On the other hand, if good forms are given a sunny position in well-worked soil they bloom much more freely and soon provide a pleasing carpet seldom without flowers all summer long. In these days a labour-saving carpeter of this kind is

† Mr. R. D. Trotter, R.H.S. Shrub Conference, 1938.

invaluable. They are humble cousins of the Oleander being members of the tropical Dogbane family, but our Periwinkles have no ill effect on dogs. They will grow well on limy soils where they may take the place of the Heaths and Evergreen Azaleas.

Vinca major, the Greater Periwinkle, is a trailing, foot-high evergreen from south Europe with blue flowers about an inch and a half across from late April or early May onwards. Once planted in good soil it can look after itself and will be found very useful for rough banks where, with an annual trim-over in early spring, it will furnish the ground attractively for many years.

Vinca minor, the Lesser Periwinkle, is more responsive to good cultivation and an even better plant for carpeting purposes and a very charming little thing indeed, worthy of more careful attention by planters. It often starts flowering as early as March and continues more sparsely all summer. There are varieties with white, pale blue, deep blue, violet and purple flowers and these make a delightful effect mingled together. Owing to the fact that almost any piece will root, with care, and that it spreads freely, rooting as it goes, it is advantageous to buy a few plants of the best and most vivid colour forms obtainable. Even the Lesser Periwinkle is, of course, too invasive for rock gardens where alpines are cultivated but it is quite satisfactory as a six-inch evergreen carpeter among the stronger shrubs. It grows quite well even in chalky and shady places and I have seen it, beautiful, about the boles of great oaks in the woodland, but its flowering is less whole-hearted there than in sunnier places. It is the ideal ground-cover.

Some named varieties are:—

V. minor "Bowles var." in colour Hyacinth Blue (H.C.C. 40/1). Flowers one and a half inches across.

V. m. atropurpurea, purple flowers.

V. m. azurea, sky-blue flowers.

V. m. alba, white flowers.

There are also several varieties with doubled flowers or variegated foliage.

The runners do not flower, so if the plants are put in 6 inches apart and cut back in midwinter spectacular massed flowering can be achieved.

Propagation is easily done at any time by detaching rooted pieces.

Vividly effective in flower, the **Forsythias** are an easygoing family very commonly planted.

Forsythia Giraldiana, from China, is one of the first to open its very pale yellow flowers and has a stronger and more shapely habit of growth than the commoner sorts, attaining about six feet in height.

In March, *F. ovata*, from Korea, often precedes it in opening its pale amber-yellow flowers, produced on a bush of lower stature and more shapely form than any. It was introduced by E. H. Wilson in 1918 and is said to be the hardiest of all the Forsythias.

Another Korean, *F. viridissima*, has a more upright habit and the bright yellow flowers have a greenish cast. The variety *koreana* is said to be superior, another—var. *bronxensis*—is a dwarf only a foot high.† Var. *elegantissima* is a good form.

F. suspensa, from China, with its flopping habit, is somewhat untidy, but the variety *Sieboldii* carries the trait so far that it has a certain attractiveness when hanging down over a cliff or draping an arbour. The flowers are Aureolin Yellow (H.C.C. 3/2).

F. s. atrocaulis is a fine and distinct variety with a more upright habit, blackish bark and large, less profuse, Primrose Yellow flowers boldly presented.

The most effective Forsythias are undoubtedly *F. intermedia* var. *spectabilis* and the more massive improved sport of this, 'Beatrix Farrand', having large Lemon Yellow flowers. If pruned after flowering to encourage new shoots the latter will often flower all along their length in a most spectacular manner. 'Lynwood' has extra large flowers.

All these Forsythias can be struck from cuttings very easily indeed, and grow well in any soil in a sunny position. They are especially valuable for gardens on limy soils.

Many of the Forsythias are highly effective when in flower, if protected with nylon netting. So much so that they are amply prominent when in flower even when placed in out-of-the-way positions in the background. These are the places to put them, for delightful as they are when in flower they are very dull and ugly bushes for the rest of the year. Care in arranging a lively and gay colour association is very well rewarded, though seldom seen; the unrelieved yellows are too startling alone. A groundwork of blue Periwinkles or the deep blue herb, *Pulmonaria angustifolia*, and contrasts with the soft orange of *Chænomeles japonica* and the white blossoms of the flowering Plums, the Yulan, the Sloe or the Spring Cherry and the softer yellow of the pollen-bearing, male form of the Pussy Willow (*Salix caprea*) and other early flowerers can afford novel and striking arrangements of great charm.

Another "ironclad" is *Ribes sanguineum*, the **Flowering Currant,** with flowers that appear a somewhat muddy pink that is difficult to

Magnolia mollicomata

Rhododendron venustum Jacksonii

Camellia japonica ' Adolphe Audusson '

Rhododendron lacteum

place near the purer and more vivid colours advocated, though actually
it is Rose Madder (H.C.C. 23/2) with Crimson buds. It was introduced
by David Douglas when collecting in western North America for the
old Horticultural Society in 1836. The var. *splendens*, having Crimson
flowers, is somewhat brighter, if less vigorous, and received the Award
of Garden Merit in 1928. 'Pulborough Scarlet' is extra good.

While we are still in the beginning of springtime we may consider
one of the earliest flowering sections of the **Magnolia** family. This is
that centred about *Magnolia stellata*, all having somewhat strap-
shaped petals and sepals (collectively sometimes called tepals) and coming from Japan. They are barely effective enough for the small garden.

Magnolia Kobus (A.G.M. 1936) is a tree said to be up to seventy
feet high in its native forests of Japan and, according to Alfred Rehder,†
it is the hardiest of the Asiatic Magnolias. It does not usually flower at
all until it is eight to nine feet in height. The northern form, *var.
borealis* is, however, a remarkably fast grower and makes a fine shapely
tree that is particularly fine when grown as a standard and much
superior to the "type" form. The larger trees in this country are
seldom more than thirty or forty feet in height and this appears to be
the maximum size that it can be expected to attain here. The flowering
time, late March or early April, is a dangerous one and the pure white
fragrant flowers, about four inches across, with thin narrow tepals,
are easily damaged by strong winds and may be destroyed overnight
by five or six degrees of frost. Unlike the other Japanese species, *M.
Kobus* will grow on limy soils.

M. salicifolia (A.G.M. 1941) is rather similar in flower. There are
two forms—the "type", which is the most handsome of the two, and
the variety *fasciata* which has a somewhat besom-like habit. The flowers
are produced on quite small trees and the willow-like leaves have a
lemon-verbena scent when crushed. It is one of the most desirable small
trees for the garden but is now scarce in commerce.

M. stellata (A.G.M. 1923) is the most valuable of the theee for really
small gardens, perhaps, as it not only flowers freely when very small
but remains a low bush for many years in most soils, although it may
ultimately reach ten or twelve feet in height. Like the other members of
the section, the flowers, with ten or more rather strap-shaped tepals
(petals and sepals) are a peculiarly pure white. This Magnolia was
brought from Japan in 1862 by Dr. George R. Hall who gave it to
Mr. S. B. Parsons of Flushing, Long Island, who distributed it as *M.*

† "Manual of Cultivated Trees and Shrubs", 2nd Edition, Macmillan, N.Y.,
U.S.A.

Halleana, and it reached England in 1877. There is a pretty variety—
var. *rosea*—with slightly rosy-flushed flowers, also var. *rubra* with pale
Fuchsia Purple flowers.

Considering the often excessive earliness of its flowering—March–
April—*M. stellata* makes a very good showing, because if the first
batch of flowers is frosted, or pounded to pieces by gales, it often
manages a second flowering a little later.

M. loebneri is a hybrid (*M. stellata* × *Kobus*) having larger leaves
and also larger flowers with about twelve petals. This excellent Magnolia
will probably become more common as new methods of propagation
are now being perfected. It grows well on chalky soils.

As regards the cultivation of these Magnolias, plenty of leaf-mould
in a deep soil and sufficient wind shelter to preserve the delicate flowers
from the worst buffetings of March gales are the first essentials. With
a very limited space available, one cannot afford the uncertainty of such
early flowers and in such circumstances much better value is offered
by the summer-flowering section of the Magnolia family, dealt with
later. In the wood-garden, on the other hand, these Magnolias and
those of the *M. denudata* section are supreme, and let us hope that
planters will soon be busy planting them in the regional gardens of
the New National Parks which should, I think, make a point of
exploiting the excellence of our climate for gardening purposes and
thus help to give future tourists something worth coming to England
to see.

Seeds, layers and cuttings (see p. 33) offer the best means of propagation.

We now come to that beautiful but much miscultivated plant
Camellia japonica (A.G.M. 1930). Introduced in 1739 by Lord Petre,
the earliest importations soon died as they were kept in a warm greenhouse. Gradually it was learnt that the plant enjoyed less warm conditions and for many years it was a popular cool greenhouse shrub.
More recently it has been discovered that some varieties are hardy out
of doors if they are grown in a really shady place in a reasonably moist
acid soil rich in humus.

In its natural state, *C. japonica* grows in the Japanese forests under
large trees. Among flowering shrubs of unusual beauty grown for
their charm as individuals as opposed to those grown for mass effect,
this Camellia holds one of the highest places. It is, indeed, also so
colourful that it is only its costliness, and the shaded and sheltered
position that it requires, that prevent this absolutely first-class flowering
shrub being used for mass effects as well.

Though there are several species, the best garden plants are provided by *C. japonica* in its innumerable garden varieties, and certain hybrids. Such is the variation of these, not only in flower, but also in habit of growth, that it is difficult to generalise on their height and appearance. On the average, a height of 10 feet and an even larger spread would appear to be about the maximum size usually attained by old plants growing under good condition. The habit varies greatly, some varieties being almost procumbent, others sturdy and upright.

The wild species is somewhat variable, there are good ones with flat, durable red flowers and bad ones with more pinkish flowers that do not open fully and soon fall off. The habit also varies, some plants being spindly and weak, others are fine compact bushes. These variations are even more pronounced, of course in the garden varieties. Far too many of these have been named so that there are now some three thousand described in the checklist. The shape of the flower is classified as single, semi-double, anemoniform, peoniform, roseform or formal double. All have both misshapen and beautiful examples, but it might be said that the larger roseform and formal double flowers are best kept under glass and that the semi-doubles have a larger proportion of shapeless, muddled flowers than other types. As regards flower colour we have a very beautiful red hue—known as Geranium Lake (H.C.C. 20). For the benefit of those without access to the Colour Chart this may be described as between Scarlet, on the oranger side, and Carmine on the bluer side (Crimson is, of course, still bluer than Carmine). Then we have a very lovely warm pink which approximates to Carmine Rose (H.C.C. 621) and there are all sorts of gradations between these colours and white and also a large number of varieties with flowers splashed with all three colours or with white.

In selecting the best garden varieties for outdoor culture we must, I am sure, pay special attention to practical qualifications. In particular we should avoid very early flowering varieties whose flowers are ruined by frost most of the time and so give us more disappointment than pleasure, also varieties of gawky and thin habit which are sure to be broken down at every heavy snowfall. Then there is the question of the adhesion of the flowers, some fall off too soon and others stay on browned and rotting until we pull them off. The presentation of the flowers on the bush needs considering too, for example the variety 'Altheaeflora' carries its flowers under the branches facing downwards; this is a poor presentation for a low compact bush, but it is going to look quite wonderful to your grandchildren when they sit under the tree! Quite sixty per cent. of the garden varieties have shapeless flowers of muddled petalage and forty per cent. open too early to avoid inevitable frost.

RED VARIETIES

' Adolphe Audusson ' is a hardy free-flowering sort with semi-double Geranium Lake flowers that are sometimes just a little too massive for the stems. (F.C.C. 1956.) The tree droops beneath the weight.

' Jupiter ' has single flowers of carmine-red with a fine central boss of buttercup-yellow stamens beautifully presented on the bush.

' Kimberley ', ' Lanarth ' and ' Takayama ' are smaller bushes of less vigorous growth than the average which makes them suitable for places where there is not room for the full development of the stronger sorts. The flowers are exquistely shaped single reds.

' Alexander Hunter ' is a slender upright grower with shapely semi-double carmine-red flowers that is also specially suitable for certain positions.

' Donckelaari ' is a husky red whose flowers are often marbled with white unless the plant is regularly fed. (A.M. 1960.)

' Lady de Saumarez ' is a self-red coloured sport of the lovely ' Tricolor ', the slightly smaller semi-double flowers are particularly well presented, making this one of the most beautiful bushes.

' Dobrei ' and ' Latifolia ' are coarser, with less shapely semi-double red flowers but strong and vigorous constitutions.

PINK VARIETIES

The most admired pink-flowered sort is probably ' Lady Clare '. Of dense prostrate habit, the huge carmine-rose, semi-double flowers are among the most sumptuous of all Camellias.

' Gloire de Nantes ' has smaller and less shapely flowers and opens regrettably earlier but it has a more slender and upright habit that makes it more suitable for a house wall. (A.M. 1956.)

Among the most exquisite of all are ' Daitairin ' ("Hatsu Sakura"), self-dead-heading, and 'Furoan'. The flowers are beautifully drawn singles of a waxy texture and a firmness of line that one looks for in vain in single Roses, with a jewel-like centre of golden stamens and petaloids. ' Elegans ' (F.C.C. 1958) is a fine stalwart variety with deep carmine anemoniform flowers that open a little on the early side on a vigorous rather spreading bush.

' C. M. Wilson ' (A.M. 56) is a pale pink sport of this and ' Shiro Chan ' a white one.

' Hana Fuki ' is a pretty, cupped, semi-double of compact upright slender habit.

SPLASHED VARIETIES

' Tricolor ' is one of the best of all garden Camellias. The semi-double flowers are white striped with pink but very variable, some being red, pink or white. The form of this with self-red flowers is called ' Lady de Saumarez ', that with red flowers splashed with white ' Lady McKinnon ' and that with red flowers with frilled edges is ' Fred Sander '. ' Tricolor ' forms a handsome, compact bush with the flowers nicely presented.

A fine formal double with similarly coloured flowers is ' Contessa Lavinia Maggi ' and ' Lady McCulloch ' and ' Lady Vansittart ' are semi-doubles that are unusually free-flowering and vigorous outdoors, eventually making superb, huge bushes.

' Kelvongtoniana ' is a vivid red splashed with white that is showy but a little untidy in the form of the flower which is a rough peoniform in shape.

WHITE VARIETIES

C. j. ' Yukimi Guruma ' is a large-flowered single white, opening flat with a bold central boss of golden stamens. Rather upright and loosely branched.

C. j. Gauntletti has large-cupped, double, white flowers with loosely grouped golden stamens, *alba grandiflora* is similar but less congested and perhaps of still better shape.

C. j. magnoliæflora. This delightful variety is well named, as the flowers have a superficial resemblance to those of *Magnolia stellata*. It is said not to be quite so strong and hardy as some, but, with me, it has suffered no damage from the severe winters of the war years. The flowers are pearly white, sometimes flushed with pink.

C. j. ' White Swan ' is a pure white, single-flowered variety with a fine central boss of golden stamens.

C. j. alba simplex is rather similar, but the flowers of these white varieties do not last long, soon turning brown and unsightly. This is regrettable as the flat-opening, waxy, pure white flowers, set off by the vivid yellow stamens, are very beautiful.

C. j. ' Devona ' has smaller semi-double, white flowers, slightly more resistant to browning.

Among the many fine Camellias not mentioned in the select list above are several that are good garden shrubs but have shapeless flowers of muddled petalage like the pink ' Fleur de Pêche ' or ' Peach-blossom ', the red ' Arejisi ' and the carmine-pink ' Preston Rose '.

Then there are many superbly-flowered varieties whose massive blooms cannot stand up to the wind and frost of outdoor life, except, of course in unusually mild seasons. ' Augusto L. Gouveia Pinto ', white-edged pink; ' Mathotiana Alba ', ' Mathotiana Rubra ', ' Mathotiana Rosea ' and ' Souvenir de Bahaud Litou ' pale carmine-rose are huge formal doubles and 'Imbricata Alba' (A.M. 1960) a little smaller but equally perfect in form are fine examples of this type. The place for these is a cool greenhouse or conservatory where, ideally, a powerful electric fan-convector is controlled by a thermostatic switch to cut in just before freezing and cut out again before it heats up the atmosphere unnecessarily. As containers to grow the plants in, earthenware garden vases, bread crocks and even old rhubarb blanchers inverted and with wire netting bottoms are excellent but at a pinch, a strong wooden box treated with Cuprinol, not creosote, which is poisonous to plants, will serve perfectly well, but the ensemble is, of course, much less decorative. In these utensils one has perfect control of soil conditions and can make up an ideal soil mixture consisting of three parts of acid turf-loam, one part of bracken-humus and one part sharp river grit. Then a light mulch of half-rotted beech leaves or squashed bracken rhizomes can be added on the surface. For watering, soft water or rainwater should be used for hard water will raise the pH and eventually make the plants sickly and chlorotic.

Camellias are in the short list of shrubs that will grow to perfection without attention in the wood-garden. The other members are Magnolias, Rhododendrons, Deciduous Azaleas, Cornels, and Eucryphias and, of course, all must be given an absolutely clean start in properly dug four-foot individual beds with a patch of clear sky directly overhead. Apart from horning by marauding cattle the chief danger is from mechanical damage by heavy snow and ice. Often this can be carefully dislodged before it breaks the bushes. Splits and partial breakages can usually be repaired with splints secured with padded ties. Plastic string is very useful for this purpose as it gives to the pressure of growth but never rots. It is easily obtainable in France but sources of supply in Britain are strangely scarce.

The garden value of *C. japonica* and its varieties is very high indeed because not only are its flowers large, beautiful, of delightful colouring and produced over a long period, but it is hardy enough to withstand over thirty degrees of frost and is an evergreen of the highest winter beauty, the shining leaves being of a rich deep green colour that is extremely attractive. It should have its place in even the smallest gardens, for every detached house has a north wall and I know no shrub that will decorate this more superbly, particularly on either side of the entrance porch. Even in the darkest courtyards this Camellia will grow perfectly so long as there is open sky overhead and the soil is made really good; and it is worth the trouble.

I find that after a hot summer these Camellias over-flower even in such completely shaded situations and have to be somewhat disbudded in late winter so as to husband their strength. In disbudding, the aim is to leave well-spaced, single buds of three sizes—large forward buds, medium-sized buds and also the very smallest and most backward. The last are the most important of all perhaps, often enabling the bush to put up a fine show later, if the first batches are spoiled by frost. In good weather this method will ensure a long season of bloom with all the buds producing good flowers for weeks on end, provided that " dead-heading " is regularly attended to and feeding is lavish.

Shade is an essential in the southern and eastern parts of Britain and a north wall has the further advantage of retarding the flowering.

The chief precaution to be taken when planting is that of removing the poor and unhealthy, lime-mortar-ridden soil usually found in such situations and replacing it with a mixture of turf loam, leaf-mould, peat, and a little of the original soil—a very rich acid loam on the heavy side being aimed at. It is also important to make sure that the roof rainwater is sensibly diverted into the beds in Spring.

A vitally important point in the growing of Camellias is regular routine feeding. They soon exhaust their soil by the enormous crops of heavy, solid flowers that they bear, particularly if these are tidied away after they fall. Not only should the spent flowers be left so that their material may be reabsorbed, but a mulch of fallen leaves should also be applied annually over the roots and, in addition, a light sprinkling of a complete fertiliser should be given. Furthermore, if the growing season is a dry one, weak liquid manure should also be applied at that time.

Camellias are very sensitive to the mineral deficiencies so easily brought about by unwisely " neutralising " the soil with lime. Iron starvation is manifested by sickly, yellow-blotched leaves and white-splashed flowers. This is curable by watering with " Murphy Sequestrene " as directed on the tin. Sometimes the yellow markings on the leaves do not disappear and this indicates that the plant has a virus infestation. This is not serious or able to spread to other plants nearby as it is only transmitted by sap contact such as occurs in grafting or budding.

In the south sun scorch is serious, in the north it may be disregarded but physical damage from heavy snow and ice is a greater danger.

Buds dropping off or flowers blotched with white are other signs of starvation. The remedy, of course, is to feed and water the plants.

Camellia propagation is difficult but with care young plants can be produced from cuttings: half-bury a slice of twig with a leaf and a bud in the axil in one-part peat and three-parts silver sand compost in March in a closed frame with bottom heat. "The American Camellia Year-Book" recommended that seeds be packed in glass jars in damp peat moss or sphagnum and kept in a greenhouse: when sprouting they are planted out in pots under glass. Good plants can be obtained if growth is kept vigorous.

Besides the admirable *C. japonica* there are a number of other species and hybrids whose charms should be exploited by those with favourable gardens.

C. reticulata is a Chinese garden variety of great beauty, with crimped, semi-double, crimson flowers 6 inches across. It is, unlike *C. japonica*, not really hardy enough for any but exceptionally warm gardens, though superb, perhaps unbeatable, as a shrub for a cold house where the worst of the frost can just be kept off. The wild form was only fairly recently found by the famous plant collector, George Forrest. It has single flowers, but half the size; unfortunately it does not appear to be any hardier than the garden variety. In the mild western coastal area of Britain, from Dorset to the north of Scotland, *C. reticulata* often does well on a south wall. The wood is well ripened and flowering is particularly free. In the south and east such a position would probably get too much sun heat.

A number of previously unknown garden varieties of this species from temple gardens in Yunnan are described and illustrated in the R.H.S. Report on the Camellia and Magnolia Conference 1950, p. 13 *et seq*. Some of these may be available in years to come.

A fine seedling of the wild form, *C. r.* var. *superba* was raised by Mr. C. Williams of Caerhays. It has eight to ten wide-spreading, vivid Carmine petals, the flower being four inches across; Illustrated in colour, *R.H.S. Journal*, Vol. LXXIV, Pt. 4, t. 41.

C. saluenensis, found by George Forrest in Yunnan in 1917, has small, but often shapely, pale rose flowers, in the forms generally obtainable in this country. It first flowered at the late Mr. J. C. Williams' famous garden at Caerhays. It is so free-flowering that "eight or nine flowers may be found on a shoot only six to eight inches long",[†] and the buds may continue to open in mild spells from January to April. It is noticeably hardier than *C. reticulata* and I have had a plant on an exposed slope seldom much damaged by frost for some years, so far as either the flower buds or the foliage is concerned, but the flowers are often spoiled, as they appear in March or early April. Seedling forms vary greatly:

[†] Lord Aberconway, C.B.E., V.M.H., "Ornamental Flowering Trees and Shrubs", p. 224, R.H.S., 1938.

some have flowers that open out flat, while other, undesirable forms never open their flowers properly. Some present their flowers beautifully in attractively massed sprays, others have them partly concealed. It is therefore important to select when in bloom.

Hybrids have been bred at Caerhays between *C. saluenensis* and the hardy *C. cuspidata* which has small white flowers, and also with *C. japonica*.

The first-mentioned cross produced the beautiful white-flowered semi-single *C.* 'Cornish Snow'. The result of the latter cross, *C. Williamsii* var. 'J. C. Williams' (A.G.M. 1949) is a plant of outstanding beauty, unusual hardiness and great freedom of flower which will surely be one of the elect garden shrubs of the future. 'J. C. Williams' is not only free-flowering to an extraordinary degree, and over a period of several weeks, but has the merit of dropping the beautifully formed pink flowers as soon as they begin to fade. Thus the shrub always looks neat and tidy, and has a hardy nature which enables it to withstand zero temperatures, at any rate against a wall, and which should make it possible to grow it anywhere in England. Cultivation, of course, has got to be good, but such a fine thing is worth every care. It strikes fairly easily from cuttings. Other hybrids by the same raiser are described in *R.H.S. Journal*, LXXIV, Pt. 8, p. 348 (1949).

One of the most widely acclaimed is C.W. var. ' Donation ' (A.G.M. 1958). This is a rather thin shrub with large, loose, double, pale bluish-pink (Tyrian Rose) flowers and is a cross between *C. saluenensis* and *C. j.* 'Donckelaari'. A very good garden climate or a sheltered, moist wood-garden is needed to preserve this rather fragile shrub. The best quality of ' Donation ' is, I think, its free-flowering nature—even as a small plant—and its readiness to strike from cuttings.

The very early-flowering habit of these Camellias (January, February, March or early April), however, leads me to doubt their being likely ever to supplant entirely the later-flowering and hardier varieties of *C. japonica*, which are really good garden plants.

C. Sasanqua is really a winter-flowering species, with single or double pink or crimson, slightly fragrant flowers, that is sometimes seen. I confess I am pained rather than pleased by these unseasonable, miserable efforts and though a good form is effective enough to be well worth while in a "cold house", it has always appeared to me a pathetic sight outdoors as it struggles to open its flowers amid the prevailing icy blasts. Some of the older varieties are apparently much less free-flowering than the more recently imported forms, but ' Hiryu ', a fine double crimson and ' Crimson King ', single, red, are superb.

An interesting allied, Chinese species is *C. oleifera* with pale green

† *R.H.S. Journal*, Vol. LXXIII, p. 283 (1948).

leaves and upright habit. The shapely, four-inch, single white flowers, slightly rosy in the bud, have a particularly sweet scent and last well on the plant or when cut. They open during early winter making this a very desirable shrub for a glassed-in veranda or a cold house. In very mild districts it may be grown outdoors. Almost extinct at one time it is now available at nurseries.

The cultivation requirements of these other Camellias are similar to those described for *C. japonica*.

Propagation, except in the case of *C. reticulata*, is somewhat easier as seeds are more freely produced and cuttings strike rather more readily.

Before Camellias went out of fashion, at the time of the first world war, a number of hybrids were bred by skilled head gardeners between *C. reticulata* and *C. japonica* varieties. Most of these, being conservatory plants, have probably been lost. Now that Camellias are again in fashion, the cross is now being repeated, although later flowering and greater hardiness would, I think be more valuable than a mere increase in the size of the individual flowers. In colour, shape of flower and hardiness, *C. japonica* is not approached by any species that I have seen.

One of the most beautiful in flower of all early-spring-flowering shrubs that will grow in a limy soil is the dwarf **Japanese Quince**, *Chænomeles japonica* (A.G.M. 1943). It is another victim of name-changing. First Thunberg, the Swedish Botanist, to whom we owe the discovery of so many lovely Japanese plants, found it in 1784 and named it *Pyrus japonica*, but the plant was not introduced into Britain until 1869 when it was imported by Messrs. Maule of Bristol and, in 1874, was distributed as *P. Maulei*, this name being given it by Dr. Masters of the *Gardeners' Chronicle*. The tall-growing commoner species vulgarly known as "the Japonica" had meanwhile usurped the name of *P. japonica*. More recent work by Alfred Rehder has shown that these red-flowered shrubs are sufficiently distinct to require a separate genus, so Lindley's original suggested name is now to be followed and the common Quince, alone, comes under Cydonia and the subject of this note becomes *Chænomeles japonica*.† Chænomeles means, literally, split apple. At the same time, as the form imported was much superior to the average wild form, we should add the varietal name ' Maulei ' to attain a still clearer definition of the original type as propagated. This dwarf Japanese Quince, then, is a low-growing cousin of the taller and commoner plant. Its hybrids with the latter, *C. speciosa*

† *R.H.S. Journal*, LXVI, Pt. 12 (Dec. 1941), p. 451.

(*C. lagenaria* Rehder), which are known as *C. superba*, include some of the most attractive of all deciduous early-flowering shrubs. These Quinces are not so often seen, used for massed effects, as they deserve to be, though they are definitely in the first class. The habit of growth of the "type" species—*C. japonica*, itself, is bushy and spreading, seldom exceeding four feet high. The flowers, over an inch across, are a soft orange-scarlet (Fire Red, H.C.C. 15/2) and borne on year-old and older shoots, and well displayed in good forms. The fruits are apple-like, yellow flushed with red and, unlike those of the taller species, make good jelly. As this Quince will grow in limy soil it is of the highest value to those whose gardens suffer from this drawback, for it provides a large part of the brilliant colour range of the Azaleas and Camellias.

On such soils the gardener will be well rewarded by trying all the varieties and giving them the careful attention that the gardener on acid soil will give to the great races of garden shrubs mentioned above.

The flowering time is unfortunately rather too early, both from the weather point of view and the æsthetic. The garden is still just too bare of leaves to do justice, as a background, to the effect. This is also particularly likely to be spoiled at this time of year by masses of purplish pink from the blossom of Almonds, Plums and Peaches. Thus, to give the Japanese Quinces full play with their vivid and lovely colourings, only white-flowered blossoming trees should be allowed near them and an occasional Forsythia and blue-violet Periwinkles. Where Camellias can also be grown the soft orange-red of the Chænomeles forms the perfect bridge between Forsythia yellow and Camellia Geranium Lake.

C. j. alpina (*Sargentii*) is a dwarf mountain form with smaller and more cup-shaped flowers less orange in hue. It is useful where a small shrub of alpine character is required but is less showy than others.

C. j. alba has white flowers that often fail to open fully on the more exposed parts of the bush if the weather is unusually cold and windy.

C. j. 'Naranja' has large orange flowers and a very dense, dwarf habit.

C. j. atrosanguinea has dark red flowers with purplish calices.

As regards cultivation *C. japonica* requires an open, sunny position that is yet sheltered from the bite of north-east winds. I find that it grows quite well in peat though less vigorously than in a good turf loam, which appears to be the ideal soil for it. Layers and seeds afford an easy means of increase for the amateur, seeds, in particular, often yielding fine plants which will flower in their second year in many cases.

Quite outstanding as first-class flowering shrubs of medium size are the varieties of the hybrid race **Chænomeles superba** (*C. japonica*

× *speciosa*). In an open position they make shapely bushes four or five feet high.

One of the finest of all the deciduous flowering shrubs that can be grown on a limy soil is, in my opinion, a well-grown bush of *Chænomeles superba* var. 'Knap Hill Scarlet'. A shapely shrub of five feet, or eight feet on a wall, it flowers with amazing freedom, well out to the tips of the branches. These flowers open fully and are 2 inches or more across and exquisitely shaped, with five petals and perfect centres filled with undistorted golden stamens. Opening a paler tint, the flowers mature to the full glory of that most lovely hue, Mandarin Red (H.C.C. 17). I have counted as many as twenty-eight of these on a 6-inch length of stem. They open about ten days later than those of most of the other varieties. Perhaps because it is rather slow-growing at first, this is one of the most undeservedly neglected of the finer varieties of common flowering shrubs. When cut and brought indoors the flowering sprays are indeed superb and last for ten days or more. Should a branch wilt, cutting off 2 inches or so of stem *under the water* with secateurs (care being taken never to allow air to come into contact with the cut end) will almost invariably cause the flowers to freshen up again completely. It is a fine example of a hybrid carrying the best qualities of both parents without their faults. (A.M. 1961.)

C. s. Simonii, another fine hybrid, is more frequently seen and received the Award of Garden Merit in 1924. The flowers are of various shapes and sizes—mostly about 1½ inches across, and deep Vermilion (H.C.C. 18/1) in colour. It has been described as " the best coloured of any in the group "† but I still think that ' Knap Hill Scarlet ' is an even more lovely colour and shape, and that it makes a finer show of colour at a distance than *Simonii*. None the less, this is a first-class shrub of good habit and high decorative qualities that is all too seldom planted.

C. s. rosea is described as having " scarlet flowers with usually six to eight petals and larger and broader leaves ". (A Rehder.)

C. s. ' Incendie ' is a new variety from Messrs. Lemoine, having Vermilion double flowers and deep green leaves tipped with red. It is of rather low and compact habit.

C. s. ' Rowallane ' makes a compact bush about 2½ feet high by three or four feet across with showy vivid red flowers. (A.G.M. 1957.)

C. s. ' Phylis Moore ' has a shapely, double flower 2 inches across, in colour Scarlet of the full hue, and is a superb, but somewhat straggling, variety for those who prefer double flowers. It is admirable for a buttonhole. Alas, it will not strike from cuttings.

† "Some Good Garden plants", R.H.S. 1946, p. 16, and photograph facing.

C. s. ' Knap Hill Radiance ' is a fine new variety with single flowers of Geranium Lake (H.C.C. 20) of similar size on a big strong plant favouring *C. speciosa* in size and habit.

C. s. ' Yae Gaki ' is dwarf with large and lovely double rosettes of Chinese Coral.

C. s. ' Rubra grandiflora ' makes a compact, low bush with large red flowers. ' Hollandia ' and ' Elly Mossel ' are similar.

A number of new varieties of *C. superba* have been bred in California by Messrs. W. B. Clarke of San José and the following is a selection:—

C. s. ' Coral Sea ' has flowers of Chinese Coral (H.C.C. 614/1) to Mandarin Red. They are described as being often $1\frac{3}{4}$ inches across and the plant is of moderate growth with small leathery leaves.

C. s. ' Crimson and Gold ' is a small plant with large cupped flowers of a blood-red colour with prominent golden stamens, already obtainable in England.

C. s. ' Early Appleblossom ' has pink and white flowers that open early.

C. s. ' Early Orange ' is a medium-sized bush with very freely borne, cupped, orange flowers. It flowers earliest of all, often being in bloom in November and December in California.

C. s. ' Juliet ' is a variety with flowers of a soft salmon colour.

C. s. ' Stanford Red ' has large flowers 2 inches in diameter opening flat and in colour Geranium Lake. It is almost thornless. Already obtainable in England.

C. s. ' Pink Lady ' has clear pink flowers that open early.

C. s. ' Ruby Glow ' has flowers of Currant Red.

C. s. ' Snow ' has large white flowers $2\frac{1}{2}$ inches across opening late in the season. It favours *C. speciosa* in habit.

Most of the above varieties will shortly be obtainable in England.

These hybrids vary somewhat in habit, a few being inclined to make larger bushes 6 feet or more across. Pruning, so as to secure ripened wood set with flowering spurs, is desirable, and pegging-down the outer branches and removing over-crowded young shoots encourages freedom of flower, but bullfinches are the bane of these lovely shrubs.

These Quinces can be propagated by spreading out and earthing-up branches and so inducing them to form roots above the main stem, by layering, or by seed.

A new race of hybrid Chænomeles has also been bred of late years by Messrs. W. B. Clarke of San José in California. It started with a seedling form of *C. superba* which was named ' Coral Glow ' and this was crossed with *C. cathayensis* (Schneider). This central Chinese species is considered to be a variety of *C. speciosa* by most authorities, but to the gardener it appears to be quite a distinct species, and Rehder stated that it is much less hardy than either of the other species†. In its typical form it is not an attractive plant in this country and has little resemblance to *C. speciosa*. It is a coarse-growing, gaunt, erect, spiky shrub of Crabapple-like appearance, flowering on young laterals, with narrow leaves and unexciting pale flowers blotched with pink. Most of us discarded it years ago. But Messrs. Clarke were clever enough to see the advantages of the characteristic of flowering on young lateral branches as opposed to that of flowering only on old wood as in *C. speciosa*. The cross mentioned was accordingly made and from 1939 onwards the following fine hybrids appeared. They are large thorny shrubs flowering very freely from the laterals and often produce three crops of bloom followed by very large fruits. Messrs. Clarke do not consider them quite so hardy as the *C. superba* hybrids in America, but their hardiness is amply sufficient for the British Isles. For this hybrid race Messrs. Clarke proposed the name *Chænomeles californica* Clarke.‡

C. californica 'Enchantress' has large rose-pink flowers, often somewhat unevenly coloured when first opening. It has the stiff branches with thorny lateral twigs and narrow leaves of *C. cathayensis*. It is obtainable in England.

C. c. 'Fire' has large, full flowers of a vivid red and is a very vigorous variety often producing three crops of bloom.

C. c. 'Masterpiece' has freely borne, rosy red flowers that open unusually early.

C. c. 'Mt. Everest' has white flowers tipped with lavender-rose flushing later to pink.

C. c. 'Afterglow' has double flowers of the same colouring.

C. c. 'Pink Beauty' is early, with pink flowers shaded with rose and often gives two further crops of flowers later.

C. c. 'Cardinal' has dark red flowers (H.C.C. Cardinal Red 822/1) and is one of the finest of this group.

C. c. 'Rosemary' is a mid-season flowering variety with pink to red flowers.

C. c. 'Sunset Glow' is similar, but the flowers are a deeper rose, maturing to darker red. This variety often gives a second crop of bloom.

C. c. 'Cynthia' (*C. japonica* × *cathayensis*) has large bicoloured flowers of pale and deep rose shades which mature to a peach pink suffused with buff. It flowers in late spring.

The above varieties will shortly be obtainable in this country.

† "Manual of Cultivated Trees and Shrubs".
‡ "Garden Aristocrats", by W. B. Clarke, II, p. 12 (1944).

Chænomeles speciosa (*C. Lagenaria* Rehder, A.G.M. 1927) is really
the correct name of *"Pyrus japonica"*, that well-known old cottage
garden favourite, the tall red-flowered Japanese Quince often called
merely "the Japonica". It is not, however, a Japanese plant but is
thought to be a native of China, being merely cultivated in Japanese
gardens.

C. speciosa was introduced as long ago as 1796, in which year it
arrived at Kew. Commonly grown against walls it has really no need of
such a position and is often even more decorative grown as a lawn
specimen. Thus placed, it offers free play for the exercise of cultural
skill, for its natural suckering habit can be kept in check with great
advantage and the older branches kept spurred-back and the plant thus
assisted to assume the full elegance of picturesque growth attainable.

None of the great plant-hunters appear to have recorded seeing the
prototype of this shrub growing wild, so far as I can discover, but it is
thought to be Chinese, and it has that look. Studying the plants of
Japan, China and America, one comes to form a picture of the "Chinese
look" in one's mind. The flower may be spectacularly beautiful, as
Magnolia denudata, *Campsis grandiflora*, or *Rhododendron Simsii* (the
greenhouse Azalea) yet there is a hint of coarseness, a faint, earthy,
toad-like quality that is absent from the Japanese or American counter-
parts. Be that as it may and common as the plant is, *C. speciosa* is a
very lovely thing, the "type" having flowers of a pale Geranium Lake
(H.C.C. 20/1 and 20/2), and many of the varieties are delightful in
both form and colour. In the rush for novelties, often much less beautiful, many of these older varieties have been lost. Still available are:—

C. s. umbilicata, rose pink, rather small flowers.
C. s. Moerloesii, white, with a rosy flush at the heart.
C. s. nivalis, pure white.
C. s. Wilsonii, flowers salmon pink, leaves reddish-furred beneath.
C. s. Cardinalis is a glorious scarlet but the flowers are sometimes
obscured by the foliage.
C. s. ' Aurora ', soft rose suffused with orange and yellow, early.
C. s. rosea fl. pl. has double salmon pink flowers freely borne on a
bushy plant. Also known as 'Falconet Charlot'.

It is in winter effect that both the species of Chænomeles and their
hybrids fail so lamentably. All winter long there is nothing to see—
just a few dim sticks, drab as the prevailing drabness; whilst the Japanese Azaleas and other flowering evergreens delight the eye with mounds
of richly varied greenery. Thus it will only be in a limy soil that precludes these more year-round-effective garden furnishings that the
Quinces will be planted *"en masse"*. Then we shall find the true dwarf,

C. japonica and *C. superba* varieties the more generally effective for massing as they can be backed with such evergreens as *Choisya ternata, Siphonosmanthus Delavayi, Ceanothus Veitchianus, Escallonia langleyensis*, and others, so as to give solidity and winter effect to the beds. Near the house, the Quinces will take the place of the Camellias so valuable for such positions on acid soils.

Indifferent as to whether the soil is limy or acid, cultivation is simple enough in any fairly open and sunny spot sheltered from the east wind, and increase may be made by detaching rooted suckers, by layers or by seed. The varieties, of course, do not come true by the last-named method but it is easily done, and seedlings are often interesting in their variations. Provided poor sorts are firmly culled no harm is caused.

Grafted plants are not satisfactory as a rule, owing to the natural suckering habit of the species.

When pruning specimens on walls, the young wood of the year may be shortened back to two buds after flowering, and open-ground plants may be similarly treated. Pegging-down long young growths is a good plan, carefully cutting out overcrowded shoots, when necessary, at ground-level. Bullfinches now nip off the buds of Chænomeles and thus ruin the flower effect. Many of the buds may be preserved by completely enveloping the bushes in the new black nylon netting, but mice also destroy many buds.

From the easy-going Quinces, conditioned to garden life by centuries of cultivation, we turn to a wilder genus that mostly still insists upon a naturally acid soil and a mild climate.

The **Tree Heaths** flower in early spring and though only one or two are possibly first class, according to the strict definition given in the Introduction, they are attractive in elevated gardens on lime-free soils where spring frosts slide away below.

Erica arborea, the Tree Heath, is not reliable, being sooner or later killed by a hard frost, but the superior form known as *E. a.* var. *alpina* (A.G.M. 1933) is, on the other hand, almost "reasonably hardy". It comes from the mountains of Spain and, from the garden point of view, may be considered a distinct species. Unlike the "type", which is always rather dingy, it forms a dense, deep green, plumy bush, usually about 6 feet high. The ashen-white fragrant flowers appear in early April and last for a considerable time. Though the scent is delightful, the fresh deep green of the bush in winter is perhaps its greatest beauty. Although reported to withstand twenty degrees of frost, it is only reliably hardy enough for use as a permanent foundation evergreen in the more favoured gardens. In such places it is superb in the composition of the winter scene, being one of the most vivid of the evergreens.

Chænomeles superba 'Knap Hill Scarlet'

Camellia japonica 'Fred Sander'

Rhododendron obtusum 'Hinomayo'

Daphne Cneorum

Any straggling branches may be pruned back so as to keep the bush densely furnished; unpruned bushes are untidy.

E. australis, the Spanish Heath, is still less hardy and is thus only suited to the south and west. It is a somewhat gaunt and gawky grower, but its cylindrical flowers are quite handsome, though the colour is difficult to place, being a bright Rhodamine Purple with black, projecting stamens, and borne in clusters on the tips of the shoots. As it is periodically almost exterminated by hard winters it is not commonly seen in gardens.

A very fine variety with white flowers, found in Southern Spain in 1912 by the late Lt. Robert Williams of Caerhays, perpetuates his name— 'Mr. Robert'. It is scarcely hardier than the "type" but is a particularly beautiful April-flowering Heath which received the A.G.M.in 1941.

E. lusitanica, the Portuguese Heath, resembles *E. arborea* but does not grow quite so tall. The foliage is a more vivid green and the white flowers are cylindrical instead of rounded, and faintly fragrant. It is less hardy than *E. arborea* var. *alpina* but particularly at home on dry, sandy or stony soils. The foxtails of white flowers with their pink stamens are very lovely, perhaps the most beautiful of those of the Tree Heaths and its lack of hardiness is therefore particularly regrettable. In the warm sandy gardens of the south and west coasts it is a delightful shrub, and at any rate it is hardier than *E. australis*.

E. Veitchii, Veitch's Heath, is a hybrid between *E. lusitanica* and *E. arborea* var. *alpina*, valuable because while it resembles the former it has the slightly greater hardiness of the latter. The fragrant flowers are intermediate in shape, and, though white, often show a rosy glow from the pink stalks and pistils. It is one of the earliest to flower, often beginning at Christmas time if the weather is mild.

E. mediterranea is a Tree Heath, coming from the Bay of Biscay, tolerant enough for planting with confidence even in limy gardens. Further, in some varieties, it is one of the more decorative and showy species. Like the others the flowering time is roughly from March to May. The honey-scented flowers appear in upright racemes several inches in length on the previous year's shoots and are, in the type form, Fuchsia Purple (H.C.C. 28/3), deepened by the dark anthers. This is, however, a poor colour for the spring garden. If the soil will grow Heaths it will * grow the glorious, clean rich coloured, large-flowered Azaleas and few will wish to have the garden relegated to unnecessary dowdiness by their omission. Fortunately there is an excellent white variety, *E. m.* var. *alba*, and a superlative one, *E. m.* var. 'W. T. Rackliff' which, with their dense evergreen habit and delightfully scented white flowers, form an admirable complement to the vivid

---

* With bracken-peat and Sequestrene where lime is virulent.

Azalea colourings. For those who prefer purplish-pink to white, irrespective of the cleanness of the tint, a grouping of the "type" and the white forms may be arranged apart somewhere. *E. mediterranea* is probably the finest of the spring-flowering Heaths for extensive planting, being a better garden plant than most of the others mentioned.

All the Tree Heaths seem to do best on warm, sandy or stony slopes where cold air and surplus water can drain freely away below.

Small Heaths transplant quite well, if firmly and somewhat deeply replanted, the opportunity being taken to lay sideways, and then bury up to within a few inches of the tips, any straggling, long branches. These will probably root and so provide more plants.

Except for *E. australis*, most Tree Heaths can be grown from cuttings taken with a "heel" of old wood in July. Unflowered side shoots are the best material. A number of such cuttings may be placed round a pot filled with peat and sand mixture finally covered with silver sand. The pots are soaked from below and then placed in a closed frame in full sun with the glass whitened with "Summer Cloud". Layering may be done by holding branches down into a prepared patch of sandy peat by means of a peg or even a brick or a sandstone rock. Care should be taken to see that the branch is reasonably young and that the "elbow" formed by bending it into the prepared hole is well covered with soil. In this way good plants are soon grown with little trouble.

Where the Heaths will grow another genus of the great family of the Ericacæ may be considered, namely **Pieris**.

Pieris floribunda, from the southern States, is a hardy flowering evergreen of attractive dense habit introduced nearly 150 years ago. The pitcher-shaped white flowers, in erect racemes, open in March or early April and so are very often destroyed by frost. When the weather is favourable it is quite attractive and is perhaps more resistant to exposure than other Pieris.

P. japonica (A.G.M. 1924) is a taller shrub than the preceding, growing up to 10 feet high and is more tree-like in habit; the racemes of similar flowers are drooping instead of erect, opening in March or early April, and more numerous and decorative than those of *P. floribunda*, but still more vulnerable to frost.

P. j. variegata is a variety with leaves neatly margined with white in an attractive manner, otherwise similar.

P. 'Forest Flame' is a lovely new hybrid with superb red spring foliage that turns to cream then green. Hardier than *P. Forrestii* (p. 140) it is smaller and more compact so most desirable for the small garden.

In gardens where spring frosts are infrequent, *P. taiwanensis* is even more beautiful in flower, like a waterfall of porcelain bells, or, rather, urns, but its early flowering habit is a grave disadvantage.

As regards cultivation, the Pieris really need Rhododendron conditions in full sun including plenty of moisture at the roots, conserved by a mulch of dead leaves. They may be increased by seeds or by cuttings.

The first section of the really hardy hybrid **Rhododendrons** opens in April. These are crosses of *Rhododendron caucasicum*, from eastern Europe, and are amongst the toughest and most wind-resisting of Rhododendrons and of dense, low habit. They are, indeed, better when grown "hard", being more compact and comely as evergreens and more decorative when in flower. Two that are commonly available are *R. venustum Jacksonii* "A"† (*R. arboreum* × *Nobleanum*) with flowers of Rose Madder (H.C.C. 23/2) and *R. caucasicum pictum*, "A", clean pale pink with red spots. There are a number of inferior clones often confused with these. They have flowers of dingy purplish pinks and, in my experience, are particularly addicted to bud-blast. Care should therefore be taken to secure the true varieties. (See illustration facing p. 48.)

These are really hardy and most valuable for cold and exposed spots; *R. caucasicum pictum*, in particular, revels in the full blast of the wind and provides a lovely sight in bloom in places where almost any other variety would be instantly torn to pieces. In the Rhododendron Handbook this Rhododendron is stigmatised by the letter "Y" which means "not up to present day standards in the British Isles". I think that is, perhaps, a case of mistaken identity as, owing to the invaluable sturdiness of the true variety it will, unlike too many choice sorts, flourish and look highly attractive as a flowering shrub in exposed garden positions. If only more of the starred varieties were up to the standard of this hardy variety *as garden plants for ordinary conditions*, the popularity of the Rhododendron with the general gardening public would receive a tremendous stimulus. R. 'Cunningham's White' is of similar type but is mentioned later as it flowers noticeably later, with the 'Mollis' Azaleas. These three varieties are of admirable size and habit for the small garden and make excellent evergreens for the centres of beds, providing both background and winter form. R. 'Cunningham's Sulphur', listed as Category "B"‡, is slightly less tough and more difficult to grow but has attractive pale creamy yellow flowers that open usually towards the end of April.

† "A" means "hardy anywhere in the British Isles" see p. 84.
‡ "B" means "hardy anywhere in the British Isles, but requires some shade to obtain best results". *Rhododendron Handbook*.

Any lime-free soil, to which some peat or leaf-mould may be added around the root-ball at planting time, seems to suit these Rhododendrons and young stock can easily be raised by layering the outer, lower branches.

The one weakness of the breed is the colour, which is merely pink in the early flowering pair, but this is less objectionable so early in the season, when it may be arranged to harmonise with Daffodils, Ribes, Aubrietas, Almonds, Peaches and early Cherries, and makes a fine show of massed flowers beautifully presented on a dense, low rounded bush in full exposure. On the other hand in shady places the growth is rank, untidy and unattractive. Such shade-loving genera as Rhododendron and Hydrangea include exceptional species that require full sun, and it is important to recognise the garden hybrids of these which have inherited this trait. We shall find other examples mentioned later.

At this time of year blossoming trees are specially welcome. The Almond (*Prunus Amygdalus*) is an early flowering tree whose positive enjoyment of urban conditions makes it invaluable. Much of this enjoyment is derived from the lack of bullfinches to strip the flower buds and the presence of a sulphurous atmosphere to discourage leaf-curl fungus. Being an Algerian native it asks only for a sunny position and free circulation of spore-free air about the branches.

P. A. macrocarpa is a very fine Almond that looks like a distinct species. It forms a shapely tree with large, faintly blushed, white flowers, each over 2 inches across, in clusters of about half a dozen which contrast pleasingly with the dark stems. The nuts of this species are, as the name implies, of unusually large size and, furthermore, are free from the bitter taste, due to the presence of hydrocyanic acid, which makes the nuts of many Almonds unpleasant and even dangerous.

A number of other varieties of the Almond have been described but do not appear to be available in commerce in Britain at the present time. Among these are:—*P. A. albo-plena*, with double white flowers; *P. A. pendula*, a weeping form, and *P. A. fragilis*, a form with a fragile nut containing a sweet kernel. A distinction is also made between the sweet and the bitter Almond. In practice it seems that these forms are so hybridised that it is difficult to find one definitely belonging to either type. Having noted which individuals in a large group of laden trees were attacked by squirrels, we harvest the nuts from these only. It requires a vice to crack them but the nuts are usually of good intermediate quality.

P. Amygdalo-persica, Pollard's Almond (*P. A. Pollardii*), a hybrid with the Peach, from Australia, has larger individual flowers of a rich pink, nearly 2 inches across, and massive dark chocolate-brown wood. It is a tree of outstanding quality, but it is essential to make certain of obtaining the true form which most deservedly received the Award of Garden Merit in 1937. Being more fastidious, however, it can never supplant the common Almond.

P. tangutica (*P. dehiscens*), introduced by E. H. Wilson, is a shrubby species, interesting because it is thought to be the subject of the charming Prunus blossom design of the Chinese Khanghsi vase. It forms a very twiggy bush, of grotesquely angled shoots, up to about 10 feet in height with fragile pale, rosy pink, solitary flowers in March. Unfortunately most of the specimens obtainable from nurseries are grafted on what appears to be Blackthorn and suckers are very troublesome, and I have neither succeeded in layering it nor striking it from cuttings. It is worth looking out for by those who like very early flowers and who are not too much troubled by bullfinches.

The dwarf Almond, *P. tenella* (*P. nana*) grows to about 3 feet high and enjoys a hot, dry spot. Some forms have richer pink flowers than others. It has the merit of being fairly easily increased by layering. As grafted plants are not satisfactory, it is best to get such plants on to their own roots in this way as soon as possible.

P. t. 'Fire Hill' form is a very distinct and attractive dwarf Almond brought back from Rumania by Lady Martineau. It forms a shapely dense bush about 3 feet high covered in early spring with carmine-pink buds opening to paler flowers. The leaves are thick and of a dark green, making it a comely bush all summer. Young plants are now available at specialist shrub nurseries.

P. triloba (A.G.M. 1935) is a delightful member of the family, if somewhat artificial-looking in its double form (*P. t. multiplex*). It was found in the gardens of North China by the collector Robert Fortune in 1855. It comes into bloom in early April and in cold districts is best grown on a south wall, although quite hardy. It is usually grafted on the Plum stock which entails endless trouble with suckers, so if a plant can be got on its own roots it is much to be preferred. The pink flowers, of very pretty shape for a double flower, having a typical, musical-comedy flavour, cover the shoots very freely if these are regularly cut back each year after flowering. There is a single-flowered form (*P. t. simplex*) which is said to be less free-flowering and long-lasting. It can be propagated, though not without some difficulty, by cuttings of fairly ripe wood.

Generally speaking the cultivation of the Almonds is a simple matter. But the repeated sprayings necessary to control leaf-curl prevent them being worth while except in limy soils where Azaleas will not grow.

Aspect is also important and an open position in full sun is necessary. Weak yellow-leaved shoots indicate infection by " dieback ", and these together with unwanted inward-growing shoots, should be removed at the end of May. Pruning at any other time should be avoided. Most species can be grown from the seeds, or nuts. In sowing, these are half buried on their sides and allowed to get well frosted in winter. If protected from mice, most will germinate the following spring.

Fragrance is a quality that must not be forgotten at this moment of the year and white flowers and a dark evergreen form may complement the slender Almonds by contrast.

Siphonosmanthus Delavayi (*Osmanthus Delavayi*) (A.G.M. 1923), a dense, bushy evergreen, 6 feet or more in height, and perhaps 10 feet wide, has small leaves and tiny, sweet-scented, white, tubular, jasmine-like flowers in clusters in early April. It has the useful quality of being an evergreen that can be grown in limy soil, but in view of the wonderfully wide choice available we must take into consideration the fact that it is a shrub of large size that has only white flowers half an inch across and these insufficiently freely borne to colour the bush solidly. *S. Delavayi*, often known as *Osmanthus Delavayi*, comes from Yunnan, whence the Abbé Delavay sent its seeds to Messrs. Vilmorin of Paris in 1890. It is a "bad mover" and not a fast grower at first. It may be propagated, it is said, by cuttings in late summer in a sand frame with bottom heat, but the amateur is well advised to buy small plants in pots, as it is not easy to strike.

When the spring weather is mild and calm, the most spectacular of the early flowering trees are undoubtedly the large-flowered **Magnolias,** but with some one has to wait a long time before they make sufficient size to flower well. On the other hand, many people enjoy planting and growing young trees, even of species that never flower effectively, and as some of the Magnolias are quick-growing and attractive merely as sapling trees, they should certainly be planted in residential areas in preference to Limes, Elms, Chestnuts, Beeches, etc.

For garden purposes the Magnolias have been conveniently sorted into groups by Lord Aberconway†. Having already described the *M. stellata* section, in this next early-flowering group I will deal with the best of those having affinity to *M. denudata*.

M. denudata, the Yulan, itself is one of the loveliest and best for the small garden. It is hardy and of strong constitution, flowers when very

† "Ornamental Flowering Trees and Shrubs", R.H.S. Conference, 1938, p. 215.

young, even at 3 feet high, and makes a handsome small tree in almost any position in good soil where it is carefully pruned to this end when young, and gets full sun. It has been cultivated by the Chinese since ancient history, and received the A.G.M. in 1936. In a favourable season it is really finer, I think, than any of its numerous garden hybrids, because the great solid flowers appear before the leaves, beautifully presented, and so all are seen with fullest effect. They are a pure creamy white and deliciously fragant. The nine petals (properly called tepals) are usually in three rows of three alternated.

Of the hybrids, the most commonly seen is *M. Soulangeana* (*M. liliflora* × *denudata*) (A.G.M. 1932), bred in France by Chevalier Soulange Bodin about the middle of the nineteenth century. It is perhaps a more vigorous grower and an even better garden plant, but the flowers open later, with the leaves, and have a purplish stain at the base, so the effect is less striking. Other hybrids of this type are *M. S. rustica rubra*, *M. S. Brozzonii*, *M. S. spectabilis*, *M. S. Alexandrina*, *M. S. Norbertii* and *M. S. triumphans*. There is really very little difference between them.

M. S. Lennei is another fine variety of similar parentage that is more distinct. Its flowers usually come still later, among the fully expanded leaves, and they are of a rich purplish pink and more globular in shape.

M. liliflora is a rather weakly and unsatisfactory grower in this country, with deep purple flowers. *M. l.* var. *nigra* is a hardier and better form, but it is of little account.

A scarce but valuable Magnolia is *M. Sprengeri* var. *diva*. It is said to be one of the hardiest of the early flowerers and was formerly known as *M. denudata* var. *purpurascens*. The flowers are Mallow Purple (H.C.C. 630/2) and cup-shaped and, if somewhat less spectacular in size than those of *M. Campbellii* and others, are more reliably and freely produced, on a more shapely tree. The seeds were originally sent back to Veitch's Nursery by E. H. Wilson. Another form, 'Wakehurst Seedling', has deeper coloured flowers.

M. Dawsoniana is a fairly bushy tree with about nine, narrower, tepals of a pale purple and has aromatic leaves. It requires some years to reach effective flowering size.

M. Campbellii, from the Himalayas, in time makes quite a large tree but does not flower until it is nearly twenty years old. It is, furthermore, such an early flowerer and grower that it gets cut by frost very frequently. None the less, the fact remains that it can provide one of the most superb sights that can be seen. The huge and notably shapely flowers are a soft rose pink, or pure white, in good forms, and when these appear in profusion on a tree of almost forest size the effect is

very lovely. In the mountain forests of Bhutan there are rare forms
with crimson flowers. Unfortunately it does not flower regularly, even
after a hot summer. One of the largest trees in the country, one that I
know well, had, I note, not a single flower bud in 1948 although the
summer of 1947 was an ideal one.

M. Veitchii is a fine hybrid between *M. denudata* and *M. Campbellii*.
There are two forms of this, one having pinkish flowers whose tepals do
not expand very widely. In the other, known as 'Isca', the large flowers
are white, tinted outside with pale purplish pink. When expanded, they
measure about 11 inches across, with eleven tepals. This Magnolia has
remarkable speed of growth so that it is very well worth planting as a
garden tree on the lawn. The only drawback is that, like so many very
fast growers, it requires some shelter from the wind as it is far from
gale-proof.

M. mollicomata, a near relative of *M. Campbellii*, from China, was
described by Reginald Farrer, with his usual vivid zest, as a tree of
supreme loveliness, under the name of *M. rostrata*, though that name
actually belongs, it has been found, to a different species. It has the
merit of glorious, if somewhat untidy, flowers, some 9 inches across,
and makes rapid growth, having flowered from seed at Lord Aberconway's famous gardens at Bodnant in twelve years. This means that
a person buying a strong sapling would not have an unconscionable
time to wait. In addition the habit of the tree is more compact than that
of *M. Campbellii*. Its pink flowers (actually pale tints of Petunia and
Mallow Purple) come a little later than those of the latter, and are more
freely and regularly borne, and thus it stands a much better chance of
making a good showing. (See illustration p. 48.)

Another early flowering tree Magnolia is *M. Sargentiana*, with large
pale purple flowers of informal shape. It requires some years to grow
to flowering size and is not very vigorous. It is, however, spindly and
tree-like, rather than bushy in habit like the following.

M. S. var. *robusta* is one of the most spectacular of all Magnolias,
though the huge, loose flowers tend to bend over to the horizontal. It
also flowers when small, plants only 4 to 6 feet high bearing flower buds.[†]
Needless to say, however, several years' growth is needed to make the
lovely display shown in recent illustrations.[‡] Seed of this Magnolia
has been sown and the seedlings are now becoming available at
nurseries.

Few trees are more interesting to grow, for the thoughtful and keen
cultivator, or the pruning enthusiast. The wood of the stem often

[†] Lord Aberconway, *R.H.S. Journal*, Vol. LXX, Pt. 6 (June 1945), p. 159.
[‡] Fig. 12, *R.H.S. Journal*, LXVIII, Pt. 2 (Feb. 1943), and frontispiece "Camellias
and Magnolias", Report of the Conference 1950.

receives a shock, in moving, from which it seldom really recovers. Consequently growth is slow. But if one can stimulate a young shoot from the base, and then boldly cut away the old stick, this young growth, provided no slugs or pests interfere with it, will shoot up at much greater speed, and make a really healthy stem, free from the die-back that so often cripples maturing specimens. I do not find any bad effects arise from firm pruning of Magnolias, either to get the plant on to fresh young wood at the start, to suppress any rival to the leader or to shorten a too presumptuous side branch.

For years I tried to make a young plant of *M. Campbellii* from an immense low bush, having several stems, but it was not happy and made slow progress. At last I cut away all but one very young shoot and this rushed up in true tree form at a prodigious rate immediately. It may seem fanciful to discuss and recommend such trees as these, when the waiting period is often so long, but they have a niche in the world of the garden from which nothing can displace them. They are the perfect long-term investment. Hundreds of much longer term speculations are made every year by persons planting Elms, Oaks, Limes, Conifers, etc. which take even more time to assume their less spectacular beauties. I would suggest that the great tree Magnolias should be planted instead of these as commemorative trees. They would be really appreciated by posterity and much more likely to be preserved than commonplace sorts. The Soulangeanas are always available in pots and will grow anywhere and for choicer and safer places *M. Veitchii* and others would be suitable.

As regards cultivation, we must remember that these tree Magnolias are forest dwellers, and so give the more delicate kinds the shelter of other trees, if possible, and a rich, woodsy soil. The Chinese species and their hybrids usually tolerate a limy soil, whilst the Japanese do not, but, as the essential is to get your young tree growing quickly, and keep it growing fast, it is worth while preparing a good plot of ground at the start, rich and deep. I have reason to think that we have not really given these trees a chance yet. The early cultivators naturally wished to hustle them into flower as soon as possible so as to know what they were like. If, on the other hand, we plant them with the primary object of growing a strong arboreal framework, allowing plenty of room and letting the flowers come when they may, I think the ultimate effect will be still better. I have no definite proof, but I have reason to believe that more regular feeding is needed. In the forest the leaf-fall feeds the trees annually with Nature's perfect food. In the garden the Magnolias are expected to go on producing barrowloads of flower-petal material with nothing put back to replace what is blown or wheeled away annually. Rather than die the tree husbands its resources. At the best a bad habit of intermittent flowering is initiated. Feed well, then, and regularly; prune to induce a shapely sapling free from the dangers of V-shaped forks of equal-sized branches, and keep the soil over the roots mulched at all times with leaves, like the forest floor.

Knowing that the Chinese have little interest in ornamental gardens compared with the Japanese, I was always puzzled at the explorers' reports of innumerable Magnolias "in cultivation" in China. On going into matters further the mystery was explained. The Magnolias were not grown to be looked at, they were grown to be cut down and destroyed so that an alleged aphrodisiac could be distilled from the sap! The nostrum obtained is said to have no scientific value and the notion is regrettable as it also leads to the destruction of many fine wild specimens.

Seeds often wait a couple of years before germinating, and even then growth is often rather slow, so perhaps layering is the easiest method of propagation for the amateur. But according to Mr. F. M. Kluis of Boskoop, *M. Soulangeana* can be propagated by means of cuttings, as follows. Small side-branches of half-ripe wood are used, taken in July, the cuttings being 3 to 5 inches long, rather slender for choice, and carefully cut at the node. A "heel" of old wood is not advantageous and sappy shoots or those that are very thick are to be avoided. The cuttings are inserted in 4-inch pots containing a mixture of half sand and half peat-dust and carefully soaked. The pots are then placed in a frame or cool greenhouse. Bottom heat is helpful, but not essential provided that the weather is fairly warm. Great care is taken to remove all fallen leaves and to keep up the moisture content of the atmosphere sufficiently to prevent wilting. Shading is provided against the sun, as the foliage must not be allowed to get dried out. Ninety per cent. have been rooted successfully by this method, under favourable conditions as to material, temperature and humidity. The cuttings were separately potted-on in six weeks from the date of insertion. 1 to 1½ feet of growth was secured in the first growing season, and 2 to 3 feet of growth in the second.

Other Magnolias do not respond well, if at all, to this method. *M. Loebneri* (*M. stellata* × *Kobus*), *M. glauca* (and, probably, *M. Veitchii*) can with care and suitable material also be rooted in this way, but *M. denudata* is slow and gives a low proportion of successes. *M. Dawsoniana*, *M. mollicomata*, *M. Sargentiana* and *M. S. robusta* are found to be very difficult.

Growth-producing substances, Mr. Kluis reports, did not cause shy-rooting material to form roots: they only induced a greater number of stronger roots.

Later, in the June section, we shall deal with the Magnolias of the

summer-flowering types centring on *M. Sieboldii* (*M. parviflora*) and
also with that splendid tree *M. obovata*.

In the meantime let us consider that very different race, the **Peaches**;
these are sun-lovers relishing an open position and a poor, dry, and
even limy, soil rather than the moist rich soil of the mountain forests.

One of the earliest is *Prunus Davidiana* (A.G.M. 1927) David's Peach,
named for the good Abbé David who sent its seeds to Paris in 1865 from
Pekin. It comes into flower about February when the white or pink
blossom often meets a somewhat chill reception. It is therefore hardly
worth a place except in large gardens, or in a sunny spot in the woodland among the early Rhododendrons.

Seedlings of the common Peach, *P. Persica*, are very easily grown
from stones and are of notably good health and remarkable vigour,
compared with grafted plants. If planted out into their permanent
places from pots they grow rapidly without check and seem almost
immune to the leaf-curl fungus which debilitates grafted plants unless
they are regularly sprayed in March with fungicide. Furthermore the
fruit from these seedlings is surprisingly often of really excellent quality
and their blossom is quite as attractive as that of any of the family.
Unlike the Cherries, I find that Peaches often suffer a severe check if
moved with bare roots unless every precaution is taken. Even then it is
wise to nip off all blossom buds during the first spring in the new position. A further advantage of these seed-grown Peaches is that one may
avoid the artificial-looking "standard" shape which one does not
always want. The drawback to this shape is that such trees need, for
several years at least, a very strong stake and a firm tie owing to their
topheavy form. The stake is not an object of beauty; in fact it quite
spoils the appearance of the trunk. A young tree put out as a tiny
sapling will grow to the wind and assume the perfect form to make the
best of its situation, assuming a rightness of look and carefree port that
the artificially shaped standard, planted when large, can never do.

A garden variety with double pink flowers is *P. P.* var. 'Clara Meyer'
(A.G.M. 1939); it is quite effective in a warm spot. *P. P. alba-plena* is a
handsome semi-double, white-flowered variety; 'Windle Weeping' is a
double pink weeper from California and 'Helen Borchers' is a semi-
double pink of similar origin.

A brilliantly coloured variety is *P. P.* 'Russell's Red'. The flowers are
large, and a beautiful rich, crimson red, but it is usually grafted on the
Plum and thus a martyr to the leaf-curl fungus unless regularly sprayed,
and therefore seldom seen in good health for long. I have, for some time,
intended to graft this superior sort on to a strong seedling Peach, to

see whether it will do better on this more consanguine host-root than on the usual Plum.† It is one of the most spectacular of all flowering trees and therefore can fully reward the attentions of the determined cultivator. 'Palace Peach' (A.M. 1939), a new variety, is equally rich in colour and it may prove to have a stronger constitution.

There is also a fine, strong healthy Peach with red foliage and pink flowers, *P. P. foliis rubris*. Two new varieties from California are: 'Aurora', semi-double pink, and 'Iceberg', semi-double white.

In cultivation the Peaches require a sunny, open position and well drained soil. Usually considered as requiring extra lime, I find nothing wrong with the vigour of their growth in acid soil if fed Growmore or with the germination of self-sown seedlings in such soil. Regular spraying with a fungicide such as 'Sulsol' is essential in early spring before the buds open, or the Peach leaf-curl fungus will cripple the trees. "Dieback" should be controlled by cutting out all sickly shoots in late May, annually.

Misunderstanding as to their cultivation has led to their neglect by all but a few thoughtful enthusiasts. Yet of all hardy blossoming trees none can give us the joyous and almost unbelievable cloud of crimson blossom of a good red Peach. Beside it the Magenta tints of the pink Cherries appear poor indeed.

Now we come to some of the most beautiful of all flowering trees as regards form as distinct from colour—the early-flowering section of the **Cherries.**

One of the first to open is *Prunus Conradinæ* discovered in Hupeh, China, by the great plantsman, E. H. Wilson, who sent seeds to the Arnold Arboretum, Boston, Massachusetts, whence they came to Kew. *P. Conradinæ* flowers in January or February, with fragrant white blossoms freely produced on the naked branches. There is a double-flowered form—var. *semi-plena* whose pink flowers, although less shapely, last longer on the tree and make a fuller distant effect. It is too early a flowerer to be generally recommended, but in a sheltered wood-garden its white blossom may fittingly complement the massive red flowers of Rhododendron 'Cornubia' or others of its kindred, amid the fresh green of Bamboos backed by the dark coniferous mass of Pine or Fir.

In the garden we need the more reliable offering of later blossoming and early April or later is quite soon enough.

† Since I wrote the above Mr. Justin Brooks, a commercial Peach grower, has confirmed the essential importance of using Peach root stocks. See *R.H.S. Journal* LXXVI, Pt. 1, p. 22 *et seq*, for a most valuable setting-out of all that concerns the grower of Peaches.

Among the early-flowering Cherries that open at this time, a good form of the variable wild Hill Cherry of Japan, formerly known as *P. serrulata* ver. *mutabilis*, now *P. s.* var. *spontanea* or 'Shiro-Yamasakura', is one of the most beautiful. This superb hardy flowering tree offers an excellent example of how mere confusion as to name can prevent a good plant becoming known and lead to its almost complete disappearance. In Japan there are avenues and groves of this Cherry, as a tree of full forest size, covered in spring with innumerable small, but beautifully formed, white or pink blossoms opening among the young, unfolding, copper-coloured leaves. By all accounts and photographs, and also many delicate and lovely Japanese paintings meticulously done with great exactitude, there must be some of the most glorious flowering trees to be seen anywhere in the world. E. H. Wilson described them so glowingly, in particular the immense veterans of the avenue of Koganei, as to excite the interest of all, but unfortunately under the name of *P. sachalinensis*. This latter Cherry has been found to be a quite different species and is also known as *P. Sargentii*. Even now the confusion is not entirely clarified for I note that in the second edition of "Manual of Cultivated Trees and Shrubs", by Alfred Rehder (The Macmillan Company, New York) which I follow in nomenclature, the poor Hill Cherry is relegated to the position of an unspecified form of *P. serrulata*, and the veterans are dead of Fire Blight.

Anyhow, as a result of this name boggle, the true Hill Cherry languished for a long time unsung, and even today it is almost unobtainable, most leading Cherry growers having given up, as no one ever asked for it. However, the few trees existing over here have begun to cast the fame of their beauty abroad and propagation is at last getting ahead. This Cherry has the merit of garden effectiveness to a high degree owing to the great mass of its little flowers and the glorious colour of the young leaves. Forms vary greatly in value and some have more shapely and pure-coloured flowers and brighter young leaves, the latter being a very important part of the effect. The best forms should be selected and *propagated under garden names* so that this lovely tree may decorate the new towns and the avenues of the future Britain now being planned. Small street-sized trees are needed for crowded places but without some trees of full forest size no landscape—urban or rural —can have proper dignity and scale. The Hill Cherry flowers when quite small but some years must pass before it can become large enough to show its true value. It is hardy and of strong constitution and seems to grow well in any reasonably good soil, though in Britain it seems unlikely to make such a tall tree as in Japan. It seeds itself freely.

P. Sargentii, Sargent's Cherry, which was sent to Kew by Professor Sargent of the Arnold Arboretum in 1893, and received the Award of

Garden Merit in 1928, has larger individual flowers of a glowing pink and also a superb autumn leaf colouring. But it is a rather more difficult plant to grow well than most other Cherries. A sapling of 6 feet that I planted in ideal conditions took nearly ten years to reach perfection, but this was well worth waiting for. The tree, nearly 20 feet high, was so densely packed with the large short-stalked bright purplish-pink flowers that it was effective at a great distance and the refinement of form made it delightful on closer examination. A rich, deep, loamy soil and a sunny but wind-sheltered position are needed for this superb Cherry to show its real quality, and it is well fitted to form the high spot of a group of the white and blush-flowered early Cherries also described in this section. Such groups need a preponderance of white to show their full brilliance; too much pink looks merely muddy. Its autumn tints do not last long.

Another species, the Spring Cherry, *P. subhirtella* (A.G.M. 1927) is hardy in all parts of England and has a great number of varieties. The variety most prominent in Japan appears to be a free-growing form, sometimes listed here as var. *ascendens*, which, over there, reaches, according to Major Collingwood Ingram, a height of 90 feet. Evidently this would be a noble Park or commemorative tree that could well be planted in preference to the uninteresting Limes and Elms too often chosen for the purpose. The commonest form over here is one which usually only makes a small rounded tree about the size of a Hawthorn. Provided that the bullfinches are kept away, it makes a fine show of white or pale pink blossom every spring. There are varieties with deeper purplish-pink flowers and doubles like 'Accolade' (A.G.M. 1961).

A notably fine variety of this Cherry is *P. s.* var. 'Fukubana' with double or semi-double flowers of quite rich and deep pink, the petals being serrated so as to give the blossoms a charming frilled appearance. At the same time, a good selected form with more abundant, single flowers is really preferable unless one has space to grow several kinds of this delightful tree. 'Ben Higan' is a fine pale pink single and 'Pandora', a cross with 'Yoshino', is very free with larger blush-pink blossom (A.G.M. 1959).

The Spring Cherry can be grown from cuttings of the season's growth placed under a bell-glass in midsummer. On their own roots the trees grow better and are more beautiful by reason of having no ugly distortion caused by the graft union. Indeed, for a beautiful and shapely tree, the cutting, and still more the selected seedling, so far surpasses any grafted plant in later life that I, for my part, am prepared to overlook a slight inferiority in shape and colour of flower to attain the handsomer tree. Such seedlings planted out as young "whips" in their permanent places grow to the wind unstaked and assume a beautiful and natural form altogether different from that of the top-heavy transplanted standard secured to its unsightly but necessary stake.

Most frequently planted, perhaps, is the variety *P. s. autumnalis* (A.G.M. 1924) which flowers at intervals during the winter. Often the poor wretch struggles to put forth its tattered semi-double flowers amid the bitter storms of January. It is certainly a wonderful testimonial to the British climate that so many gardeners relish winter-borne flowers. But if one compares the glorious spring picture made by this Cherry among the Daffodils and Primroses of April with the unhappy haze of bedraggled blossom dimly seen against grey skies and naked branches in winter I think most will prefer it, as I do, in its normal form.

The weeping variety, var. *pendula*, can be a very beautiful tree when carefully trained. Failing a seedling tree, I think the best effect is obtained when it is top-grafted on a very tall pole of the Gean (our native wild Cherry) but even then it is necessary to tie up the branches at first so as to get a beautiful gradual curve downwards rather than merely letting the branches hang straight down. There are pink and white forms of the weeping kind, some having starry, thin flowers and others shapely and full ones, and there is also much variation in habit, some having such weak and trailing branches that only a permanent wire umbrella would keep them from hanging straight down in an ugly tangle. Care should therefore be taken to select a good form. It is not a very healthy species in this country, often suffering from "die-back" in parts, or even total sudden death for no cause that I can ascertain.†

The Cutleaf Cherry, *P. incisa* (A.G.M. 1926) is one of the most indispensable delights among the early Cherries for small gardens. It is a good garden plant and will even stand quite severe cutting back, which is often disastrous with the other Cherries. *P. incisa* flowers profusely every spring with solid little white blossoms that look rosy pink at a distance owing to the red calyx (this being the name given to the leafy base surrounding most flowers). Eventually it will make a rounded little tree up to 20 feet, it is said, although usually no more than 12, but it may easily be kept down to a rounded bush 4 or 5 feet high if desired. It flowers freely when only a foot or two in height, and is a treasure of the first order. It is easily grown from seed.

Two outstanding garden-bred Cherries tail along with the early section as to their flowering time and so had best be mentioned at this point.

The first is *P. serrulata* var. 'Yoshino' (*P. Yedoensis*) (A.G.M. 1930). It is thought to be a hybrid between *P. serrulata* and *P. subhirtella*, but

---

† Instancing this, the remarkable specimen illustrated opposite p. 21 in *The Flowering Shrub Garden* (2nd Edition) by the writer, died outright in the ensuing winter.

in dealing with Japanese garden plants that have been cultivated for hundreds of years there is much uncertainty and it is most convenient to have a handy garden name, whenever the rules allow. ' Yoshino ', then, is a fine Cherry with white flowers, often faintly blushed, that cover the naked branches in early spring. It is a good garden plant growing vigorously into a handsome, firm tree in good soil, but it should be selected in flower for there are many very poor forms about that are not worth growing.

P. serrulata var. 'Tai Haku' is a very large-flowered variety of absolutely outstanding beauty, pre-eminent among the first six that one would choose for that quality from the many Japanese garden-bred sorts. The shapely single blossoms, each two inches across, are white and appear among the rich bronze-copper colour of the unfolding young leaves. It is a particularly strong and healthful tree, having double the number of chromosomes of *P. serrulata*, and is perfectly happy grafted upon the roots of our native Gean as its unusual vigour matches that of this stock better than most. It flowers a little later than 'Yoshino' and this is the time of year when the first real display of flowers in our gardens had best begin.

Such a spectacularly lovely thing as this Cherry is worthy to take part in an association of harmonious flowerers, one of those delightful colour groupings that distinguish the garden planned with artistry from the mere collection. The building up of these associations is one of the greater joys of the art. An arrangement possible only under the perfect conditions of a good acid sandy loam, where any shrub will flourish, will have alternatives of lesser perfection possible in cold limy clays where the selection is much more limited. At this time, when the big white Cherry blooms, we have a wide choice of complementary plantings.

Among the most beautiful shrubs in bloom at this time are the dwarf mountain Rhododendrons. A charming example that is a really good garden plant is the hybrid 'Blue Tit'. This offspring of *R. impeditum* crossed with *R. Augustinii* was rightly given the four stars of merit, that constitute the highest encomium, by the Rhododendron Association. It forms a shapely mound perhaps a yard across and nearly as high. I started with a little sprig kindly given me by Mr. James Comber, and, a few years later, when I moved the plant, which I had grown under optimum conditions, I was able to divide it into four goodly specimens and also to remove a ring of twelve lusty little seedlings from its perimeter. It is thus a plant that pays its rent very handsomely. The charming evergreen dome covers itself almost completely with flowers of a delightful Aster Violet tint and in the kindly shade of the Cherry, these last long in beauty.

Charming as is an association of two harmonious colours the addition of a third can yield a higher perfection. The colour sought to make up this picture was that of the Primrose, and for years these humble plants have served well enough, but now we find the dwarf Broom, *Cytisus Kewensis*, or the larger *C. prœcox*, even lovelier in combination owing to the denser mass of colour they provide.

There are a great number of highly interesting, early flowering wild Cherry species described in detail in "Ornamental Cherries", by Major Collingwood Ingram (*Country Life*, 1948). Most of these are, however, on the whole less effective for the small garden than the varieties described above, but a number of superlative forms, which will, it is hoped, be propagated as clones under garden names, are especially worth noting. Among these are: a seedling form of *Prunus serrulata* var. *pubescens* with "intensely vivid scarlet" autumn tints; a double-flowered sport of the tender *P. campanulata*, interesting for warm gardens; also certain hybrids of this crimson-flowered species and *P. incisa*. A seedling of this cross kindly given me by the author cited above showed amazing vigour in growth but its bright pink blossoms open in March, which is rather too early for safety and the young leaves, unfolding at the same time, fall an easy prey to frost. *Rhododendron prœcox*, *Daphne mezereum* and *Pieris japonica* associate pleasantly with it, contrasted with white 'Mirabelle', but one of these mild March spells of calm weather is necessary for the enjoyment of such precocious effects.

Unfortunately *P. cerasoides* var. *rubea* a 100-foot crimson-flowered Himalayan tree is not yet with us, and indeed it never seems to set seed (according to Mr. R. C. Sheriff) in its native habitat.

I have never thought the Bird Cherry, *P. Padus*, really worth growing in the small garden but the variety *Albertii* may be noted as an outstandingly attractive member of an otherwise rather dull family. *P. P. Watereri* (A.G.M. 1930) is also an improvement on the type owing to its longer racemes.

The Chinese Bush Cherry, *P. glandulosa*, is, in most gardens, too much of a martyr to attack by "dieback" to be a good garden plant. On the other hand, when on its own roots in an open, sunny spot in a hot, sandy or chalky garden, this little Cherry may grow healthfully enough for its pretty musical comedy appearance to be quite enjoyable. Var. *albi-plena* is a pretty double white variety.

The little Rock Cherry, *P. prostrata*, so widely found wild in the mountains of the world and so seldom seen in the garden, would also be quite delightful if we could only bake and freeze it enough to make it flower really freely. In most gardens it is not very effective.

The wide-ranging roots of the Gean are so troublesome that

grafted Cherries should not be planted in shrub beds, if this can be avoided by planting them as lawn specimens. Bullfinches often spoil the flower display.

On the other hand they require an open position, apart from other trees if possible. Spraying to control lichen and black aphis is necessary.

Propagation is described in the special chapter thus headed on page 35. Pruning is restricted to cutting off small branches that are badly placed for the building up of a shapely tree. Rubbing off ill-placed young shoots is even better as fungus attack is the chief enemy of the Cherries. Care should be taken to attend to any wounds caused by broken branches at once, carefully paring away all damaged tissue and painting over the exposed surfaces immediately.

Daphne Mezereum (A.G.M. 1929), a common cottage-garden plant, has great charm. The mauve-pink flowers appear on the naked branches early in the year and smell delicious. It is thought to have been a native but was "collected" to the verge of extinction. Seedlings appear freely from the bright red berries produced among the leaves in summer. There is a rather poor white variety *D. M. alba*, of more open habit, and also a notably good one, var. *grandiflora*, which flowers from October onwards with brighter purple and larger flowers. There is also the lovely new 'Snow Queen' with big white flowers.

One of the most attractive of early flowerers is *D. odora* var. *elegantissima*, a rounded evergreen usually about two or three feet in height with yellow-margined leaves and clusters of pale rosy purple, intensely fragrant flowers during mild spells in late winter or early spring. It is reputed tender but I have found it undamaged in many gardens by the severe winters of the past decade and indeed it has long outlived *D. Cneorum* and other supposedly more hardy kinds. It has usually the benefit of the foot of a south wall, it is true, but it is at any rate a plant worth chancing owing to the charming nosegays it produces in earliest spring. *D. odora* itself (*D. odora indica*), is a more tender, sprawling, less hardy plant with plain green leaves.

In colder gardens, the hybrids, which go under the names of *D. Fioniana* and *D. Dauphinii*, may be grown. According to the late Alfred Rehder these are, botanically, forms of *D. hybrida*, a cross with *D. collina*.

D. collina var. *neapolitana* is a three-foot shrub that is an excellent garden plant for a moist but well-drained, loamy soil either limy or acid, with narrower, more glaucous leaves and smaller, rose pink flowers than the hybrid sold as *D. Dauphinii* which is very similar to *D. odora* but considerably hardier and more erect, robust and bushy. These

Daphnes will all grow on limy soils and are not particular as to aspect either. The species may be reproduced slowly but surely from seeds.

Another lime tolerator is *Spiræa arguta* (A.G.M. 1927), the 'Bridal Wreath', a hybrid between *S. Thunbergii* and *S. multiflora* which makes a shapely deciduous bush about 7 feet high and its masses of little white flowers are aglow in April. It is best as a single specimen where its graceful habit is shown to better advantage than when crowded in with other plants, and is generally considered the finest of the spring-flowering Spiræas. It will grow in any fairly good loam, whether limy or not, and is easily propagated from layers.

We have mentioned the excellent little Rhododendron 'Blue Tit' in association with Cherries and now, having done justice to the limy garden, come to consider the great clan of **Dwarf Alpine Rhododendrons** that are among the most fascinating of all garden plants for a lime-free soil.

There are a great number of these delightful little shrubs and it would be a long business to enumerate them all. Grown, as I have seen them all too often, alone without association with other shrubs, their effect is less than that of the common *R. ponticum* which at least boasts a more vivid green leaf. But planted here and there among big boulders in the open, and *complementary plants of other genera*, they are jewels of the highest value. One of the most vital essentials to good planting design is just this embroidery of evergreens of contrasting leaf tones with deciduous shrubs.

Some have condemned the winter value of evergreen Rhododendron foliage as dull, likely to curl up in hard weather and generally unsatisfactory for winter effect. It is too sweeping a statement and with complete confidence I must contradict it. Some species are among the most beautiful of all evergreens, quite apart from the effect of their flowers. If Rhododendrons are isolated in beds by themselves the effect is dreary and dull certainly, and so it would be if Laurels, Hollies, Box or any other evergreens were so tastelessly lumped together. Again, one can hardly expect the best garden landscape to look lovely during a howling east wind with ten degrees or more of frost, but our British winters abound in mild days and on every one of those your hardy Rhododendron foliage sparkles, unfolded, green and lush. Who cares if amid the snow and ice the wise plants huddle down and curl their leaves against the blast? To me it looks a most fitting gesture.

To return to the alpine shrublets, I shall describe only a few of the more outstanding early-flowering members of the various "series" that can be bought from nurseries, leaving out the evergreen Azaleas until later. These Azaleas, I should point out, are the most important section of all for the ordinary garden and are technically known as the "sub-series" *obtusum* of the Azalea "series".

Owing to their great numbers, the system of dividing the Rhododendron species into series of kinship, carried out by the late Sir Isaac Bayley Balfour, has been of the greatest help to all. Thus the innumerable species have been conveniently sorted out into groups showing a family resemblance, and the gardener who knows one member of a series will have some idea of the type of the other members.

Another most helpful short cut is the system of indicating relative hardiness by the letters "A", "B", "C" or "D" which we owe to the Rhododendron Year-Books. "A" means "Hardy anywhere in the British Isles and *can be planted in full exposure* if desired". In practice Rhododendrons so qualified are, of course, by far the most valuable, as they can be grown in the open garden *where they are wanted*, provided the soil is right. "B" means "Hardy anywhere in the British Isles but requires some shade to obtain the best results". These are therefore less valuable, and, in practice, shelter from wind is also often necessary, but shade can usually be arranged. "C" means "Hardy along the seaboard and in warm gardens inland". Not all of the "C" class necessarily want shade, as for example *R. indicum* ("*Azalea macrantha*"), but the category letter means that the plant may suffer from cold and exposure, and consequently some care must be taken in its placing and it is not to be recommended for unfavourable gardens. "D" means "Hardy in the south and west but requires shelter even in warm gardens inland". This is clearly a danger signal.

So as to maintain as much order as possible, without sacrificing the essential feature of grouping them according to their flowering time in the garden year, I will go steadily through the various series mentioning those in flower during early spring and April. Throughout this book I omit many superb new hybrids, privately bred, because they will not be available in the nursery trade for some years to come, if ever.

From one to four stars of merit are awarded to extra fine species by the Rhododendron Group, and this offers a useful guide.

First, in the Boothii series, which is rather a difficult and tender section on the whole, we have the lovely *R. tephropeplum* *** (*R. deleiense*). This was awarded the three stars of merit by the Rhododendron Association but placed in hardiness category "C", which means "hardy along the seaboard and in warm gardens inland", only. Thus if it were not a particularly beautiful species easily grown from seed,

delightfully fragrant and flowering at two or three years old, we should
not trouble with it. But the best form of this species has these qualifications and in my garden has proved reasonably hardy and a good
garden plant, undamaged by all the hard winters of the war when,
alongside, Ceanothus, Cistus and Escallonia all perished.

R. *tephropeplum*, in its best form, makes rather an open bush, about
2 feet high when fully exposed, with informal trusses of about six or
seven flowers which are of a Rose Bengal (H.C.C. 25/3), not magenta-
rose as in poor forms, and wide-open and beautifully full and rounded.
The fragrance, which incidentally I have not seen mentioned anywhere,
is most enjoyable and scents the air around. In a hundred seedlings
there is very little variation, and they are usually in bloom in late April.
The form known as R. *deleiense* was found in the Delei valley of Assam
"in exposed places on rocky ridges" by Captain Kingdon Ward, but
my seed was actually sent back by another collector, George Forrest,
under the name of R. *tephropeplum*.

Another charming member of this series, much fancied by Cornish
gardeners in R. *leucaspis*, also awarded three stars. This is a smaller and
denser shrub with large white flowers with chocolate stamens, but they
come much too early to be really useful, in February or March—but
in some seasons they are nicely synchronised with those of R. *ciliatum*
which also grows easily from seed and flowers within three years of
sowing.

Also in this very early-flowering group, in its own series, is the
charming R. *moupinense*, a nice little bush with Box-like leaves and
coral buds that open to large, speckled, white, scented flowers. There
is a very good illustration of it in Captain Kingdon Ward's "Rhododendrons for Everyone" (*The Gardeners' Chronicle*, 1926). It flowers
from seed in three years but such early spring flowerers are really better
grown in the Alpine House than fully exposed to March weather.

The next series is the Cephalanthum series, now to be known as the
Anthopogon series† and it contains some delightful little bushlets,
with tiny Daphne-like flowers that, at first glance, few would recognise
as members of the Rhododendron family. The one we grow is R.
trichostomum var. *ledoides* "C" *** which comes from the lovely, but
mosquito-ridden, land of Yunnan where it grows in open scrub. The
bush is dense and nearly 2 feet high with miniature spherical trusses
of tiny pale pink flowers in April or May. It is so free flowering that it
makes a real effect and is so dainty and delightful as an individual that

† Dr. MacQueen Cowan and H. H. Davidian, B.Sc., *Rhododendron Year-Book*,
1947, p. 55 *et seq.*

everybody enjoys it. *R. sphæranthum* and *R. cephalanthum* are very similar and equally charming.

The Glaucum series contains the curious *R. pemakoense* **, "A" class, (which means "hardy anywhere in the British Isles and may be planted in full exposure if desired"). This little shrub is almost a joke, with its tiny framework and relatively huge flowers, which are, regretably, an unpleasing pale Mallow Purple in colour (H.C.C. 630/3). It is said to make suckers like a Pernettya but my plants do not do this. Although it starts blooming when only a few inches high, usually being at its best in late March or early April, it eventually makes a bush over a foot high.

Now we come to the largest and most important series of these dwarfs—the Laponnicum series, but, as with the other series, we will deal here only with the early-flowering batch that will be in bloom together, as far as possible leaving the later-flowering sorts for our May and June sections. *R. lapponicum* itself, circles the globe around the North Pole and the others are moorland plants, taking the place of heather on their native mountains and tundras. They mostly tend to a mauve, "ponticum", colouring and, therefore, particular care is needed to diversify the effect with pale citron yellow and white which is often best supplied by other genera; otherwise the effect can be dreary.

R. russatum "A" **** (A.G.M. 1938) with Amethyst Violet (H.C.C. 35/2) or purple-blue, white-throated flowers, forms a rather open, stiff bush said to reach 4 feet although it usually remains more dwarf in an open situation. It is quite an attractive little shrub but requires shelter. *R. cantabile*, a distinct, smaller form with rusty-green leaves, is now, regrettably, merged with it as to name. The general appearance of this plant is very bronzy in tone but its sturdy, compact form and the vividness of the Amethyst Violet flowers (H.C.C. 35/1) make it one of the finest of the mountain dwarfs, though it is sometimes less free-flowering than others. It stands up to exposure much better than *R. russatum*.

R. chryseum "A" **, grows to about 1 foot 6 inches high in the open and has untidy yellow flowers sometimes a little too late in opening to contrast effectively with most of the members of this batch. Forms vary somewhat, but on the whole it is one of the best yellows, but scarce.

R. fastigiatum "A" ***, has light purple flowers and a rather upright habit. I do not find it so beautiful as many others, but it is, at least, more easily obtainable than most.

R. flavidum "A" **** has pale yellow flowers that sometimes open as early as March, too early for the bulk of the other Lapponicums and often too late for the very early section of the other dwarfs such as *R. leucaspis*, etc.

R. hippophæoides "A" **** (A.G.M. 1925) is perhaps the easiest to grow of all, making a tallish shrub of up to 3 feet in height. The shapely little flowers are, however, only a pale lilac. It should be grown in an open situation and firmly pegged down at the start or it is a poor gangling thing.

R. impeditum "A" *** is a typically good Lapponicum with a dense mounded habit and, in a good form, has very lovely sparkling Amethyst Violet (H.C.C. 35/1) flowers that completely cover the bush, and beautiful sea-green young foliage. It comes from open moorland at 15,000 feet elevation in western Szechwan but is perfectly happy on my open, peaty slope at 500 feet elevation in Sussex. It is a most delightful plant and in my opinion one of the most beautiful of all miniature evergreens in winter. *R. intricatum* "A" *** is rather similar but less fine.

Of the hybrids of these blue sorts, 'Blue Tit' *** (*Augustinii* × *impeditum*) has already been mentioned. It is a lively grower and rather early, but the flowers will not stand as much exposure as those of either of its parents. 'Blue Bird' *** (*intricatum* × *Augustinii*) has actually the bluest (Veronica Violet, H.C.C. 639/1) and one of the shapeliest flowers, but it is not quite as free-flowering as one would wish, and it flowers rather early. 'Sapphire' *** is said to stand more exposure but I have not seen it looking spectacular. 'Intrifast' * (*fastigiatum* × *intricatum*) will stand exposure, and looks like a bluer flowered and bluer leaved *impeditum* but has not quite the freedom of flower of the best form of that species. Its offspring with *Augustinii*—'Blue Diamond' **** (F.C.C. 1939)—is the finest of all the dwarf blue hybrids owing to the reliable profusion of its Aster Violet (H.C.C. 38/3) flowers and compact, busy habit, but it needs shelter from sun and cold wind. This does not really matter because shelter is also required for its best associates, those pale yellow flowered hybrids such as 'Unique', 'Dairymaid', 'Moongold' or 'Adriaan Koster' that, together, make one of the most exquisite colour schemes of the year.

R. scintillans "A" ****, has a poor habit but fine flowers in the best form which gained a First-Class Certificate, as these are almost a Royal Blue. It is comparatively easily struck from cuttings and though small, slender and fragile, it is a fairly quick grower so that it is regrettable that it is much less effective in the garden landscape than *impeditum* or the hybrids 'Intrifast', 'Bluebird', 'Blue Diamond' and 'Blue Tit', with their neat, compact, bushy forms. *R. scintillans* comes from open pastures on the Lichiang Range at up to 14,000 feet elevation.

R. microleucum "A" *** is a delightful white-flowered Lapponicum species, blooming in late April and growing about a foot high. It thus provides a useful foil to the other colourings and lights up the effect (F.C.C. 1938).

In the Maddenii series we have an easily seed-propagated Rhododendron in *R. ciliatum*. But the big pale rose flowers, that seem almost too large for the little bushes, often come in March and, though a large bed of seedlings in fullest exposure makes a great bowl overflowing with a rosy foam of flower, I find it too riskily early in effect and too weak in colour to be worth while in the new small garden, and have therefore discarded it. If grown in the wood, this Rhododendron loses its dwarf form and makes a bush several feet high which is not, in my opinion, particularly attractive.

The series *neriiflorum* contains an interesting dwarf creeping species —*R. repens* "A" **** (F.C.C.) with big red flowers but it is too shy-flowering. Some of its hybrids, though, are just the sort of Rhododendrons that are wanted for the small gardens of today. Specially notable are:—

'Elizabeth' (F.C.C. *Griersonianum* × *repens*). Exquisite, shapely big scarlet flowers on a neat bush 4 feet high by 6 across. An outstandingly beautiful variety.

'Little Ben' (F.C.C. *repens* × *neriiflorum*) is dwarfer, smaller-flowered and earlier.

Then we have hardier and slightly later-flowering varieties from crosses with hardy hybrids:—

'Spring Magic', with dark, twisted leaves and deeper red, more bell-shaped flowers, opening in early May in little trusses of six or so on a bush 3 feet high and 5 across ultimately.

'Spring Day'. The leaves are vivid green and the flowers earlier, brighter red and opening flatter on a 2½ feet by 4 feet bush.

'Scarlet Wonder', a particularly handsome bush of shapely leafage, less free-flowering when young but always good-looking.

In the Thomsonii series the only member possibly qualifying for inclusion in this section of April-flowering dwarfs suitable for open positions is *R. Williamsianum*, "C" ****. I am afraid that the "C" is very justly attributed, so I mention it only for a sheltered corner. It is quite a pleasing little Rhododendron with a dense, mounded habit, seldom much more than a foot high. The rounded leaves are pale-coloured below and the young growths chocolate brown. The loose trusses of about two large, pale pink, nodding flowers are beautifully formed and, though owing to its very weak colouring it makes no great effect, it is, perhaps, too charming as an individual to be left out.

Again, the hybrids are an improvement from the garden angle and it seems, curiously enough, that these have a much greater tolerance of limy soil conditions than is usual among Rhododendrons. Only *R. hirsutum*, a form of the Alpenrose found on limestone formations and Azalea 'Satsuki' appear to share this quality. These hybrids are bred from an extra hardy and free-flowering form of *R. Williamsianum*:—

'Spring Pearl' has a charming pale pink flower opening flat on a bush about 4 feet high and broad.

'Spring Rose' has a more bell-shaped, deeper pink flower and a darker leaf of a smoky-purplish tint.

In the Virgatum series, *R. racemosum*, "A" **** (A.G.M. 1930) in its various forms is the most useful. The excessively early flowering variety *oleifolium* is, I think, to be avoided, as it opens in March when the weather prevents its being effective more often than not. *R. racemosum* is perfectly hardy in the open and the masses of pale apple-blossom-pink flowers in April are quite pleasing, if sadly weak in colour. It is best in a fully exposed position, as in a shady and sheltered place it grows tall and leggy and does not flower properly. On the whole it is a somewhat over-rated species, but it is useful for bleak places where the more lovely and vivid kinds cannot be grown.

As regards the cultivation of all these delightful little shrubs, a peaty slope with sandstone rocks and a northerly rather than a full south exposure, seems to be the ideal. But in the ordinary garden, on any acid soil, they grow well enough provided that they are pegged down when planted and given water if dry after flowering, and are planted in a fairly moist area made up with black humus and sunken sandstone rocks. Peat or leaf-mould, or just the dark soil from a lime-free Beech wood, all serve equally well. They do not really like woodland conditions and, in my opinion, never look right there, although the shade of distant tall trees is helpful in the dry eastern section of the country to avoid over-roasting when we get one of our hot summers and the frost protection afforded by a canopy of tree branches may be essential in a low-lying garden.

To grow the larger Rhododendrons from seed is a long business, it is true, although the rewards are great. But, with these little fellows that flower within two or three years of sowing, it is obviously well worth everybody's while. The best way of growing them from seed is to collect this carefully when ripe, in November or December, and sow in January in pans of sifted, damp, peat-moss litter, with the bottom half nearly all drainage crocks. Sow the seed on the flattened surface and sift on a scattering of silver sand. This sanding must be repeated when the seedlings appear, to help to anchor them. Air is gradually given, and the pans kept uniformly moist and shaded. Watering is done by partly immersing the pans in a tank of water so that the moisture seeps up from below. When the seedlings are large enough to handle they are very carefully pricked off into boxes and grown on.

With the easier sorts such as 'Blue Tit', I find that sowing in selected spots in the woodland, where a shady bank offers likely conditions, is often quite effective; no reliance can be placed on results, of course, but it is amusing when it succeeds. Cuttings, too, can be rooted without great difficulty and as small plants of good forms now often cost 12s. 6d. apiece it is evidently a rewarding proposition for the amateur. Short firm shoots with a trimmed heel firmly set in sharp sand and peat mixture under a shaded bell-glass in early winter usually respond; but for a masterly exposition of this complex subject in detail, see F. Hanger, *R.H.S. Journal*, Vol. LXX, p. 359.

Those fortunate enough to have a small piece of wooded ground, and an acid soil, may adventure happily with some of the larger woodland Rhododendron species. Some of these flower in April, but as early May is a safer flowering time the greater number of those specially recommended flower then or later still. Consequently a selection of these is grouped under early May (p. 132) together with cultural directions.

Turning now from these acid soil shrubs to a family that is indifferent to soil conditions, we note that several attractive members of the **Viburnum** family flower in spring, usually in April.

Viburnum Carlesii (A.G.M. 1923) comes from Korea and was introduced to Kew in 1902. In the open it forms a bushy, fairly symmetrical, rounded, deciduous shrub, usually about 4 or 5 feet high, with dusty-looking leaves and bun-shaped trusses of very sweet-scented, small, white Daphne-like flowers, fairly freely borne and well displayed, but making little distant effect. Its weak points are that the leaves are rather unattractive until they colour in autumn and that often each of the cymes† of flower has a number of browned florets that spoil their charm. But the young leaves are attractively fresh and green when they expand with the delightful pinkish flower buds in early April.

Various hybrids have been bred with the object of improving upon the vigour of *V. Carlesii*. *V. Burkwoodii* (A.G.M. 1956) is a cross with *V. utile* and can be very beautiful as a ten-foot wall-plant but is now often attacked by a virus which prevents the flowers developing properly.

V. Juddii (A.G.M. 1960) is a hybrid with *V. bitchiuense* and has a more graceful habit and better resistance to pests than *Carlesii* and as it grows better from cuttings the endless nuisance of grafted plants can be avoided.

V. 'Anne Russell' (A.M. 1959) and V. 'Fullbrook' (A.M. 1957) have the parentage of *V. Carlesii × Burkwoodii* and are improvements on both their parents being charming graceful shrubs with pink buds and fragrant white flowers.

V. carlcephalum (*V. Carlesii × macrocephalum*, wild form) has larger leaves similar to *Carlesii*, and the habit is compact and vigorous. The domed, tightly packed flower cluster is 4 to 5 inches across and very fragrant. Its flowering time is usually slightly later than that of *V. Carlesii*. On a limy soil near the coast this should be one of the first choices among spring-flowering shrubs. It is by far the best of the early Viburnums.

V. bitchiuense is a taller shrub of more open habit at first, finally making a large bush, 9 feet high or more, when it may almost equal *V. Carlesii* with the freedom of its brighter, equally fragrant, but smaller flowers. The flowering time is usually early April.

These Viburnums might be described as some of the finest of second-class shrubs; possibly first-class in favoured spots. The flowers being white, they cannot clash with any colour scheme, but assist all, and their fragrance is quite delightful. But one or two plants are enough; one bush is as good to look at as a dozen. They are not particular as to soil, even growing well on chalk, but respond well to a mulch of cow manure; and an open sunny position with shelter from cutting winds is required. Although said to be easily increased by leaf-cuttings, I have not found them to strike very readily or to grow on well. Ordinary cuttings taken at the end of May before the wood gets too hard strike easily but are also very slow-growing. Many make no headway for a whole season. Nurseries usually supply plants grafted on *V. lantana* and these grow well enough, provided that any suckers from the stock are removed at once. The members of this group of the Viburnums do not transplant very well.

† A cyme is a broad, more or less flat-topped, flower cluster, with the central flowers opening first.

Several beautiful members of the **Clematis** family flower in spring and these are mostly rampant climbers suitable for large house walls or, better still, unimportant trees such as ragged old male Hollies or conifers. Among the finest are the following:—

Clematis montana (A.G.M. 1930) in its finer forms is superb, the great masses of shapely white or pink flowers giving a beautiful effect. Fine varieties are: 'Elizabeth' with pale pink fragrant flowers, the new 'Tetrarose' with huge deep pink flowers and 'Grandiflora' with white flowers.

C. m. rubens is a fine pink-flowered form with large, anemone-like, pale purplish-pink flowers. 'Pink Perfection' is a deeper pink.

These Clematis are best planted with their roots shaded but where they can climb up into the sun. They grow well among builders' rubble, and in limy soils generally, and are therefore specially valuable to clothe unsightly new buildings or to decorate an arbor when quick-growing and effective furnishings are required.

Propagation is really best left to the nurserymen as seedlings usually vary in quality for the worse. Layering, however, can sometimes be effected by burying portions of low young branches. No pruning is necessary provided that care has been taken to train out the growth at the start in a well-spaced fan formation covering the required area.

Ulex europæus plenus (A.G.M. 1929), the **Double Gorse,** is one of those innumerable shrubs which nearly achieve great beauty, but just fail. There are always a lot of unattractive dead spines to be seen, the doubled flower is rather a muddle and the habit is very gawky. A poor, hungry soil is needed, or it immediately grows too leggy. Examples of rabbit-topiary of the wild Gorse on the moors are often very attractive, but too much clipping of course prevents free blooming. Though the Gorse makes good windbreaks it is far too inflammable to be safe near valuable shrubs, so perhaps it is best to keep it out of the garden, except for the dwarf species, the 'Petty Whin', whose apricot spires are very welcome in late summer.

In old gardens there is often buried treasure in the form of priceless plants swamped by rubbish. Too often new owners are too hasty in destroying everything in order to make a fresh start. However good the new plan may be, its realisation would probably be both earlier and better if modified so as to include some established features already grown to mellowness and majesty. Among the finds worth keeping at all costs, at any rate until the new work has become furnished, are large evergreens; in particular ancient **Rhododendrons.**

Such an old hardy hybrid Rhododendron is ' Rendall's Scarlet ', formerly known as "*Smithii*", a cross between the early, tender, red Himalayan *R. arboreum* and *R. ponticum*. It is customary to put this old variety down as a "has-been" or "no longer worthy of cultivation", owing to the fact that its flowers are really of rather a purplish pink colour. But after seeing superb aged specimens in open parkland gnawed by cattle to the "browsing line", and been greatly impressed by the picturesque habit of these fine flowering evergreen trees, I am not at all sure that this is right. A non-gardening friend, whose artistic taste is widely respected, once told me that, though I had shown him several hundred different choice varieties of Rhododendrons in the great Leonardslee gardens during the afternoon, he found that these gnarled trees were really the most beautiful of all. Forcing myself, with an effort, to cast aside all horticultural bias for a moment, I had to agree, but the beauty is possibly that of age, rather than of the variety. Some Rhododendron hybrids, of course, will never make trees; they always remain bushes, but this is not invariably such an advantage as is sometimes thought. Few gardens are so minute that a tree of any kind is unsuitable, and the most beautiful small trees I have ever seen, anywhere, are old trees, 30 feet high, of *R. arboreum*, *R. Thomsonii* and *R. Luscombei*. The flowers are glorious but the clean, marbled, pink trunks and weeping branches set with blue-green foliage are a delight even when the corollas lie in carpets of rose, red and crimson beneath. So let the old hybrid be spared by all who are lucky enough to find one on their land, and should a specimen of *R. Thomsonii* or any of its hybrids *having a smooth bark*, be thought too "leggy" to be worth keeping, I would plead especially for its life. As this type will not "break" freely again if cut down, the only alternative is to treat it as a tree and encourage it to grow in this way. The trunk is as decorative as that of any of the much boosted trees grown solely for the beauty of their bark, but too much clearing must not be done, as, unless the ground is shaded and mulched, the plant soon gets wizened and dried up, and is no longer an object of beauty. In sheltered spots, immense plants of the old hybrids, feathered to the ground, are sometimes found in Rhododendron districts and, rather than destroy them, the wise course is to plant a complementary flower effect, taking advantage of the invaluable shelter *without ground-robbing*, that these shrubs provide so well. Crabs, Plums, Cherries and Narcissi, alone, can build up in a very short time a group of great splendour around such a main feature, which would otherwise require a lifetime for its attainment.

Name changes are often irritating but there are times when they are very welcome. Let us be thankful that the wretched situation of having

Pyrus as the generic name of "Japonicas" (Chænomeles), Pears, Rowans, Apples and Aronias is now brought to an end by general consent. Malus is now the accepted generic name for the **Crab-apples**.

As flowering trees, the Crabs have many handsome species for the garden. They are less beautiful in the individual blossom, as a rule, than the Cherries, and form less shapely trees in the landscape when out of bloom, but their coloured fruits are often brilliant in autumn.

The dull-purple-leaved forms *Malus purpurea Eleyi* (A.G.M. 1925) and *M. p. Lemoinei* (A.G.M. 1937) are very commonly planted, but not everybody finds either the foliage or the somewhat muddy, vinous-pink flowers altogether attractive, and the fruits which are of much the same somewhat uninteresting tint make no great display. *M. purpurea* itself (A.G.M. 1923) has more richly coloured blossom of a bright crimson tint (H.C.C. 22/1) but the dull, reddish-purple foliage, again, makes the tree difficult to place in the summer garden.

M. p. floribunda (A.G.M. 1923), so rightly named, is one of the most beautiful of the Crabs, with its masses of pink buds and white flowers. It should really be allowed to grow as a large bush as it does not make a shapely tree. ' Hillieri ' is a fine late-flowering pink variety.

M. hupehensis (M. theifera) (A.G.M. 1930) is a very handsome Crab with a better, more tree-like habit than the foregoing. It comes from China, whence it was sent back by E. H. Wilson in 1900. The flowers are large, $1\frac{1}{2}$ inches across, and white, or blush pink in the variety *rosea*, and the globular fruits are yellow and red. It is one of the most attractive members of the family.

M. spectabilis, another tall, upright tree of around 20 feet or more, has red buds opening to blush pink flowers, and yellowish fruits. The variety *Riversii* (or *flore pleno*) is particularly fine. Var. *albi plena* is a superb double white and one of the finest of all Crabs.

M. micromalus makes a smaller, more upright tree, with small pink blossoms in great profusion followed by red fruits.

A singularly fine Crab is *M. baccata mandschurica*, a bigger and more ragged tree with white blossom, violet-scented, very late in the season—towards the end of May. Some forms have abundant vivid red fruits and are especially worth looking out for.

M. prunifolia is one of the best Crabs for fruit as the red and yellow apples remain long on the tree. An interesting variety is *M. p. fastigiata* with an upright habit and fine pink blossom which make it suitable for street planting. 'Cheal's Crimson' has exceptionally vivid fruits.

M. 'Golden Hornet' is a hybrid Crab of erect habit with round, pale yellow, cherry-sized fruits freely borne.

M. 'Cheal's Golden Gem' has attractive, pale blushed flowers followed by small yellow fruits, and 'Gibbs' Golden Gage' is rather similar.

The most delightful bush Crab is *M. Sargenti* (A.G.M. 1927), with shapely white blossom in abundance followed by round red fruits that remain over winter, and a good autumn effect from the colouring of the leaves. The bush is seldom more than 4 or 5 feet high and, anyhow, can be kept to this size quite easily, if desired, by a little pruning.

M. toringoides (A.G.M. 1929) has white blossom followed by very handsome, waxy, red and yellow fruits, but is usually a wretchedly shaped tree.

M. 'John Downie' can make a fine shapely tree with white blossom and bright red and yellow fruits. It is still one of the best of the red-fruited Crabs and unlike many of the others its natural habit leaves little to be desired.

Several fine Crabs have appeared recently. *M. robusta* is a strong tree with white or pink-flushed blossom and a fine long-lasting display of red fruits. *M.* 'Profusion' is an improvement on *Lemoinei* with more and brighter flowers. *M.* 'Almey' has red flowers with a white centre.

The Crabs are indifferent to soil so long as it is deep and reasonably well drained. For long, Apples were thought to prefer a limy soil, but of late it has been found that the "freezing up" of available iron, caused by alkalinity, has a bad effect and this is sometimes remedied by injecting iron pills into the trunks. A good mild tonic for a Crab that is not growing well is a light hoeing followed by a top dressing of fresh wood-ash or Growmore. Like the Cherries, Crabs need regular spraying with both winter-wash and Derris or, sooner or later, they will be made unsightly and checked in growth by a massed assault by caterpillars. In view of spraying dangers to evergreens, the trees are best kept away from the beds of shrubs, being either grown as specimens, complementing groups of flowering Cherries perhaps, or as an irregular line of shade trees for the beds.

Another pink-blossomed lime-tolerating subject in flower at this season is a member of the **Bladder-nut** family.

Staphylæa holocarpa rosea is the best form of this Chinese species which makes a twiggy and rather undistinguished bush about 8 feet high, very pretty when in flower in late April with its innumerable pale purplish-pink flowers. Only introduced from China in 1908 by E. H. Wilson it is still uncommon, but this quality should not lead us to place it in too prominent a position as it is of little ornamental value when out of flower. It is, however, very useful for gardens with a limy soil as it grows perfectly well under such conditions. For gardens with neutral or acid soils there are innumerable shrubs even more brilliantly in flower at this time of year that will, when their flowers are over, still be beautiful parts of the garden composition with pleasing forms and evergreen or autumn-colouring foliage. This Bladder-nut is hardy and can be increased from cuttings of half-ripe shoots treated in the usual manner.

It is in the later part of the early springtime period that the first section of my favourites of all the flowering shrubs come into bloom. They are a very choice family, rich beyond any in plants that have all the qualities for the gardener who seeks the maximum of charm in his garden landscape in miniature. They are the **Evergreen Azaleas** of Japan and their allies, and they give us one of the first displays of densely massed flower colour for the ordinary garden on lime-free soil.

As with the Cherries, the Tree Peonies, the Camellias and the Hydrangeas, these superb garden plants have been so long bred and cultivated by Japanese gardeners that to determine the true original wild prototypes and to trace the crossings that have taken place is an almost impossible task for the botanist. That great plantsman, E. H. Wilson, studied these Azaleas particularly and introduced the lovely 'Kurumes', a cultivated race emanating from the district of that name, to America. But, owing to the fact that intermediate forms between the many extreme types, which appear to gardeners to be quite distinct species, still survived as wild plants among their native hills, he lumped a number of horticulturally distinct kinds together under the name of *Rhododendron obtusum*. We gardeners cannot so generalise, as some are hardy and some are not; some have flowers which fade quickly in the full sun necessary for the health of the plants; others do not fade; some are "mimps" (plants which never really get going); others are first-class garden plants.

When the specific name thus loses horticultural significance the varietal name becomes very important. A good colloquial name is "Evergreen Azalea" and I find the Japanese garden names of the varieties on the whole rather less troublesome than such Latin ones as *Chamæcyparis pisifera plumosa nana aurea Rogersii*, or even French names of the type of 'Souvenir de Claudius Denoyel', 'Petite Sœur Thérèse de l'Enfant Jésus', etc.

As pet plants for the small garden, charming all the year round and having, each, a distinct personality of its own and delightful to have living close to us, few shrubs can compare with the Evergreen Azaleas.

Furthermore, no evergreens that I know have such neatness and beauty of form in the landscape, and in the great gardens of this country, places that are unmatched anywhere in the world today, they are lavishly used in such a manner that this delightful quality is fully exploited.

According to E. H. Wilson,[†] the original "type" form of *R. obtusum* was a red-flowered garden form now seldom seen in Britain, named by Jules Emile Planchon, and grown in Japanese gardens for centuries. It is so floriferous that "the whole plant appears blood-red" and its Japanese garden name is "Hiryu", but, to add the usual complications, we learn that around Kurume it is called "Hino tsukasa". Furthermore, it was first introduced from near Shanghai, China, by Robert Fortune who sent it to the Horticultural Society of London in 1844. Wilson states that this Azalea is derived from a wild plant common on Mount Kirishima which has also given birth to the dense, dark, tiered, fully evergreen, purple-flowered var. *amœnum*, to the tall open-habited, partly deciduous, ultra hardy, orange-flowered var. *Kœmpferi*, and the two quite distinct forms which many have grown from wild seed sent from Japan. Now, however, we are glad to discard this theory, which never looked right to those who grew and lived with these plants and to follow Professor Hiroshi Hara who gave species status to *R. Kœmpferi* and *R. kiusianum* also; these species being the chief ancestors of the hybrid garden races generally known as *R. obtusum*.[‡]

At the same time we should note that two horticulturally distinct types of Azaleas are raised from wild Japanese seed: (1) the type known as *R. obtusum* Planchon, a wild form with bright rose-red flowers with dark purple anthers, flowering too early for safety and incapable either of withstanding full exposure in Britain or of growing healthfully for long in shade and shelter; and (2) the type known as *R. kiusianum* Makino, flowering in late May with purple or deep rose, widely opened corollas with a short tube and revelling in full exposure to sun and wind so that the growths are well ripened and thus hardy and resistant to frost. Although these are not clearly recognisable botanical distinctions, they are vital ones to the gardener who is, after all, the most interested party with regard to these fascinating plants.

The important point is that, being hybrids of multiple parentage like the Hydrangeas also bred for centuries by the Japanese, the varieties differ very widely in hardiness, depending upon which parent they favour in this respect.

The natural habitat of the wild type of *R. kiusianum* is interesting, for it gives us some guidance to its culture in our gardens. Apparently it grows mostly on windswept slopes on the mountains above the

[†] "A Monograph of Azaleas", by Ernest Henry Wilson and Alfred Rehder, University Press, Cambridge, 1921, p. 30.

[‡] "Occurrence of Rhododendrons in Japan", by Hiroshi Hara, *Rhododendron Year-Book*, pp. 112–127 (1948).

tree-level in full sun among coarse grasses and other low shrubs. *R. Kœmpferi* has a more northern distribution and often inhabits shady woods.

Two kinds of leaves are produced by these Azaleas: large, deciduous summer leaves, and smaller, firmer, persisting ones. The commonest colour of *R. kiusianum* in the wild is a rosy-mauve, but all the other colours mentioned in dealing with the varieties are said to be also, if more rarely, found in nature. The fragrance of the flowers is also variable, though actually I have not found this to be appreciable in the cultivated forms.

E. H. Wilson sent a selection of fifty of what were considered the best of the evergreen Japanese Azaleas cultivated at Kurume to the Arnold Arboretum in 1919. Of these only about five had been commonly obtainable in England up to now, although as many as eighteen are listed by one well-known Surrey nursery. The R.H.S. have, fortunately, now been presented with a complete set of these,† from the original American stock, by Mr. Charles Williams, and as their increase from layers or cuttings is easily practicable we may hope that ere long they will all be readily obtainable.

Of the Kurume types, the following particularly good varieties appear to be commonly available in commerce:—

'Kureno Yuki', white "hose-in-hose" (one flower within another).
'Irohayama', white flushed mauve, exquisite. (A.M. 1952).
'Takasago', pale Carmine (H.C.C. 21/2) flowers.
'Azuma Kagami'—large peach-pink flowers, (Neyron Rose H.C.C. 623/2) hose-in-hose.
'Kirin', flowers bell-shaped, (Neyron Rose H.C.C. 623/2), early.
'Hinodegiri', bright crimson flowers, a very good strong grower with beautiful coppery winter foliage, and one of the best.
'Hinomayo', pure pink, lovely but not very tough.
'Hatsugiri', bushy and free but magenta.
'Helena' a good clear double pink.
'Blaauws Pink' hose-in-hose warm pink.
'Blue Danube', bright purple, contrasting nicely.
'Bikini', flesh pink flowers, lettuce green foliage.
'Salmon Sander', can reach over 6 feet high!
'Shin Sekai, creamy white, flowers soon turning brown.
'Kumo No Uye', flowers pale Vermilion or "salmon".
'Purple Triumph', deep purple.
'Tsuta Momiji', flowers deep vermilion red.
'Rasho Mon', flowers scarlet, regrettably early.

† See Wilson's "Monograph", footnote p. 202, for the complete list.

The chief weakness of the older Evergreen Azalea varieties is their early flowering which risks spoiling their display, and their lack of sufficient basic hardiness to make them proof against damage in hard winters. Thus, when we started breeding Evergreen Azaleas our objectives were obvious. Now, the hardiest Evergreen Azalea is *R. Kœmpferi* and its latest flowering form 'Daimio' is one of the last of all to bloom. From the other parent we wanted to achieve a more wide-open, substantial, sun-resisting flower and a more evergreen leafage, for *Kœmpferi* is almost deciduous. The Chinese species *R. Simsii*, parent of the Dutch greenhouse Azaleas, was obviously a good candidate. But most forms are rather tender so only the hardiest, most northerly form of the species could be suitable. This was finally found and the cross made and many seedlings raised. As so often happens with a brainchild, the result of much thought to obtain a definite objective, the results exceeded our expectations.

The following have been named and registered:—

'Bengal Beauty' (A.M. after Trial). Bengal Rose in colour, large flowers, hardy, free and late.

'Pinkabelle', large flowers of deeper pink.

'Moon Maiden', compact, huge white flower.

'Coral Beauty', large rich orange flowers.

The above flower in May so should really be in that section, but they are more apt to be overlooked there so that older and less effective varieties are ordered instead.

The variety *amœnum* is very distinct, being notably hardy and of superb form as an evergreen shrub, having a cedar-like habit with dense tiers of branches more persistently evergreen than most. Unfortunately the charming little hose-in-hose flowers are of a Rhodamine Purple very difficult to place. This defect, however, is absent in the gloriously decorative branch-sport sometimes known as Azalea 'Tyrian Rose' (see illustration facing p. 113) and also in the rare crimson-flowered variety *coccineum* which is prominent at Wisley. Sometimes a purple-flowered branch appears, but if this is cut out at the base further trouble seldom occurs. In old gardens splendid specimens of the purple form are sometimes to be found up to 6 feet in height, which leads one to think that this was one of the earliest varieties to be introduced. This Azalea is a particularly good garden plant and grows well in any acid soil with added peat or black mould, rooting "layers" with the least encouragement.

Many other varieties are available but suffer from the grave disadvantage of having flowers whose colourings quickly fade in the sun.

This failing prevents my being able to recommend them for general garden use. This is because, in my experience, unless these Azaleas are grown fully exposed to sun and air they fail to ripen their wood sufficiently to resist autumnal frosts. Thus, instead of being hardy plants they are reduced to the status of rather tender plants. Furthermore, in sheltered shady places these Azaleas are killed-back and disfigured by lichen and fungoid growths.

In the Orient, legend has it, this difficulty was got over by growing the orange-flowered sorts in full sun and air and having small boys on duty with straw-thatched parasols during the time the flowers were open. When the owner appeared to view the flowers these attendants withdrew gracefully to take up their task again later, so long as the sun shone brightly. In our gardens the best course is the compromise of planting these varieties near a Cherry or other specimen flowering tree so that the Azalea receives shade from the midday sun, but is yet in a comparatively airy and open position.

Among these varieties of more fugitive colouring which require shade and are in cultivation in this country, are:—

R. *obtusum* 'Beni Kiren', a bushy variety with medium-sized double flowers of a deep salmon hue flowering a little later than the others.

R. *o*. 'Hino-tsukasa', with flowers of a deep vermilion red freely borne on a spreading and vigorous bush.

R. *o*. 'Ima-Shojo', with small, vivid, crimson flowers, of "hose-in-hose" shape.

R. *o*. 'Koran Yuki', a dense plant with beautiful orange-salmon flowers, fragrant.

R. *o*. 'Kurai No Himo', with flowers of carmine red, hose-in-hose.

R. *o*. 'Sakata', having larger, Geranium Lake flowers on a strong-growing vigorous bush.

R. *o*. 'Suiyohi', with flesh-coloured flowers.

R. *o*. 'Tama No Utena', with pale salmon flowers.

R. *o*. 'Ukamuse', with orange-vermilion flowers.

Further information covering all the known varieties is to be found in Wilson's monograph already cited (p. 97), in the *Rhododendron Handbooks* published by the Rhododendron Group of the R.H.S., and in an article in *R.H.S. Journal*, Vol. LXXIV, p. 144 (1949) by J. P. C. Russell, "Hardy Evergreen Azaleas for the Garden".

Much suitably prepared, open-ground space and considerable labour, expense and careful recording would be needed to make full tests of the couple of hundred existing varieties. Many are unsuitable for general planting in this country, being less hardy and vigorous in constitution than others, or having flowers which will not stand up to the full exposure to sun and wind necessary to produce winter hardy growth. In my opinion a shaded trial-ground would not provide the essential data. Indeed, the results might well be misleading and tend to cause undeserved setbacks to the popularity of these beautiful plants. Greater hardiness is the vital factor (see p. 145).

Many seedlings are being bred at the present time and there is very wide variation in the unfading quality of their flower colours and the durability of the material of the corollas. As an example it may be mentioned that the flowers of 'Hinomayo' remain fresh for five weeks or more in full sun while those of 'Shin Sekai' are browned and shrivelled in a few hours. These qualities have little botanical significance but they are of primary horticultural importance.

R. Kæmpferi. This horticulturally distinct species is only partly ever-green and has certain important characteristics. In the first place it is evidently hardy anywhere in the British Isles as it grows well at the Arnold Arboretum, Boston, Mass., where the climate is too severe for our native Ivy and Holly. Unlike *R. kiusianum* it is abundant on most of the Japanese hills and mountains. The flowers are larger—nearly twice the size of most of those of the varieties of *R. obtusum* and in clusters instead of in pairs, as is usual. This Azalea has also two varieties which are of considerable importance to the gardener owing to the fact that they come into bloom in early July instead of April. These are known as 'Mikado' and 'Daimio' and are available at a number of nurseries. They are not described in any of the works on the genus previously cited, though commonly listed by the trade. I will say more of them under the July headings. Some seedling forms of *Kæmpferi* flower disastrously early and I have seen these destroyed by March frosts. In favourable years such plants are very pretty with the pale violet of R. 'Blue Tit', etc., but on the whole it is better to play safe and select the later-flowering forms. Among other important points is the wide variation in the durability of the colour and texture of the corollas. Some seedlings of this species are quite useless, as their flowers fade in a few hours—others remain long in beauty. Again, some are unusually evergreen and maintain superbly autumn-tinted leaves for a very long period; others drop nearly all their leaves at once, before they colour in autumn. (See illustration facing p. 128 for my best form.)

R. Kæmpferi has produced, with a hybrid clone called *malvatica*, a number of excellent garden hybrids of nearly equal hardiness to *Kæmpferi*. The latter is given as category "A" in the *Rhododendron Year-Book* while that of the true 'Kurumes' is listed as "C". These hybrids are quite good garden plants, but most require shade to preserve their flower colours and many lack the fully evergreen quality so valuable in the best Japanese varieties and also something of their perfection of refinement of flower form. When flowers are the perfect size in proportion to the bush nothing is gained by making them any bigger. The origin of *malvatica*, a clone with single, mauve flowers, is not known.

The following is a selection of *Kæmpferi* hybrids:—

'Addy Wery' ***, A.M. 1950. Deep brownish vermilion, fls. 1½ ins. across. Rather tender.

'Alice' **, geranium lake (H.C.C. 20/1), fls. 2 ins. across.

'Anny' *, A.M. 1948, deep brownish vermilion, fls. 2 ins. across.

'Atalanta' **, orchid purple (H.C.C. 31/2), fls. 2¼ ins. across.

'Betty' *, orange-pink, scarce.

'Fedora' †, ** deep rose madder (F.C.C. 1960) fls. 2½ ins. across.

'Gerda' ‡, * bright rose madder (H.C.C. 23/2) fls .2¼ ins. across.

'Jeanette' ***, rose madder (H.C.C. 23/2) fls. 2½ ins. across.

'John Cairns' ***, A.G.M. 1952, deep brownish scarlet, very shapely fls. 2 ins. across.

'Mother's Day' **, crimson (A.M. 1959), compact, dwarf.

'Vuyks Scarlet' ***, flowers wavy-edged, crimson (A.M. 59).

'Willy' ***, the best pink, as Jeanette, but later and sturdier.

With the exception of 'Mother's Day' and 'Vuyks Scarlet', these hybrids lose nearly all their leaves in winter. They are mostly in the "A" category for hardiness but need to be shaded by a light canopy of branches, as *Genista aetnensis*, to preserve their flower colourings.

Crosses have also been made with "Mollis" Azaleas and the name *Vuykiana* is suggested for this new race. One of the best of these is 'Palestrina' a fine white-flowered evergreen variety.

'Hinodegiri' has been crossed with *R. Kæmpferi* producing, among others, the fine variety 'Orange Beauty' ** with rather early, orange-red flowers. A batch of seedlings of this cross will be found to resemble this variety closely, and if care has been taken to select a sun-resistant, long-lasting form of *R. Kæmpferi* as parent, some may be found to improve upon it. These Azaleas are some of the finest of all shrubs for autumn colour, as the richly tinted leaves remain on the bushes right up to Christmas, while those of many species recommended for such effects last only a few days.

Now for the garden arrangement of this early-flowering section. They are such delightful little plants and so singularly decorative all the year round that many of those fortunate enough to have an acid soil will choose them for the first massed colour display of their garden year. There are two colour arrangements that look particularly satisfying.

* Stars represent my own rating as garden plants.

† Audrey Wyniatt, Fidelio and others are similar.

‡ Pink Treasure, Juliana, William Lawrence, Kathleen and Pekoe are all similar, but slightly less bold in flower.

The first is to give full play to the extraordinarily clean and clear pinks so lavishly provided owing to the hyaline, or translucent, quality of the corollas and add merely white-flowered varieties and blue Forget-me-nots, with a bush or two of, say, *Magnolia stellata* to add its remarkably pure white to this assembly of rich but unmuddied colours. *R. Kæmpferi* and the orange-flowered sorts are kept apart in shady places where the sun will not burn away their delicate salmony tones and the crimson 'Hinodegiri' can be grouped elsewhere with a white-flowered shrub, whilst the purple *amænum* is grown as a specimen in some other part of the garden where its unsociable colour will not clash with other spring bloomers and its noble, darkly bronzed, evergreen habit will adorn the winter scene.

The other method, which I prefer, is to mix all the colours so thoroughly that no large blocks of one tint are able to start a fight. This needs plenty of plants and *all* the colours and a certain boldness in treatment. Thus, if one adds *Kæmpferi* and the salmon and orange 'Kurumes' and the mountain dwarf Rhododendrons with their blue-violets and yellows, and also *Cytisus kewensis* and *C. Beanii*, the palette is practically complete, and it only remains for the artist-gardener to arrange the picture. In this instance he can be absolutely confident of success, because these charming shrublets are so highly portable that trial and error must give the perfect result in the end.

For those who mutter darkly that these Azaleas must be too tender for their gardens it will, I hope, be an encouragement to observe the illustration facing p. 454 in C. G. Bowers' " Rhododendrons and Azaleas " (Macmillan, 1938) showing them in full beauty in the much more exacting climate of New England. More abundant and lovely flowers no shrubs possess and these have the daintiness, the subtle fragrance, the perfection of drawing, the pure and delicate colourings and the hyaline texture that are the very qualities that epitomise the charm that flowers have for us.

No gardeners on lime-free soil in these islands need be condemned to the second-rate; it is purely a question of whether they wish to take the necessary trouble. All are free to grow, in this most favourably situated group of islands, their own choice from amongst the richest garden floras in the temperate world. Some few deliberately seek a certain practical ugliness and no one may blame them, for the pleasure that the growing gives the grower is the criterion, and competition is only for those who wish to compete. As Farrer said once (I cannot remember where) of a fancier of "monstrous Chrysanthemums like mops dipped in lobster-sauce"—"there is not a weed that man treads beneath his feet on his way home from work that is not more beautiful than these." But that is no real point. Gardening for pleasure should have no stern exhortations to growing this or that. I can but indicate certain beauties and hope that the path shown may bring new fields of delight to those who seek that way and would welcome some short-cut which the long and twisted trail I have trodden may enable me to lay bare.

Some eyes are offended at the rich and somewhat "Russian ballet" flavour of orange, magenta, red, white and pink with added blue-violet, but amid the complementary green of spring grass I have found it most enjoyable. The pinks may lose something, perhaps, but the general effect is fascinating, and, all winter, the bright and varied ever-green mounds are a delightful feature of the garden composition.

So supreme are these Azaleas as plants to live with, beautiful every moment of the year, that, in the case of a small garden or courtyard with polluted, muddy, unsuitable soil I know no earth-shifting operation so rewarding as its complete removal and the substitution of a mixture of peat or "woodsy" black mould and sharp sand. In a tiny garden to have only the best is more than ever essential. Such a clean, weed-free soil, that is delightful to work and that will grow these superlative garden furnishings and also the newer types of deep blue, violet, crimson and pale blue Hydrangeas, gives better value than many costlier earth-shiftings that only move bad soil from one position in the garden to another, and there prop it up with expensive stone walls.

In low-lying districts the Evergreen Azaleas may lose their lives in a hard winter and they may be temporarily badly damaged by an unusually hard and late spring frost coming after a long spell of mild weather. But they seldom die, they recover amazingly rapidly and in quite a short time will have regained their old bushiness and vigour provided that they are growing in an open position and in suitable soil.

The cultivation of these Azaleas, garden-bred for centuries, presents few unsurmountable difficulties. A humus-rich, well-drained acid soil arranged so that it does not dry out in summer (see p. 24), plenty of sun and air, and pegging-down as advised for dwarf Rhododendrons seem to be the chief requirements. In too sheltered and shady places lichen attacks the plants and cripples them so that they make poor growth, with the unnaturally small leaves that betoken ill health in members of the Rhododendron family. Thus it is important to select those varieties whose flowers do not fade in the sun.

These Azaleas can be grown from cuttings, although they often take some time to form roots. On the other hand, any branch trodden into peaty ground frequently surprises me by rooting nicely and layers are at any rate a simple and consistently successful means of propagation.

Seeds sown as prescribed on p. 90 are also an excellent method but the varieties, of course, do not come true. Self-sown seedlings often appear in my garden.

Some hold that true heather peat is not essential for these little plants, but it is an easily obtained and safe material to incorporate with existing soil. Old, black, woods-mould is almost indistinguishable in appearance from peat, though, being richer, it is even better and is so much more quickly colonised by the roots than even a good loam that I always plant these Azaleas in a mixture of this material at the start. Commercial "peat-moss litter" is also effective, and, unless the soil is naturally a suitable black sandy stuff, I would advise adding a half-part of this to the topsoil and well mixing together.

To plant these Azaleas so that the top portion of the ball of roots is covered by ordinary soil is, usually, to ensure their early death. It is wise to keep a few sackfuls of natural forest peat and fine black rotted leaf-mould for the final sprinkling over the root-ball, and never, I would advise, put ordinary soil above the root-ball at any time. These roots require more air than those of most other plants, but sandstone rocks over them do not seem to be objected to, and they certainly help to retain moisture. A mulch of chopped bracken should be supplied every autumn if maximum growth is required.

In this treatise we have only begun the almost summer-long pageant of these Azaleas; in the sections that follow we shall list those that flower in later May, June and July.

The **evergreen Barberries** are a very valuable group for limy soils giving us both evergreen winter furnishing and vivid yellow and orange flowers very potent in the spring garden landscape.

Berberis Darwinii (A.G.M. 1930), a rather gangling, sparkling, spiny evergreen with orange flowers followed by bluish-purple berries is too well known to need further description. It was introduced from the strange and misty island of Chiloe, off the west coast of Chile, by William Lobb for Messrs. Veitch in 1894. Though ubiquitous, it is only "reasonably hardy" and it is often difficult to make it form a compact and shapely bush. Coming from south of the equator many find its appearance too alien to the northern flora to group really well with them unless special care is taken, and I must confess to being one of these.

A good example of my reasons for using the names of the flower colours, as given and shown in the Horticultural Colour Chart, is provided by this well-known garden shrub. As a rule the colour of the flowers is described as golden. The Chart reveals that they are Orpiment Orange (H.C.C. 10), which is about as pure an orange colour as one can get. I think that anyone holding a piece of orange skin near to a gold wedding ring will probably agree with me that gold and orange are two totally different colours.

This group of Barberries is far the most important of the genus for flower effect and there are a number of very fine varieties among them. Most of these we owe to the skill of that great old plantsman, the late T. Smith of Daisy Hill, Newry, who raised *Irwinii*, *gracilis*, 'Brilliant', *corallina*, 'Fireflame' and many others.

Mr. W. J. Marchant of Wimborne and Messrs. Cheal of Crawley have also raised fine hybrids.

The ability of the flowers to withstand quite sharp frosts unharmed is a valuable feature of many of the varieties and hybrids, some of the best of which are described below. *B. Darwinii*, like other Berberis, will grow on either acid or limy soils and its chief value will be for use in gardens with the latter type of soil. Its self-sown seedlings appear everywhere and thus propagation is self evident, though I find them bad movers.

There are a great number of improved seedling forms propagated as clones such as vars. 'Flame', 'Gold', 'Fireflame', etc. Another variety —*nana*—is seldom free-flowering.

Early nipping and pegging down improves the habit of *B. Darwinii*, and even its most bushy-habited hybrids such as *B. stenophylla corallina* are benefited by shearing back any shoots that tend to straggle.

B. stenophylla (*B. Darwinii × empetrifolia*) (A.G.M. 1923), a ten-foot mass of spiny twigs with fairly profuse, small yellow flowers in late April greatly admired by many, is perfectly "reasonably hardy", of very tough constitution and very commonly planted. It is excellent as a barrier where a gap has to be completely closed up, but it is too often seen as an ugly, leggy bush with a dense but sprawling and top-heavy head. In my opinion there are better forms for gardeners prepared to give the necessary extra care in cultivation. *B. stenophylla* must be propagated by cuttings, seedlings do not come true. Any necessary pruning is best done immediately after flowering.

B. s. gracilis is a lower-growing and more compact variety with arching branches and soft yellow flowers often not opening until early May.

B. s. 'Brilliant' is a dwarf, drooping form with very richly coloured flowers and rather yellowish-green foliage.

B. Irwinii is a dense and bushy hybrid with curious shield-shaped leaves and arching branches, otherwise resembling *B. Darwinii*, having flowers of a similar hue but slightly lighter in tint. It is one of the best of this type. Dr. Ahrendt considers that this hybrid should not carry the name *stenophylla*, being distinct in certain characters†.

B. stenophylla var. *coccinea*, in the finest form I have, which was received long ago as a tiny sprig as part of an R.H.S. Wisley plant

† "Berberis stenophylla Hybrids", by Rev. Leslie W. A. Ahrendt, *R.H.S. Journal*, LXXIV, Pt. 1, p. 36.

distribution, is an even more decorative shrub, being of dense, bushy habit, about three or four feet high, with crimson buds opening to Cadmium Orange flowers that make quite an attractive display of rich soft colour most valuable for limy gardens in the warmer districts. Unfortunately it is not quite hardy enough to be absolutely reliable, fine specimens being very badly damaged by frost alongside Japanese Azaleas, *Rhododendron deleiense*, *Hydrangea macrophylla* varieties, etc. which, often considered as rather tender, were comparatively unharmed by the low temperatures that destroyed this Berberis. Nothing is more annoying than to have specimen-grown bushes, that after some years have reached perfection, ruined overnight. Some branches in the centre of each dense, twiggy mass remained precariously alive and, by pruning away dead wood and pegging down and shaping up the remains, it has been possible to rehabilitate the specimens. But if more reliable substitutes can be found it is better to use these and avoid such worries.

B. s. ' Crawley Gem ', raised by Messrs. Cheal of Crawley and seen by me as small plants, appears to be rather similar in flower but it unfortunately lacks the fine, upright, but bushy, form which makes the last-mentioned variety so pleasing. The branches are wide spreading and loosely arching. 'Crawley Gem' is, however, said to be "reasonably hardy ", like *B. Darwinii*.

All these hybrid forms require to be propagated from cuttings, as seeds usually provide plants reverting to one or other of the parents, usually *B. Darwinii*. Cuttings of some of the hybrids are not very easy to strike.

In gardens with limy soils these Berberis may play a fine part with *Kerria japonica Chænomeles superba*, *C. japonica*, *Spiræa arguta*, Forsythias, *Cytisus purgans*, *C. præcox*, etc., in providing a spring display of vivid yellow and orange flower colour for those who prefer this warm-toned theme to the commoner pink and white theme which is also available.

Berberis linearifolia, introduced by Mr. H. F. Comber in 1927, has larger and brighter-coloured flowers than *B. Darwinii* and evergreen, entire, linear leaves. It is not a very vigorous grower in most gardens and requires a moist woodland soil and situation. In such places the large-flowered Azaleas give a better return but the Berberis is useful to diversify the effect and in gardens just too limy for Azaleas it is very valuable.

B. lologensis is a natural hybrid between the preceding and *B. Darwinii*, also collected by Mr. H. F. Comber, in the Andes. According to the collector's father, Mr. J. Comber (*R.H.S. Journal, Vol. LXV, Pt. 7, 218*) it has the rich flower colouring of *B. linearifolia* and the hardiness of *B. Darwinii*. This is borne out by the fact that, though severely injured, it survived frosts at Dawyck, N.B. which killed *Hoheria glabrata, Pyracantha atalantioides, Escallonia langleyensis, Ceanothus dentatus* and almost all kinds of Brooms†. There are various forms of this hybrid, such as 'Orange King', and care should be taken to secure the best.

B. buxifolia nana is a useful species for limy soils where it provides an attractive dense, two-foot, evergreen bush of a dark bluish-green, bearing scattered, solitary, amber-yellow flowers towards the end of April.

Here we will mention an admirable old cottage-garden favourite—*Kerria japonica* (A.G.M. 1928), also long cultivated in Japanese gardens, though actually wild only in China. It has two forms so different that few would recognise them as the same species. The double-flowered form—a gangling, leggy plant with small, pointed, toothed leaves and round balls of confused Saffron Yellow (H.C.C. 7/1) petals for its flowers, was introduced to Kew by William Kerr in 1804. As the deformed flowers had no "works" to them no one knew what the plant was. In 1834 John Russell Reeves introduced the single-flowered form which is a charming, twiggy, dense bush bearing rather bramble-like, pure Buttercup Yellow flowers from late April or early May onwards, and that great naturalist A. P. de Candolle accordingly placed it in the Rose Order under the name of Kerria. The single-flowered form is really much the better shrub and perfectly hardy and indifferent as to soil. There are both golden-variegated and silver-variegated varieties, but they are, I think, much inferior to the green-leaved single-flowered type. It is a very pleasing shrub and especially valuable for a soil too chalky for the Azaleas, where, with *Chænomeles superba, Ch. japonica, Berberis Darwinii, B. stenophylla coccinea. Genista hispanica, Spiræa arguta, Helianthemum vulgare* vars., *Viburnum tomentosum* and others, it will help to provide a substitute display for the warm and vivid Azalea colourings.

The only really bad feature of the British climate from a flowering shrub's point of view is its habit of making perpetual false promises. The wily Ash of the hedgerows, actually as tender in leaf as most of the exotics of which I write, knows how to discount such deceptions. However balmy the March airs, it keeps its young leaves safely coiled within the black bud-scales. They emerge only when things ought to be pretty safe, and treacherous late frosts are unlikely. Not so the sanguine

† *R.H.S. Journal*, LXVI, Pt. 7, p. 230 et seq.

Moutan, or Tree Peony, most splendid of lime-tolerant deciduous shrubs. At any really mild interval, after the turn of the year, it may sprout hopefully forth and usually receives a dreadful snubbing for its pains. The Rose and the Hydrangea are almost as easily deceived and lured into too-early growth.

All we can do, to avoid the consequences, is to study our garden climate, and select as backward a spot as possible or take advantage of a tree canopy or good katabatics.† Katabatics determine the incidence of late, or early, frosts in accordance with the lie of the land. To be very brief, cold air is heavy and slides, if it can do so freely, away downhill. Consequently elevated sites, with free "air drainage", do not suffer very much from spring frosts. Curiously enough this is one of the few fundamentals, comprehensible by mere observation without scientific knowledge, that our grandfathers apparently knew nothing about. This was, I suppose, because folks did not care to live up on a hill if they could avoid it, and, if they had to, they did not wake up early in the morning to have a look at their plants and those of their neighbours below. Nowadays many of us like to live on hills, and, almost any time when we look out of the window in early spring or autumn in the early morning, we see quite clearly that our friends in the valleys below are smothered in white fog and frost while we are up in the clear sun-light. To profit by these recently discovered phenomena we cannot all go and live up in the hills, perhaps, but very many gardeners on sloping lands can improve their garden climates out of all knowledge merely by removing obstructions to free air-flow on the downward side.

Those of us who have to garden in valleys and hollows must either avoid these over-sanguine growers or grow them under a canopy of branches where they are protected, or else in north-facing places where they get no encouragement to start growth until it is late enough to be reasonably safe. Cold, late districts suit the Tree Peony.

The Tree Peony, *Pæonia suffruticosa* (*P. Moutan*) first came to us, like so many oriental shrubs, as a garden plant long cultivated in China and Japan. In the earliest days of the missionaries to China the fame of the beautiful Moutan, that decorates many Chinese paintings and pottery designs, was spread abroad.

It was Sir Joseph Banks, who also introduced the Hortensia and many other valuable plants, who first secured a specimen for Kew from China through a Dr. Duncan in 1787. Robert Fortune, when sent to China by the Horticultural Society in 1843, also sent back many Tree Peonies from nurseries there, and these, according to William Robinson in "The English Flower Garden", were better garden plants than many

† See p. 25 for further data on garden climate.

of the over-elaborate varieties evolved later, in the florist era. They became quite popular and were widely distributed.

Although a rather similar plant had been imported by Sir Abraham Hume in 1802,† the wild ancestor was only discovered in its natural habitat by that fine writer and keen plant enthusiast, Reginald Farrer, in 1913. In "On the Eaves of the World" he wrote—"I was setting eyes on *Pæonia Moutan* as a wild plant. . . . that single enormous blossom waved and crimped into the boldest grace of line, of absolutely pure white, with feathering of deepest maroon radiating at the base of the petals from the boss of golden fluff at the flower's heart." He was not, however, able to introduce the plant or send back botanical material. It was only in 1925 when Dr. J. F. Rock sent back seeds which he collected from a lamasery garden, which afterwards proved to be apparently similar to Farrer's plant, that the wild Peony arrived. Plants of this origin grew and flowered in Colonel F. C. Stern's famous garden at Highdown near Worthing. There is an excellent photograph of this lovely shrub in bloom, p. 552, *R.H.S. Journal*, Vol. LXIV, Pt. 12 (Dec. 1939). From this and flowers exhibited at the Chelsea Show in 1949, we may see that the wild form is as good as, if not better than, many of the garden varieties as a decorative shrub *for appraisal as it grows*, rather than as a cut flower. Of its fragrance, Farrer recorded "the breath of them went out upon the twilight as sweet as any Rose". It was therefore greatly to be hoped that nurserymen would be able to propagate this fine plant in quantity from seed so that it might be made readily available to all. Unfortunately, however, the wild *Moutan* has proved to be far from vigorous as a garden plant, succumbing all too often to botrytis fungus attack.‡

At last we have many beautiful Japanese Tree Peonies safely imported and, though the labels all too often bear the name of the variety ordered rather than that actually applicable, most of the finer varieties are available. The faults that I think we should avoid in selecting garden varieties are:—Overdouble heavy flower-heads that bend over into the mud; flimsy, over-large, ragged petalled sorts whose flowers are dishevelled at the first gust of wind; pallid magenta flower colours. The following is a selection of good Japanese sorts:—

Benichidori, semi-double carmine-rose, good centre of jewel-like golden anthers.

Bijou de Chusan, see illustration p. 112.

† *R.H.S. Journal*, Vol. LXVI, Pt. 9, p. 310 (1941): "In 24 years this original plant has formed a bush 7 feet high and 14 feet in circumference producing 660 buds".

‡ See also "A study of the Genus Pæonia", by F. C. Stern, published by R.H.S. (1947), and "The Moutan or Tree Peony", by the author, Constable, 1963.

Hakugan, double white flushed rose.
Hakuo-jisi, double white, purple base, fine centre.
Hatsu-hinode, semi-double, carmine, fine centre.
Horaisan, semi-double, cupped lilac-rose, good centre.
Ima-shojo, semi-double, carmine-crimson.
Kajura-jisi (" Mme. S. Low "), double, carmine, fringed petals.
Kamada-fuji, double lilac-purple.
Kintei, this is L'Esperance, see p. 164 for the later-flowering varieties.
Lactea, single, white.
Momoyama, semi-double, large shapely flesh pink.
Nishiki-jima, semi-double, flesh pink.
Nissho, double, carmine, fine centre.
Ranzan, semi-double, carmine-pink, frilled.
Renkaku, white, semi-double, good centre.
Rimpo, deep purple, semi-double.
Ruriban, deep maroon, single, good centre.
Saishoji, semi-double, carmine-pink.
Setsugetsuka, double, white frilled petals, good centre.
Shirotae, white saucer-shaped flowers, frilled edges.
Sitifukujin, carmine, double, fine centre.
Taiyo, carmine-crimson, semi-double.
Tama-fuyo, pink, double, fine centre.
Tama-midori, scarlet, semi-double.
Tama-sudare, white semi-double, fine gold centre.
Yae-sakura, lilac-pink single, large, fine centre.

These varieties are root-grafted. We have also raised large numbers of single and semi-double-flowered varieties from seeds and these appear extremely promising as they are more resistant to botrytis fungus attack and grow very rapidly, often flowering in their third year. Grafted plants, if deeply planted, are also good strong growers and usually flower in the second year after planting.

The great danger is fungus infection. Every tiny bit of dead stem or leaf must be cut cleanly away to live wood and dusted with fungicide such as sulphur or treated with a spray such as Bordeaux Mixture.

In cultivation the Moutan requires skill and care. It is perfectly hardy, so far as winter cold is concerned, but as already explained, is a martyr to late spring frosts. Finer specimens are to be seen in the cold north-east than in the alternately mild and frost-ridden Thames valley. Accordingly, it is wise to select as backward a spot as possible, where the sun comes only in the afternoon. It is a gross feeder and appreciates farmyard manure and bonemeal applied after flowering.

It can be propagated by layering or even sometimes by cuttings taken in July and given bottom heat. Plants are often grafted on herbaceous Peonies, and in such cases one can only try everything possible to get these to root above the graft or to layer them all round.

The double varieties seldom set seeds, unfortunately, but single varieties often do so, and these seeds are precious and should never be wasted. After the pod splits, sow as soon as the seeds have lost their first stickiness and become *partly* dry. Dried seeds seldom germinate. A good loam or John Innes Compost is best, and the young plants should not be disturbed for two years.

On the whole, as with Camellias, Roses and Hydrangeas, the garden varieties of the Tree Peony have been grown for the florist rather than for the shrub gardener and I, for my part, would far rather have something nearer the wild form† than some of the varieties with badly presented, over-massive, very double flowers that cannot hold themselves up properly. The florist wants a flower with, say, a hundred petals —we gardeners would prefer, I think, ten flowers instead, with only ten petals each. Most of the petals of these over-double flowers are wasted —we can't see them and the beautiful form of the true, functional flower is lost. This is, I think, why so many experienced gardeners will only grow true species; they are disgusted at the coarseness and enormity of the florists' varieties. But the early crosses and selected seedling forms of the species are, in my opinion, often even more decorative than wild species, and are usually better garden plants.

The Moutan will, under favourable circumstances, make quite a large, picturesque bush having been reported up to 8 feet high and 10 in diameter.

Since the last edition was published the botrytis fungus infection has now become so lethal and widespread, even in the Japanese rootstocks, that my nursery has had to give up selling Tree Peonies. Both here and almost everywhere else fine old plants, even seedlings on their own roots, have died suddenly in the most heart-rending manner, and no effective cure has so far been found.

The splendid family of the **Brooms** are now beginning their continuous sequence of flower and the first to open now claim our attention.

Cytisus purgans is a bushy and dense, though almost leafless, Broom up to 4 feet high, giving us a brilliant mass of very intense yellow flowers in late April or early May. To keep it low and shapely, both pegging-down and shearing should be done annually. The colour is almost too

---

† See *The Moutan or Tree Peony* Plate IX (Constable, by the author), for a perfect portrait of this exquisite flower.

Pæonia suffruticosa 'Bijou de Chusan'

Rhododendron 'Elizabeth'

Rhododendron obtusum 'Tyrian Rose'

Genista lydia

startling to place easily and needs careful planning so that one may lead up to it with whites, paler yellows and blue-purples. This species comes from southern Europe and is reasonably hardy. Perhaps its best associates are *C. multiflorus* and the presumed offspring of these two, *C. præcox*, whose description follows:—

C. præcox (A.G.M. 1933) (*C. purgans* × *multiflorus*) is a bushy Broom with pale Empire Yellow (H.C.C. 603/1) flowers in April or early May which have rather a heavy and unpleasant smell. The colour, however, is a very valuable one for contrast and for interposing to neutralise possible colour clashes. It originated as a chance seedling in a nursery at Warminster about 1867. With a little trimming, it forms a good, dense, rounded bush about 4 feet high, and is very free-flowering.

Unlike the Brooms of the *C. scoparius* section, *C. purgans* and *C. præcox* will grow well on limy soils.

The cultivation required includes the selection of an open, warm spot, with a soil rather on the poor, dry side for choice, frequent nipping back when young, and, if possible, shearing back and the removal of seed pods the moment flowering is over. Seeds of the hybrid result in variable progeny but *C. purgans* is reliably true as a rule. Cuttings of side-shoots with a carefully trimmed "heel" can be struck in the sand-box in August with a fair proportion of successes.

The **Lilacs** are very commonly planted, and although they are first-class as "cut flowers", with the leaves removed, they are certainly surpassed by very many other flowering shrubs for garden decoration *as they grow*. Their foliage is hardly beautiful, their habit of growth somewhat unattractive and, except for some of the white varieties such as *Syringa* 'Vestale', the colouring of the flowers is so muddy that it does not show up decoratively in comparison with that of many other species. On the other hand, they have their value for gardens on limy soils or in very bleak and cold districts.

Syringa vulgaris, the Common Lilac, is a deciduous bush from S.E. Europe up to 20 feet high with pale Cyclamen Purple flowers in short, blunt spikes in late April or early May.

Of the single-flowered varieties, the following are worth special mention:—

S. v. ' Congo ', lilac-red.
S. v. ' Etna ', wine coloured buds, opening pink.
S. v. ' Massena ', tall, large panicles of wine-purple flowers (A.G.M. 1930).

H

S. v. ' Maréchal Foch ', tall vigorous bush, reddish-purple flowers, well presented.

S. v. ' Philemon ', reddish-purple.

S. v. ' President Lincoln ', light bluish-lilac.

S. v. ' Primrose ', pale Empire Yellow flowers.

S. v. ' Réaumur ', Petunia Purple, moderate height.

S. v. ' Souvenir de Louis Spæth ', deep purple (A.G.M. 1930).

S. v. ' Vestale ' (A.G.M. 1931), a fine white of good, bushy habit.

The doubles have several good varieties in:—

S. v. ' Edouard André ', the best pink for colour.

S. v. ' Clarkes Giant ', about the best blue for colour.

S. v. ' Kathleen Havemeyer ', a fine pyramidal truss, purplish-lavender.

S. v. ' Mme A. Buchner ', a tall, later, red-purple with deeper buds.

S. v. ' Mme Lemoine ', white (A.G.M. 1937).

S. v. ' Mrs. E. Harding ', pinkish wine colour.

S. v. ' Paul Thirion ', lilac-pink, late.

S. v. ' Président Loubet ', deep reddish-purple.

For a fuller list of varieties of the Common Lilac see Mr. H. G. Hillier's article cited in footnote.†

S. vulgaris varieties can, if on their own roots, be propagated from suckers, otherwise they may be layered.

The Lilacs are not easily placed in the shrub garden owing to their awkward habit of growth. In too sunny a position "few flowers fade more quickly if exposed to light"† and in shady places growth is sometimes rank and shy-flowering. On the whole a north slope, or a position where the rays of the midday sun are tempered by tall distant trees are the best aspects.

With regard to cultivation, the Lilacs really like a rich soil although they will grow well enough on limy soils in a moderately warm position. Faded flowers should always be removed as soon as possible, to prevent seed formation. If, on the Common Lilac, grafted plants are trouble-some owing to suckers, cuttings or layers are an improvement.

Pruning, apart from cutting flowered branchlets back to the first good wood-buds in late May, follows the lines adopted for Apples, aiming at a strong, shapely tree without overcrowded or intercrossing branches. Scraggy specimens may be sawn down to within 2 feet of the ground in November and regrown.

This shrub is at its finest, perhaps, in Scandinavia, where, budded on Privet, it is carefully trained into an arboreal form and much grown as a street tree. The most attractive individual Lilac I have seen was a

† H. G. Hillier in "Flowering Trees and Shrubs", p. 102, R.H.S. (1938).

specimen of the single-blue-flowered form grown as a tree. To achieve this some authorities hold that the best of all root-stocks is the Common Privet, as then there is no trouble with suckers which will emerge even from Lilacs on their own roots. Unless great care is taken, however, the Lilac grows poorly and the union is unsightly.

Many of the other species and hybrids of the Lilac family are interesting. As they flower later, they are dealt with in the later seasonal sections, pages 171 and 202.

The first section to open, of the large-flowered deciduous hybrid Azaleas, are those generally known as the 'Mollis' Azaleas. Before the last war when good seedlings for naturalising in open woodland spots were obtainable at eighteenpence apiece it was a very valuable acquisition, but the flowers come rather too early to be safe in most gardens and it has a weak strain in its composition. This is because the plant is the offspring of the hardy, tough, smooth, orange-red-flowered R. japonicum and the soft, downy, rather tender and "miffy", yellow-flowered R. molle (R. sinense) which is a martyr to dieback.

In beauty it is one of the elect of all shrubs, and few flowers of any kind have more rich and lovely colourings. Given its requirements of lime-free, open soil, moist and rich in humus, light shade and shelter from cold winds, shallow planting, a leafy mulch and a site where spring frosts are infrequent, it is a good garden plant provided that it is on its own roots. But grafted plants on high, dry beds, planted 2 or 3 inches too deep, with heavy soil piled over the roots, have dwindled and died by the hundred and the plant has accordingly got a bad name as a shrub for general use.

The Dutch, who know a good plant when they see one, were the first mass-producers of these Azaleas and started in 1880, and they are still sending them all over the world today. The firm of Anthony Koster & Sons of Boskoop were the originators and Rhododendron Kosterianum is really the correct name for this group of Azaleas; and furthermore, Messrs. Koster are still producing them. The reason why the soft Chinese species was crossed with R. japonicum was, I think, because the former is more responsive to forcing. In North America the Chinese strain makes the hybrid too tender to bear their colder winters, although R. japonicum itself does well enough in all but the coldest districts. Even in Britain its superiority as an outdoor shrub is very evident.

In English gardens, favourably situated, the hybrid "Mollises" are a very lovely sight when thoughtfully arranged with bulbs, Welsh Poppies and Forget-me-nots among white-flowered Cherries and Birches. One of the best ways, I find, is simply to plant them out 10 feet apart, each plant in a carefully made circular bed 5 feet in diameter, in thin wood-land. One can then practically forget them and they increase in beauty year by year. At least 60 per cent. of yellow-flowered sorts is essential if the effect is to be really pleasing.

For the open garden, their flowers lack the toughness of those of the Evergreen Azaleas, succumbing quickly to spring north-easters, and as the two kinds do not go very well together it is often best, in the small garden, to have the invaluable evergreen types and to leave out the ' Mollises '. Three other sections of large-flowered rather similar Azaleas—the ' Knap Hills ', the ' Occidentales ' and the ' Ghents ' come into bloom later, when most of the Evergreen kinds are over, and, for a main effect, these offer the average garden far better value than the ' Mollises ', in view of late frosts, and provide a better succession.

There are innumerable varieties of the ' Mollises ' but care should be taken to insist on "layers", or even seedlings, rather than grafted plants which are apt either to dwindle owing to failure to make the essential new wood or to give endless trouble by suckers of the wild yellow stock. A healthy Azalea grows like a Black Currant—it is perpetu-ally in course of renewing itself from the base. When really suited they make, I note, shoots three feet long terminating in a coronet of flower-buds but many ' Mollises ' suffer from inherent die-back.

Some outstanding varieties are:—

' Adriaan Koster ' ***, deep yellow.
' Koster's Brilliant Red ' **, "salmon", (Azalea Pink, H.C.C. 618).
' Floradora ' **, orange, late.
' Anthony Koster ' *, Cadmium Orange (H.C.C. 8/2).
' Golden Oriole ' *, bright yellow.
' Clara Butt ' **, deep pink.
' Mrs. L. J. Endtz ' **, clear yellow.
' Mrs. Oliver Slocock ' **, orange-yellow, a variety of outstanding quality.
' Dr. M. Oosthoek ' **, vivid unfading orange-red.
' J. C. van Thol ' *, Fire Red (H.C.C. 15/2).
' Spek's Orange ', large flowers, orange-red with yellow anthers.
' Marmion ' ***, pale yellow, deeper flare.
' Mrs. G. A. van Noordt ' **, salmon pink.

* Stars of Merit awarded by the Rhododendron Group of the Royal Horti-cultural Society.

These fine varieties may well form the high spots of groups of cheaper and less richly coloured seedlings with, above all, an ample interplanting of the common yellow R. luteum, moving the plants after a season's flowering, so as to get the best colour grouping. So long as the root-ball is kept intact and moist they do not mind being moved at all, at any age.

There are certain essentials that I believe must be faithfully observed to ensure the well-being of these Azaleas, and I would venture to advise accordingly. In the first place, when planting, do not put *soil above* the ball of roots. The plants merely suffocate if you do. If the soil is sandy and well drained set them so that the upper surface of the root-ball is about an inch below the soil level and then put only half an inch of light leaf-mould or well-soaked ordinary peat-moss litter on the top of the root-ball. If the soil is clayey, efficient and thorough drainage must be provided, as waterlogging quickly kills the roots. It is desirable to add also a generous dosage of rotted leaf-mould or peat to the soil and mix in well. It is essential to keep the beds mulched with forest leaves at all times. Give such light shade as is afforded by Cherries, etc. growing south of the beds or by light shrubs of friendly growth such as *Genista virgata, G. æthnensis,* etc. growing in the beds along with the Azaleas. Well-grown plants in light shade do not need to have seed pods removed after flowering, but young ones, or those in very dry and sunny positions, are benefited. Limy soil is not suitable for Azaleas of any kind, of course.

No pruning is needed but when really well grown and on their own roots these Azaleas will send up shoots from the base about 3 feet long and as thick as a fountain pen. If these shoots are gently arched over, and pegged down, or the penultimate 6 inches are buried and the end bent up, flower buds are formed all along the shoots in quite a spectacular manner provided that they are in a fairly open position. To feed well to induce strong basal shoots, and then peg them down, rather than prune growth away, is one of the secrets of good cultivation.

The removal of seed pods *before they swell* is always helpful to growth, as the material otherwise put into these is used, instead, to make stronger shoots for next year's flowers. The benefit is only obtained if the deseeding is done the moment the flowers fade. Care has to be taken not to damage the ring of dormant and sprouting buds immediately below. Varieties differ enormously in the ease with which the work can be done. With some, the stalks are sticky and tough, others are easily snapped off at the right place. For the difficult ones, snipping off the cluster of seeds with secateurs is one of the quickest and easiest methods. One snip for each bunch is usually enough, as, if the stalk is even mutilated, the seed capsule does not swell and exhaust the plant.

An excellent dense-growing, ultra hardy, cheap Rhododendron very pretty with the 'Mollis' Azaleas, as it flowers at the same time, is R. 'Cunningham's White' "A". The flowers are white, with a "flare" of orange at the heart. It is a good wind-resister and can be planted practically anywhere in the lime-free garden provided the soil is made right. It can even be grown from cuttings fairly easily.

Few plantings within our power are more lovely in effect than a well-diversified group of 'Mollis' Azaleas, where yellow is carefully kept the dominating colour leading up to an occasional burst of soft flame intensified at a few points by vivid orange reds that are cooled by the old 'Cunningham's White'. Few plantings are more crude and unpleasing than a mere row of one lobster-coloured variety affronting the woodland.

A member of the great **Cornel** family, *Cornus Nuttallii*, flowers, as a rule, towards the end of April. It comes from western North America where it makes a tree reported at sometimes 80 feet high, "so beautiful that it is even spared by the settlers". In this country it usually stops short at about 15 feet even if pruned to tree habit, otherwise it forms a large shrub. The clematis-like flowers, at first yellowish and then white, are formed of about six large petal-like bracts surrounding the central, greenish button which is actually the true flower. This button, incidentally, erupts into a bunch of tiny flowers which resemble minute replicas of the inflorescence. The autumn colour of the leaves is a further adornment, and, with its beautifully presented, long-lasting, large fragrant flowers, this lovely tree is quite as valuable as *C. Kousa*, which see under June (page 225). Unlike the latter species and *C. florida*, it does not move well when of any size and I have lost some good specimens when transplanting although the other species mentioned all survived without check. Large plants, also, often die suddenly for no apparent reason. *C. Nuttallii* was introduced by David Douglas about 1826 from seeds, gathered in British Columbia, sent back to the old Horticultural Society of London.

This Cornel will grow on a limy soil, if this is well enriched with leaf-mould. The best plan would be to give the young plant a good start with a few barrowloads of turf loam, with which some of the natural soil should be mixed, otherwise it will probably be very slow to get going in the chalk. It is very scarce in commerce.

A graceful little tree, about 20 feet high, flowering in April is *Amelanchier canadensis*, (A.G.M. 1927). It is sometimes called the "Snowy Mespilus". This English name is also occasionally used for the less attractive *A. vulgaris*. *A. canadensis* is snowy indeed when sheeted with its white blossom which makes a lovely, if short-lived, display among the pinkish, expanding leaves. In autumn the foliage turns to a rich red or yellow and thus the tree gives a double dividend

very acceptable in the small garden. It is quite hardy and not particular
as to soil though it prefers the acid greensand districts where it seeds
itself freely and has even become naturalised. It was introduced about
the middle of the eighteenth century. There are a number of other
species of Amelanchier but they are, on the whole, of inferior decorative value. The less attractive *A. lævis* is sometimes confused with it,
but may be distinguished by the young leaves being quite smooth, not
downy on both sides, as in the more decorative species.

Of all the flowering trees of early spring the Cherries, and most
particularly the Oriental varieties grouped under *Prunus serrulata* are
the most spectacularly beautiful. Though their soft rose or white tones
are charming in the vernal landscape, this beauty is one of form rather
than of colour—it is the exquisite, delicate design of the massed flowers
and the picturesque habit of the trees that appeals to us most strongly.

In dealing with my suggestions for the best associations for the choicer
Cherries I am grouping them roughly into sections, as nearly as possible
in flowering order. These sections, of course, merge into one another
and there are times when one or another variety will flower unusually
early or late, but the system forms none the less a useful rough guide
for group planting.

I have followed the names used in Major Collingwood Ingram's
Ornamental Cherries (*Country Life*, 1948).

One of the loveliest in form, of the double-flowered kinds, is *Prunus
serrulata* 'Hokusai'. So graceful is the habit of the blossoming sprays
contrasted with the dark branches, so exquisite the shape of each
individual flower that even very young specimens are highly decorative,
but in its maturer years it makes a splendid round-topped tree particularly healthful and long-lived. The colour, however, is such a pale
blush-pink that it appears rather washed-out as a landscape effect.
'Hokusai' is therefore best planted where its charm of detail can be
enjoyed at close range rather than as a park tree.

P. s. 'Shirotæ' (also known as 'Mt. Fuji' or 'Kojima') has an altogether different habit, being inclined to be low and sprawling, and it is
by nature rather soft. If left to its own devices it forms a huge rounded
bush rather than a tree. Provided ground space is available this is not
a disadvantage and the great mass of its large single or semi-double
white flowers turn such a specimen into a mound of snow at blossoming
time which will be one of the finest sights in any garden. It is not always
long-lived, not having a very strong constitution and I have sometimes
lost a specimen from no ascertainable cause.

Another distinct Cherry of high garden value is *P. s.* 'Takasago' (also known as *Sieboldii*, *pubescens*, etc.). It does not make a tall tree, seldom exceeding 20 feet and is easily distinguished by its downy young leaves. The variety *Watereri* is particularly floriferous and markedly superior to the ordinary form which is slower in growth and rather shy-flowering, though the usual cause of this state of affairs is simply bullfinches, destroying the flower buds. The blossoms are pink and mostly semi-double, the young leaves appearing at the same time being of a reddish bronze. E. H. Wilson stated that this variety will root from cuttings and as it flowers when quite small this method of increase should be worth trying.

The true *P. s.* 'Hisakura' is a rare and rather delicate Cherry with small, single, pink flowers opening among reddish-copper young leaves —a delightful combination.

P. s. 'Yedo sakura' (*P. s. nobilis*) is a very slow-growing, but highly decorative variety, with clusters of pale pink double flowers, that often open before the leaves appear. These slow growers are usually worth waiting for and the best way to hustle them is to grow them in top-spit meadow loam and to pinch off their flower buds before they open.

One of the next varieties to flower is *P. s.* 'Mikuruma-gæshi'. It is of notably graceful, upstanding port with the compact, single, pale-pink flowers thickly clustered all along the stems. About the same time *P. s.* 'Ariake', of stiffer, more restricted growth, will open its large, single white blooms.

April is now drawing to a close in our calendar of Cherry blossom and the coppery-pink buds of the slow-growing *P. s.* 'Horinji' are so attractive contrasted with the dark calices among the red bracts and rufous-bronze young leaves that one feels that even the semi-double flowers that will follow could not surpass them. When they open we shall not be disappointed and the last section of the Cherries to flower will have begun. They will be described in our next chapter and there, too, will be given cultural directions.

Unfortunately most of these Cherries are grafted on the Gean stock. This, our native Cherry species, is, curiously enough, less healthy than the wild Japanese Cherry—*Prunus mutabilis*—in this country, being subject to canker, witches' broom and black aphis attack. As a stock it is so surface-rooting and prone to sucker that it is unwise to grow grafted Cherries in beds of other flowering shrubs. The trees are better sited as lawn or drive-side specimens. Of late, the arrival in this country of the Fire Blight which has killed so many fine trees in America and Japan has discouraged us in planting Cherries. Then, again, the vastly increased severity of the Tortrix Caterpillar plague caused by the destruction of the more valuable insectivorous birds—such as the warblers, by the use of D.D.T.—has meant the ruin of both flowers and foliage almost every year.

The time when April ends and May begins is so busy with promising buds and opening flowers and so unusually sensitive to the particular complexion of the weather, that ordains an early or a late season, that it is difficult to draw a demarcation line. The other months of the flowering season are much more readily separated.

In most gardens this is the time of greatest danger from frost damage. All too often a promising mild spell followed by a sudden hard frost ruins opening flowers and tender growths. This is so discouraging as to spoil much of our pleasure in the garden. It is therefore very important to study carefully how we may best avoid such disappointments.

Air drainage, tree canopy and nearness to the sea are absolutely decisive advantages but backward sites that discourage too early a start in growth also play a part and backward districts where spring warmth comes late have good points that may be exploited. For every garden it is a different problem and sometimes the factors are so involved that only trial and error can provide the solution.

More often than not, many of the April flowerers escape; it is the May bloomers that suffer most. Hence this chapter is a more bulky one than the following.

CHAPTER IV

MAY

*Means that the plant tolerates limy soil.

123

MAY

WHEN the early spring flowerers are over, the plants that bloom in the second flowering period are ready to take over the display, provided that they escape a treacherous late frost.

In this period of the flowering season the largest number of particularly beautiful shrubs are in bloom. Consequently if our gardens are to be equally attractive later on, as they easily may be if we so wish and are ready to take the trouble to plant for that part of the season, we must exercise restraint in the numbers of May flowerers that we plant. Thus we have to be more selective than ever to pick out only the finest possible for our own particular garden conditions.

For acid-soiled or neutral-soiled gardens the claims of the Evergreen Azaleas and the Rhododendrons are again very strong this month, owing to their effective flowering coupled with all-the-year-round decorative value, but we must be vigilant to avoid excessive concentrations of these fine things that, unrelieved by other growth, lose most of their charm and beauty in the landscape.

In limy-soiled gardens we have a choice of dwarf Brooms and Genistas, Daphnes, Choisya, Rouen Lilacs, hybrid Tree Peonies, Ceanothus, Viburnums, Spiræas and the Burnet Roses and allied kinds, assisted by many of the Berberis and the Chænomeles, Periwinkles and Kerria that, although they begin in April, will usually carry on well into the middle of May.

In the last chapter we left April with **Japanese Cherries** in flower and there are more to come this month. Forerunners among these will be the daintily shaped, even, blush-pink rosettes of *Prunus serrulata* 'Ichiyo', each becomingly decorated with one or two tiny green leaves in the centre. Like the earlier-flowering 'Hokusai', this is a Cherry which appeals more for its perfection of drawing when seen near at hand than for its form and colour in the distant landscape. It is free-flowering and elegant to a degree and makes an excellent, healthful, upright-spreading specimen where it can be admired at close range.

P. s. 'Ama-no-gawa' (A.G.M. 1931), being so closely upright in habit as almost to constitute a fastigiate form of the Japanese Cherry, is invaluable in small gardens and confined spaces. The semi-single, blush-pink flowers, borne in clusters, solidly massed, are finely shaped and most agreeably scented. It must, however, be nipped and pinched-back continually in the early stages and annually pruned back in late May at the top, and also regularly sprayed with a fungicide such as "Bouisol" to control the fungus that otherwise destroys the invaluable lower wood-buds. Unless this treatment is religiously carried out it is apt to make a thin, gaunt, awkward-looking, besom-shaped tree instead of the rosy cylinder of outwardly facing blossom which it is our aim to produce. As their achievement requires considerable trouble, such perfect specimens are all too rare.

The original oriental Cherry (*Prunus serrulata*) is a Chinese garden variety which, unfortunately for botanical seemliness, has to stand as the "type" form of the Japanese Cherries owing to being the first to be introduced. It is absolutely the opposite of 'Ama-no-gawa' in appearance, forming a low, wide-spreading tree of the highly picturesque heaviness characteristic of many Chinese garden plants as opposed to the more delicate grace and extreme refinement characteristic of Japanese plants. Obviously this Cherry requires a good deal of space, but the singular architecture of the tree and the profusion of the small, double, white blossoms give it a very high decorative value in the landscape. There are superb specimens at Kew and in many old gardens.

The valuable *double-flowered* form of our native Gean, *P. avium plena* (A.G.M. 1924), flowers at about the same time, considerably later than the wild, single-flowered type, making a stronger, taller tree than any of the Japanese varieties usually do in our climate. It is thus particularly useful as a shade tree, and in some seasons its autumn colour rivals that of Sargent's Cherry. A sub-variety *P. a. grandiflora* exhibited by Messrs. Waterer Sons & Crisp is a particularly fine form.

At this time we may expect the single white blossoms of *P. s.* 'Jo-nioi' and, though the tree is a sturdy and shapely one of very free-flowering habit, it is valued still more for the delicious fragrance of its flowers than for their appearance. A good form of this variety will perfume the air for a considerable distance around, and the scent is always delicate and attractive, never becoming heavy or oppressive.

P. s. 'Ukon' (also known as var. *grandiflora*), the best known of the yellow Cherries, will be out when May is well under way. At first sight it is often rather a disappointing Cherry, for the fact must be faced that it is a very pale, and even rather a greenish yellow. Then, again, it is only when the tree has reached a certain size that it makes any effect at all, and a dark background is particularly essential. Given these requirements the planter's patience is well rewarded in the end. As regards a complementary planting, we can pick up the yellow tone a little more vividly with an early pale yellow Broom, such as *Cytisus præcox*, and then intensify it by contrast with the blue-lavender of one

of the little alpine Rhododendrons or a blue form of the larger-growing
R. *campanulatum*, if only we can make that shy plant flower freely.

P. s. 'Pink Perfection' is a lovely double pink-flowered Cherry bred
by Messrs. Waterer, Sons & Crisp in 1935. It is very free-flowering and
a valuable addition to the Japanese varieties.

P. s. 'Ojochin' bears white, single flowers with a darker centre and
such outstandingly attractive "drawing" that this makes its portrait
in "Ornamental Cherries" the most pleasing of all in a delightful
selection. The form grown at the R.H.S. gardens at Wisley seems to me
to be a particularly fine one, though the tree in question is not in a
sufficiently open position to show itself to advantage.

We are now nearing the end of the Cherry time but a number of very
choice late varieties are still to come. Of these, *P. s.* 'Kirin' is a notably
magnificent Cherry of the very front rank. In sunlight the flowers are
apparently of a rich and beautiful pink (though actually of the palest
tint of Magenta) very double but more finely formed, if not quite so
deep in colour *when on the tree*, as those of the better-known *P. s.*
'Kanzan'. They are borne more evenly along the branches rather than
in dense clusters.

'Kanzan', or 'Sekiyama' (A.G.M. 1930) for so long confused with
'Hisakura', is almost too well known to require description, for it is
the most commonly planted of all the Japanese varieties as a street
tree. It is a fine vigorous Cherry with the richest coloured flowers of
any of these owing to the fact that the delightful coppery young foliage
casts a warm glow on their pale Magenta tint. 'Kanzan' also often
provides a particularly fine autumn leaf colour. If it has a fault it is
that the individual flowers rather lack form and that when top-grafted
standard-high it is not an attractively shaped tree for a good many
years, being of an inverted-pyramid shape, until the crown has filled
out laterally. On the other hand, when grafted or budded low down
it is one of the best for landscape effect and with 'Jo-nioi', 'Shimidsu'
and 'Shirofugen' to provide the white which is so helpful in enhancing
the vividness of the purplish pink colouring, we can contrive a very
rich and harmonious grouping.

As 'Kanzan' fades, one of the last, but certainly one of the loveliest
of all the Japanese varieties, opens. This is the Cherry for long grown in
England as *P. s.* 'Oku-miyako' or var. *longipes*, and in America as
'Sho-get-su'. Now its name is changed to 'Shimidsu' ("The Gardeners'
Chronicle", 1941, p. 240). It received the Award of Garden Merit in
1933, and has a good constitution, but is not a fast grower unless too
shaded to flower freely, the habit being dwarf and spreading yet rather
dense. It is easily recognised by the long stalks on which hang the daisy-
like, double white flowers. It is an exceedingly floriferous variety, indeed,

so much so as to limit its growth, and is of the highest decorative value, even in early youth. 'Shimidsu' groups well, being white in colour, with almost any of the other shrubs in bloom at the same time, such as the 'Knap Hill' Azaleas with their yellow, orange and pink tones, or the blue of *Ceanothus Veitchii.*

About the same time *P. s.* 'Fugenzo' ("J. H. Veitch") will be in flower; it is one of the oldest varieties and almost as commonly planted as 'Kanzan'. It is a compact, sturdy tree of rounded form, best grown as a lawn specimen in an open situation. The double flowers are of a pale magenta pink that is not very clean in tone; they last well on the tree, however, and are attractively formed with a nice open centre from which project two green leafy carpels. This Cherry is not, in my experience, satisfactory in a rich soil in a sheltered situation as it then runs to leaf and shoot growth.

Last of all comes 'Shirofugen' (sometimes known as *albo-rosea*); it is a strong and rapid grower, and easily outstripped all the other varieties of equal age except 'Tai Haku' and 'Yoshino' which I planted at the same time. Such rapid growth in the early stages usually means that flowering will be somewhat deferred and 'Shirofugen' has to reach a fair size before it flowers really freely. Once well started it is very reliably free with its faintly blushed blossom which turns white when fully expanded, to blush again before it falls. It has the coppery young foliage which is an added attraction to so many of the Japanese Cherries and makes a wide-spreading stately specimen which provides a fitting "finale" to the season. It is one of the varieties which are quite attractive when top-grafted on a strong pole of the wild Gean as its chief beauty is seen when looking up at the pendent blossoms from below, (A.G.M. 1959).

A late-flowering Cherry whose beauty has much impressed me is the variety ' Morello ' of *Prunus Cerasus* whose fruit is so delicious as jam, or in that delicious confection "Kirschkuchen". When it is grown as an open-ground tree the habit is good, the abundant white blossom quite delightful, and the ensuing red fruits are both decorative and valuable. The double-flowered variety *P. c. Rhexii*, on the other hand is, in my experience, not half so decorative and is doubtfully worth growing, as the congested little flowers are more sparsely borne and do not show up well. *P. c. semperflorens* is also inferior, merely producing odd racemes during the summer.

As to soil, the Cherries seem to prefer a good fibrous turf-loam though they also do well both on limy soils and the acid peaty green-sands. They are more exacting as to position, insisting on one that is open and sunny. Strong winds spoil the blossom all too quickly, it is true, and it is here that the Pines, recommended for background and

Lithospermum diffusum 'Grace Ward'

Rhododendron Kæmpferi

Daphne retusa

Cornus Nuttallii

contrast, may perform a third useful function by affording shelter from the north and the south-west.

Cherries may be increased by grafting or budding as described in the chapter dealing with Propagation (p. 35). A complete spraying programme, as for Apples, is really very beneficial to them. In this country aged Cherries often die from fungus attack and are debilitated by lichen. In Japan, small boys whose naked feet do not damage the tender bark, are sent aloft every year to scrub off the lichens and attend to any wounds caused by the wind and thus their Cherries live to a great age and attain a picturesque beauty of the highest order.

A flowering tree too seldom seen is *Paulownia tomentosa*. It is a fast-growing stalwart 30-foot tree with lovely blue foxglove flowers of persistent and delightful fragrance opening before the huge catalpa-like leaves in spring. Alternatively it may be cut down annually when it will send up shoots with enormous tropical-looking foliage. Thus it is a lusty plant of spectacular character and I am surprised that parks and large gardens do not plant this beautiful tree more frequently. Best in a sunny spot to get the growth started early, with some thoughtful pinching and a poorish soil to keep the tree small.

Rubus deliciosus should really do duty here for the whole Bramble family, for if one of them is worth growing it is certainly this species. Its dry and tasteless fruits could hardly be called delicious, unless so steeped in choice liqueurs as to function merely as a texture. Its wild-rose-like flowers, of purest white, so profusely borne among the black-currant-like leaves as to make quite a splash, are a couple of inches across, five-petalled and glamorously presented. It comes from the Rocky Mountains whence it was introduced in 1870. The difficulty of propagating it has, however, kept it scarce ever since. Furthermore the best-flowered form is even more troublesome to root, even from layers, than the commoner one which has smaller flowers.

A sunny spot with sandy, or at least loamy, soil is needed and the older branches will require removal at ground-level occasionally to keep the plant youthful and vigorous.

R. 'Tridel' is a hybrid between the above and Mexican *R. trilobus*. The best form of this is named 'Benenden' by the raiser, Major

Collingwood Ingram V.M.H. It appears to be superior to the best form
of *R. deliciosus* and is now available in Nurseries. The arching branches
recall a well-flowered wild white Rose and it is well worthy of a place
in all good shrub gardens where, with *Viburnum tomentosum*, it can
light up the red, yellow and orange masses of the Azaleas.

Let us now examine the **Exochordas,** a genus of tall, deciduous,
white-flowered shrubs from northern Asia, distantly related to the
Spiræas.

Exochorda racemosa (*E. grandiflora*) grows eventually to 10 feet or
more in height, with many stems springing from the ground. The five-
petalled pure white flowers, about 1½ inches across, appear in May on
short, upright racemes at the ends of the branches of the previous year.
It is a beautiful shrub in flower but its habit is not decorative in winter.

E. Giraldi Wilsonii resembles the preceding but the flowers are larger,
if slightly less numerous. It seems to require a warmer spot and greater
care than *E. racemosa.*

E. Korolkowi (*E. Albertii*) (A.G.M. 1933) is an upright, 12-foot bush
with inch-wide, white flowers less freely produced than those of *E.
racemosa.* It is, however, a very robust and hardy species. The finest
form is *E. K.* var. *Wilsonii.*

E. macrantha (*E. Korolkowi* × *racemosa*) is a fine hybrid raised by
Messrs. V. Lemoine of Nancy at the beginning of this century. In freedom of flower this is the finest of the family. The white is a singularly
pure one and the racemes of about eight flowers are so numerous that
it is very effective in early May.

The Exochordas are hardy and indifferent as to whether the soil is
limy or acid. A sunny, open position suits them best. After flowering
the flowered twigs may be cut back and, if the stems are very densely
set, some thinning may be done by removing old or weak ones.

Cuttings do not root very readily. Seeds are a good method of
increase.

Let us turn now from these plants that are suitable for limy soils to
a section of great beauty that will only grow on acid soils. Fortunately
the greater acreage of the soil of Britain is acid, but unfortunately many
gardeners, misled by directions to apply lime as though it were a
universal fertiliser, have gravely damaged the soil of their ornamental
gardens. Originally the practice arose as a means of correcting the over-
manuring of kitchen gardens. Gradually it came to be a stock directive;
the ridiculous phrase "lime-deficient" was used for any soils not

definitely limy, as though there was something wrong with Nature's acid soil that had to be put right by man to make it fertile. This may be desirable for the purpose of growing coarse fodder-grasses or certain peculiarly constituted lime-loving vegetables, but it is a complete fallacy so far as ornamental plants, trees and shrubs are concerned. By liming acid soil, the essential minerals cannot be assimilated by the plants so that many of the finest genera cannot grow at all.† Among these are the Rhododendrons.

Rhododendron yunnanense "B" **** is one of the few pure **Rhododendron species** of the larger-sized sort that appears to be admirably adapted for gardens just as it is. It is a shapely, slender-twigged bush with small leaves and delightful masses of Azalea-like white flowers, orange-throated or spotted with red, towards the end of May. It is a treasure that no reasonably favourable lime-free garden will wish to do without. It comes from 9,000-foot elevations in Yunnan. In hard winters it loses many of its leaves and if too much shaded and not pruned back when young is sometimes rather thin in habit. Otherwise it is difficult to find fault with it. The flower colour of seedlings is variable and some are of a purplish-pink which is not pleasing; others, and these should be selected, have white flowers with an orange flare on the upper lobe (A.G.M. 1934).

R. yunnanense, like all its family, insists upon an acid soil rich in humus. It may be propagated by seed, cutting or layers. I think the most perfect position is when this lovely bush is sited as a lawn specimen in a sheltered but not overshaded spot. In flower it will hold the stage against all competitors and, unlike most wild species, may be considered as an ordinary garden plant for general use.

Specially favoured gardens, that is to say, those that have an acid soil rich in humus, trees to afford light shade and sufficient relative elevation (see Katabatics, p. 25) to avoid the worst spring frosts, may grow certain other Rhododendron species of supreme year-round beauty. Some of these flower in April and some not until June or July, but, as early May is the peak flowering time of this section and also because their culture is rather a thing apart from ordinary gardening, they are grouped here for convenience.

"A" means "Hardy anywhere in the British Isles."
"B" means "Hardy anywhere in the British Isles but requires some shade to attain best results."
"C" means "Hardy along the seaboard and in favourable gardens inland."

† Even farm grassland should not be limier than pH 6.50, which is acid. See National Agricultural Advisory Service Conference, March 1957.

The stars indicate relative merit adjudged by the Rhododendron Groups of the R.H.S.

R. apodectum "A" *** is a relative of *R. dichroanthum* with dull orange or red flowers in June; in an open position it makes a bush of about 4 feet.

R. Augustinii " C " ****. This exquisite species is evaluated by the degree of blueness of its flowers. The bluest I have seen were of the lovely, violet-blue known as Aster Violet (H.C.C. 38/2). Most forms are nearer violet. It is not very attractive as an evergreen when out of flower and needs a sheltered and favourable spot. In time it may reach 10 feet, each way, and it flowers in early May. A good form is one of the most spectacularly beautiful of all shrubs, when in bloom (A.G.M. 1924).

R. chasmanthum " C " **** is very similar.

R. campylocarpum " B " ****, in the original type form makes a fairly dense bush usually about 4 or 5 feet high in the open. It is generally considered one of the best yellow-flowered Rhododendrons, but the colour, which I estimate to be Dresden Yellow (H.C.C. 64/2) is not very brilliant compared with that of a good yellow Azalea and the flowers are not very well presented. The variety *elatum* is quite distinct and has pink buds and a warmer but paler flower colour. The bush is taller and looser and the flowers are well presented and have a red centre. Grown near R. ' Blue Diamond ' the colour combination is a special delight. This variety also differs from the type in being quite happy in a comparatively open, sunny position, and the flowers last well.

R. cinnabarinum " B " **** has blue-green leaves and dull red, clear rosy red, or yellow, tubular bell-shaped flowers. Its habit is rather thin and upright at first. Var. *æstivale* is specially valuable as, unlike the type, which flowers in late May, it flowers in July. Var. Blandfordiæ-florum is a fine form with large Poppy-red (H.C.C. 16/2) flowers.

R. concatenans " C " *** has bell-shaped apricot flowers in early May and beautiful aromatic blue-green foliage but requires care.

R. decorum " C " ** has exquisitely shaped, fragrant seven-lobed white flowers in May and sea-green foliage. It seeds itself so freely and stands full exposure so well that I mention it here although it is not so exciting as others. There are tender forms that are useless.

R. dichroanthum " B " *** has been described elsewhere in this work (p.185). A further feature of this curious plant is that it strikes from cuttings and thus certain specialist nurseries are able to supply the finest orange-flowered forms on their own roots.

R. didymum " B " ** is a 3-foot bush with black-crimson flowers in late June. It is a good " doer " but needs side or back lighting to illumine its dark flowers.

R. discolor "B" ***. This is a big bush with large, fragile, scented, seven-lobed, white flowers with a red centre in July. Some forms are able to stand the severest cold if grown in a sunnier place than one would choose for most other Rhododendrons. My private hardiness-rating would be category "A". See also under July, p. 280.

R. fictolacteum "B" ***. The massive foliage is superb, deep sage green and vividly russet-felted beneath, and the white, dark-eyed flowers in April or early May are very attractive. Care must be taken to get a good, large-flowered, bud-hardy form. There are bud-tender, useless forms. It is a tall shrub or small tree growing up to 30 feet ultimately.

R. Griersonianum "C" **** has been described elsewhere in the work (p. 206). I find that it really grows best in full exposure without any shelter whatever. Under such conditions it is almost category "A" in the south provided that Katabatics are good, (see p. 26). But it is useless except as a tub-plant in low-lying places.

R. hæmatodes "B" **** is a small, wide bush of about 3 feet with brilliant scarlet-crimson flowers in May. Although slow to flower, it is a treasure worth waiting for.

R. lacteum "C" ****. This, the finest yellow Rhododendron, is slow-growing and difficult, very variable in quality and flowers dangerously early, in April, but a good form is a noble and massive plant of fascinating individuality. (See illustration facing p. 49.) It is one of the few Rhododendrons that apparently grow better when root-grafted on *R. ponticum* than when on their own roots. Thus grown there is no danger of suckers from the stock and the deadly Honey Fungus which often attacks *R. lacteum* may more easily be avoided.

R. neriiflorum "C" **** is a small neat bush of about 4 feet as a rule, with white-undersurfaced leaves and scarlet-red flowers in April.

R. orbiculare "B" **** is a dense bush with round leaves and large, delightfully shaped but nodding, purplish-pink, campanula-like flowers in April.

R. rubiginosum "A" ***, a small tree completely covering itself with purplish-pink flowers in April, will grow almost anywhere and has a most attractive habit. It would be a most valuable Rhododendron if a form with flowers of more attractive colouring could be obtained.

R. Thomsonii "B" ****. This beautiful bush with rounded blue-green leaves that make it highly decorative at all times, has superb, long-lasting, waxy, blood-red flowers in April and early May. In an open position it forms a dense shrub about 6 feet high but if drawn up by nearby forest trees may make a tree of 15 to 20 feet (A.G.M. 1925).

R. Wardii "C" *** is a shrub up to about 15 feet with exquisite saucer-shaped clear yellow flowers in May, beautifully presented on a shapely bush. It is also the parent of many lovely hybrids.

R. yakusimanum is a superb new species. When it becomes available and if it proves hardy it will be of the highest value. It is a dense, low bush with spoon-shaped leaves felted below and delightful trusses of pink buds opening to shapely white, wide-open, bell flowers in amazing profusion. Its charm is typical of a pure wild species.

The above twenty species are a selection out of over seven hundred grown in this country. They are chosen for their distinction, their effectiveness and their strongly marked individuality and charm. The woodland, rather than the garden, is really their proper home. They can be grown in a suitable piece of woodland with far less labour than that required to grow any plant in the open garden, *provided that they are originally installed with the full specification laid down for this genus.* There is no gardening adventure that I know more pleasurable than to be able to plant these delightful things as specimens in a little woodland corner. Once the planting is faithfully done there is no drudgery and all is enjoyment. Unfortunately few of us have the opportunity, but this treatise, limited as it is, would have been incomplete if I had entirely missed out this fascinating by-way of horticulture. Further suggestions for the late summer effects for such a venture will be found under *Hydrangea serrata* and in that section (pp. 305 and 309).

There are a few large, fairly hardy, hybrid Rhododendrons with yellow flowers, but unfortunately many of these are hardly robust enough for the wind and the sun of the ordinary open garden, being either category "B" or "C". Where, however, there is light shade, good shelter from wind and, of course, a lime-free soil, some of these may be grown. It must be admitted that, compared with the Azaleas, the yellow is often rather a pale, greenish-sulphury tint of no very great decorative value in the landscape. As *R. campylocarpum* ("B" or "C", Thomsonii series, usually flowering in April) figures largely in the parentage of the majority, they are for the most part rather early flowerers, which adds to the difficulty of growing them really well. None the less, whilst the Evergreen and later, the deciduous Azaleas furnish the main colour mass in the garden landscape at this time, the association of these delicate off-yellow and off-blue tones is so supremely beautiful and out of the ordinary that it is worth while struggling to grow the shelter necessary to achieve it. 'Carita' and 'Damaris' usually synchronise their flowering with that of the exquisite 'Blue Diamond' (*augustinii* × 'Intrifast') (see p. 87) whilst 'Alice Street', 'Letty Edwards' and 'Souvenir of W. C. Slocock' are well timed with the violet 'Susan'.

'Alice Street' (*wardii* × 'Zuyder Zee'), vivid yellow bells, first class.
'Butterfly' "B" *** ('Mrs Milner' × *R. campylocarpum*), very pale lemon, brown eye, shy-flowering.
'Carita' "B" large shapely truss, pale yellow.

'Dairymaid' "B" ***, very pale lemon, flushed pink, of very good, sturdy habit and very free flowering.

'Damaris' "B" ***, fresh yellow, a lovely bush, needs a sheltered position.

'Devonshire Cream' "B" *, very pale yellow, red eye, very pretty and of good compact habit.

'Diane', palest sulphur yellow, sickly and addicted to "fly".

'Fabia' "B" *** (*R. dichroanthum* × *Griersonianum*), orange salmon, is very fine indeed, but still scarce and expensive. It is worthy of every care. Var. 'Tangerine' is vermilion.

'Goldfort' "B" ***, pale creamy yellow.

'Goldsworth Orange' "A" ***, Maize Yellow (H.C.C. 607/1), a fine Rhododendron. My private rating is "C".

'Goldsworth Yellow' "B" (*R. caucasicum* × *campylocarpum*), pale Empire Yellow, spotted with green and bronze, rather a straggling habit.

'Hawk' (*R. Wardii* × 'Lady Bessborough') "C", a lovely yellow, requiring a moist, sheltered, shady position.

'Idealist' ***, cream, large shapely flowers, late.

'Lady Bessborough' "B" **** (*R. discolor* × *campylocarpum*), very pale yellow.

'Lady Primrose' "B" ***, pale lemon, red spots.

'Letty Edwards' "B" *** (*R. Fortunei* × *campylocarpum*), very pale sulphur yellow, a better grower than most and has more attractive foliage, but needs protection from wind. Very lovely.

'Margaret Bean' "B" **, pale yellow, blushed pink.

'Mrs. Ashley Slocock' "B" **, pale cream, suffused apricot.

'Mrs. W. C. Slocock' "B" ***, pale apricot pink, shaded yellow.

'Moongold', creamy yellow bells.

'Penjerrick' "C" **** (*R. campylocarpum* × *Griffithianum*), creamy yellow in best forms, very shapely flowers. One of the loveliest of all Rhododendrons in a wood.

'Queen Souriya' "B" * (*R. Fortunei* × *camplyocarpum*), pale ochre, mauve edge, shapely flowers.

'Souvenir of W. C. Slocock' "B" ***, Maize Yellow (H.C.C. 607/3), fading to pale yellow, larger truss and slightly later than most.

'Unique' "B" **** (Slocock's form), very pale yellow, orange-pink buds, a very good, compact habit.

'Unique' "B" ** (Wallace's form), pale orange fading to buff, attractive in colour.

'Zuyder Zee' "B"** (R. 'Mrs. Lindsay Smith × *campylocarpum*), pale lemon yellow, red spots.

In addition to the positional requirements previously mentioned, the soil should be well enriched with peat or leaf-mould and these Rhododendrons should be kept mulched with fallen leaves over the whole area beneath their branches. They grow so much better in a wood-garden that, on the whole, I would advise growing them in that way, keeping to the "A" class hardy hybrids for the ordinary open garden. Those who do not mind taking a chance on a long-term venture may plant selected, small, low, bushy plants in more exposed places, but shade is desirable in the south-eastern part of the country to prevent scorching of the foliage and bleaching of the delicate flower colours. Both the 'Uniques', 'Dairymaid', 'Goldsworth Orange' and 'Goldsworth Yellow' are particularly suitable for such an experiment.

All these *campylocarpum* hybrids appear to be rather susceptible to attacks by the Rhododendron Fly and, if the pest is seen, need dusting carefully so as to cover the undersides of the leaves several times in early summer wherever the plants are not shaded. Shade generally prevents the "fly" causing much trouble as it seems unable to multiply under these conditions. Pyrethrum/Derris is effective.

Two attractive hybrids that make a charming association with a pale yellow variety such as 'Dairymaid' are 'Mount Everest' "B" **, a sturdy bush with shapely, cupped, white flowers, and 'Susan' "B" ***, an Amethyst Violet flowering at the same time. A sheltered but fairly open position shaded by large trees is, I think, the ideal for this type of Rhododendron as they then form shapely and dense bushes well set with flowers, as at Wisley, on Battleston Hill.

I would never advise the making of Rhododendron beds where the larger sorts are herded together by themselves. Culturally it is unnecessary. Æsthetically it is bad because the ultimate result is a dank, gloomy cavern whose outer roof is decorated by largely invisible flowers. The intervening stage is not attractive, either, because Rhododendron foliage demands association with the more vivid leaves and later flowers of deciduous trees and shrubs. Plant Rhododendrons, then, as single specimens grouped among less valuable and less permanent shrubs and all the centuries of their lives they will be rounded, beautiful bushes furnished evenly to the ground. No gloomy groves will make dull the late summer scene. "What is that lovely thing?—Oh, I do believe it's a Rhododendron!" should be the comment evoked, rather than the usual perfunctory response to an overpowering concentration.

To do proper justice to the limy garden and also to mark my insistence that the different sections of the Rhododendron family are as distinct, from the garden angle, as if they were members of different genera, we break off to examine a plant of very different character.

An early-flowering evergreen climber, introduced by E. H. Wilson from China in 1900 is *Clematis Armandi* (A.G.M. 1938). The fragrant white flowers, produced in clusters in the axils of the leaves, are 2½ inches across in the best forms. There are, however, many poor seedling forms about, whose flowers are small and dingy. There is also a very pretty variety, 'Apple Blossom' with pink flowers. In warm gardens this Clematis may be grown on a tree stump or a tripod of poles with delightful effect, but in most places a warm wall is desirable. Plants are reported 30 feet high on suitable walls where the soil, either loamy or acid, is moist and rich, but well drained. No pruning is desirable except for the removal of dead wood. Seeds germinate readily, but there is great variation in the value of the seedlings, so the best forms should be propagated from cuttings. Like many climbers, *C. Armandi* tends to become bare at the base, and it is therefore a good plan to train the young growths out sideways at the start, and to take the opportunity of tying out, similarly, any subsequent young shoots that may appear. Alas, the good forms are now almost extinct.

There are several charming **wild Azalea species** that flower, as a rule, towards the end of April and in early May. For convenience I group them here.

Rhododendron Albrechti "B" **** forms a twiggy bush 3 or 4 feet high with 2-inch-wide exquisitely shaped Fuchsine Pink (H.C.C. 627/1) flowers that open in April or early May before the leaves. It comes from Japan where it grows in woodland on steep slopes and was introduced by Professor Sargent of the Arnold Arboretum and later by E. H. Wilson.

R. Schlippenbachii "C" **** (F.C.C. 1944) is perhaps more attractive than the previous species. It is a taller shrub, said to be up to 15 feet high in its native Korean hills where it is extraordinarily abundant, giving, according to E. H. Wilson, "miles and miles of the purest pink from the millions of flowers of this Azalea". The fragrant flowers (Rhodamine Pink, H.C.C. 527/2) are borne in April in clusters of about five and open before or with the large, heart-shaped leaves. There are good and bad forms, some of the worst being very weak in colour. The plant was first introduced by J. H. Veitch in 1893 from a Japanese garden. It is hardy at the Arnold Arboretum, Boston, Mass., and may therefore be considered quite hardy in Britain so far as cold is concerned, but a moist, lime-free soil, rich in humus, and light shade with shelter from wind, appear to be necessary for the well-being of this lovely plant over here. The autumn leaf colour is very fine and so two pleasing effects are provided.

R. pentaphyllum "C" **** is a large bush, 6 to 12 feet high in the hanging woods of Nikko where Wilson, who surely saw more flowers than any man before or since, said: "I shall never forget the charm of that splash of lovely colour among the leafless plants of a well-wooded, steep slope". The leaves are in whorls of five at the end of the branchlets, hence the name, and turn to gorgeous tints in autumn. The solitary, or paired, flowers are pure rose pink, unspotted and about 2 inches across, opening April–May. It is rather a difficult plant requiring specially favourable conditions.

R. reticulatum "A" ***, on the other hand, is hardy and easy-going by comparison, and as abundant as the previous species is rare. The flowers are a magenta or purplish-pink colour and appear before the leaves.

R. Vaseyi "B" **** (A.G.M. 1927) is notably beautiful and usually flowers a little later in May. The flowers, of the exquisite finish typical of these Azaleas, are smaller and of a pure pale pink, or nearly white, and open before the leaves. In habit, *R. Vaseyi* is rather upright, growing up eventually to 12 feet or more. Light shade, and well mulched, moist soil with plenty of humus are required to grow it well.

The best place for these Azaleas is really the wood-garden where their individual charm is displayed to the full when in flower, and their bare brown stems melt into the prevailing brushwood in winter. For the open garden the more richly coloured and reliable 'Knap Hill' and 'Ghent' hybrids, flowering later, are much more satisfactory.

China and Australasia have been fairly thoroughly explored by our plant-hunters though more "finds" may possibly yet be made. Japan and North and South America, to our certain knowledge, contain considerable numbers of absolutely first-class hardy flowering shrubs, not to mention many herbs, which we lack. Among these several of the most glorious of the known Azaleas are prominent. Unlike the oriental species mentioned, many of the Americans have really good colourings —vivid blood-reds, oranges and yellows instead of purplish-pinks, and, furthermore, several come into bloom at critical periods of the flower sequence of the garden year when such superb colours are particularly desirable. In the hope that the required importations *of good forms* may be made ere long I give below brief particulars of some of these:—

Rhododendron alabamense, a hardy, May-flowering Azalea species with fragrant white flowers, is in commerce here in the "type" form. Some more desirable varieties are, however, described as having apricot-coloured flowers† and these would be a great acquisition to our gardens.

† Mrs. J. Norman Henry, *R.H.S. Journal*, LXII, Pt. 10, p. 388.

R. atlanticum var. A hardy dwarf form of this species, a foot high, with rose-scented white flowers in late May, grey-green leaves and carmine stems (*loc. cit. sup.*).

R. speciosum "A" ** is, in its best forms, amazingly free-flowering with orange to blood-red flowers.

R. austrinum is, in my garden, a rather undistinguished, early June bloomer, but Bowers† states that it blooms in early spring with the expanding leaves. According to Mrs. Henry it bears its yellow or orange flowers, in the wild state, before the leaves unfold.

R. cumberlandense, formerly thought to be a form of *R. calendulaceum*, has brilliant blood-red flowers.

R. prunifolium *** has the immensely valuable characteristic of producing its blood-red flowers, which are said to be the largest of all Azaleas, *in July*. That brilliant plant-hunter, Mrs. Norman Henry, (*loc. cit. sup.*) said: "It fairly took my breath away the first time I saw it in bloom . . . twelve feet tall and fifteen feet in diameter".

For my part I would rather have a good specimen of this Azalea in my garden than almost any shrub I can think of. The importation of seed of the really good form described above would earn the gratitude of all gardeners enjoying an acid or neutral soil.

Turning for a moment from these choice and rare creatures to a commoner and more easily grown shrub of very different character, let us record the excellence of a member of the Spiræa family.

Spiræa prunifolia plena is a Japanese garden form of a Chinese shrub.

It is a graceful, dense, 5-foot bush with arching branches laden in early May with intensely double, white, pompon flowers like "bachelors' buttons". It is specially useful as it will grow on limy soil where it may follow *S. arguta* in bloom and associate with the Kerrias, Berberis and other shrubs of similar size in bloom at this time.

This Spiræa may be increased by detaching rooted suckers from old plants, carefully potting these and growing them on in a fairly warm frame.

Less hardy, but equally easily satisfied as to soil, *Fremontia californica* is a soft, partly evergreen shrub of doubtful hardiness and "miffy" nature, like so many Californians in this country. The brilliant golden-

† "Rhododendrons and Azaleas", by Clement Gray Bowers, Macmillian, N.Y., 1936.

yellow Mallow-like flowers, 2½ inches across, are spectacularly free from May onwards but it is only to be recommended for favourable gardens.

A warm, sunny, well-drained spot on a south slope, rather than against a wall, is probably the best place for it and increase is easily attained by seeds. Established plants usually die if moved.

A new variety, 'California Glory' is hardier and more free-flowering than the "type".

More as a warning than a recommendation I mention *Davidia involucrata,* the Dove Tree, a rather Lime-like, 50-foot Chinese tree with large bright green leaves and dark ascending branches. The curious flowers, consisting of a small pompon with a large white bract hanging like a huge petal on either side, just fail, I think, to be really beautiful. They hang down among the leaves and are seldom very well presented and are too roughly formed, so that, in May, from a slight distance, the tree merely looks as though it had a lot of waste paper caught up in it. As a street or park tree it is quite attractive.

The Davidia likes a moist, loamy soil and is apparently hardy. Seeds are the best method of increase.

The finest of the **Pieris** flowers in early May and is a distinguished plant that requires care.

Pieris formosa (a Himalayan species) is too tender for any but the more favoured gardens; it is, in any event, eclipsed by its Yunnanese and Burmese form, *P. f. Forrestii* (A.G.M. 1944) whose flowers appear whiter, having a white instead of a green calyx, and whose young leaves are of such vivid red as to make a most spectacular effect.

A more recent arrival, being first introduced in 1910, it was exhibited in flower at the R.H.S. Chelsea Show in 1924. It is a strikingly beautiful shrub growing up to 10 feet high, with fine, dark, evergreen foliage, and large pyramidal panicles of fragrant pure white urn-shaped flowers among the brilliant red young leaves in early May. This latter feature is extremely decorative, and the fine 'Wakehurst Variety' rivals the Azaleas in brightness of colours. 'Wakehurst' is hardy but others are not really hardy and many good specimens have succumbed entirely to recent cold winters. It is, however, so outstandingly beautiful as to be worth trying in favoured gardens on lime-free soil in a sunny spot with moist soil. Cuttings or seeds are the best methods of increase.

In those favoured gardens where shade and shelter from wind and a lime-free soil are combined with reasonable freedom from spring frosts owing to good katabatics, the hardier of the **Rhododendron Hybrids** having the "blood" of the great Himalayan Lily-laurel, *R. Griffithianum*, can be effectively grown.

The finest of these is undoubtedly the hybrid with the fragrant, seven-lobed, pale purplish-pink flowered *R. Fortunei*, known as *R. Loderi* "C" ****. The stars are stars of relative merit awarded by the Rhododendron Group of the R.H.S. The "C" means "Hardy along the seaboard and in warm gardens inland", and it is a very salutary precaution always to include the hardiness-category-letter in naming any Rhododendron. The *necessary* conditions to grow a "C" plant are enumerated above.

R. Loderi is one of the loveliest of all flowering shrubs and, where it can be grown, it is worthy of the most important position, such as at the foot of the north wall of the house, rather than tucked away somewhere or lumped up with other Rhododendrons in some dismal concentration. A fine specimen adorned a north wall near the entrance to my old house to the great enjoyment of all. In time it makes a shrub of some 8 feet or more, but a finer occupant of the required space in a lime-free garden could not be found. The immense pearly-white flowers, 6 inches across, are fragrant, though not powerfully so, and expand from pink buds.

There are a number of different clonal forms of the hybrid, as the cross has been made several times. 'King George' is the most generally available at present. It has large and firmly carried flowers in a fine truss. Some seedling forms of the cross are inferior in various ways, some have very lax flower-trusses and others are markedly more tender. Such a tender form, sometimes known as 'Sir Joseph Hooker', with remarkably beautiful, light, bright green foliage, veined with darker green, and having early pink flowers, is often seen. We have very large plants in our favoured wood-garden but it could not be recommended for the open garden. Care must therefore be taken to make sure that one of the hardier forms (many of which have received awards) is secured.

Gardens subject to late spring frosts that destroy the flowers and young growth of *R. Loderi* may well substitute R. 'Angelo' "C" (*R. Griffithianum* × *discolor*). There are many varieties of this later-flowering hybrid, which otherwise much resembles *R. Loderi*. A wide selection in my wood-garden has, through the years, given a better return owing to the flowers escaping frost more frequently as they do not open until the end of May or early in June. At the same time neither the habit of growth nor the form of the flowers of 'Angelo' is quite so decorative as in *R. Loderi*. In poor conditions both these fine hybrids grow better if root-grafted on *ponticum* rather than as layers.

A degree hardier, but still requiring light shade, regular mulching with leaves, and shelter from wind, are the "B" category hybrids, once removed, so to speak, from *R. Loderi*. This section may be typified by the well-known 'Pink Pearl' "B" **. "B" means "Hardy anywhere in the British Isles but requires some shade to obtain best results", but some amplification and explanation is needed. Briefly the varieties in this section flower early and are consequently at the mercy of spring frosts; they will just tolerate a favourable garden, but grow twice as well in woodland and there become superb plants with huge bold leaves and immense trusses, so different from the usual, shrivelled, garden occupants as to be almost unrecognisable. Any who doubt this statement are referred to the plants themselves which will give a very emphatic confirmation if given the chance. Having given due warning, let us review the different varieties that will flower simultaneously in harmonising colours, assuming that a sheltered spot shaded say, by tall trees to the south, and having a good, acid, sandy loam enriched with leaf-mould, is available:—

'Albatross' ***, white, scented.
'Alice' **, rose madder, earlier than 'Pink Pearl'.
'Beauty of Littleworth' ****, huge fls., white, spotted maroon.
'Betty Wormald' ****, rosy pink, dark eye.
'Boddaertianum' ***, arboreum, type, white, spotted maroon.
'China' ***, pale yellow, bold foliage.
'Corona' ****, pale crimson, exquisite wide bells.
'Countess of Derby' ***, rose pink, large truss.
'Cynthia' **, purplish deep pink.
'David' ***, blood red, early.
'Fabia' ***, orange, hanging bells.
'Grosclaude' ***, scarlet, late.
'King George' ***, bright crimson-red, fine truss (illustn. p. 112).
'Luscombei' ***, carmine, a lovely bush.
'Mother of Pearl' ***, blush to white.
'Mrs. A. C. Kenrick' **, rose pink.
'Mrs. A. T. de la Mare' ***, white with green eye.
'Mrs. Charles Pearson' ****, blush-mauve spotted brown.
'Mrs. G. W. Leak' ***, pink, brown-purple eye.
'Mrs. Lindsay Smith' **, lovely white but leggy habit.
'Mrs. Philip Martineau' ***, pink, pale yellow flare.
'Mrs. R. S. Holford' **, warm rich pink, almost "A".
'Mrs. Walter Burns' **, pink, vivid red eye.
'Naomi' ***, pink flushed green and lilac.
'Pink Pearl' ***, rose pink, fading soon in sun.
'Rose Perfection' **, carmine.

'Sir John Ramsden' ****, yellow suffused pink.
'Susan' ***, blue-mauve, early.
'Unknown Warrior' *, crimson, early.
'White Pearl' **, blush to white.

A particularly lovely hybrid that flowers before the above group is R. 'Loder's White' "C" **** (A.G.M. 1931). It was raised by Sir Edmund Loder of Leonardslee near Horsham, and is of rather similar parentage to R. *Loderi* but is perhaps more wind-resisting. It is so free-flowering as to give the effect of a cloud of snow, but, as with all the above-mentioned, must be given care and a favourable position as previously described to do well.

Until recently Rhododendrons have been the most pest-free and disease-resistant of all flowering shrubs. Of late, however, a most serious fungus infestation has begun to spread. This is generally called "bud-blast". In late autumn—even if no frost has yet manifested itself —a number of flower buds may be found to be browned and dead. They have been attacked by the fungus—believed to be *Sporocybe azaleæ*† and, unless these infected buds are removed with a small portion of the stem, all subsequent ones nearby are likely to be infected and thus spoiled. Once the fungus gets hold of large plantations the position is grave and I know of superb gardens whose display is sometimes ruined by this pest. On the other hand, with constant vigilance there is no serious danger. We do not yet know much about this new enemy and some form of timed, fungicidal spraying may be found to provide an effective control. In the meantime, the gardener will do well to remove all dead flower buds promptly by early November. Some species such as R. *campylocarpum* and R. *Griersonianum* are reported to be immune (*loc. cit. sup.*). In my view R. *caucasicum* is particularly susceptible.

The first display of **Evergreen Azaleas** is over, the second is under way. One of the members of this later chorus is "Azalea ledifolia", correctly known as *Rhododendron mucronatum* "C" ****, with large, fragrant, white flowers. It has been cultivated in Japan for 300 years. The noble company of fragrant white-flowered shrubs have few more beautiful representatives than this lovely Azalea. The habit is compact and mounded and the evergreen leaves, dark and pointed, show up the massed flowers to perfection. Apparently it was first introduced into England through a collector named Joseph Poole, who sent it from China to his employers, Brookes' Nurseries, at Ball's Pond in 1819. This Azalea is a good garden plant growing to nearly 6 feet high and

† *The Rhododendron Year-Book*, 1949, p. 25 et seq.

15 feet across in favourable gardens, and is reasonably hardy in suitable soil anywhere, but, like all its family, it grows best where the atmosphere is fairly moist. In the ordinary garden it is usually 2 or 3 feet high only, but of much larger spread. Its flowering has apparently been almost everywhere unaffected by recent severe winters. The flowers last longer in the shade of distant trees, but an airy situation and a clear sky overhead is desirable for compact and healthy growth.

The origin of this Azalea is uncertain, being lost in antiquity. No wild species exactly corresponding is known. Professor Hara considers this group to be of hybrid parentage.†

Varieties:—

R. m. *Noordtianum* has larger flowers, but, as a growing shrub, is no improvement on the "type".

R. m. *narcissiflorum* is a double-flowered form, and, again, is no improvement.

R. m. 'Sekidera' (*magnificum*) is white, spotted with rose, and is a fine hardy variety.

R. m. 'Akebono' white, flushed and spotted mauve.

R. m. *amethystinum* with smaller flowers spotted and flushed with lilac, is evidently a hybrid and flowers much earlier.

R. m. 'Fujimanyo' with double, Orchid Purple (H.C.C. 31/3) flowers, introduced along with the type, is of more open habit and has a slightly later flowering time. It is probably a hybrid.

R. m. *ripense*, purple flowers.

A convenient associate for the charming R. *mucronatum* is 'Azalea Maxwellii' (R. *pulchrum* var. *Maxwellii*) "C" **. The wild form is not known; this variety is a Japanese clone with large, deep Phlox Pink (H.C.C. 625) single flowers that open at about the same time. Though the flower colour is poor it is a sturdy evergreen Azalea and makes a pleasing contrast with its white-flowered relative (A.M. 1960). Our superb new Azalea 'Moon Maiden' has wide-open white flowers two inches across in great profusion on a dense, low bush. Flowers have a yellow-green centre and some may have a purple streak.

Various new hybrids synchronise their flowering with the foregoing. One of the best is 'Nettie' with semi-double flowers of that enchanting Camellia pink—Geranium Lake (H.C.C. 20/2). Sometimes slightly earlier in opening are 'Leo', like a prostrate vivid orange *kœmpferi*; 'Louise', deep scarlet, like a later 'John Cairns'; 'Marie', carmine with bristling stamens; 'Naomi', flowers large, frail, pale orange-pink,

† *The Rhododendron Year-Book*, 1948, p. 123.

Viburnum tomentosum sterile

Azalea 'Mrs. Oliver Slocock'

Azalea 'Devon'

Philadelphus 'Belle Etoile'

the new 'Mother's Day', with huge red flowers, apparently a *Simsii* hybrid, and 'Rose Greeley' with large white flowers, 'Bengal Beauty' with large pink flowers.

Our new 'Coral Beauty' ('Daimio' × *Simsii* hardy F.C.C. form) has profuse, large, orange-pink flowers on a compact, evergreen bush that appears to be hardy if given the usual requirement of moist peaty soil etc.

'Gumpo' has large white flowers; *album giganteum* has larger ones that are not so well presented; 'Gumpo Red' has large pale pink flowers; 'Titugetsuse' has purplish-pink flowers and so has 'Yugiri', but they have darker spots, they are all rather shy-flowering.

Another small but valuable group is tentatively named *Wadai* after the Japanese nurseryman Mr. K. Wada who exported so many beautiful plants to this country before the war. 'Asakanonare' is a beautiful Azalea with large salmon-red flowers opening late in May; 'Bungoni-shiki' has terracotta semi-double flowers and may have *R. indicum* in its parentage, and 'Chichibu' ** is rather like 'Gumpo', with large white flowers. 'Higoromo' is shy-flowering.

As a further adornment to this grouping there may be added, although it sometimes flowers earlier, the dwarf-growing form of the yellow-flowered *Rhododendron Hanceanum* "C". One would have expected this form to have been awarded quite a constellation of stars, as that highly experienced judge, Mr. Francis Hanger, the Curator of Wisley gardens, stated that it was his favourite of all the yellow-flowered dwarfs.† But there are many different forms, among them a richer yellow one rarely exceeding a foot in height which is unfortunately very scarce, dwarf forms with whitish flowers, and the "type" form which makes a shrub of 3 feet and is also not particularly attractive, having small, very pale yellow flowers. It is a member of the Triflorum series and comes from the Western Szechwan mountains, China.

Another miniature, blooming in May, is *R. Sargentianum* "C" **, a member of the Anthopogon series. It has pale lemon-yellow flowers and is figured in *The Rhododendron Year-Book* for 1947. Though not so showy as some, it has the dainty individual personality that is such an attractive feature of these little species although rather a delicate plant, coming from the same habitat as the preceding.

R. 'Yellow Hammer' (*R. flavidum* × *sulphureum*) has small, somewhat tubular, yellow flowers and small neat foliage of a rather dull purplish tone. It is remarkable in the length of its flowering season which beings in early May but it seldom has sufficient flowers out at one time to make a real display. In habit it is thin and upright (attaining seven feet in height) unless grown fully exposed, with all straggling shoots pegged-down.

† "Miniature Rhododendron Species", *R.H.S. Journal*, LXIX, Pt. 2, p. 40.

The May-flowering Alpine Rhododendrons run much to undesirable purplish pinks. Though not recommended they are described below for those who do not object to these colourings.

R. calostrotum "A" *** is a russet-green-leaved bushlet from the Saluenense series. The flowers, usually in pairs, open out flat and are of an awkward purplish colour (Petunia Purple 52/1) which, lacking the hyaline sparkling intensity of those of the Petunia herself, are not easy to place. *R. calostrotum* comes from 11,000 or 12,000 feet altitudes in the mountains of north-eastern Burma whence it was first introduced by Reginald Farrer. It is very free flowering, but possibly not very long-lived.

Reduced to a variety of this is *R. calciphilum* "A". It is a prostrate dwarf with rosy purple flowers towards the end of May or in early June, interesting because it is said to be found only on limestone in Nature. Those stalwarts who struggle to grow Rhododendrons in chalky districts might find it worth trying.

R. radicans " B " ****, Saluenense series, is a very tiny, dwarf and compact grower of attractive habit, but regrettably, magenta-pink flowers, that often delays its flowering until June.

R. imperator "A" ***, of the Uniflorum series, is a creeping shrub that needs some care and in warm gardens grows best in the shade of distant trees. It only rises a few inches from the ground but it will make a little mat, sometimes nearly 2 feet across when it is happy. In early May it is so free flowering that the mat becomes a solidly floral one, composed of the ½-inch wide, often six-lobed, rosy flowers. It comes from 10,000-foot elevations in Burma and was introduced by Captain Kingdon Ward from his 1926 expedition. It was illustrated in the *Gardeners' Chronicle*, March 13, 1948, p. 85.

R. aperantum "B" ** is in the Neriiflorum series. So far we have not mentioned a really difficult species, but Reginald Farrer's watercolour of this Rhododendron ("The Plant Introductions of Reginald Farrer", p. 68) is so enchanting that I do not think that anyone who has seen the picture could fail to wish to struggle with the problem of growing the plant. Both the shape of the flower and the colouring vary enormously, but all appear beautiful; either the trumpets or the wide-open bells, and the yellow, orange, red or fresh pink tints of the corollas. Apparently the plant is rather a "miff" in cultivation and this is sad indeed, for it seems to have every good quality otherwise. The Rhododendron Group Year-Book's mention of "mats up to 20 feet across" is certainly exciting and, if only we can go on growing this species from seed, sooner or later a good steady grower should appear.

Before we leave these delightful shrublets of rock garden size, mention must be made of *R. myrtilloides* "A" ***. It is not really effective, but it is very amusing, being only a few inches in height and covered, if a good form, with magenta-rose bell-flowers of a shape that reminds one of *Campanula cæspitosa*. There is a superb illustration of this species in *R. H. S. Journal*, LXIX, Pt. 2, Fig. 6 (1944). It is often not in flower until nearly the middle of June.

For the propagation details of these miniatures see end of April-flowering section of dwarf Rhododendrons, p. 90.

Too often one sees the mountain dwarfs as thin, weedy-looking bushes planted alongside woodland paths, ineffective when in bloom amid the larger-flowered woodlanders and unthrifty and ugly when out of flower. On the other hand, grouped with dwarf shrubs of other genera, such as those described later, among boulders *right out in the open*, on little sloping banks, they are a delight at all times—compact mounds of violet, yellow or purple in spring, dense, blue-green, emerald or bronzy cushions in winter. To attain this, plant them in humus with buried sandstone rocks, with moisture provided as described on pp. 167 and 190. Peg down every possible branch flat on the ground, with bamboo or wire pegs. The centre then grows vigorously and fills up, the whole plant seems suddenly invigorated and in a season or two you have your dense, comely cushion. The simplest pegs are those made by cutting up Bamboo (*Sinarundinaria nitida*) canes with secateurs. When the main stems are cut to size and inverted it will be found that the shortened side growths of the Bamboo hook over the Rhododendron stems most conveniently.

An alternative is to layer the outer branches, but, though good increase is thus secured, the compact dome is not so quickly attained.

Whilst we are still among the little shrubs that are so delightful for the open parts of the garden where a low, cushiony effect is needed, we must not forget the members of another great and valuable family, the Brooms. As everyone knows, most of them are yellow-flowered, but it is often a very good yellow. This is a very beautiful and a very showy colour, when embroidered among whites and, either pure and strong colours, or pale colours, depending upon whether the yellow itself is pure and strong or pale. For perfection both associations should be boldly interlaced.

Cytisus Ardoinii, from south-eastern France, usually flowers in early May, growing only from 4 to 8 inches high. It is a free-flowering and pretty little thing with bright yellow flowers.

An outstanding dwarf Broom flowering in May is *C. Beanii* (*C. Ardoini* × *purgans*) with profuse yellow flowers. It grows about one foot or more in height and makes a bright and attractive patch of colour.

C. kewensis is another dwarf hybrid Broom (*C. Ardoini* × *multiflorus*), slightly later in blooming, with flowers of a more creamy yellow (Empire Yellow, H.C.C. 603/1), which is the same as that of *C. præcox*. It is more prostrate, but is a particularly lovely shrub when seen in flower in a well-raised position above the cool violet of R. 'Blue Tit'. These dwarf Brooms will grow quite well on limy soils, but of course do so equally well on acid soils. The soft yellow colouring of *C. kewensis* is particularly delightful with the mauves and violets of the mountain Rhododendrons, providing the perfect complement.

C. emeriflorus (*C.* or *Genista, glabrescens*) from Switzerland and north Italy, has an attractive habit, forming a mound about eighteen inches high, completely covered with shining yellow flowers in the latter part of May. It has been rather scarce over here, but I note that it is now listed by several nurserymen specialising in flowering shrubs. One of the loveliest of the dwarf Brooms, it is worth taking some trouble to secure it.

C. procumbens is a less neat tussock, alight with yellow pea-flowers at this season. Rather larger, it will reach 2 feet in height and flowers over quite a long period.

Those who can look after very small plants may add the Hedgehog Broom, *Erinacea pungens* (*E. anthyllis*) from Spain and Morocco. This spiny little hummock, eventually perhaps a foot high and a yard wide, is usually seen no more than mole-heap size, and of a young mole at that. The spines have an attractive silvery sheen and the clear, purplish-blue pea-flowers, two or three together, but not quite as numerous as one might wish as a rule, usually appear in early May. It is quite hardy in a warm dry place where it grows slowly but steadily year by year.

There are a number of other interesting dwarf Brooms, less commonly found, such as *Cytisus versicolor*, a hybrid of *C. purpureus* which has purplish and yellowish tinted flowers; *C. purpureus* itself with rosy-purple flowers in the "type" form and white-flowered and pink-flowered varieties; *C. hirsutus* with yellow flowers stained with brown and also its variety *hirsutissimus* with more downy and vigorous growth.

As regards cultivation, all these Brooms like an acid, sandy soil with good drainage and full sun, but will stand a slight degree of liminess. Many can be struck from cuttings, but it is tricky work and on the whole the amateur is well advised either to buy them in pots or to grow them from seed. As they are tap-rooted and suffer badly if the roots are disturbed it is best to sow three seeds only in each small pot, and, if all come up, either treat the result as one plant or pinch out all but one seedling. The Brooms, apart from *Erinacea pungens*, are quick growers, most desirable for the rapid furnishing of new gardens but they are seldom really permanent, long-lived plants like the Chænomeles,

Azaleas, Rhododendrons, Camellias, Cherries, Hydrangeas, etc.; consequently it is wise to keep a replacement service going. Their lives can be appreciably lengthened by regular pruning-back of the young wood after flowering and by pegging down and layering any suitable branches.

Another dwarf shrub which associates delightfully with the foregoing is *Lithospermum diffusum* 'Heavenly Blue' (A.G.M. 1925), a small, prostrate evergreen with brilliant blue flowers (Gentian Blue, H.C.C. 42) in May and onwards into June and even later. It likes to trail down among sandstone rocks and strikes fairly easily from cuttings placed under a bell-glass in July. Unfortunately, like so many good shrubs, it will not tolerate a limy soil. One of the best of carpeters, it always looks attractive, though to get a mass of blue, as shown in the illustration opposite p. 128, requires some skill. Top-dressing is necessary or the flowers dwindle to half the proper size and growth becomes stunted. Pegging down keeps the plants compact and healthy, but it is a fastidious and difficult plant and very sensitive to drought or untimely frost.

The variety 'Grace Ward' has flowers of a slightly darker blue, perhaps, and the habit is generally more upright, though this feature depends much on feeding and pegging down when a close, bushy habit is desired. An interesting feature is that this variety is reputed to tolerate a less acid soil than the " type ", though my own experience is otherwise. Both varieties grow unusually well in Close Boskage beds (see p. 20) where they can run through other shrubs.

There is a white variety which I have not seen, var. *album*.

Another pleasing bushlet is *Phyllodoce empetriformis*, a delightful little Heathlike shrub from Western North America. The reddish-purple, pitcher-shaped flowers cover the 9-inch bushes in late April and May and it grows well in any acid, sandy soil suitable for Heaths.

P. nipponica is less easy-going, if even more attractive with its white bell-flowers, with wavy edges, at the tips of the sprigs. Such little treasures as this, exquisite on a near inspection, are among the rewards of the stroller rather than components of the main colour groupings.

The **Genistas,** such close allies of the Brooms that only the botanists can separate them, give us several dwarf growers flowering in May which are conveniently mentioned here.

Genista lydia though seldom mentioned, is a dainty little Balkan species that is absolutely first class, with its densely massed clear yellow flowers covering the gracefully arching branches. It seldom exceeds 2 feet and its life-span seems to be short; a warm place, well elevated, seems to suit it best. It flowers towards the end of May, as a rule, often remaining in flower during June. Alas, it does not set seed or strike very readily from cuttings. (See illustration facing p. 113.)

G. hispanica is one of the most useful of all the low-growing members of the Legume family, making dense pouffes of foot-high, spiny branches completely covered in late May and early June with the rich golden yellow flowers. Not quite reliably hardy in the cold north-eastern and midland parts of our country, it is sound enough anywhere in the south-western half and is a shrub that no chalky garden can well do without. It is a good garden plant provided that it is planted in poor soil, and it is increased easily from rooted fragments, cuttings or seeds.

G. pilosa is a straggling but easily grown dwarf Broom and a native of sandy Heaths in parts of England, it is said, but I have never been lucky enough to find it wild. A more compact form, the best for the garden, is often described as var. *nana* (A.G.M. 1939). It forms a mass of twiggy shoots about 1 foot 6 inches high, sometimes 6 feet across. In May it provides a fine mass of yellow and is very effective on dry banks, carpeting the ground and spreading freely. It may, according to Mr. J. Comber (R.H.S. Shrub Conference, 1938), be propagated from pieces several inches long, put three parts in the ground in February, before growth starts, in the manner used for Sage. It can be grown in a fairly limy soil. Var. *procumbens* is too dwarf for shrub beds.

G. × 'Pyjams' (*G. pilosa* × *januensis*) is a new hybrid of great promise, being free-flowering and neat in habit, forming a bush about 18 inches high.

G. januensis also from south Europe, has a spreading, procumbent habit and is seldom more than a foot high. It has curious triangular stems and the bright yellow flowers rather like those of *G. virgata*, appear in racemes along the ends of the shoots in May and June. It is not so hardy as the others but is very decorative.

Most of these Genistas can be grown from seed, if and when they produce it. Cuttings are not very easy for the amateur.

Leiophyllum buxifolium, the Sand Myrtle, is a pleasant little North American evergreen shrub of the Heath family. Its white, myrtle-like flowers opening from rosy buds, are very freely borne in May and June and its neat, domed habit, rarely more than a foot in height, makes it very suitable for association with the other dwarf bushes mentioned.

It needs a lime-free soil and may be propagated from layers.

The Daphnes, chancy and uncertain plants of poor flower colouring, liable to "miff off" without apparent excuse as they are, have yet a delightful personality of their own and give us a charming May-flowering species in *Daphne Cneorum* (A.G.M. 1927) from South Europe. The abundant trusses of pale Tyrian Rose ultra fragrant flowers almost conceal the low-spreading, lax, evergreen branches that seldom rise more than a foot from the ground. In my experience a sandy turf-loam, on the acid side, and a lightly-shaded position suit this plant well, but good specimens of this, and indeed all the Daphnes, are seen, at least for a time, in almost all kinds of soils. They are pets for odd corners rather than components of the main flower effects.

D. C. grandiflora and *D. C. eximia* are much superior to the "type", being more vigorous in growth and having flowers of larger size and warmer colouring. *D. C. alba* is a weakly dwarf form with small white flowers. A virus disease now further enfeebles this species.

Placing sandstone rocks over the longer branches helps the plants to remain compact and renew their growth and a light scattering of a complete fertiliser should be given each spring, but, sooner or later, they usually die off suddenly. (See illustration facing p. 65.)

D. Burkwoodii, a vigorous hybrid between *D. caucasica*, a deciduous Daphne, and the preceding species, is a well-rounded, semi-evergreen shrub, about 2 or 3 feet high, dappled all over with little trusses of paler, rosy-pink, fragrant flowers in spring. It is fairly robust and easy-going. *D. B.* 'Somerset' appears to be very similar but lower and more spreading in habit.

One of the finest and the most enduring of all Daphnes is *D. retusa*, an evergreen with leathery, oval leaves (there is said to be a deciduous form), and a dense, stout and picturesque habit, most impressive when seen as a large bush 3 or 4 feet high and equally wide (see illustration facing p. 129). It comes from the mountains of Western China whence it was introduced by E. H. Wilson in 1901. The large flowers, in clusters at the ends of the shoots, are pale mauve, with the interior white, and are deliciously lilac-scented. It is probably the best long-term investment among the Daphnes for a sunny position, but the tragedy of the sudden loss of a fine, permanent-looking shrub, just grown to perfection, always threatens. It is surprisingly easily raised from seeds sown as soon as ripe, though the seedlings grow very slowly, and it can be struck from cuttings placed under a bell-glass in July. This Daphne grows best in a position where its head is in the sun but the roots are shaded, an arrangement easily provided with the help of neighbouring, low shrubs. The Daphne family is one which can mostly be grown in limy soils provided that a little fine leaf-soil is added. On the other hand they grow well in acid soils and the addition of lime mortar to the soil, often recommended, does not, in my experience, do the plants any good at all, but a light dressing of 'Growmore' is helpful.

D. tangutica (A.G.M. 1949) very much resembles *D. retusa* but it has slightly narrower leaves and the flowers are rather more purple in colour. It was introduced from Kansu by Reginald Farrer in 1914. He described it as "a dense low shrub of very dark glossy foliage about 12 inches high and twice as much through. Dotted in open turf on the slopes, 9,000–10,000 feet, in deep calcareous loam or vegetable mould". According to Mr. E. H. M. Cox,† like *D. retusa,* though hardy, it is both very slow-growing and slow to flower. One of Farrer's plants had 'rose-pink' flowers and the other creamy-white. But the *R.H.S. Journal* (LXXV, Pt. 2, p. 76, 1950) records *D. tangutica* as having flowers rosy-purple outside and white inside, and as free-flowering even when small and the forms available in this country all appear to be of this type. This species flowers rather earlier than *D. retusa,* often opening in early April. Consequently *D. retusa* is probably the better species.

The arrangement of all these dwarf shrubs is most effective on an undulating piece of ground with plenty of mounds, hummocks and little ravines, running downhill if this is possible, so as to let cold air drain freely away. In such a setting a few large, picturesque boulders are invaluable. Æsthetically, such a little landscape is more interesting and attractive than a flat one, and culturally it is of the greatest advantage as it gives many varying aspects suited to the different types of plants. Thus the cooler, northerly slopes suit the mountain dwarf Rhododendrons, the flatter areas the Evergreen Azaleas, the elevated sunny summits the Brooms, and the hot south slopes the essential June-flowering Helianthemums and Halimiums that will be mentioned later, while larger slopes and outskirts may be "lawned" with Heaths, quietly green, until, in August, their turn comes to take over the display. In this way the garden landscape is a miniature, concentrated expression of the beauties of nature and each "alp", perhaps 2 or 3 feet high, supports a different vegetation on its various faces in accordance with their climate. The more showy plants are so placed as to be visible from garden-house, windows and other viewpoints and those chosen for their interesting individual personalities where they can be closely viewed from the paths that invite a walk.

Occasionally a specimen shrub of dense, bushy habit slightly larger than the others, may emerge from such a low planting—*Kalmia latifolia myrtifolia* (see p. 240) is the type I have in mind—and in such cases we should make sure that the immediately surrounding shrublets are

† "The Plant Introductions of Reginald Farrer."

either plants that will become time-expired by the time the specimen needs more room, or such easily portable little shrubs as Evergreen Azaleas or Alpine Rhododendrons.

The **Wisterias** are beautiful and vigorous climbers all too seldom sufficiently pruned and trained to show their racemes of violet or white flowers to the greatest advantage. Every whip-shoot left on means one raceme of flower less.

Wisteria floribunda macrobotrys (*W. multijuga*), the best form of the Japanese Wisteria, has very long racemes of the fragrant, bean-like, violet flowers opening in late May. It is less effective, perhaps, for house walls than its Chinese relative but very attractive grown on strong trellis, pergolas or trees. In Japan it is often trained out over water on poles and screens, when the ropes of flowers hang beautifully sil-houetted, perhaps a yard long. The wild type from which this garden form is descended has shorter racemes and is less decorative. By hard weekly pruning, this Wisteria can be made to form a picturesque specimen shrub or small tree. The flowers open gradually from the bases of the racemes which makes the display longer lasting but less spectacular than that of the Chinese species. Occasional flowers open throughout the summer in favourable seasons. It is the hardiest of the Wisterias.

W. f. alba is a white variety.

W. f. rosea has pink flowers tipped with purple.

W. f. violaceo-plena has violet, double flowers less freely borne. But, judging from photographs, there appears to be a free-flowering double form in some Japanese gardens.

Wisteria sinensis (A.G.M. 1928), the Chinese Wisteria, has shorter and thicker racemes of a more vivid heliotrope colouring. It is the most decorative of the family on a wall but is less so than others, perhaps, on pergolas, arches or trees. Great care is needed in early training to ensure the form of an immense fan on a wide wall or an espalier to decorate the spaces of a house-wall, between the windows, in an orderly manner. The flowers open somewhat earlier in May and as they all unfold at once the display is very striking. It will grow on limy soils provided that rotted manure or leaf-mould is added.

W. s. alba has white flowers.

W. formosa is a hybrid between the two preceding species, favouring the latter in appearance.

W. venusta is a Japanese garden form of a wild Chinese species not yet introduced. The short racemes of large, fragrant white flowers are substantial and long-lasting, very attractive, and produced in May on very downy stalks. It was introduced in 1912. When pruned and grown as a shrub it is particularly effective.

W. macrostachya. This American species is not often seen but is quite attractive. The flowers are fragrant and lilac-purple, in racemes up to a foot long, and usually do not open until June. It is not so rampant as the others and may therefore be planted where there is not room for the larger-growing sorts.

W. japonica, a July and August flowering species, is mentioned in the section devoted to that month.

The Wisterias all seem to prefer a moist and rich soil and full sun on the upper growth. They may be increased by layering. Seeds are ripened in warm summers in long, bean-like pods but the resulting seedlings are usually disappointing, compared with the selected superior varieties.

Pruning is important and early training even more so. Well-spaced shoots should be tied early into their permanent positions and any not required should be cut away. Afterwards all unwanted shoots may be spurred back as with vines. The difference between the unsightly tangle of untrained wall plants and those that have been properly guided is very great. When the Wisteria is used as a tree climber one stout shoot should first be trained up spirally without competition, later it may be allowed to grow as it wills. If required to form an open-ground bush, a strong single stem is first built up and then short strong branches are allowed to develop a certain length each year.

The spring-flowering members of the **Ceanothus** family have their headquarters on the Pacific Coast Range and among the hills of California and, unfortunately, like most shrubs from that part of the world, are rarely hardy enough for these islands. None the less, they are very commonly grown, usually as wall plants, although they are naturally open-ground shrubs, carpeting the baking slopes with their masses of small and rather coarse blue, purplish-lilac or white flowers. Nature's last few sanctuaries are menaced there now, as everywhere else, although good people struggle to protect them.

One of the hardiest species is *Ceanothus thyrsiflorus,* introduced in 1815, which has the habit of a small tree, up to 15 or 20 feet high, with clusters of pale blue, sometimes slaty blue or even whitish, flowers in May. It will grow on a limy soil. Like others of its kind it is liable to be wind-rocked and killed unless either firmly supported and anchored by layering stones, or staked and always pruned back after flowering. It is particularly attractive grown in association with Azaleas as, indeed, often occurs in the wild.

A variety of unusual hardiness and vigour is *C. thyrsiflorus* 'Cascade'; the flowers are sea blue. It was introduced by Messrs. George Jackman of Woking, Surrey, as was *C. t. repens*, an extra hardy dwarf form reaching 4½ feet in height with a spread of 9 feet. Admirable beneath a south window.

C. Burtonensis (*C. impressus* × *thyrsiflorus*) is also extra hardy and looks like becoming a great acquisition, even surviving away from a wall.

C. Veitchianus (A.G.M. 1925) was sent back to Messrs. Veitch by their collector, William Lobb, in 1853 and is thought to be a natural hybrid between *C. thyrsiflorus* and *C. rigidus*. It has apparently not been seen since in a wild state.

With their comparatively bright blue flowers and free growth these are some of the most effective of this spring-flowering section and have the merit of striking fairly easily from cuttings. As evergreen shrubs they are sometimes unattractively encumbered with dead twigs unless carefully "manicured". A light soil, quick drainage and a sunny position all help the hardiness and consequently the permanence of the plants, but I have often lost them after hard winters. Most Ceanothus suffer in transplanting and it is better, even, to strike the cuttings in separate small pots, if possible, to avoid a check. On the other hand, potbound plants whose main tap-root has got twisted round do not anchor themselves properly as they cannot develop a spreading root system. Many deaths occur from this cause.

C. t. griseus, the Carmel Ceanothus, is a form with bluish-white or pale lilac flowers and larger leaves, and is reputed less hardy. It is very fast-growing and can make a fine bush in four years from a cutting.†
It is said to be the commonest species on the Monterey peninsula and to have blue-flowered forms whose "blunt-nosed blobs"‡ have cream-coloured anthers.

C. cyaneus, the San Diego Ceanothus is more refined in flower than most and an outstanding species for warm coastal gardens, with notably bright blue flowers on long spikes and small shining green leaves on green shoots but a lanky and ragged habit. It is listed by several British nurseries.

C. 'Edinburgh' is a valuable new hybrid with long sprays of vivid blue on a compact bush of unusual hardiness which can even be grown away from a wall.

C. papillosus is one of the less tall-growing species with long strap-like bright green leaves and clustered flowers of quite a pleasing lavender-blue, about the third week in May. Seeds were sent back by

† F. G. Preston, *The Gardeners' Chronicle*, 3245, Vol. CXXV, p. 99, also fig. 48, idem.
‡ Lester Rowntree, "The Native Ceanothus of California", *Gardening Illustrated*, 1098, August 1947.

William Lobb from California. The resulting young plants first flowered "in the open border" at Messrs. Veitch's nursery in Devon in 1854. Although considered one of the hardier species, it died out, except for a plant carefully conserved at Kew and a few specimens in favoured Devon gardens. From these sources it has been redistributed and is now commonly available from nurseries specialising in flowering shrubs. It is notable for its remarkably free-flowering habit. *C. p. Roweanus* is a variety with narrow, creased, sticky leaves growing usually to less than 3 feet high and having deep blue flowers which is increasingly popular in America. It is one of the more spectacular blues.

C. rigidus, a somewhat stiff and sparse-branched shrub, with purplish or dark slaty-blue flowers, originally thought to be too tender for the open, is generally grown against sunny walls where it flowers freely. Curiously enough it has survived recent severe winters far better than most other species, so it is worth trying on a warm slope in the open where it makes a fairly dense 3 to 4 foot bush.

C. 'A. T. Johnson' is one of the newer hybrids with flowers of a good blue, often giving a second display in late summer.

C. 'Delight', a hybrid between *C. papillosus* and *C. rigidus*, has flowers of a deep, greyish blue on long-stalked panicles and is a vigorous and hardy variety. (A.G.M. 1957.)

C. dentatus is of bushy habit and has pale grey-blue flowers in small bottle-brush clusters.

A form generally known as *C. d. Russellianus* is a particularly good variety, growing more freely and having clusters of bright blue flowers. It survived the 1968/69 winter undamaged.

C. impressus (A.M. 1944) is an allied species of most attractive habit with profuse, short-stalked flower-clusters of a bright blue in mid May and little round, puckered orbicular leaves. Quite one of the best.

Owing to confusion as to the correct names of the species, which merge into one another, being only signposted by an occasional extreme type clearly botanically distinct, it is often difficult to determine whether one has the true plant or not. As with the Evergreen Azaleas, the oriental Cherries and the Hydrangeas, the best solution will probably be to treat the forms available as clones with garden names. Most of the other species, of which there are over fifty, are of lesser garden value, but superlative forms of these have already been collected and propagated by Californian nurserymen. One of these, according to Mr. Lester Rowntree (*loc. sit. sup.*) is a form of *C. impressus* growing 2 feet high and 9 feet across, with abundant, vivid, electric-blue flowers and small wrinkled leaves. A similar form now available in this country, is proving to be one of the hardier spring-flowering Ceanothus making, with pruning, a sturdy bush of very neat habit.

The later-flowering, Mexican, hybrid section are dealt with later under seasonal headings.

It is regrettable that the Ceanothus are so tender and unresistant to wind, as there is no doubt that their spring blue is highly desirable in the garden. Though not really pure in their case, it is a lovely and rare colour and very beautiful with pale citron or sulphury yellows, such as the Azaleas and the Brooms supply. In late summer, on acid soils, the purest true blues are easily attained by the Hydrangeas, but early in the season it is much more difficult to provide this colour. A sunny position such as a south slope or the foot of a south wall, good air drainage, a light and well-drained soil, and attention to keeping the plants firmly anchored against wind damage, are all factors affecting the longevity of the Ceanothus, but if the temperature drops below the danger point the plants die. As the danger point for the genus is one often reached and passed in these islands, the mortality is high and, after a time, many turn to more reliably permanent shrubs with relief. Most of the species can be grown on limy soils.

The larger **Brooms** now claim attention and this family contains many beautiful shrubs flowering in May.

Cytisus multiflorus (*C. albus*), the Portugal Broom, (A.G.M. 1926), is a delightful white-flowered species that is a good garden plant and useful for supplying light shade as, like the other Legumes, it has deep roots that are out of the way and in any case do not rob the soil of nitrogen. This food is manufactured for it from the atmosphere by symbiotic (which means "living-friendlily-together") bacteria which form nodules on the roots without which, indeed, the plant cannot grow. The Portugal Broom grows quickly from seed and needs, like all the taller Brooms, much regular nipping-back when young to induce a bushy habit and good framework. On the other hand, if required to shade smaller shrubs, it may be kept to a single, tree-like stem. In height it will reach 8 to 10 feet ultimately, but is usually somewhat battered, gaunt and leggy by that time. There is a variety, *rosea*, with pale pink flowers that is sometimes seen.

A little later on, the many forms, varieties and hybrids of the common Scots Broom, *C. scoparius*, are in bloom, offering many fine yellows, creams, oranges and coppery reds. The wild type varies greatly in habit, but very little in flower colour. This is, however, a most beautiful clear yellow, being often a combination of Lemon and Buttercup, and in the garden landscape it is really much more effective than many of the garden forms. This is because so many of these are "bicolours" and the colours tend to cancel one another out at a distance. I have even destroyed quite large bushes of named varieties, at times, and replaced them with the common yellow with great advantage to the garden picture as a whole.

The work of producing the multi-coloured garden forms began when a Monsieur André found a wild form in Normandy in 1884 with wing-petals of a brownish-crimson. Then, in 1900, Kew, by artificial cross-fertilisation, produced the first hybrid between this form and *C. multiflorus*, named *C. Dallimorei*. The flowers were of a pinkish-crimson in general effect. The late T. Smith of Daisy Hill, Newry, was one of the first nurseryman breeders and he produced many new forms of attractive mixed colourings. The Donard Nursery and others followed later and a selection of these varieties which come under the heading of *C. scoparius Andreanus* is given below:—

'Daisy Hill splendens', buff standards, lower petals madder crimson.
'Diana', white standard, yellow keel, notably effective at a distance.
'Donard Seedling', pale pink standard, terracotta keel.
'Dragonfly', large yellow standard, bronze, crimson and yellow lower petals.
'Firefly', similar to above but more orange-tinted at a distance, the best of this type.
fulgens, amber standard, russet keel.
'Lord Lambourne', dull red wings, pale cream standards.
'Dorothy Walpole', brownish-crimson wings, rose standard.
Burkwoodii, maroon red, larger flowers than preceding.
'Lady Moore', brownish fiery red and buff.

Most of these, with the exception of 'Firefly' and 'Diana', although amusingly gay on close inspection, make little show at a distance. Much more effective for this purpose is *C. s. sulphureus*, the "Moonlight Broom". This has large pale lemon-yellow flowers which make a mass of fine colour, attractive in association with almost any blue-purple flowers in season. Besides the Ceanothus, *Rhododendron Augustinii* "C" **** is an example, where it can be given the necessary shelter nearby. *C. s. sulphureus* has a bushier and more naturally compact habit than most.

Another beautiful Broom is *C. s.* 'Cornish Cream', raised in Cornwall. The buds are cream-coloured and open into flowers with white standards and rich yellow wings.

Great as is the value of the Brooms for the delightful flower effects they provide in spring, their quality as all-the-year-round garden furnishings is even more outstanding. Clipped firmly several times in their first growing seasons, and annually trimmed after flowering, they form shapely mounds of beautiful verdure owing to the dense mass of their deep green twigs. In the winter landscape they rival the Evergreen Azaleas in the comeliness of their forms in all weathers. Owing to their wider tolerance of poor soil conditions the Brooms are flowering shrubs of the highest importance to an even greater number of gardeners and their culture, pruning and selection thus merit particular care. Many gardens unable to take advantage of the most beautiful of the flowering evergreens owing to the fact that their soil is just too limy for Rhododendrons, Kalmias, Camellias, Azaleas or Heaths, can grow these Brooms successfully. In such places I know few plants that can equal them as flowering shrubs of year-round beauty in the garden landscape.

Unfortunately the garden varieties are usually grafted on Laburnum seedlings or on the common Broom and this seems to affect their longevity, and cuttings are also often short-lived owing to decay of the pith.

Seedlings do not come true to variety of course, but their flowers are often extremely attractive, if seeds are taken from rich-coloured sorts, and the important point is that they make healthier and more long-lived plants. Two or three seeds may be sown in small pots and the seedlings planted out, and, when they bloom, the inferior ones may be pulled out. Young Brooms, I will repeat, unlike almost any other shrubs, *must* be sheared back all over, again and again, so as to make them form the dense, velvety green mounds so beautiful in the winter landscape and highly effective when in bloom. Old wood cannot be cut without death, or at least serious damage, to the plant, so not only should the young plants be sheared back but it is also advisable to shear back the young twigs of older specimens every year after flowering. The Brooms of this section unfortunately do not grow well on very limy soils. The Genistas, of course, do grow well on such soils.

A most charming evergreen flowering shrub whose praises are seldom sung is *Choisya ternata*, the Mexican Orange, a member of the Rose family. Given proper space it forms a nice, dense, rounded, shapely bush usually about 3 feet high, but it can attain to 9 feet, in time. It has three-lobed evergreen leaves and a succession of clusters of fragrant, white, five-petalled flowers from spring onwards. *C. ternata* was named for a Swiss botanist, Monsieur J. D. Choisy, 1799–1859, and introduced in 1866. Remarkably hardy for a Mexican, being in what I term the "reasonably hardy" class, it has often safely withstood temperatures below zero. Furthermore, it will grow under trees, even, according to the late J. C. Williams, under Beeches, and it flourishes in London. It was killed by forty-two degrees of frost near Selkirk in 1940, but, as all Rambler Roses, and almost everything else, suffered the same fate, this is not surprising. The Choisya is a valuable evergreen for situations too warm for Rhododendrons, enjoying a sunny, well-drained spot. *C. ternata* can be propagated by cuttings of rather ripe wood in the sand-frame and will grow on limy soils.

Another fine shrub from the western hemisphere, **Cornus florida,** the American Dogwood, flowers usually towards the latter part of May. It forms a small tree or large bush, usually about 8 to 10 feet high in this country but sometimes, particularly in the white-flowered "type" form, up to 15 feet or more when pruned to the tree habit. The true flowers are merely small green pompons but they are surrounded by about four large petaloid bracts which make a sizable inflorescence about 4 inches across. Forms vary in the shapeliness, colour, texture and size of these bracts, but most have them of too irregular and ragged a shape for the flower to compare favourably, in individual beauty, with that of a good form of *C. Kousa*. The variety *rubra* is generally considered the finest, but this really depends upon whether one prefers a pure white or a pale crimson-pink flower. In my opinion, a really good white form with symmetrical and shapely bracts is even more beautiful than the pink clone available in commerce here, which has the bracts somewhat irregularly formed. Two newly imported outstanding varieties are the white ' Cherokee Princess ' and the red-flowered ' Cherokee Chief '. These may prove to have shapelier and brighter flowers.

In America this Cornel, in the white or pale pink-flowered wild forms, is a small tree of great beauty and there, when making new gardens in the South, darkies are sometimes sent out into the woods to collect young trees. The method is to hack out a lump of root just around the base of the stem and then behead the tree at about 6 feet. Thus an easily portable "set" is secured that can be carried back on the shoulder. I have seen all stages of growth and the final one is a shapely standard tree with a fine bushy head, four years later. I shall not easily forget the sight of such trees near Lake Hall, Tallahassee, covered with the huge white "flowers" shading, with Pines cunningly interplanted, a foaming carpet of the Chinese *R. Simsii* (our florist's potted "Indian Azalea"). But in our climate with its spring frosts and weak spring sun, made still weaker in effect by the prevailing north-easters of May, *C. florida* is usually but a poor shadow of its real self. After a hot summer, however, it is a glorious thing with all the amazing freedom of flower seen in its native land. A neutral or acid soil is required.

In large gardens sufficiently elevated to avoid spring frosts this Cornel is very well worth planting more frequently for its distinct habit

Embothrium lanceolatum, Norquinco

Magnolia Sieboldii

Rhododendron 'Tondelayo'

Ghent Azalea 'Graf Alf von Nipping'

and fine autumn colour. The flowers open on the naked branches, unlike those of its rival, *C. Kousa*, which appear among the full leafage and yet by reason of their greater numbers and superb presentation make an even greater display.

Very different from the gentle Dogwood is *Poncirus trifoliata* (*Ægle sepiaria*) the **Hardy Orange,** which comes from Japan and is a curious and, in warm gardens, quite an attractive shrub. It forms a fairly dense, deciduous bush usually about 5 feet high, sparsely foliaged but profusely armed with the most terrible olive-green spines 2 or 3 inches long. In May the fragrant white orange-blossom flowers appear, often in such numbers as to make a very nice display. Later the fruits, like small inedible oranges, are formed. These contain good seeds from which a person requiring an unusual, but highly effective, hedge might easily raise enough plants for this purpose. It stands clipping well enough, though not hard cutting into the old wood, and is quite reasonably hardy, revelling particularly in the sandy soils of Surrey. It is not, however, over-particular as to soil provided that it has a sunny position and free drainage.

One of the most spectacular of all flowering trees is *Embothrium coccineum* and more particularly *E. c. longifolium* and *E. c. lanceolatum* —"Norquinco Valley Form".

The various forms are so distinct in both hardiness and decorative quality that it is best to deal with them separately although botanical distinctions are less clear.

Embothrium coccineum is a native of Chile introduced by William Lobb for Messrs. Veitch of Exeter in 1846 and it first flowered there in May, 1853. It is a sturdy but somewhat thin tree about 15 or 20 feet high with small, oval, evergreen leaves. In late May small clusters of the brilliant scarlet honeysuckle flowers appear on the ends of the branches. In spite of their vivid colouring the flowers, on typical trees under observation, are not really numerous enough to make much of an effect. On the other hand this form appears to be quite "reasonably hardy", no winter damage having been noticed for at least the last ten years. This plant comes from the most southerly, and thus coldest, part of Chile at a corresponding latitude south to Liverpool north.

In the wild, around the Straits of Magellan, it seldom exceeds the dimensions of a tall shrub and is often not more than 1 or 2 feet in height.† Dr. Wilfrid Fox of Hascombe, Surrey, obtained seeds of an

† R. O. Cunningham, "Natural History of the Straits of Magellan".

L
?" The Chilean Fire-brush" ?   E.F.S.

absolutely hardy form from Tierra del Fuego, an island lying even further south than the straits.† He kindly gave me a young plant, and its slower and sturdier growth and shorter, blunter leaves are very distinct from the rapid sappy growth and long narrow leaves of *E. c. longifolium* nearby.

E. c. longifolium. According to Messrs. Marchant of Wimborne, who have shown fine specimens at many of the R.H.S. meetings and shows, this form is one long cultivated in Irish gardens. The oldest plant, according to Mr. H. Armytage Moore‡ of Rowallane, is at Rostrevor where it is surrounded by sucker growths at the base. Growth is not slow, hard and twiggy like that of the preceding, but rapid, soft and slender, so that a rather insecure tree is quickly formed. Whether this form is a separate species or not I cannot say, but it is distinct enough from the gardener's point of view to require a distinguishing label. The reason being that *E. c. longifolium* has the valuable quality of producing flowers all along its branches instead of merely at their ends. Furthermore, the flowering season is more prolonged, starting earlier and finishing later, and both fertile seed and numerous basal suckers provide ready means of increase. *E. c. longifolium* is apparently not quite so hardy as *E. coccineum* but it is a faster grower and more vigorous. While I would put the latter in the "reasonably hardy" category I cannot do so in the case of the former. None the less the splendid speed of growth and the sustained and spectacular brilliance of its flowering make *E. c. longifolium* one of those plants that it is worth taking a chance on. There used to be a saying among the old hands with large gardens: "Do you grow Embothriums? If so, you have a garden—if not, you haven't." I think it is possible to have a real garden without them but I agree that anyone who has a fine flowering specimen of this tree has really got a garden, whatever the rest of it is like. The leaves of *E. c. longifolium* are, as the name suggests, longer and narrower than those of *E. coccineum.*

E. c. lanceolatum. Seed of this sub-species was collected 5,000 feet elevations in the Argentine by H. F. Comber about 1927. The leaves are still longer and narrower and the flowers, in great fox-brushes of flaming scarlet, even more numerous and effective. The form 'Ñorquinco Valley' is the finest Embothrium I have seen (see illustration facing p. 160). Most authorities are agreed that this form, which Lord Aberconway stated to have withstood 34 degrees of frost,§ is practically as hardy as *E. coccineum.* When 'Ñorquinco' becomes generally available it should be tried in every likely garden for it is the most

† *R.H.S. Journal,* LXX, p. 289.
‡ *Gardening Illustrated,* Jan. 21, 1939, p. 37.
§ Lord Aberconway, *R.H.S. Journal,* LXX, p. 191.

spectacularly brilliant flowering tree that can be grown in these islands. Like most of the plants from the Southern Hemisphere it has a slightly strange look but, rather than segregate it, as is sometimes suggested, I think the best effect is, probably, to intensify its brilliance by letting it take part in an association with the late-flowering forms of the Scots Laburnum (*L. alpinum*), the white-flowered Manchurian Crab and the Knap Hill Azaleas. Viewed entirely alone its queerness is intensified and the garden as a whole is less assisted. (Illustn. p. 160.)

In years to come, when hardy forms of the best flowering qualities have been bred and selected, the Embothriums will take their proper place as reasonably hardy shrubs or small trees adding to the gaiety of all southern and coastal gardens. In the meantime, like the Eucryphias and Hydrangeas, they are plants that wealthy Local Authorities in tourist areas should plant for the decoration of their resorts. I think that such spectacularly beautiful little trees would pay a very handsome dividend, for by the time they come to flowering size healthful competition in such places might well have been restored.

As regards cultivation *E. coccineum* and its sub-species require a moist acid soil well enriched with leaf-mould. Observing the compact bushy specimens produced in their native land by the frost-killing of those branches that rise above the deep snow, I cut down a tall unstable tree 4 feet above the ground. This has now formed a huge bush which may prove more effective than the tree form. Some protection from cutting winds is desirable as the plant is apt to come into growth rather early in the season.

Propagation may be by means of the rooted suckers which can often be secured from trees growing in cultivated ground, or by seeds. Seed raising is not easy, as many of the young plants, being sensitive to root disturbance, succumb in the pricking off. Possibly, therefore, it would be a good plan to avoid this danger by sowing the seeds singly in small pots. Once established, 'Ñorquinco' grows three feet in a year.

Another species from the southern hemisphere, *Tricuspidaria lanceolata*, a South American evergreen shrub or small tree introduced by William Lobb for Messrs. Veitch in 1848, is too tender to be effective in any but very favoured gardens or along the south and west coasts, particularly up the west coast of Scotland where the moist atmosphere seems to suit it. None the less, it is commonly attempted. Among the dark green leaves the fleshy, bud-like rich crimson flowers depend on long stalks, reminding one of miniature Chinese lanterns. Every summer it grows vigorously, every winter it is disastrously cut back, almost, but seldom quite, to destruction. Thus its appearance is usually anything but decorative as a growing shrub. In the woodland, provided that the katabatics are good, it survives in better shape, but I must repeat that it is, unlike *Embothrium coccineum*, too tender to be effective in the ordinary garden as a rule. There are exceptional places where, growing perhaps against a whitewashed west wall where the soil is not very rich and air drainage is good, it may provide a spectacular effect; but the vast majority of the many specimens known to me are a sorry sight.

Later flowering **Tree Peonies** would be a valuable acquisition and, indeed, there are already quite a number of such hybrid varieties, derived from *Pæonia lutea* and *P. Delavayi* crossed with the Moutan, such as one with the regrettably long name of 'Souvenir du Professeur Maxime Cornu'. They are attractive in their warm orangy tints but some are afflicted with a shape of flower which reminds one painfully of the grosser and more malodorous members of the Composite family and others have their flowers hidden among the leaves.

On the other hand, there are beautiful varieties with sweetly scented flowers that hold their heads up nicely. Among these are L'Espérance, a lovely single yellow with a red centre to the petals and a shapely boss of golden stamens; 'Mme Louis Henry' (*lutea* × 'Reine Elizabeth'), a yellow flushed red flower of lovely form and 'Satin Rouge', red, with orangy lights.

These *P. lutea* hybrids, of which just a few root-grafted plants are available every year, are rather stronger in consitution than the Moutan hybrids. A three-year-old plant of the exquisite 'L'Espérance' may carry five or more flowers, and these open in late May when the weather is more favourable than earlier on. Any seeds produced should be carefully gathered just after the pod splits open to show them, but the hybrids are mostly sterile.†

It is a good plan to sow each seed in a small pot and plunge this outdoors as the seedlings require two years without root disturbance. After this, they may be moved into larger pots and again plunged. At five years old from seed they will flower and, according to Japanese growers, the seedlings are almost invariably of high quality though, of course, different from the parent. Indeed, it is very difficult to see how any seedling of *P. fruticosa* could go far wrong because the flower of the original wild plant is quite exquisite in shape and design. One feels that a later flowering date and a better colour are the only improvements possible, apart from resistance to fungus attack.

† "Hybrid Yellow Tree Pæonies", by John C. Wister, *R.H.S. Journal*, LXXIII, Pt. 6, p. 190.

The Tree Peony is far the most important shrub, in the grand manner, for the owners of gardens in cold districts with unkindly soils which deny them the charms of the greater Rhododendrons, such as abound in Essex, East Anglia, north east Yorkshire and Midlothian. Indeed, some of the finest specimens in Britain were recorded precisely in these areas. One such is described (*The Garden*, Oct. 18, 1890) as "eight feet high and twelve yards in circumference and during twenty-five years never failed to perfect several hundreds of flowers". The largest and handsomest trees in Midlothian (*The Garden*, Jan. 22, 1887) "grow on sloping banks of light and deep soil well exposed to the sun and protected from fierce winds. During the time they are in bloom their wealth of colour carries all before them". For warmer districts I have recommended more backward positions but the sunny aspect is desirable in such cold districts where fungus attack is less rife.

Thus Local Authorities and Parks Departments might well get started on the propagation and culture of such beautiful permanent material instead of spending hundreds of pounds annually on lorry-loads of second-rate temporary plants whose destruction at the end of each season leaves the grounds no better off than before.

The Tibetan form of *P. lutea* recently introduced by Messrs. Ludlow and Sheriff appears to be much superior to the older (1883) Chinese form, being of a more firm and graceful habit, growing up to six feet high and presenting its flowers properly, above the foliage. These flowers are twice as large and of a real butter yellow. Unfortunately, however, it flowers three weeks earlier than the old Chinese form.†
It may perhaps be valuable in hybridising, as it is hardy and vigorous and grows well from seeds.

We now come to the flowering time of one of the most gorgeously coloured sections of all flowering shrubs for lime-free soils and one in which both individual charm of a high order and outstanding garden effectiveness are combined. The **Modern Hybrid Azaleas** are perhaps the finest of all, so far as the individual flowers are concerned, and are the result of a lifetime's work of patient breeding and culling on the part of the late Anthony Waterer in the early part of this century. Since then I and other breeders have bred on from the finest of the original varieties. The basic hybrid vigour seems to have come from the crossing of the hardy, large-flowered oriental *R. japonicum* with the occidental 'Ghent' progenitor *R. calendulaceum* and the red *R. speciosum*, and the solid flat flower from an infusion of *R. occidentale*.

† F. C. Stern, "The Tibetan form of *Pæonia lutea*", *R.H.S. Journal*, LXXII, Pt. 10, p. 394.

On the whole the Modern Hybrids flower in May after the 'Mollises' already described, and before the 'Ghents', reviewed later, but some varieties are a little ahead and others behind the normal. Where the soil is lime-free and leaf-mould or forest-peat can be added, they, and their cousins the 'Ghents', are pre-eminent for the main display of colour in the month of May. As their hues are mostly pure and unsullied by any muddiness, only equally pure colours and whites go well with them. Some of the cleaner-coloured deep purple hardy hybrid Rhododendrons add a fine note to the scheme, but magenta pinks and purplish-crimsons are to be avoided at all costs and even the very clean pure pinks of some of the Modern Hybrids themselves are really best kept away from the salmon, orange, yellow and red varieties. Since these Azaleas were first described by the writer in "The Flowering Shrub Garden"† a number of further varieties have been exhibited and named:—

'Brazil', nasturtium red fls. 2½ ins. across.

'Devon', (A.M. Trial 52) fine red Ghent type. (Illustn. facing p. 145.)

'Farall Orangea' (selected for Trial Chelsea 68) strong grower, fragrant orange fls.

'Farall Pink', peach pink (H.C.C. 22/2) fls. 3 ins. across.

'Farall Yellow', (A.M. Trial 57) vivid chrome yellow massive frilled fls. 3½ ins. across.

'Fireglow', rich orange-vermilion.

'Gog', (R. calendulaceum × japonicum) vermilion, early, young foliage flame-red.

'George Reynolds', (A.M. 36) buttercup yellow, deep blotch.

'Gibraltar', orange-red frilled flowers.

'Harvest Moon' (A.M. Trial 53) exquisite pale primrose flowers lovely with R. 'Purple Splendour'.

'Knaphill Pink', orange-pink, good grower.

'Noondream' (selected for Trial Chelsea 68) vivid yellow.

'Persil', superb white, yellow flare.

'Pink Delight', warm pure pink.

'Satan', splendid fragrant vivid red.

'Sunte Nectarine', fine new orange-pink.

† "Country Life", 1st edition 1939, and for further varieties see second edition 1947.

'Seville', orange.

'Tunis', orange and red, late, fine autumn leaf colour.

'Yaffle', Geranium Lake, yellowish blotch, late.

'Unique', buff-yellow flushed orange.

altaclarense, yellow, flushed orange.

'Nancy Waterer', golden yellow, deeper flare.

The last three mentioned are older varieties sometimes classed with the Ghent Azaleas but they are, I think, of Modern Hybrid type.

The cultivation required for these Azaleas is similar to that described for the 'Mollis' group (p. 117), but a further word of caution may be added in the treatment of new plants. Restraint in permitting the flowering of newly planted Rhododendrons or Azaleas is well rewarded by much stronger growth, giving a far finer effect the following season. For optimum growth put bracken-peat mixed with a little sharp sand all round the root-ball—not below it—and put just an inch of it on the top. Do not stamp on the roots with the feet, just a very gentle sideways push is all that is really required. If a dry summer follows, spring-planted specimens will need watering to ensure full growth. The best way to do this is to form a ridge of added peat, like a saucer rim, around the spread of each plant, then the "saucer" may be filled several times so as to soak the soil thoroughly or, best of all, the hosepipe may be allowed to deliver a tiny trickle all night. At all times a mulch of leaves or bracken should be kept over the roots. It is essential that the plants should be very carefully installed and make full growth during that vital first growing season. If this is successfully achieved they can, provided of course, that they are on their own roots, practically take care of themselves, with mere minor attentions, such as mulching, for the rest of their lives.

Besides the Rhododendrons, 'Purple Splendour' (a Doge Purple variety with pale-yellow-tipped anthers), very lovely in association with 'Harvest Moon', and 'Royal Purple' another very hardy variety with rich purple flowers, charming associates for the Azalea groups are provided by the contrasting flower-forms of several outstanding **Viburnums**.

Viburnum plicatum, a Japanese and Chinese shrub, is best in the superior selected forms mentioned below. The "type" being of some-what gangling habit and less attractive in flower.

V. p. Mariesii (A.G.M., July 1929) is one of the loveliest of all white-flowered deciduous shrubs. The horizontal, arching branches bear, all along their length, pairs of the lace-like flat flower-heads, 4 inches across, composed of a central portion containing the true, functional flowers and showy ray-florets of large size around the margin, like a much finer form of our native Viburnum the 'Guelder Rose', or, for that matter, like the wild Hydrangeas. So numerous are the flowers that the effect is that of a shawl of white lace on a green velvet gown. The bush grows ultimately to 8 feet high or more, though usually seen only about 4 feet high, and has the further merit of turning its leaves to a striking deep wine-colour in autumn. Introduced by Charles Maries from Japan, it first flowered at Messrs. Veitch's Nursery at Coombe Wood, Devon, in June, 1875. 'Lanarth' is very similar.

V. p. 'Rowallane Variety' was exhibited by Collingwood Ingram, Esq., Benenden, Kent, in 1942. This variety is quite distinct and very valuable, being later in coming into flower. The inflorescence is more compact and of domed shape and the shrub is of more dwarf habit which is a further advantage for small gardens. Figured in *R.H.S. Journal*, LXVII, Pt. 10 (October 1942). (A.M. 1942, F.C.C. 1956.)

V. p. sterile, the "Japanese Snowball", is a variety with balls of all-sterile white flowers like the Hortensia types of the Hydrangeas. It is one of the most beautiful of the flowering shrubs of artificial appearance. (See illustration facing p. 144.) As a bush it has not the handsome habit of *V. p. Mariesii*, but is apt to sprawl anyhow, unless pruned and tied to ensure a good framework when young. Robert Fortune introduced the plant over a century ago but its use in the open air only became general of recent years. It usually flowers in the latter part of May.

V. p. var. *rotundifolium* is similar, but earlier flowering by about a fortnight, which just alters the combinations possible with other shrubs. There are said to be two other varieties of the same sort, *parvifolium* and *lanceatum*, but I cannot trace these as being offered for sale in this country at the present time.

Unfortunately, it has recently been disclosed that this is one of those awkward cases where the garden variety was, like the Hydrangea, named by Thunberg before the wild form of the same species. Thus, by the priority rule the latter becomes a variety of the former.

Viburnum plicatum grandiflorum is a form with coarser flowers, but is a slower grower with more rounded leaves, forming a denser bush. It colours its leaves very early in autumn, (A.M. 1961).

V. macrocephalum sterile. The "Chinese Snowball" has very large balls of white flowers, so large, in fact, as to make the appearance of the bush somewhat clumsy. It flowers towards the end of May as a rule and, even in Surrey, seems to require a wall. The scentless sterile form was introduced by Robert Fortune from China in 1844. This shrub grows to about 8 feet high, as a rule, and lasts some weeks in flower but its more tender nature and coarser appearance make the Japanese varieties a still better investment. The wild form, which I have not seen, has only the inch-wide outer ray florets surrounding the small fragrant fertile central flowers, thus forming a flat head 4 to 6 inches across. It is said to be hardier.

V. Opulus, our native Guelder Rose, is attractive in the wild with its translucent red berries and fine autumn leaf colour. In the garden the sterile-flowered or mop-headed form *V. O. sterile* is the more suitable. It is ultra-hardy and grows anywhere, but in view of this it is surprising how seldom it is that one sees a really fine specimen. Messrs. Nottcutt of Woodbridge, Suffolk, introduced a specially fine form of the wild type with improved flowers.

Fortunately the Viburnum family will grow on limy soils and under such conditions other species of this genus may be grown in addition to those described. Many are attractive though they do not quite measure up to the standard of flowering laid down for inclusion in this book. Particulars of these may be found in "Ornamental Flowering Trees and Shrubs", R.H.S. Conference 1938, p. 78 *et seq.* in the section written by the late Lionel de Rothschild.

A curious advantage of the flat-headed types over the globose-headed types with only sterile flowers is that the fertile flowers alone are fragrant. The Hydrangea varieties share this characteristic and thus many growers who have dealt only with the solely sterile-flowered, globose-headed varieties of these genera are probably unaware that the wild, flat-headed forms have a delightful fragrance.

The Viburnums mentioned grow best in ground where plenty of humus is present, and either a mulch or light shade, to retain moisture, seems to help them. They must have moist soil in summer.

As regards propagation, most will root from cuttings taken in late July or August and placed in a sand-frame, if possible with bottom heat. Layering, especially in the case of *V. plicatum*, is an easier and more certain method for the amateur.

At this time the Scots or **Burnet Roses,** varieties of *Rosa spinosissima*, open. These compact, dwarf bushes have a delightful habit of growth that is all too rare among the wilder Roses and the yellow-flowered varieties are invaluable, particularly to gardeners on limy soils, as a part substitute for the brilliantly coloured Azaleas. Such is the healthful nature of these Roses that we may grow them in natural ways among other flowering shrubs without censure from anyone for robbing them of the full hideosity of the "Rose-bed". Further more, on their own roots, they are good, permanent shrubs that may be relied on to keep their places without endless fuss and replacement. On the other hand, the Burnets only flower once and the best single and semi-double varieties of the Floribunda Roses are therefore a better investment for the smaller shrub gardens.

The wild species inhabits a vast area that includes Britain and Asia and usually has creamy-white flowers, though pinks and splashed forms are sometimes seen. It is important to get this Rose on its own roots rather than grafted, as its suckering habit is one of its advantages, enabling it to fill out a bed nicely and provide young plants when wanted, as well as renewing its own strength and youth in a natural way.

Like the Camellia and the Hydrangea this Rose was developed during the Victorian era when deformed flowers of large size were in demand and the beautiful, functional design of the normal "single" flower was not esteemed. Most of the innumerable old varieties have become extinct and even the few that survive are not commonly listed by nurserymen.

There are a number of new continental-bred varieties and among these are 'Frühlingsgold', an eight-foot hybrid with fragrant semi-double, 4-inch saucer-shaped blooms of Mimosa Yellow—and 'Frühlingsmorgen' with pink, creamy-based petals and dark mahogany stamens, flowering later, in June, and sometimes again in September.†

The following is a selection of the older sorts:—

Rosa Harisonii or Harison's 'Yellow' is really a hybrid with the Persian Yellow Rose (*R. fœtida persiana*); it grows taller than *R. spinosissima* and does not sucker so freely. The flowers are a fresh Buttercup Yellow (H.C.C. 5/1) and very decorative though they are apt to "ball" in wet weather.

R. s. lutea, a single Lemon Yellow (H.C.C. 4/1) with rather cup-shaped flowers, is somewhat scarce; the flowers are about $1\frac{1}{2}$ inches across, and the bush about 4 feet high or more ultimately, when well grown. There is also a double form sometimes known as "double yellow Ayrshire" that is otherwise rather similar, but less vigorous in growth.

R. s. maxima lutea has larger, single flowers, but possibly a rather less healthful and vigorous constitution when grafted. On its own roots it is very a fine variety and its flowers open out flat and are very shapely.

R. s. rosea is a pink-flowered form of the "type".

R. s. altaica (A.G.M. 1925), is a Siberian form of much taller growth, up to about 6 feet and has yellowish-white flowers.

R. s. 'William III' has double crimson flowers of a brownish cast and is of rather dwarf growth.

R. s. 'Stanwell Perpetual' is a fragrant pink-flowered, semi-double hybrid flowering all summer. It is a useful Rose, but the shape of the flower is too muddled-up to be really beautiful in my opinion.

R. s. 'Brightness' is a double crimson-purple.

† "Shrub Roses", by G. S. Thomas, *R.H.S. Journal*, LXXV, Pt. 1, p. 10 (1950).

R. hispida is a closely allied species (figured, *R. H. S. Journal*, January 1943) making a 4-foot, spiny bush, suckering freely. The flowers are 3 inches across, ivory white in colour and very lovely.

In the wild the Burnet Rose favours a sandy soil and full exposure to wind, and so makes light of such conditions in the garden and grows well on limy soils. Unlike evergreens, deciduous shrubs cannot be expected to keep down weeds beneath them unless a heavy mulch of leaves, chopped bracken, or mowings, is applied. For these Roses a mulch of lawn-mowings, straight from the box, but carefully spread and patted down so as not to interfere with the stems, is a wise precaution. Otherwise the task of weeding among their fiercely armed stems can be a nightmare that, once suffered, will be avoided at all costs ever afterwards.

All Roses need spraying against aphis and caterpillar attack and must be constantly looked over in their early stages. In places where there are many trees or adjacent woods they are not shrubs that can be left to their own devices. They are too palatable to pests. The pocket dust-gun, at least, has to be applied regularly or reinfestation ruins even bushes that have been carefully kept clean from the start and are perhaps thought to be safe for the season. I find it best, therefore, to restrict even these hardy, half-wild types to places near the house where they can receive the necessary little attentions in odd moments snatched from other work.

In addition to the above, gardeners in warm, limy-soiled gardens, unsuitable for Azaleas, may well adventure with the glorious-flowered but difficult 'Austrian Copper', *R. fœtida bicolor*. The English name is misleading as the species comes from Western Asia. The large single flowers are a glowing Signal Red (H.C.C. 719/1) so far as I can judge, but the petals have a hyaline quality, a translucent orangy fieriness, that no colour on paper can quite equal. A warm, sunny spot, with added humus and bonemeal, free drainage, and timely spraying against each disease or pest the moment it threatens, are the only hints that I can give but I must confess to having always failed to grow this Rose really well. It is often superb in Scotland.

Rosa Primula, described on p. 198, usually flowers in May. It is a very lovely primrose-yellow-flowered species and worthy of high recommendation. It was superbly illustrated in *Gardening Illustrated*, Vol. LXIV, No. 3318, p. 651 (Sept. 1945).

Syringa persica, the Persian Lilac, a 6-foot Chinese shrub with upright arching branches and pale lilac flowers in broad, loose panicles, opening in May, is not very spectacular. It is, however, hardy and not particular as to soil or position. It was introduced in the seventeenth century.

A better plant is the hybrid known as the 'Rouen Lilac', *S. chinensis* (*S. persica* × *vulgaris*) introduced in 1795, which is justly popular. It is a shrub of more lax habit of growth than the common Lilac, with looser flower panicles usually produced in May with remarkable freedom, making it one of the finest flowering shrubs in this family. It was supposed to have originated at Rouen in the eighteenth century but was apparently also long known in China.† The type has purplish-lilac flowers and there are varieties as follows:—

S. c. *alba*, white flowers.
S. c. *metensis*, lilac flowers.
S. c. *Saugeana*, lilac-red flowers.
S. c. *duplex*, double, purplish lilac flowers.

Syringa Palibiniana is a little dwarf Lilac that is one of the best of this genus for small gardens making a neat little bushlet perhaps 2 feet high covered with fragrant pale lilac flowers.

Coronilla glauca is hard to place in this work, as so long as it thrives it is always in flower. On the other hand it needs a warm south-facing chimney-stack wall or some such favourable spot if it is to last long, as it is scarcely hardy enough to flourish unprotected in the open. The grey-green pinnate leaves and sweet scented yellow pea-flowers are very attractive. In very mild districts, or if grown in a tub and taken in in winter, it may reach eight feet in height, but it is easily pruned to a smaller size if required.

C. Emerus (A.G.M. 1930), the Scorpion Senna, is hardy enough for any position but it has not the quality for an important place. It will attain six feet in both directions and the small yellow pea-flowers borne from May to frost are tipped with rusty red. Useful for rough places.

Cuttings and seeds will increase both species and a sunny position in any soil suits them well.

Actinidia Kolomikta cannot well be left out. It is a very effective climber and it does flower, but this has little to do with its effectiveness. It is the beautifully painted leaves of the male plant, bright rose-pink, white and green that are the great beauty of this species. The shy, sweet-scented little white flowers hide coyly among the leaves while these are

† Mr. F. G. Preston, *The Gardeners' Chronicle*, 3245, Vol. CXXV, p. 99 and fig. 47. See also "Lilacs", by H. G. Hillier, *R.H.S. Journal*, LXI, Pt. 11, p. 449.

still green and have not yet assumed their delightful colourings which usually appear later in the season. Often slow to exceed a modest six feet, this plant has been sometimes reported as attaining twenty feet. It is now rather uncommon although introduced from Japan by Maximowicz, the Tzar's gardener, in 1859. Seeds and cuttings may provide increase and a sunny wall suits it best.

This is one of the many unusual and attractive plants that can do so much to change a dreary town backyard into a pleasure and an ornament to the house. The walls must first be prepared if the best effect is to be attained. Assuming a wall of London Stock bricks in all their grimy "greenery yallery" hideousness, the first step will be the application, with a whitewash brush, of a thick coat of slurry made with one part of Portland cement and three parts of sand thoroughly mixed dry, and then moistened with enough water to provide a creamy consistency that will brush on easily. This is worked in and laid on vertically and then laid off with careful horizontal strokes. When set, the wall may be colour-washed, and then a painted trellis is affixed and the climber may be planted as soon as the foot of the wall has been thoroughly enriched with peat or black rotted leafmould.

It is difficult to place large families with innumerable garden varieties in their proper seasonal flowering order. One must either group them, choosing a time when the majority are in flower, or one must chop and change too distractingly from one genus to another. In my view, however, the significance of flowering time is so important with flowering shrubs that the advantages, for the reader, outweigh the disadvantages.

The **Clematis** family provide one of the most awkward problems in this respect. Their glorious great flowers most generously reward the skilful cultivator and like the Roses, Azaleas, Camellias, Moutans, Rhododendrons and Hydrangeas they enslave their devotees in a happy bondage which, at least, ensures that never again in all their lives will they know the curse of boredom for an instant.

Clematis patens, an 8-foot Japanese climber introduced by Von Siebold in 1836, is seldom seen but has produced a number of fine garden hybrids. Many of these flower in May and June and are attractive when scrambling up strong-growing shrubs or decorating trellis screens or posts near the garden-house or Loggia. Among the hybrid varieties, commonly available in nurseries are:—

'Barbara Jackman', barred violet flowers, yellow stamens.

'Daniel Deronda', semi-double blue-purple.

'Edouard Désfosse', violet, "the finest large-flowered Clematis."†

† "Clematis", by Ernest Markham, "Country Life", 1935.

'King of the Belgians', light mauve with purple bars.

'La Lorraine', pale purplish-pink flowers and strong growth.

'Lasurstern', very fine deep blue-purple.

'Miss Bateman', white flowers with red-brown anthers.

'Mrs. George Jackman', full pearly white flowers.

'Nellie Moser', large pale mauve-pink flowers, sometimes considered
  as a *C. lanuginosa* hybrid.

'President', rather later-flowering and continuing into autumn, deep
  violet flowers very freely borne, sometimes considered a variety
  of the Jackmani section.

Many of these beautiful kinds flower at intervals over a long period,
being of hybrid origin. Accordingly more detailed mention is made of
these in the late summer section where the garden Clematis are dealt
with.

These Clematis will all grow well on limy soils and are thus of very
special value to those gardening under such conditions. Gardeners
with neutral or acid soils, though they can also grow them perfectly will
have this flowering season so strongly catered for by the Brooms,
Azaleas, and Rhododendrons that they will have less need of these
more exacting early-flowering climbers. For them the later-flowering
section is probably the more valuable.

In planting a Clematis, care should be taken to set the plant on the
shady side of the support and to allow the growth to emerge into the
sunlight. A strong piece of wire netting is, I think, essential to protect
the highly vulnerable emerging stem. Occasional treatment with "Meta"
slugicide is necessary in the growing season or slugs may spoil every
emerging shoot. The shoots should be frequently tied out in fan formation, as they grow, or they soon form an unsightly muddle with
little chance of bearing the abundant, huge, and beautiful flowers
which are the great asset of these rather troublesome and fragile
plants. The well-grown and trained specimen does, however, most
amply reward the gardener's pains. Further details on the family are
to be found in the late-summer section, pp. 215 and 263.

Pruning, for this section, is best confined to the removal of unripened
tips and slight thinning if necessary. On acid soils Clematis often root
whenever they touch the ground. A Clematis planted near a non-
flowering bush can convert this into a gorgeous-flowering subject.

Stalwart shrubs that can act as hosts for Clematis have their uses.
One of these is a **Staphylea**, *S. colchica Coulombieri grandiflora*, a
member of the Bladdernut family. It is a deciduous bush of possibly

hybrid origin which appeared in the famous arboretum of Segrez in France about 1870. Usually seen about 8 feet high, it is quite handsome when decked in late May with the drooping panicles of white flowers followed by the large, bladder-like, inflated fruits. While it plays no useful part as an all-the-year-round garden decorator, it is graceful and pretty when in flower and useful for limy gardens as it will grow well on this type of soil. Increase can be effected by cuttings. ' Elegans ', a newer hybrid (A.M. 1961) is rather more effective.

Jasminum Mesnyi is an evergreen scrambler which most of us know under the more pleasing name of *J. primulinum*. It is a strange and puzzling plant that has so far not been found wild or bearing seed. E. H. Wilson found it in a garden in Western China in 1900. It resembles the common winter-flowering yellow Jasmine but it is just twice as fine and it flowers in May. The clear yellow flowers, borne singly, are semi-double and an inch and a half or nearly 2 inches across. Unfortunately this Jasmine has not the hardiness of the old favourite and requires a warm and sheltered wall in the south and a cool greenhouse farther north. A blue Clematis makes a charming neighbour for it.

Cuttings or layers may be rooted fairly easily in the usual manner.

Were all gardens of the small size I should not mention here many species which do not quite fulfill the requirements for such small spaces, where the maximum of charm attainable must be closely concentrated. There are, however, many extensive gardens in country places whose upkeep, owing to a well-planned naturalistic layout, is no greater than that of many a plot a tenth of the size. Full advantage is taken of mulching and shade as weed deterrents, and groups composed of separate, single specimen trees and shrubs, rather than closely planted beds, are the rule. The motor-scythe, used perhaps only two or three times a year, takes the place of the mowing machine and the swap-hook, or sickle, replaces the border fork. In such places flowering trees are the ideal plant material.

Halesia carolina, the **Snowdrop Tree**, comes from the south-western United States, whence it was introduced in 1756, and is a wide-spreading, irregular, shrubby little tree seldom more than 20 feet high at most. In May, the clusters of short-stalked pendent white bell-shaped flowers decorate almost every naked twig in the most delightful manner. Were it a shapely tree when out of flower we should see it, no doubt, more commonly planted, but unfortunately it is one of those that have not the attractive all-the-year-round appearance so necessary for the small gardens of today. A hybrid form, *H. c. Meehanii*, is a bushy, upright shrub with smaller, more deeply divided flowers.

The Snowdrop Tree requires an acid or neutral soil, preferably sandy. It is hardy, but flowers best in a sunny spot and can be propagated from seed and by layers.

H. monticola. The Mountain Snowdrop Tree is a taller and even hardier American tree species, making a shapely, full-sized tree with longer stalked and larger, white flowers. It is also a more rapid grower and flowers when quite young. It is not readily available yet over here, but is mentioned as it seems to be a tree of great possibilities for the future.

H. m. var. *rosea* is a form described as having pink flowers.

Known here for three centuries yet rarely planted, *Cercis Siliquastrum* (A.G.M. 1927), the 'Judas Tree' from south Europe, is only seen at its best in the warmer gardens in England. It is, however, remarkably beautiful in Italy and Spain where it is often used as a street tree. The tree, perhaps 15 or 20 feet high, erupts from the naked wood of twig, and even stem, into a cloud of rosy purple pea-flowers in late May. The heart-shaped leaves and bean-like seed pods follow. The Judas Tree is of attractive habit, but, being a bad mover when over 2 feet high, it is rather a long-term investment.

A warm position on a south slope is required, but either chalky or acid soils suit it equally well. Seeds are the best method of increase.

The even more beautiful Redbud, *C. canadensis*, though superb in America, unfortunately declines to show its real qualities in our more uncertain climate.

"Ne'er cast a clout till **May** is out" seems to me to refer to the plant rather than the calendar. It is, at all events, in that sense that I have always obeyed the adage.

Cratægus Oxyacantha, the Hawthorn or May, is one of the most beautiful of our native flowering trees, especially when in an open position on chalky soil. Aged specimens have a picturesque habit that can be greatly helped by a little careful "manicuring".

The garden varieties are very commonly planted, yet it is seldom that one sees well-flowered specimens of the finest sorts. Among the best are:—

C. O. rosea, a tree of shapely, twiggy and rounded form, in a properly isolated position, with profuse, pale rose-pink single flowers.

C. O. punicea. This variety appears to me to provide the most colourful effect of any, with its single crimson flowers, though these are not always borne as freely as one could wish.

C. O. Pauli (*C. O. plena coccinea*, 'Paul's double scarlet'). The colour of this fine Thorn bears no resemblance to scarlet, being a rosy crimson. Curiously enough, owing to rapid fading of the flower colour, the effect is often less brilliant than that of the preceding.

C. O. plena has double white flowers that become pinkish with age. In my view a fine selected form of the wild type with large and shapely single white flowers and bright red anthers is often even more beautiful. Such a form would be worth propagating as a clone, as the variation in beauty of flower among wild specimens is very wide.

C. O. candida plena, is a scarce, double, white-flowered form that does not turn pinkish.

C. O. Maskei is a variety with charming double, pale-pink flowers.

To flower really freely the Hawthorns require more open positions than they are usually given. When the white, and just a few pink, varieties are grouped where they have sufficient room, the effect is delightful and makes them one of the best of flowering trees for chalky or limy soils. Careful pruning is needed in the early stages to form a shapely tree with a short trunk and characteristically bushy head. Bushes rather than standards are really best, for when attempts are made to keep the tree to a tall clear stem and small head this shape is so foreign to the nature of the Thorn that results are seldom good, or permanent.

As lawn or park trees in chalky districts forming 20-foot domes of fragrant flower in late May, the Hawthorns are superb. On light, very acid soils, unlike almost all other flowering trees that I know, they are less vigorous and also less free-fruiting and the fruits are apparently less vivid in colour.

The garden forms are grafted or budded on the common type and layers, which may occasionally be got where low branches reach the ground, are the best means of propagation for the ordinary amateur. The Hedge Thorn or Quick is of a different species (*C. monogyna*) and this is quite easily grown from seed if required for hedging though it is much quicker, of course, to buy young plants.

Two hybrid members of the Hawthorn family provide us with pleasing small trees for the garden. Judged on flowers alone they would hardly be called effective, but they add the qualities of decorative fruits and autumn-tinted leaves and thus qualify for inclusion.

C. Lavallei (A.G.M. 1925) (*C. Carrierei*) is a hybrid Thorn making a tree about 20 feet high with dull-white flowers about an inch across in late May or early June. These are followed by large orange-red fruits

M   E.F.S.

which last well on the tree in winter. In autumn the leaves turn red before falling. Thus, without ever being spectacularly brilliant, the little tree is a steady worker in the cause of garden decoration.

C. prunifolia is another hybrid of doubtful origin. Unlike the previous variety there are times when this Thorn is one of the most vividly brilliant objects in the garden. Making a rounded tree, furnished to the ground, about 20 feet high, its clusters of white flowers appear, nearly three-quarters of an inch across, in late May or early June among the roundish-oval, brilliant dark green leaves. The round red fruits, about five-eighths of an inch long are often described as falling in October, but having frequent occasion to pass a couple of dozen specimens most admirably planted on the Guildford and Kingston by-pass roads by the Roads Beautifying Association I have been able to note that a large proportion of these often remain decoratively on the trees during the winter. These particular specimens do not colour to any very spectacular extent in autumn. But other specimens under my observation, whose fruits do fall in October, colour their leaves to the most superb brilliant red and orange tones. I have gathered some of the fruits littering the sides of these roads and grown seedlings quite easily. It is as yet too early to say whether they will have the good qualities of the seed parent, but the leaves all appear to be identical.

This fine Thorn, like other members of its family, will grow on limy soils and appears to be perfectly hardy.

The **Laburnums** are among the most spectacular of flowering trees that can be grown in our climate, but their ubiquity and the fact that complementary plantings are hardly ever specially arranged causes them to be held in comparatively little esteem.

Laburnum anagyroides (*L. vulgare*), the common Laburnum from South Europe, opens early in May and the racemes of Canary Yellow flowers are short and do not last very long in beauty. It is, however, very lovely with the white-flowered Cherries, particularly when the colour scheme is kept to white, blue-violet, soft orange and yellow without any pink in sight.

The variety *L. a. aureum* has yellow leaves and is very striking, but not commonly seen.

L. alpinum, the Scotch Laburnum, flowers a fortnight later, as a rule, and some especially desirable seedling forms flower later still. This makes possible a very vivid association with the flaming scarlet flowers of the Embothriums. This is the sort of real "eyeful" that the milder coastal resorts should try out, I feel, instead of the Salvias and other bedding plants which the public are getting tired of. Unlike the common

Laburnum, *L. alpinum* forms a particularly fine, shapely and strong tree and the short racemes are so numerous and well presented that, in my opinion, it is far the most beautiful member of the family. Unlike other sorts, it is perfectly wind-firm.

L. Vossii (A.G.M. 1928) is usually in flower a little before the later forms of *L. alpinum*, and is a hybrid between the two species mentioned. The racemes of flowers, of similar Canary Yellow, are very long indeed and provide a fine contrast when the tree is trained over a pergola with Wisterias. It is the finest in the individual flower raceme, but, making only a poor weak tree, is not so valuable in the garden scene, perhaps, as the latest-flowering forms of *L. alpinum*. *L. Watereri* is rather similar but distinct. The buff seed-pods are decorative in winter sunlight.

There has been, until recently, little encouragement for the nurserymen to select and propagate the later-flowering forms of *L. alpinum* so invaluable to the gardener seeking continuity in his garden decoration. Such forms, indeed, transfer a beautiful flower effect from a period when there is too much available to one which is short of good material. To my mind a fine mass of flower is much more acceptable in the dreary "June gap" when most gardens are dull in the extreme, although then at their most climatically enjoyable, than in the bleak days of winter when flowers seem out of place.

The Laburnums are easily raised from seed and are not particular as to soil, even growing well on very chalky land. Careful training and pruning and firm staking in the early stages are needed to secure a fine shapely tree capable of supporting the great weight of a heavy crop of flowers in later years.

Euryops acraeus, from S. Africa is a lovely miniature bushlet of moleheap size with beautiful flowers—well-drawn, solid, vivid yellow Daisies—and highly decorative silver foliage that looks like hoarfrost on a sunny morning. This little treasure, beautifully illustrated in colour in *R.H.S. Journal*, October 1964, p. 419, is worthy of every care, an ideal denizen of one of those delightful groups in the ultra-modern manner so conveniently arranged where, instead of the usual tiresome grass—greasy for half the year—fine gravel on sterile subsoil is the main coverage.

At this point, when June is about to begin, we may lament the passing of a most useful **Broom** which also provided a fine mass of yellow, that most brilliant of all colours at a distance. The late T. Smith of Daisy Hill, Newry, used to grow seedlings from the latest flowering specimens

of *Cytisus scoparius* each year and, after a while, a very reliable June-
and July-flowering strain was evolved. These Brooms are still to be
found occasionally in old gardens in many parts of the country where
they enliven the midsummer scene in the most spectacular manner.
Unfortunately the strain has been lost in commerce, though I have
hopes of inducing some firm to put them on the market again. Even
amid the galaxy of May flowers the common Broom is a very lovely
shrub; in the dogdays of June it is a riot. Furthermore, by constant
shearing back of the young wood the plants form dense velvety green
domes very decorative at all times of year.

Eucalyptus gunnii is the flowering tree chosen to fill this little space
made available by reprinting. Coming from the cool mountains of
Tasmania this species of Eucalyptus alone deserves the title of hardy
in the British Isles. It is among the fastest growing of known species,
specimens planted in 1950 being, seven years later, beautiful thirty-
foot evergreen trees with an enchanting pattern of willow-like leaves.
Its young foliage in May, of russet, silver and lilac, has the highest
decorative quality, and the white, heavy-scented flowers in late summer
soon set the bees roaring. Beneath this friendly tree shade-loving
shrubs grow particularly happily, and its value for the rapid screening
of unsightly objects is evident.

Before closing the section devoted to the flowers of May I should
remind readers that in late May some species described along with
their kindred in the June section will often be already in flower.
Styrax Obassia, Rosa Hugonis, Dipelta yunnanensis, Magnolia sinensis
and *M. Sieboldii* are examples. Several Potentillas (see page 267) are
also in bloom.

Then, too, the phenomenally long-lasting qualities of the flowers
of some kinds of flowering shrubs enable them to play almost as fine
a part in May as they did in the previous month. Azalea ' Hinomayo ',
for example, I record as having held its flowers in decorative condition
in full exposure for exactly five weeks from the time the first buds
opened. The evergreen Barberries, Camellias, Moutans, early alpine
Rhododendrons and the Periwinkles will also carry on their display
well into next month.

CHAPTER V
JUNE

*Means that the plant tolerates limy soil.

JUNE

AFTER the late spring-flowering shrubs are over the flowers of early summer open. This time is usually one of the dullest in gardens, though, as the weather is usually then at its best, it should surely be one of the gayest. There are plenty of beautiful shrubs that flower in June—more than enough to fill any ordinary-sized garden completely, but they are too late for the great Chelsea Show, unless unnaturally forced. Thus their names appear comparatively rarely in the nurserymen's order books, and consequently in only small numbers in their propagating lists.

In my view this time of year merits the keenest attention by planters. There is no need for their gardens to drop to a deplorable dullness the moment the rush of spring bloomers is over. Yet the neglect in planning for June is astonishingly widespread. I have ranged the great gardens of England at that time more than at any other, herbaceous borders and all, in search of flowers. There have been many days when the only plants I have found in bloom have been *Campanula glomerata*, *Lilium umbellatum* and a few little oddments. Through the years I have found at last the shrubs to give me flowers in what were flowerless days, and I cherish and enjoy them more than any and judge the garden most critically at this time.

When we have new plantings in mind then, let this be the moment when we visit the nurseries, go flower-hunting in others' gardens where we may, and keep the notebook close at hand. Then, when the results mature, we shall find this lovely time of year in our gardens as flowery as the spring.

Formerly the "herbaceous border" was supposed to take over the decoration of the garden at this stage. But even if one assumed that herbs, unnaturally and densely concentrated in a carefully contrived assortment in one or more rectangular beds, could be an artistic and beautiful feature showing off these handsome plants effectively, the artificiality of the thing is so marked that it upsets the naturalistic atmosphere of the garden at once. The continuity of the whole composition is destroyed by such an unnatural concentration and, indeed, a "shrub border" set down in an otherwise shrubless garden is just as bad. But, unlike herbs, shrubs are storm-proof.

Many of the herbs are beautiful plants of fine, individual drawing and attractive flower colour, but they are out of scale with small shrubs.

183

They are in scale in the composition with trees. In small groups of one fine but varied sort, such as Peony, Campanula, Iris, Lupin, Poppy, Japanese Anemone or Phlox, they can be superb at the foot of a grove or even near large shrubs of a greater height then theirs. But if the garden scene is to be really harmonious, evenly decorated and beautiful all through the year we must really do without that rectangular concentration of herbs. Consequently we should best look to our shrubs, however many or few we have, to spread their blossoming evenly over the flowering season from the end of March to the beginning of October. This they can do with ease and brilliance; there need be no let-up whatever in the sequence of flower, the whole scene remains beautifully knit and gaily decorated, and there are no cultural complications.

On acid soils, of course, the whole listed selection is available, but the hardy hybrid Rhododendrons, the Evergreen Azaleas of the *R. indicum* section and the Ghent Azaleas make the finest display in the early part of the month and *Cornus Kousa* and Magnolias will be outstanding among the taller subjects. Later on the Roses will take over.

On limy soils Genistas, Roses, Tree Lupins, Cistus, Halimiums, Helianthemums, Senecios and Philadelphus offer ample fine plant material to make this month as fine as any. One or other of these genera will be found especially suited to the particular garden conditions of soil and climate and therefore suggest itself for special exploitation.

Intensified beauty, in the language of Nature,† in the garden landscape satisfies our longing for the natural landscape that is now almost everywhere destroyed, for the wild flowers we can no longer gather and the "homes of the wild creatures now far away from us in their own solitude".

Among the indispensables for the lime-free garden are the **Hardy Hybrid Rhododendrons**. There are two fairly clearly marked sections of these which should, I venture to think, be kept entirely separate both in nurserymen's catalogues and in the planter's mind. If this were done much disappointment would be avoided; this is because the earlier flowering section, typified by the well-known *Rhododendron* 'Pink Pearl', "B", or 'Loder's White', "C", is markedly less suited to withstand the wind-buffetings and sun-scorchings of the ordinary open garden than the "ironclad" later-flowering section typified by *R.* 'Purple Splendour', "A", or 'Mrs. P. D. Williams', "A".

In the wonderful galaxy of colour of the superbly beautiful new hybrid Rhododendrons, the old ultra-hardy types are sometimes put

† As one might say a good building is carried out *in the language of architecture*.

down as quite outclassed; and so they are, *as cut flowers or as denizens of the Wood-garden*, a special type of garden really outside the scope of this work (see p. 134). But, as flowering shrubs to decorate the ordinary little gardens of the majority, many of the new beauties just fail to compete at all. They can only be effectively grown in what approximates, culturally, to a wood. In the opinion of many, a wood-garden is far the nicest kind of garden, but the fact remains that, in these over-populated islands, only a favoured few can have one. Consequently, I hold that no Rhododendron that is not Category "A" ("Hardy anywhere in the British Isles *and may be planted in full exposure*") should be considered as capable of competing with the existing Category "A" Rhododendrons. Having grown all types under varied conditions and made many experiments, these latter are the only ones that I can recommend for the ordinary, but of course lime-free, open garden. Admittedly, the bulk of these varieties have flowers of rather poor and muddy colours compared with the more tender novelties, but there are whites, purples, warm pinks, lavender-blues, crimsons and even an orange-yellow which are reasonably clean in tone. They are all we have got, anyway, and, indeed, if adjudged purely as flowering shrubs for the open garden against other species of flowering shrubs, they are absolutely first-class. Flowering evergreens work all the time and are therefore the most valuable of all shrubs and the hardy hybrid Rhododendrons are some of the finest of these. The late Anthony Waterer, who bred many of the first Rhododendrons and Azaleas that are still unsurpassed, refused to recognise as a *good garden Rhododendron* any which did not possess the following qualifications:—

A strong constitution.
Large, firm foliage.
A compact and conical flower head not easily injured by wind or rain.
Flowering in June or later, thus avoiding frost damage.

In my view, this is as true today as ever.

In a few years' time there will be available a new range of brilliant colours in the truly hardy, "A" category, types. They will be due to an infusion of the "blood" of that remarkable Rhododendron *R. dichroanthum*, "B". In itself this species from "dry, open, rocky meadows" in Yunnan at 11,000–12,000 feet altitudes, does not appear particularly attractive. A low, fairly dense bush with a thin, lax truss of long-stalked, tubular-bell-shaped, small, fleshy flowers of a dull orangy tint, it is not at all striking. Yet this little plant carries the genes that provide the answer to the Rhododendron breeder's prayer. There are hidden fires in that meaty-looking little corolla for, crossed even with the magenta-flushed *R. Fortunei*, the latent orange colour is so dominant that, instead of the purplish-tinged progeny that results from crossing *R. Fortunei* with almost any other mate, a Geranium Lake and Indian Yellow-flowered hybrid can be got. When *R. dichroanthum* is crossed with a red hardy hybrid with a strong, full, upright truss of wide-open flowers, the very first generation, such as 'Berryrose' and 'Limerick', seem to me to be quite remarkably lovely as they are, but no doubt still further perfection will be reached in the second and third generations by skilful breeding. 'Zanna', dwarf orange-pink, is already available in commerce and I think it is the forerunner of a superb race of hardy hybrids in rich and lovely warm colourings as fine as those of the Ghent Azaleas.

But now let us review the best of those at present available in commerce here, leaving out the more objectionable magenta-pinks, and taking the late May or June-flowering sorts only for this section. All are category "A" unless otherwise stated. Plants from layers are best.

album elegans, palest mauve, a splendid grower and wind resister.

'Blue Ensign' **, pale purplish-mauve, dark centre.

'Blue Peter' ***, pale mauve (H.C.C. 633/2), dark centre, needs shade to avoid "fly".

'Cetewayo' *, dark purple.

'Chionides', creamy white.

fastuosum flore-pleno, double mauve, must have shade or gets "fly" badly.

'Frank Galsworthy', full Solferino Purple (H.C.C. 26), yellow spots, a fine deep colour.

'Garibaldi', salmon-red.

'Goldsworth Orange' **, Maize Yellow (H.C.C. 607/1), flushed orange, very attractive. Not so hardy as others.

'Goldsworth Purple', vivid purple.

'John Walter', crimson.

'Joseph Whitworth' *, deep purple-lake, very dark in tone.

'Lady Annette de Trafford', clear, fresh pink, chocolate blotch, very shapely flowers.

'Lady Clementine Mitford' **, a peach-pink effect, actually palest Crimson (H.C.C. 22/3), attractive foliage.

'Lady Eleanour Cathcart' ***, clear rich pink in effect, actually Rose Madder (H.C.C. 23/2), chocolate spots, good, *R. maximum* hybrid.

'Lord Fairhaven' *, shrimp-pink suffused yellow, very lovely.

'Lord Roberts', crimson, blackish centre, very good for an extremely exposed position, superb foliage.

'Tondelayo', white with red flare, late.

'Midsummer', rosy pink, yellow eye, late.

'Mrs. Anthony Waterer' *, white, yellow flare.

'Mrs. Davies Evans' *, blue-mauve.

'Mrs. Furnival' ***, "B". Pink with a crimson flare, very dense and free flowering, really midway between this section and the 'Pink Pearl' types.

'Mrs. J. C. Williams' **, blush, red spots.

'Mrs. J. G. Millais' **, white with a big flare of gold, fine truss, very lovely with late Azaleas.

'Mrs. John Clutton', white, yellow flare, late.

'Mrs. P. D. Williams' ***, ivory white, greenish-brown eye, very beautiful in an open position.

'Mrs. T. H. Lowinsky' *, "B" (Category "A" in my experience), white suffused with the palest flush of cyclamen overlaid on the upper half of the flower with a great orchidaceous flare feathered with saffron, gold and geranium.

multimaculatum, white with orange and black spots, late, a ponticum hybrid and a very beautiful shrub in full sun, deservedly a favourite of the late Miss Jekyll, the inventor of the herbaceous border.

'Old Port', Fuchsia Purple (H.C.C. 28), also good with late Azaleas.

'Orion', clean rose pink, scarlet flare, good.

'Purple Splendour' ***, Doge Purple, black centre, yellow anthers, a very beautiful colour when well associated, as with Azalea 'Harvest Moon'.

'Royal Purple', warm purple, yellow centre, *R. ponticum* hybrid.

'Zanna' (*dichroanthum × catawbiense compactum*), dwarf habit, orange-pink bells.

It will be seen that, after all, there is quite a fine selection of "iron-clads", bred for the purpose, that may be safely planted in open positions in the ordinary garden with confidence, provided, of course, that the soil is not limy and that peat and leaf-mould are added to improve the humus supply when planting as described on p. 189. In the larger gardens these are the ideal plants for providing the solid backgrounds and mounds of winter green without which the garden landscape would be but bare earth and naked branches for half the year. Unlike some evergreens they may be planted right in the beds with no fear of their robbing the soil for the essential complementary shrubs. The compact root-ball requires only water, tinctured by the leaf-mould of the mulch and the peat, or rotted mould, used at planting time to surround the ball. When, in a limy garden, other kinds of evergreens have to be used to give solidity to the groups, they compete actively with the marginal deciduous shrubs and, the effect can, for this reason, seldom be quite so good.

Beds of garden-bred grafted Rhododendrons segregated alone are just bad gardening that will not satisfy the amateur gardener of taste, today, on any pretext. The worst effects are the result of the greater carelessness, when varieties of different flowering-times are lumped together in gloomy, humped beds that can never make any but a spotty effect, for lack of the care and craftsmanship to sort out these easily moved plants from the muddle produced by a thoughtless plant order to the local nurseryman. Such concentrations form a ready breeding ground for the new scourge "Bud Blast" fungus infestation typified by dead flower-buds sprouting black hairs. The best treatment is to cut out infested branches six inches back from the very first dead bud which started the trouble. Equally vulnerable and dull are the puddings seen in some gardens where Rhododendrons particularly flourish, where innumerable plants of the "B" class, almost hardy, but not sufficiently sun-and-wind-resisting, such as 'Pink Pearl', or 'Cynthia', have been planted in beds solidly of one variety. Thus exposed, the wizened plants flower freely enough, but the colours bleach in the hot sun and are soon withered to brown, and the unrelieved masses, when out of bloom, are a notable cause of "Rhododendrophobia". As Reginald Farrer so aptly quoted, "at these repulsive pies, our offended gorges rise!"

The most attractive colour effects can be obtained, whenever there is space to plant a good breadth of hardy hybrids, by making an evergreen "spine" to a bed, or to fill a corner. These are attained by fairly close planting of those which bloom at precisely the same time, and so form an embroidery of interwoven colours.

In the colour scheme, either crimson, pink, white or purple, with plenty of pale colours to lead up to the richer tints, or, in a sheltered garden, a warmer scheme of reds, whites, orange-pinks and purples again assisted by paler tones, may be chosen. Usually, in practice, only purplish-crimson and scarlet when juxtaposed in large blocks will be found to make a serious clash.

Where the pure, but brilliant colours of the large-flowered Azaleas are used, the background Rhododendrons are best limited to the many superb whites, often with flares of gold which pick up the Azalea colours again, and to the pale mauves and purples. Scarlet Rhododendrons, of course, blend perfectly with the Azaleas, but I do not know a true scarlet in the "A" category.

In those favoured gardens where conditions of soil, shade, and wind-shelter are good enough for the "B" class, that superb landscape

colour, red, can be used with fine effect. Among the truer reds
are:—

'Britannia' "B" ***, Turkey Red fading almost to Rose Madder.
'Damozel', red, long lasting.
'Doncaster' "B" **, Turkey Red. Rather dwarf and compact.
'Earl of Donoughmore', red, *griersonianum* hybrid.
'Grand Finale' "B", late red (illustration facing p. 209).
'Jean Mary Montague', vivid red, good habit.
'Kluis Sensation', a splendid red.
'Mme de Bruin', good red.
'Mars' "B" ****, Turkey Red, a very fine variety.
'Mrs. A. M. Williams' "B" ***, bright Turkey Red.
'Pygmalion' "B" **, crimson-red, black spots, late.
'Red Riding Hood' "B" **, red.
'Scandinavia', "B" **, crimson-red.
'Souvenir of A. Waterer' "B" **, warm carmine.
'Vulcan' "B" **, carmine.

And flowering later, well into the latter part of June:—

'Baron de Bruin' "B" **, a fine dark red, but of rather straggling
habit unless nipped-back when young.
'Essex Scarlet' "B" *, deep crimson-scarlet, very good.
'G. A. Sims' "B" *, ditto, habit more straggly.

The cultivation of the "A" class ultra-hardy hybrids offers few
difficulties if, at planting time, the soil is generously enriched with leaf-
mould or peat until its healthy acidity and high humus content is
beyond all doubt. Some say that peat is doubtfully desirable but I
have always found it highly beneficial and, indeed, necessary, placed
above the root-ball. It has the merit of being clean, free of weed seeds,
and easily and cheaply bought anywhere, as handy bales of "Peat-Moss
Litter". The only proviso is that it should not be used until the bone-
dry material that arrives has been completely saturated with lime-free
water; if it can be spread out in the rain a considerable time before
using, so much the better. Care should be taken that no *soil* is ever
placed over the root-ball, a scattering of peat or leaf-mould, only,
should be put *over* the roots and then a mulch of dead leaves or bracken.
Neither pure peat nor dead leaves should be put below the root ball
when planting.
   If grafted plants must be used, it is often best to set the plant a
little deep in the ground, so that it stands in a "saucer" which can

be kept well mulched with an extra depth of fallen leaves and chopped bracken which will tempt the variety to form its own roots above the graft. Unlike baled peat, bracken-peat has real feeding value.†

Nowadays the problem is to give the plants enough lime-free water. The later-flowering Rhododendrons bloom at a time when very hot weather often occurs. Unless sufficient watering is done to keep the roots moist the buds cannot expand properly and the display will be spoiled.

Layers, that is, plants on their own roots, are very much more valuable to the owner-gardener than grafted plants, as with the former there is no trouble with constantly emerging suckers from the *ponticum* root-stock. On the other hand, in unfavourable soils, *root-grafted* plants which are sometimes available are often advantageous as the *ponticum* roots are very tolerant and cannot produce suckers.

The resistance to wind of the hardy "A" class is ample for all requirements but in very exposed places it is best to start with low, bushy plants. In nurseries they are usually grown fully exposed so there is no difficulty in securing these. If grown in too sheltered and shady places the old hybrids make too much soft growth and sprawl about in a very unattractive manner. For such spots the ' Pink Pearl ' types and other " B " and " C " class Rhododendrons are much more suitable.

The " fly " mentioned is a dirty, semi-transparent-looking insect that infests the undersides of the leaves of Rhododendrons, particularly those having the " blood " of the ultra-hardy *R. catawbiense* or the yellow *R. campylocarpum*. It seems that it likes the smooth concave undersurface of this type of leaf and can only flourish if the host plant is growing in the sun. The pest is, in general, only difficult to control where there are large numbers of Catawba hybrids grown in full sun, as in nurseries. Certain varieties are martyrs to the " fly " and act as sources of re-infection. Consequently these should either be avoided or grown in the shade. Almost any of the proprietary insecticide sprays or dusts are effective, if applied so as to cover the *undersurfaces* of the leaves in early summer when the juvenile stages of the fly can be seen. Care should be taken, though, to obtain a dust which does not have lime, or ground chalk, incorporated as a " spreader ".

Sometimes, particularly near Oaks, the Tortix Moth caterpillar destroys the young leaves of Rhododendrons. Derris dust, applied with a proper dust-gun is a convenient method of destroying these, and the leaf-hoppers that are believed to start the fungus infection that destroys the flower-buds.

" Bud blast ", a recently noted plague, has now arrived to spoil the remarkable health record of these sturdy, trouble-free plants. In early

† See " The Flowering Shrub Garden Today ", p. 34.

winter, browned flower-buds betray the attack of the fungus responsible.
These should be cut off, with an inch or two of stem, at once, and burnt.
If this is regularly done it is thought, although the pest is not yet fully
studied, that the spread of the infestation is prevented. In large plantations this treatment is hardly practicable and it is to be hoped that, ere
long, we shall have a spraying programme worked out to combat this
new menace. For my part I use green sulphur dust applied in August
with a big rotary dust-gun to protect especially valuable specimens. In
conjunction with the hygiene measures mentioned above the treatment
appears to be effective. At least I have seen no blasted buds for some
years.

The species and varieties of **Deutzia** now claim attention. This is,
incidentally, one of the more perplexing of plant names as to its pro-
nunciation. Those who have learned German usually call it "Doytzia",
others "Dootzia". One should be consistent, without doubt, and
though I am in the first category regarding the name of this shrub I
must admit that I boggle at "Fooh'sia", "Mingizzia", "Mineyolia"
and "Esckaliownia". Presumably, then, the "Dootzias" are right, and,
indeed, a stern anglicising is the rule ordained by custom, though it is
too late for many of us to change our ways.

The Deutzias are a large race of deciduous shrubs belonging to a
section of the Saxifrage family, which some now hold should, with
the Philadelphus and Hydrangea, comprise the Hydrangea family,
with white or pale purplish-pink flowers in early June, and mostly come
from China. If they flowered in early May, amid the huge selection of
beautiful shrubs in bloom at that time, we should not wish to trouble
with them but any effective flowering shrub at its best in June is worthy
of our attention. There are about twenty species of possible garden
value and a larger number of hybrids propagated as clones. A few of
the most decorative have been selected for mention below. Further
particulars may be found in an article by Mr. H. G. Hillier, p 118 *et
seq.*, "Ornamental Flowering Trees and Shrubs", R.H.S. Conference,
1938.

Deutzia albida, a 12-foot, bushy species introduced by Reginald
Farrer from Kansu, China, flowers in early June. The inch-wide, bell-
shaped white flowers, in clusters, whiten the bush in a whole-hearted
manner and it appears to be reasonably hardy so long as it escapes a
late spring frost.

D. longifolia Veitchii is a shrub of about 5 feet with one-inch-wide,
purplish-pink flowers in crowded clusters, during the last half of
June, and narrow, pointed leaves.

D. Monbeigii is a particularly decorative Deutzia flowering in early July, so free with its tiny white flowers as to colour the 6-foot bush. It was found in Yunnan by Forrest in 1927. It requires a loamy soil.

D. pulchra from Formosa, is taller, reaching 12 feet in height with long arching sprays of Lily-of-the-Valley flowers. It is one of the most beautiful members of the family.

D. scabra (A.G.M. 1928) is a useful old Japanese species introduced in 1822. It will grow anywhere, and the white or pinkish flowers, rather like half-open lawn-daisies, are quite attractive in a quiet way in late June. Var. *compacta* is a 3 foot bush with Hawthorn-like, later, flowers.

D. setchuenensis from China is a very pretty, dwarf, late-flowering species usually seen about 3 or 4 feet high, with starry white flowers in clusters. *D. s.* var. *corymbiflora* is even more attractive and is a plant of great charm and refinement, but very scarce.

D. Sieboldiana is another small species with orange-anthered white flowers with a faint sweet fragrance.

The hybrid Deutzias are of course less distinct and refined in form, if somewhat more vigorous in growth and bolder in flower.

D. elegantissima has purplish-pink flowers.

D. kalmiæflora has cup-shaped, pinkish flowers.

D. magnifica (A.G.M. 1926) is a taller shrub with double white flowers in clusters densely set along the branches.

A very fine sub-variety is *D. magnifica* var. *latifolia* with single flowers 1½ inches across in great profusion.

D. rosea carminea (*D. gracilis* var. *carminea*) has fragrant flowers of a purplish-pink colour in June.

The Deutzias, although they prefer a good loam, will grow on limy soils and, indeed, are not particular as to situation either, though they suffer sometimes from the effects of late spring frosts. They flower on shoots made the previous year, so that pruning, except for the removal of flowered branchlets the moment the flowers are over, is done at the expense of flower. None the less, the oldest branches may also be removed at intervals of a few years with advantage. Cuttings of half-ripened shoots can be struck sometimes in the sand-box, but bottom heat is really required to secure a good percentage of rooted plants.

Buddleia alternifolia (A.G.M. 1924), a hardy, rambling, slender-twigged species with narrow, greyish leaves and abundant clusters of Mauve flowers in late May or early June, is one of the more attractive members of a rather dull family. Introduced by Reginald Farrer in 1914, it was described with his usual remarkable flair as "like a gracious

Magnolia Watsonii

Cytisus Battandieri

Cornus Kousa

Rhododendron indicum macranthum

small-leaved weeping-willow when it is not in flower, and a sheer
waterfall of soft purple when it is." Unfortunately the habit of growth
has the family weaknesses: it flowers on two-year-old wood which
makes pruning unprofitable and soon forms a bush 6 feet high and 16
across. Being an insecure rooter, the weeping-willow-tree form is seldom
attainable in the garden and its winter appearance is far from decorative. A dry sunny spot on either acid or limy soil suits this Buddleia best
and cuttings of half-ripe shoots taken in July are an easy means of
propagation.

Very similar in its preferences as to aspect and its indifference to
soil conditions is *Caragana aurantiaca*, a member of the Pea family.
It is a deciduous shrub about 3 or 4 feet high with small, narrow leaves
and plentiful orange-yellow, gorse-like flowers in dense rows beneath
the arching branches in late May or early June. It is hardy and an easy
doer in any well-drained sunny spot in either type of soil. Thus it is a
useful shrub for limy gardens where it may take part in the substitute
display of Azalea colourings.

Seeds, and July cuttings treated in the usual manner, are the best
means of increase.

The **Leptospermums** are a group of beautiful, small-leaved slender-
branched evergreens of the Myrtle family, found in Australasia. They
are, most unfortunately, too tender for any but unusually warm coastal
gardens and these must be further favoured by having acid soil. In west
Sussex survivors from 1963 succumbed in 1965/6.

Leptospermum scoparium, the Manuka or "Tea Tree", is the national
flower of New Zealand. The common wild form is a slender-twigged,
dense, upright, round-topped bush with small narrow, pointed, evergreen leaves and dull-white flowers, about half an inch or less across,
in early June. Specimens over here are usually seen about 5 feet high,
but, along the south and west coasts, bushes may be seen up to 18 feet in
height.

When wreathed with their masses of white, pink or crimson, May-
blossom-like flowers the varieties of this Leptospermum are singularly
lovely and the other species described later will provide a succession of
bloom almost until summer ends.

The great beauty of the family is a crimson-flowered sport, found
about the beginning of this century, named *L. s. Nichollsii*. It was
introduced in 1908 and is a beautiful shrub that should be tried in all
favoured gardens. It revels in sunny and windy spots rather than in
more sheltered situations.

N   E.F.S.

L. s. eximium, a Tasmanian variety with rounder leaves found by H. F. Comber, has larger flowers of a purer white than the "type".

L. s. 'Red Damask' has crimson double flowers, very tender.

L. s. prostratum is a dwarf, prostrate form which is notably hardier than others. It has small white flowers.

L. s. Chapmanni is a variety with singularly large pink flowers.

L. lanigerum, with silky, grey-green foliage and profuse white flowers in late June or early July, follows the previously mentioned species in flowering time.

L. l. 'Giblin's var.' is a fine Tasmanian form of this species. It was collected by H. F. Comber.†

L. Rodwayanum, of more rigid growth, larger, darker green leaves and large, white, fragrant flowers over an inch across, blooms later still, in late July or in August.

L. Liversidgei is a slender small-leaved species with drooping branches and very small white flowers.

L. pubescens is notable for being hardier than many of the other members of this family. It is of slender, erect habit, being spire-like rather than round-topped like *L. scoparium*. The flowers, about half an inch or more across, are white.

L. flavescens is described as a tall white-flowered species flowering in July.

The Leptospermums require a well-drained, open, sunny position and a neutral or acid soil, on the light side for choice. They do not seem to mind wind at all, a useful quality shared by many New Zealand shrubs. Once planted they cannot be moved with safety which is somewhat surprising in view of the fact that they can be so readily grown from cuttings treated in the usual manner. Seeds sown as advised for dwarf Rhododendrons (p. 90) are also a good means of increase, but the unusually rich-coloured *L. s. Nichollsii* usually gives white or pink-flowered seedlings.

Few trees have more beautiful foliage than *Robinia Pseudoacacia*, the 'Common Acacia'. This American species introduced long ago, in 1640, has had its ups and downs in popularity but it has great qualities as a street or garden tree. The brilliant green, divided leaves come late and hold their fresh colour most attractively when most others are already dull with age and the fatigue of summer.

The racemes of delightfully fragrant white or pink pea-flowers are borne in June when they are particularly welcome and the tree submits to lopping to almost any desired size with perfect good nature. On the

† *Gardeners' Chronicle*, Sept. 5, 1936, Fig. 74.

debit side, it tends to run at the root, though, being a legume, even the most hidebound old tree-hater cannot charge it with "robbing the soil". Normally growing to about 30 or 40 feet high, it is easily kept, as a pollard, to half that height if desired. The branches are unfortunately very brittle, which is a serious drawback in windy places, but by growing the tree on one clean stem and then pollarding, so that a fair-sized head will provide the right height, this trouble is greatly minimised. The new golden-leaved variety 'Frisia' makes a spectacular mass of vivid yellow.

R. p. Decaisneana is similar to the type but has pale pink flowers.

R. hispida, the Rose Acacia, is a more tender species. Introduced into this country in 1758, it comes from the Pinewoods of Carolina where it grows to a height of 20 feet. It is even less windproof than the other members of the family, though very lovely when covered with its short, thick racemes of purplish-crimson pea-flowers about 6 inches long and two across. In warm and sheltered places it is very attractive grown as a grafted standard tree carefully trained. In colder and more exposed spots it should be given the protection of a wall where it makes an unusual and attractive decoration. An improved form, *R. h. macrophylla* has larger, brighter flowers and larger leaflets.

In Nature this species runs at the root, covering wide areas in Tennessee by this method. This being so, it might be a good plan to get the plant on its own roots and to let it grow in this way.

R. Kelseyi is another sadly brittle but attractive shrub of the same type from North Carolina, with bright rose-coloured flowers in June. Unlike the last, this species sometimes produces fertile seeds in cultivation. Unfortunately, however, it is usually grafted on *R. Pseudoacacia* and is thus seldom safe from destruction by the wind. Plants on their own roots, on the other hand, could renew themselves in this event in a natural way.

The Robinias are not particular as to soil and indeed the poorer this is the better as otherwise they make soft growth more easily broken by the wind. The Goat Moth sometimes destroys the trees by the tunnellings of its huge caterpillars in the centre of the stems. When the tree is on its own roots increase is possible by rooted suckers.

An interesting wall plant is *Solanum crispum* (A.G.M. 1939), a climber of the **Nightshade** family. It is barely up to hardiness requirements in the open, but is so quick-growing and floriferous that it is worth trying in any sunny spot against a wall. It was introduced from the island of Chiloe in 1829 and produces its fragrant, pale Heliotrope, inch-wide, potato-like flowers with their projecting yellow-anthered centres from June to the end of summer.

Pruning is not necessary unless it is desired to grow this shrub as an open-ground bush. In this case it requires spurring back each year. It is not particular as to soil and indeed this is probably better if on the poor side as it induces firmer and shorter growth.

An even more beautiful relation, *S. jasminoides*, with pale blue-violet flowers, is slighter in growth and more tender. A form of this with white flowers, var. *album*, is more commonly seen than the "type". They are delightful climbers for unusually favoured places in the south and west but seldom grow well enough to be worth while elsewhere.

The Nightshades may be propagated from cuttings in the usual manner. The Latin name comes from *solari*—to quiet, referring no doubt to the permanently quietening effect caused by eating the poisonous berries.

Among the **Hydrangeas** *H. petiolaris* (A.G.M. 1924) is a hardy climber from Japan with strong rough-barked stems clinging by aerial roots like Ivy. The leaves are bright green and smooth on the upper surface and in June the flattish corymbs of white flowers open. The centre part is composed of the small fertile flowers and on longer stalks around the margin are scattered the larger sterile ray-flowers. The form available here is hardly showy enough for a wall, where so many decorative species compete for our attention, but on a tree stump, or climbing up a tree, this Hydrangea has a picturesque habit that makes it very attractive. There appears to be a superior form of this climber in Japan with much larger flowers and there are many species of climbing evergreen Hydrangeas with red, violet, primrose yellow, pink or white flowers not yet introduced.†

H. anomala comes from the Himalayas and also from Formosa (*H. glabra* Hayata). Resembling the preceding, it suffers from the same drawback, namely that the form we have in this country is not the finest in flower. Herbarium specimens sent back by E. H. Wilson have fine corymbs with many bold and shapely ray-flowers. The form we have has few, and rather small, ray-flowers, but it is a vigorous grower though less hardy than the preceding, requiring a sheltered wall.

These climbing Hydrangeas have the merit of supporting themselves well on walls and thus act as useful hosts for more fragile and larger-flowered climbers such as hybrid Clematis, *Tropæolum speciosum*, Morning Glory, etc. They are not very particular as to soil but, of course, grow better when this is well enriched with humus.

They may be propagated from cuttings in the usual manner although they do not strike quite so readily as the cultivated hybrid races of

† For description, see "The Hydrangeas", by the author, Constable & Co. (1950).

Hydrangea. Seeds, sown as advised for dwarf Rhododendrons (see p. 90) might easily provide better forms than those now available in commerce. Wilson recorded the delightful fragrance of the finer forms of *H. anomala*, and as these climbers can be crossed with the red Hortensias, there are great possibilities for the hybridist.

Another interesting climber, self-clinging and evergreen, is *H. integerrima*. The Cornidia section of the Hydrangeas, to which it belongs, comprises some of the strangest, the loveliest and the least known of all plants, and few Europeans have seen them alive. They are powerful evergreen climbers mostly having large ovate or elliptic leaves. The flower umbel is at first enclosed in bracts so that it looks like the bud of one large flower. When it opens a large umbel of the small fertile flowers with many large and often vividly coloured ray-flowers expends.

There are over twenty different species in Central America and nearly as many in Formosa, the Philippines and the East Indies. Those from both hemispheres have a remarkably close family resemblance yet most species are evidently quite distinct from one another. Some are patently of no garden value, lacking the showy ray-flowers that are the chief beauty of the plant, but others are evidently of the very highest value having gorgeous red, violet, primrose-yellow or white flowers.

These climbers usually resemble Ivy in having two different states; the juvenile climbing state with small, differently shaped leaves and aerial roots on the stems, and the free, bushy, flowering state with large entire leaves.

The other species are described in the monograph on the Hydrangeas already cited. We must return to the one species of the family that we have already got in cultivation in this country.

Hydrangea integerrima (*Cornidia serratifolia*) resembles the other members of the Cornidia section, being a powerful liana with elliptic evergreen leaves, ascending to the tops of tall trees, but unfortunately the inflorescence of the form seen and sent back by that capable collector, J. F. Comber, is rather a poor one. The inflorescence opens from a large, bracted bud enclosing the whole thing with numerous small yellowish-white fertile flowers but the ray-flowers are each reduced to one irregular, leaf-like sepal which is white tinged with green.

Judging by herbarium material, forms of this species do, however, exist having the essential valuable feature of four or five well-formed four-sepalled ray-flowers to each inflorescence. None the less the important point is that this evergreen climber is reasonably hardy in favourable gardens in this country. Thus, if the more vivid-flowered species were secured, we might expect remarkable results from hybridisation.

Like so many South American plants it dislikes drought or sun heat in this country. My plant has reached the roof.

A sheltered wall with moist rich soil, a damp atmosphere and light shade appears to suit this evergreen climbing Hydrangea best and increase may be made from the rooted offsets often found round established plants.

In gardens whose limy soil precludes the growing of the Azaleas with their vivid orange, red and yellow flowers at this season, the various **Rose species** are of particular interest. They flower at different times but it is more convenient to group them in this section as it is about the normal time for their flowering to begin.

Whilst they do not provide the effective mass of bloom over a long season that is such a valuable characteristic of the Floribunda Roses dealt with later, they have often a singularly attractive foliage and habit. Certain of the yellow-flowered kinds provide some of the best substitutes for the later-flowering Azaleas where these cannot be grown.

Among the more outstanding species and hybrids are the following:—

R. Ecæ. This Rose has been confused with *R. xanthina* and *R. Primula*, but the true plant is quite distinct, being a fairly tall shrub with small Buttercup Yellow, five-petalled flowers, red-brown wood and foliage that is not aromatic. It was found in the Kurrum Valley of Afghanistan by Dr. Aitchison in 1880. R. Ecae is quite easily grown but is rare in cultivation, as it is difficult to propagate except by suckers. The puzzling name is based on the intitials of the doctor's wife.

A Rose often sent out under this name, which is really *R. Primula* (from Samarkand), is a more easily propagated species forming a 6- to 8-foot bush with spicy, aromatic foliage, red-brown wood, red shoots and thorns, small round leaflets and 1-inch-wide very pale Primrose Yellow flowers in May†. At first it is rather shy, but becomes very free-flowering when well established and is a very lovely shrub notable for the beautiful presentation of its flowers and long flowering season (see also p. 171).

R. Hugonis (A.G.M. 1925) is, unfortunately, a disappointing shrub in many gardens. In my own experience it was one of the very few flowering shrubs that died out completely in a favourable garden under the enforced neglect of the "emergency" years. The cause was a form of "dieback" to which this Rose seems liable in places where the atmosphere is moist and favourable for fungal growths. In some districts it grows quite satisfactorily and is then very attractive, making a tall bush of about

† For further discussion of these distinctions, see B. O. Mulligan, "Rosa Primula and Rosa xanthina Kokanica", *Gardening Illustrated*, p. 218 (April 27, 1940).

8 feet high with arching branches thickly set with the lovely ferny masses of foliage and 2-inch, pale yellow flowers in May. It takes its name from "Pater Hugo", Father Hugh Scallan, a missionary in China, who first sent its seeds to Kew in 1899.

Much superior as a garden plant is the shapely, palest yellow hybrid *R. cantabrigiensis* (*R. Hugonis* × *sericea*). This Rose is fairly free from "dieback" and is more free-flowering, and the flowers open fully in late May or early June, which those of *R. Hugonis* often do not do.

Another hybrid, *R.* 'Dr. E. M. Mills' (*R. Hugonis* × *rugosa*), is a 4-foot, spreading bush with semi-double cup-shaped flowers of a blushed primrose.

R. 'Canary Bird' is a most attractive, but very early-flowering Rose of *Hugonis* type, with fragrant flowers 2½ inches across of bright Canary Yellow. (See A.M. under *R. xanthina*, p. 202.)

R. Moyesii (A.G.M. 1925), introduced by E. H. Wilson from Western China in 1904, is, in the superlative, red-flowered clonal form, one of the loveliest of all Rose species. It makes a 9- or 10-foot, rather "leggy" bush, with gracefully arching branches, admirable as a shade tree for orange Kurumes or Hydrangeas. The blood-red flowers are superbly formed in one of the most beautiful of all flower shapes, that of the Heraldic Rose, with five petals and an exquisitely formed "old gold" centre. Unfortunately, although sometimes over 3 inches across, the flowers are often sparsely borne for the large framework of the shrub. They do not quite "colour the bush" and thus it usually just fails to be really splendid. The numerous red fruits are very colourful in autumn.

I have not yet fully tested the matter, but I would wager that a good way to grow this Rose so as to induce freer flowering would be to arch-over and peg-down the long growths from the start so as to induce flowers and foliage from every possible bud. Great care in handling the brittle shoots would have to be used but the flowers are so lovely that success would be worth a lot of trouble.

R. M. highdownensis, a variety produced by Colonel Stern of High-down, near Worthing, has even more decorative and numerous heps than the type and the best form is very effective indeed. *R. M.* 'Geranium' and *R. M.* 'Underway' are also fine varieties as regards this quality.

R. 'Nevada', a hybrid with 'La Giralda', is an almost perpetual flowering, shapely, strong bush with 4-inch creamy-white flowers (figured *R. H. S. Journal*, LXXV, Pt. 1, 1950).

R. moschata, the Musk Rose, is a delightful climber for a wood, where it may be allowed to scramble up a tree at will. It is too hearty, perhaps, for the small garden where its masses of creamy-white flowers would not quite atone for the amount of room demanded. It will climb 30 feet or more without difficulty and an established specimen is a fine sight.

R. Rubus, a less strong-growing semi-climber, introduced from Western China by both E. H. Wilson and Reginald Farrer, is of the Musk type. The fragrant white or faintly blushed flowers, 1½ inches across are borne in large loose clusters from June to August. Hardy and vigorous and flowering very profusely this is a fine but rather neglected Rose. The red heps are decorative in autumn and this species appears to have no particular fads about soil or position so long as it gets full sunlight.

R. Roxburghii (*R. microphylla*) forms a large, handsome bush 7 or 8 feet high and is very dense, picturesque and sturdy. The fragrant pale purplish-pink flowers are about 3 inches or more across in a good form, and in spite of the weak colouring are so freely produced and so well presented, in an open position, as to be quite effective at a distance.

R. Eglanteria (*R. rubiginosa*), the charming Sweet Briar, is too well known to need description. The improved garden hybrids known as the "Penzance Briars" include a number of quite attractive shrubs, pleasant to have in the wilder parts of the larger gardens. None are, however, in the front rank, in my experience, as they only flower once, and those that are good growers have only pink flowers. 'Meg Merrilees', a sturdy bush with rose Madder flowers, 'Hebe's Lip', white with a pink edge, and 'Lady Penzance', orange-pink but a more weakly and unhealthy grower, are examples. Unlike other Roses the Sweet Briars prefer a limy soil but their growth on acid soils is perfectly adequate.

R. rubrifolia has attractive pinkish-grey leaves but the red flowers are few and inconspicuous.

R. anemonoides (*R. sinica anemone*) is a distinct Rose of doubtful origin. It is a beautiful climber with very large, single, palest purplish-pink flowers in May. For a south wall it is quite pretty but is, of course, eclipsed by the great climbing H. T. Roses, the Campsis, Clematis, Bignonias, etc. which are a still better investment for such a choice position. Much depends, of course, on the colour of the wall surface, but *R. anemonoides* is a Rose that needs some care and, in my experience, resents pruning and sometimes suffers from "dieback". *R. a.* 'Ramona' (A.M. 1950) is a deeper coloured sport.

R. rugosa. The Japanese, or Ramanas Rose is one of the most promising flowering shrubs among the Rose species. The habit is handsome and compact, the leaves have a good autumn colouring, and the tomato-like fruits are highly decorative, but the colour of the flowers is unfortunately very poor indeed. It is a wretched purplish pink that apparently bars any improvement in the direction of true scarlets, oranges, or yellows but yields one or two good dark crimson-red and some white varieties. A number of hybrids are available with large, coarse flowers of a feeble, washy pink or pale fawn colour, such as 'Conrad Meyer', 'Nova Zembla' and 'Dr. Eckener'.

Some beautiful varieties and hybrids of *R. rugosa* now, alas, hard to find, are:—

'Ruskin', a single red.

'Carmen', with 2-inch, single flowers in rich damask red.

'Schneezwerg' (a hybrid with *R. bracteata*), with snow-white flowers in clusters of six to eight, it was raised by P. Lambert, Trier, Germany in 1912.

'Red Grootendorst', with small, fringed, red, double flowers in clusters.

'Pink Grootendorst' is similar, but pink in colour, and makes the charming little bouquets one sees for sale in Swiss flower shops. It sometimes occurs as a branch sport on the red, but may be obtained under its own name.

'Lady Curzon', a single pink, with thin-textured flowers 4 inches across, is thought to be a hybrid with *R. macrantha* and, if well nipped back, makes quite an attractive bush.

'Blanc double de Coubert', this double white variety is particularly lovely and fragrant and, except in a very wet summer when it balls its flowers, is quite effective.

'Mrs. Anthony Waterer', has semi-double, deep crimson flowers.

'Parfum de l'Hay' has double deep rose flowers, and is a fragrant and charming hybrid.

Atropurpurea, deep purplish red.

The *rugosa* family have a good golden yellow autumn leaf colour and their healthy and perpetual flowering nature is most commendable. They grow even in the sea-sand on the beaches, yet they are seldom seen in seaside gardens.

R. pomifera is not remarkable, but a variety of this species, *R. p. duplex*, originally found in the late Mr. Wolley Dod's garden, is very beautiful, with large, soft pink flowers and grey-green foliage followed by hairy fruits.

R. macrantha has single, pink flowers and a bushy habit and flowers for a longer period than most, from May onwards.

R. fœtida, the yellow Persian Rose and its brilliant scarlet variety 'Austrian Copper' are important as the part-ancestors of most of our best garden Roses in these colours. As flowering shrubs they are too difficult to make much of a showing in most gardens, but 'Austrian

Copper' is worth any amount of trouble. It is more fully mentioned in the section comprising the Burnet Roses and their allies, p. 171.

R. Banksiæ. The Banksian Rose is the pride of the gardens of the Riviera, but I have never seen it do well enough in this climate to look really attractive, compared with the other species and hybrids available. The violet-scented wild form recorded by Reginald Farrer does not appear to have been introduced.

R. virginiana has the merit of flowering late and has a lovely pink, double-flowered, possibly hybrid, variety, the 'Rose d'Amour' which is now hard to find. There is also a white-flowered form. This species has notably rich autumn leaf colouring which, with the scarlet heps, give it a second season of beauty.

R. xanthina is a garden form and comes from Korea and North China. This Rose and *R. Primula, R. Moyesii* and *R. cantabrigensis* are, I think, the best of this group for the average small garden. The Rose sent out under this name makes a fairly compact and very free-flowering bush about 8 feet high with semi-double yellow flowers about 2 inches across in early June. The wild form, var. *spontanea* Rehder, is of weaker constitution and has smaller, paler, single flowers. Unlike most, this Rose seems to need a sheltered position, and may suffer in hard winters.

An A.M. was awarded to *R.? × xanthina* on May 1, 1945. Unless it was forced, the flowering date seems wrong for this species.

One of the best of all places for these Rose species is probably an open position in a wild garden. There, if the soil is chalky, with Cistuses, Genistas, Halimiums, etc., they may take the place of the Ericaceous families so effective on acid soils. For the Roses, it would be advisable to add turf-loam when planting, or fresh inverted turves, buried below the roots, would serve almost equally well. If it is possible to mulch the bushes with bracken or fallen leaves this is most helpful to healthy growth, as alkaline conditions, and particularly artificially added lime, seems to lower the resistance of the Rose to "Black Spot". Great care should be taken to set the plants in the ground exactly at such a depth that the "burl", or growing point, is only just under the soil. The usual cause of failure is their being planted too shallowly on unmulched ground. Bonemeal is appreciated as a tonic in peaty soils.

Most of the species can be propagated from seed and the varieties may be layered or struck from hard-wood cuttings, formed of flowered shoots about 6 to 8 or more inches long, three parts sunk in sandy soil in the open or, better, in the shade of a north wall.

Some of the wild **Lilacs** are worthy of note as their flowers have the delicate lines and shapely individual formation characteristic of many wild species, avoiding the undistinguished, mongrel look of the typical garden hybrid. For the most part, they also flower much later than the common Lilac which is a further advantage for Lilac lovers, as they prolong the season.

Syringa microphylla, a rounded compact bush up to six feet, has profuse clusters of pale lilac, or in var. ' Superba ', pink flowers in June and, often, again in August: one of the best of Lilacs (A.M. 57).

S. Sweginzowii superba, a long-introduced Chinese species, has small, pale, pinkish-lilac, fragrant flowers which are quite attractive when cut, but the bush is no great ornament to the garden landscape.

S. villosa, another Chinese species, is comparatively free-flowering and compact in habit, with pale rosy-lilac flowers late in the season.

S. amurensis (*S. japonica*) a Japanese and Chinese species, is useful owing to its habit of flowering at the end of June, when good flowering shrubs are scarce. The Japanese form *S. a. japonica*, is particularly fine, attaining, in its native land, it is said, a tree-like habit up to 30 feet in height, with abundant panicles of creamy-white flowers.

S. Julianæ is an attractive and easily grown species introduced by Messrs. Veitch in 1900 and later from Kansu, China, by Reginald Farrer. From lilac buds the fragrant white flowers open in early June in such numbers as to colour the bush, which reaches to 10 feet in height in cultivation. Sometimes it flowers again, less profusely, in August. Farrer described it as growing "in sheer limestone cliff" and it has duly proved to be a good plant for a warm chalky garden.

S. Potanini is another Chinese species from the same district, with very fragrant white flowers with yellow anthers. Farrer also sent back seeds of this previously known species and the plants over here are mostly from their sowing. It is also a limestone shrub, flowering in June and interesting for warm, chalky gardens, the deep green, lanceolate leaves setting off the white flowers to great advantage.

S. yunnanensis, usually of little decorative value, has superior forms with brighter purplish-pink flowers than the type, but the habit of the shrub has all the family weaknesses.

In a cold and chalky garden some of these Lilacs might well be thought worth growing for their coverage of the "June gap"; for a complete description of all available species, see H. G. Hillier, *R. H. S. Journal*, 61 (1936) p. 450 *et seq.* and also the same author, p. 101 *et seq.* "Ornamental Flowering Trees and Shrubs", R.H.S. 1938.

A number of late-blooming hybrid Lilacs derived from *S. reflexa*, *S. villosa*, *S. Josikæa*, *S. Sweginzowii*, *S. Wolfii*, etc. have been bred at Ottawa by Miss Isabella Preston. The original cross, *S. Prestoniæ* (*S. villosa* × *reflexa*), is commercially propagated in Canada in the varieties 'Oberon' with panicles of very pale pinkish-lilac flowers, and 'Romeo' with phlox-pink flowers on reddish-brown stalks.

S. 'Bellicent' (*S. josiflexa* seedling) is described as a graceful 7- to 8-foot bush with small panicles on the lateral branches and a large central truss of the pink flowers terminating the main branches in late May or early June. In Britain the growth of this variety has usually been less tall, reaching only 5 feet in seven years.

Other varieties, mostly of *S. josiflexa* parentage, are 'Guinevere', "a graceful bush of seven feet"; 'Enid', "nine feet high" and 'Desdemona', "seven feet by seven feet"†. They are growing in heavy chalky soil at Stansted Park, and were brought back from Canada by Lord Bessborough in 1935.

S. Prestoniæ 'Isabella' (*S. villosa* × *reflexa*) has narrowly tubular flowers of Mallow Purple (H.C.C. 630/3) borne in large groups of open panicles nearly a foot in length at the ends of strong shoots set with large dark green leaves. I must state, however, that of the entire range of colours shown in the Horticultural Colour Chart, I think that this hue is the most unattractive that a flower can possibly be.

A number of further crosses have been made with successful results. A seedling of *S. reflexa* × *Sweginzowii* was crossed back to *S. reflexa* producing a very attractive hybrid, *S.* 'Fountain', illustrated in the article cited, the chief improvement being that the flowers do not split and turn brown soon after opening, like those of *S. reflexa*, although they have not the rich pink colouring of that species, being only a pale purplish-lilac colour.‡

Although these Lilacs display their panicles of flower boldly above the foliage with a good presentation, these are mostly of muddy pink or purplish-pink colours, such as would ensure that any new Rhododendron that dared to flower with such a tint would instantly be labelled "unworthy of cultivation", and consigned to the bonfire, but they have a value for very cold, limy-soiled gardens where the more vivid-flowered shrubs unfortunately cannot be made to grow. Their habit is much superior to that of the common Lilac, as basal growths keep the bushes well furnished to the ground. As regards cultivation, the Lilacs are indifferent to the alkalinity or acidity of the soil so long as it is in good, free, aerated condition, but they need some sun to ripen the growths well and a mulch of dead leaves promotes vigour.

---

† "Notes on New Hybrid Syringas", by T. E. Tomalin, p. 312, *R.H.S. Journal*, Vol. LXVI, Pt. 9 (1941).

‡ "New Hybrid Lilacs", by Isabella Preston. *Gardening Illustrated*, 952 (Dec. 1946).

Wall plants and climbers also provide their sequence of flowers but *Jasminum officinale*, the common **Jasmine**, grown for its delightfully fragrant white flowers from June onwards, makes no great effect on a wall as a rule, and is rather untidy as a climber unless very carefully trained fanwise at the outset. This may be facilitated by driving one large, strong staple into the wall a foot above the spot where it is planted and then driving a number of smaller staples into the rafters, or the roof-plate if this is of wood. When the upper staples are connected to the lower one by wires a ready-made fan is provided to which the young growths may be tied. The first shoots are best secured to the outermost wires as this is more likely to encourage a greater number to spring from the base.

If kept stubbed back to an initial framework of branches, like a Wisteria, this Jasmine may be made to form an open-ground shrub.

J. stephanense is a hybrid with *J. Beesianum* with pale pink flowers.

J. polyanthum is like the common Jasmine but much finer in every way, but unfortunately only hardy enough for very favourable gardens.

J. humile revolutum, a less spectacular species, is hardier. It is not really climbing in habit, having stronger, shorter stems and clusters of numerous yellow flowers from June onwards on the young shoots of the year. It does not, however, make the fine display of that grand old species, *J. nudiflorum*, the most spectacular of winter-flowering shrubs.

The Jasmines are not particular as to soil and can be grown from cuttings of half-ripe shoots placed under a bell-glass in July.

Quite a different type of shrub flowering at this time is **Thymus nitidus**. It is a little gray-green bushlet with pleasing pale pink flowers in June and is the most shrub-like member of the family. It comes easily from seed though it is not very long-lived; thus it is valuable as a "filler" among the many charming dwarf shrubs for undulating open spaces in the garden where the low and rather flat effect of an embroidered mantle for the ground is wanted. The arrangement of such spaces is one of the secrets of good composition that gives the spice of contrast to the taller groupings.

The **Dipeltas** barely attain the requirements of effective flowering shrubs for garden decoration: their tolerance of limy soils and charm as cut sprays for indoors weigh, however, in their favour.

Dipelta floribunda, a member of the Honeysuckle family, is a tantalising shrub from China that was introduced by E. H. Wilson in 1902. The abundant and fragrant flowers, in free and picturesque sprays in late May or early June, are white or pinkish, with a yellow throat and somewhat like small foxgloves in shape. Cut and brought indoors they are a delight, but the bush that grows them is a gaunt, shambling, 10-foot-high brute of a thing, with dirty brown bark peeling off in flakes everywhere so as to defy the "manicurist", and branches sprouting in odd directions all over the place. Thus it is a shrub that the wise planter will keep in the background in some well-jungled corner whence he may emerge at the right moment bearing beautiful sprays of the gay, lacy flowers to the great pleasure of his household. In fact, I have never seen a more pleasing flower arrangement than one I once contrived in a great majolica vase upon a dark and ancient table, with the Dipelta aided by the apricot flavouring of the pink and gold Ghent Azalea 'Aurore de Royghem' and spiced with the fragrant pearly chalices of *Magnolia Sieboldii*.

D. ventricosa, also a Wilson introduction, is an allied species from Western China with larger but narrower downy leaves and sparser flowers of similar colouring. It is hardy and easy going and grows better on limy soils than *D. floribunda*.

D. yunnanensis was found in Yunnan in 1886 by the good Abbé Delavay, to whom we owe the discovery of so many Chinese shrubs. It flowers a little earlier than the other species, often in late May. Less tall than the preceding, about 8 or 9 feet is the usual height. The creamy-white flowers, flushed with pink and with an orange throat, are clustered on the ends of short shoots from the previous year's growths and have the usual foxglove shape of the family. In habit it is more graceful and spreading than *D. floribunda* but does not really produce such masses of flower. On a limy soil it is preferable as it is more vigorous in growth under such conditions.

On the whole, the Dipeltas are hardy and easy-going shrubs that are not fastidious as to soil or aspect. They are, however, so difficult to propagate that *D. floribunda* is now almost unobtainable.

Where the soil is acid June offers us a confusingly large number of Rhododendrons but some species are so outstanding and unlike their kindred that they require special mention. **Rhododendron Griersonianum** "D" ****, is I think, much hardier than is generally supposed. Indeed, it stands far better in a warm, open spot in poor soil than when sheltered in the woodland conditions that suit other kinds so well. It forms a dense bush with bright green, lanceolate leaves red-furred and silvered below. In June the brilliant scarlet flowers appear but unfortunately the sun, so necessary to ripen the wood of the late-maturing young growths, soon browns the corollas if the weather is clear at the time. Early autumn frosts are the bane of this species and, as it happens, my katabatic† position preserves me from these. This late growth of the bright young shoots is regrettable, but it is singularly decorative in the September scene. The plant is so easily and quickly raised from seed that it is not at all an expensive Rhododendron for the skilful cultivator and it is my belief that it has great possibilities for tub culture. The plants could be placed in shade as the flowers opened, and, as *R. Griersonianum* is remarkably drought-resisting it could be taken under cover in autumn without the need for much attention. In the open it is worth trying in all gardens where early autumn frosts are not severe, and the effect of a group of seedlings ablaze with their shapely and vivid flowers is one of the finest that June can afford us.

Certain kinds of that long-lasting, high flower-power shrub the **Hydrangea** flower in June and they are notable for their effectiveness in the garden landscape.

Hydrangea acuminata. The best Japanese forms of this are most valuable garden shrubs giving, in moist acid soil, a mass of exquisite blue flowers at midsummer on a neat bush of two or three feet easily raised from cuttings. 'Diadem' is notably hardy and beautiful.

Hydrangea paniculata var. 'Praecox' (A.M. 1956). This bone-hardy massive, rounded eight foot bush is enveloped in creamy lacy flowers in late June in the most spectacular manner. When red Roses such as 'Firedance' or 'Donald Prior' are added the effect is one that remains long in the memory. *H. paniculata* does not do well in limy soil and is not always easily struck from cuttings. Layering, however, is perfectly successful though the young plants may have to be cut back several times to make bushy specimens.

The genus **Styrax** covers quite a long season with a succession of flowers. As the most valuable members flower in mid June, however, we may well consider them at this moment of our floral calendar.

Styrax Obassia, a Japanese flowering tree of great charm, introduced by Charles Maries for Messrs. Veitch in 1879, bears its racemes of snowdrop-like flowers in amazing abundance in late May or the first

† See pp. 26 and 109.
‡ "The Plant Introductions of Reginald Farrer", by E. H. M. Cox, *New Flora* and Silva, 1930.

days of June. It forms a shapely little tree up to 20 feet high and is attractive as a lawn specimen, but the flowers are much hidden by the foliage and they only last about three days in beauty, though the snowy carpet of flowers beneath the tree on about the fifth day is very decorative.

S. Hemsleyana, a Chinese species, introduced by E. H. Wilson in 1900, is very similar but longer-lasting, and would, I expect, grow on a limy soil which the Japanese species probably would not. It flowers, as a rule, after the foregoing species is over and the racemes are less pendent and therefore more boldly displayed, making it the better species.

S. japonica is the great beauty of the family and it flowers about a fortnight later—right in the June gap when rivals are few. One of the most beautiful trees that I have ever seen was a specimen of this species grown as a tall standard. One looked up into the faces of thousands of snowdrop-like flowers that hung in rows from every twig. *S. japonica* is usually seen as a dense, bushy, little tree about 8 or 9 feet high but it will grow to 25 feet, in time, in a good soil. It was introduced as long ago as 1862 and it is surprising that it is so seldom seen as it is apparently quite hardy, though sometimes cut by late spring frosts. Like the other Styrax the flowers are white and thus, though *S. japonica* has great individual charm and beautiful "drawing", it is to other genera that we must look for vivid June colour in the shrub garden.

The Styrax, except *S. Hemsleyana*, need an acid or neutral soil rich in humus, to do well, and some shelter from the full blast of the wind. Seeds are the best method of increase. Regular mulching is very necessary to replenish the nourishment expended in the production of heavy crops of flowers. I have seen fine specimens of *S. japonica* dwindling to death from mere starvation.

The most valuable section of the **Magnolia** family flowers in late May or, more often, from early June onwards. They are somewhat vulnerable, alas, to spring frosts, and so are among the delights of elevated or coastal gardens rather than absolutely reliable subjects for general planting in cold districts.

Magnolia obovata (*M. hypoleuca, M. officinalis*) is a tree attaining about 30 feet or more in height and undoubtedly one of the most beautiful that can be grown in the British Isles. The large leaves, shaped as the name suggests, are of a brilliant green and most attractive to the eye. The flowers are very large with cream-coloured petals and sepals surrounding a rosette of red stamens from which emerges a club of carpels. The fragrance is very fruity and delightful. Owing to the fact that the flowers open a few at a time, over quite a long period,

Rhododendron indicum 'Satsuki'

Cistus lusitanicus decumbens

Helianthemum 'Magnificence'

Rhododendron 'Grand Finale'

the tree gives no great distant flower effect but is yet notably good to look at at all times and in particular in autumn when set with fine red fruits. Though it takes time to grow to its full majesty, and does not flower when young, it is quick growing and handsome as a sapling, provided that the situation is open but reasonably sheltered from wind, that the soil is moist and well enriched with leaf-mould and that a fresh leader is grown up after transplanting. In the perfect garden of one's dreams it is the tree to whose shade one brings the tea-things on a warm summer evening. It appears to be reasonably hardy, though in its old age it requires care, and regular feeding, particularly in dry years, is essential. This Magnolia is now placed in a different section from the following species ("A Survey of the Genus Magnolia" by J. E. Dandy, *Camellias and Magnolias*, R.H.S., 1950) but from the horticultural standpoint it has an affinity to them.

M. Sieboldii (*M. parviflora*) (A.G.M. 1935) is another superb Magnolia of the highest value for all gardens. Usually a small tree or large shrub about 15 feet high and of wide-spreading habit, it can be kept to a smaller size by occasionally pruning away the oldest stems at ground-level if desired. *M. Sieboldii* usually has quite a crop of flowers at the end of May or in early June and then goes on flowering only slightly more sparsely until August. The flowers have usually nine waxy-white petals and sepals with a red rosette and a green club in the centre. Their fragrance is quite delightful and they are produced by comparatively young trees. The finer forms have the central rosette of a rich red, inferior ones of magenta pink, but even the magenta-centred ones are highly attractive. Spring frosts are the only serious enemy of this Magnolia which is otherwise a good garden plant in enriched soil *on the acid side*. (See illustration facing p. 160.)

M. Watsoni is generally considered to be a hybrid between the two previously mentioned species and in my opinion has the most beautiful flowers of any Magnolia, and the most remarkable perfume. But unfortunately it is a plant of inherently weak constitution, almost invariably dying back badly after it has reached a certain age. I have formed the opinion that this weakness probably results from a deep-seated failing of the stem, caused by moving. Grown up on a new young stem, *in situ*, I think we should get a healthier and more long-lived tree. *M. Watsoni* has otherwise all the good qualities of its parents and flowers when comparatively young. It is to be hoped that it will again become available in commerce ere long, though it is so difficult to propagate that this is doubtful. If the cross could only be made again a seedling of better constitution might appear which would enable this superb hybrid to take its rightful place as the most popular of all Magnolias. (See illustration facing p. 192.)

O   E F.S.

M. sinensis is a Chinese cousin of *M. Sieboldii* and notable in that it can be grown on a limy soil. It forms a fairly tall, symmetrical, bushy tree, rather than a rambling shrub like the latter. The otherwise rather similar flowers hang down, facing the ground, instead of being only slightly inclined from the horizontal, and they open out to a flat saucer shape. I have counted as many as fourteen of the pearly-white tepals (midway between sepals and petals) surrounding the rosette of crimson stamens. The central club of carpels is green. So many different seedling forms exist, however, that there is surely some hybridity with the following species to be described. Characteristically the leaves are large and obovate compared with the furry-backed lance-shaped ones of *M. Wilsonii* and the flowers are bolder and broader petalled. *M. sinensis* is reputed, when matured, to flower throughout the summer, like *M. Sieboldii*, but plants under my observation have always flowered very freely in late May or early June and then ceased and set abundant seed. The fruits are very decorative and of a bright crimson, and later the scarlet seeds emerge and remain for some time clinging on gossamer strands to the seed vessels before falling. I now have self-sown seedlings but the conditions appear ideal for their germination.

M. Wilsonii. This somewhat similar Magnolia has furry young shoots and more lance-shaped, smaller, narrower leaves and narrower petals and sepals and is of less vigorous growth. Extreme forms of the type are markedly inferior to *M. sinensis*, but of recent years specimens under the name of *M. Wilsonii*, equalling *M. sinensis* in size and beauty of flower, but furred and with narrower leaves, have been commonly exhibited by well-known amateur growers of these trees.

These fine hybrids should probably be named *M. highdownensis* (*M. sinensis* × *Wilsonii*). This forms a bushy tree up to 20 feet high with flowers equalling those of *M. sinensis* and is a vigorous grower in the chalk soil at Highdown, near Worthing.

M. globosa is an allied species from the Eastern Himalayas with ovate leaves, red-furred beneath when young, and more globular flowers. It is probably rather less hardy than the other species of this group.

Most of the Magnolias of this group require a good loam, rich in forest humus, to grow fast, as they should to reach a good size quickly, and to bear big crops of flowers. They may be grown from seed, but it is a slow process and not altogether easy. In cultivation the first essential is to get the plant growing strongly, then any necessary pruning to ensure a fresh start with the production of a new shoot from the base that will form a healthy, shapely tree, may be done in March with safety. Many have stated their fears to me of any cutting of Magnolia wood, and to reassure myself I have even pruned mine unnecessarily hard, but I have seen no ill results on trees of good growth. A mulch of forest leaves should at all times be kept over the roots both for their general well-being and to replenish the soil after heavy crops of flower.

M. macrophylla (in spite of its flowers, 16 inches across), *M. Fraseri*, *M. tripetala*, *M. acuminata*, *M. cordata* and *M. Thomsoniana* are really of insufficient garden value relative to their great size for description here. Data regarding these may be found in *Camellias and Magnolias*, Conference Report, R.H.S. 1950. *M. virginiana* and *M. grandiflora* are dealt with later in these pages (p. 294).

From these fragile but exquisite trees, the real aristocrats of the garden, we return, starting with the Genistas, to small convenient bushes suitable for restricted spaces and giving the quick results increasingly insisted upon today.

Genista silvestris pungens, generally known as *G. dalmatica*, is a neat, dense bushlet 8 inches or a foot high with thin hairy, spiny branches and a profuse covering of yellow pea-flowers in June and July. It comes from the dry pinewoods of Dalmatia and requires a warm and well-drained spot though it is quite happy in light shade.

It is one of those delightfull, low, dwarf shrubs so pleasing when grown in association with other kinds of similar habit to form a close carpet of flower and foliage.

The Dalmatian Genista is not particular as to soil and strikes freely from cuttings placed under a bell-glass or in a propagating box in late July.

Another member of the family, *G. radiata*, also flowers in June. It is not spectacular, but the density of its thin green twigs gives it the winter value of an evergreen bush of the convenient height of 3 feet. Although it comes from south Europe it is reasonably hardy and a good plant for a very hot and dry bank. The small deep yellow flowers are borne in terminal heads only about an inch across and thus its display is hardly up to first-class standards, but in a very dry and warm season when many plants flag, it puts up a superior performance that earns it a position here. This species is easily raised from seeds and is not fastidious.

A large Tree-Broom flowering at this time is *Cytisus Battandieri* (A.G.M. 1938), introduced from the mountains of Morocco in 1921. It has silvery leaves and Aureolin Yellow flowers with an apple-loft fragrance, in corn-cob-shaped spikes. These silvery leaves are rather sparse and the habit is ragged and lanky unless controlled by perpetual early pinching-back. It takes some years to reach flowering size, but a well-grown bush can make quite a good showing though not, I think, up to the very high standard of the July-flowering species mentioned later. (See illustration facing p. 192.)

A sunny position suits this Broom and it is notable in that it does not object to a moderately limy soil, though it is more vigorous in an acid one. It can be increased by seeds. I have not been successful with cuttings.

Another member of the great Legume family that plays its part in June is *Lupinus arboreus*, the familiar **Tree Lupin,** which comes from the Californian coast. It carries a smaller version of the well-known Lupin type of flower-spike in sulphur yellow, palest yellow, pale purple or white, according to variety. The Tree Lupin's remarkably quick growth makes it very useful in new gardens for furnishing the spaces between more permanent and slower-growing species. It is very beautiful at its best, when the delicately formed, divided, evergreen leaves and yellow flower spikes make a pleasing combination on a bushy young specimen that has been well pinched back in the early stages to induce a good framework. All too soon the Tree Lupin gets top-heavy and, inevitably, wind-damaged, dying probably in the following winter from the effect of some frost which it would easily have withstood in its younger days. Fortunately it is easily grown from seed sown in a reserve bed. The seedlings do not move well except when small enough to be moved with a ball of soil adhering to the roots. A rich soil is not desirable as the plants then make excessively soft and rank growth which does not stand the winter so well. They will grow quite well on moderately limy soils.

Perhaps the best position for the Tree Lupin is as a lawn specimen where it can share a little bed with a young specimen tree. Being a Legume, far from robbing the soil of its companion it will advantageously shade the ground and the infant's stem, also helping the young tree materially in later years, when, the top of the now time-expired Lupin being removed, the sapling will profit by the nitrogen stored in the roots of the corpse. Another good association is provided when the white and pale yellow varieties are planted near large existing plantations of *Rhododendron ponticum*. The purple flowers of the latter seem to take on a bluer tone and the combined effect of these two common shrubs is really very enjoyable.

In June the last and the most valuable section of the hardy hybrid deciduous Azaleas, known as the "Ghent" Azaleas, come into flower. Derived from hardy species and flowering so late, they are almost immune from damage by spring frosts. Thus, with the really hardy category "A" Rhododendrons, they provide one of the first absolutely reliable massed flower effects that are safe from damage by spring frosts. As with other members of the family, grafted plants are weakly and troublesome and, until layered all round, difficult to make into large permanent bushes. Bought as layers, on the other hand, they are easily encouraged to send up strong basal shoots by liberal feeding, and these are advantageously drawn out, arched over and pegged down, when they will usually produce young branches all along their length and thus eventually make fine bushes of dense, mounded habit. By June the cold north-east winds, so often a feature of May weather, have usually gone and thus the Ghents have another advantage over the other types of large-flowered hybrid Azaleas, as they avoid weather conditions which quickly spoil the delicate Azalea flowers.

Varieties differ a little, but the bushes are usually seen about 4 or 5 feet high, and of equal or greater breadth, when well grown and on their own roots. In the shadier places they grow much taller, but are thinner in habit. Under good conditions their ultimate size is about 8 feet high and 12 feet across. Their cultigen name is *R. gandavense*.

Some good varieties are:—

'Aurore de Royghem', orange yellow and pink.

'Chieftain', apricot and brown-orange.

'Graf Alf von Nipping', Chinese yellow and vermilion, another old variety of unexcelled beauty of form.

coccinea speciosa ***, orange-red.

Daviesii ***, white, yellow flare. Very fragrant.

'Devon' ***, deep vermilion, A.M. 1952, the finest red, see illustn. p. 145.

'Dr. Charles Baumann', *, vermilion.

'Fanny', *, magenta-pink.

'Fritz Quihoui', vermilion.

'Géant des Batailles', deep vermilion.

gloria mundi, **, orange-red.

'Mrs. H. White', white, pink and yellow, late.

'Pallas', **, crimson and yellow, very fine.

'Prince Henri des Pays Bas', light crimson, orange flare, late, a beautiful variety.

'Sang de Ghentbrugge', *, deep crimson, rather small flower, late.

'Satan', ***, vivid red, fragrant, superb.

'Volcano', deep red, orange eye, very late.

'William III', *, orange.

'Flamenco', orange, July-flowering.

'Flamingo', pure orange, very late, good autumn colour.

All these varieties, and dozens that I have not mentioned, are extremely beautiful but a special mention must be made of the last named as unfortunately one of the new Knap Hill Azaleas has since been given the same name. The Ghent 'Flamingo' is the older and, as it happens, the more valuable plant as it flowers long after most others are over. The dreaded "June gap" is apt to be a dull moment even in the better regulated gardens unless special care is taken to plant some of the neglected beauties that flower precisely at that time. 'Flamingo' is one of the most brilliant of these and can provide a most lovely effect grouped with *Cornus Kousa* and the rare and precious Japanese Evergreen Azalea so inappropriately named *Rhododendron indicum*.

The other Ghents, flowering a little earlier, are so lovely as individual flowering shrubs and their colours are so effective that, on an acid soil, they can carry the whole garden during their season. Light shade, such as Silver Birches, Cherries or *Cornus Kousa* afford, is helpful in preventing the hot summer sun bleaching the flowers and it is well worth while taking the measures advised, under the heading of the Mollis Azaleas (see p. 117), for soil improvement and exact planting depth.

Gardens on limy soils have to do without the Ghents and make the best show possible with Roses, *Cornus Kousa*, var. *chinensis*, Helianthemums, Cistus, Halimiums, *Cytisus Battandieri*, etc., but few garden plants produce a greater profusion of more vivid, shapely and fragrant flowers than the Ghents and their absence is painfully marked. For the average lime-free garden these are the most suitable of all the large-flowered Azaleas comprised in the groups Mollis, Knap Hill, occidentale and Ghent. Their hardiness and vigour is outstanding and their flowering-time a most convenient one to follow the Japanese Evergreen early section of the Azaleas. I do not know a deciduous flowering shrub that is a more perfect example of all the good qualities combined. Beauty of form, fragrance and colour are added to sturdiness, freedom from diseases and pests and free-flowering qualities that are all that could be desired.

Owing to lack of demand many lovely old varieties are becoming extinct, particularly the more honeysuckle-like, late-blooming, types with flowers of soft but pure colouring and delightful fragrance.

The true Ghent type has even more perfect "drawing" and finish than either the Mollises or the Knap Hills and owing to its denser flowering, is more effective in the landscape than the latter. As they are so near to that superb species *R. calendulaceum*, the Ghents avoid the coarse and hybrid look, having about nine exquisitely shaped flowers beautifully grouped in a close truss of flattened dome shape, the valuable "top flower" filling the centre superbly, with the lovely foliage and attractive habit of the wild species mentioned. I have seen a great many flowering shrubs but I believe that the most beautiful that I know are two superb old Ghent Azalea specimens, 'Aurore de Royghem' and 'Graf Alf von Nipping'. By some, these old varieties are thought to be outclassed today, and no doubt the foot-rule would endorse this, but never, I think, the eye of the lover of beautiful things when comparing them as growing plants. Both are now unobtainable.

The varieties 'Unique', *altaclarense* and 'Nancy Waterer' usually classed as "Ghents" are, in my opinion, "Knap Hill" types and are therefore listed in that section.

The hybrid Azalea varieties having a strong strain of *Rhododendron occidentale* in their composition form another distinct section. They are particularly valuable owing to their ability to grow well in full sun and exposure. Thus placed the Occidentales make rounded, dense, 3- and 4-foot bushes so solidly set with flowers that hardly a leaf can be seen. Their colourings are, however, rather pale and weak. Like their relations, the "Knap Hill" Azaleas, they come under the cultigen group of *Rhododendron albicans*. Most commonly seen are the following:—

> *delicatissima*, creamy blush-pink.
> *exquisita*, creamy white and yellow.
> *graciosa*, creamy pink with an orange flare.
> *magnifica*, creamy blush-pink.
> *superba*, pale pink with an orange flare.

The wild type of *R. occidentale* flowers later than most of these hybrid varieties. It makes a taller and looser bush and the more star-shaped white flowers, with a yellow flare, are in a more open truss. Their fragrance is more pronounced than that of the hybrids. It is a variable species and some forms are much more beautiful than others. In a shady position this charming Azalea is not very free-flowering, so a sunny position is best.

The race of **Clematis,** members of the Buttercup family, provide several fine climbers flowering about midsummer in addition to the large-flowered hybrids dealt with later.

Clematis montana Wilsoni is a Chinese variety of that spring-flowering species, that blooms in June and July. The large white flowers, 3 inches across, have gracefully twisted sepals and are borne on downy stalks. It is now very scarce in commerce.

C. chrysocoma is a Chinese species discovered in 1884 by the Abbé Delavay and introduced to Kew from France in 1910. It is not an ulta-hardy species but is most decorative in appearance with its pale magenta flowers on long stalks in June and later, and golden downy growths. It grew particularly well at Gravetye Manor, in the late William Robinson's garden near East Grinstead, Sussex, where it was allowed to scramble up trees and bushes, succeeding *C. montana* with an almost equal display over a much longer period. It is easily and quickly raised from seeds.

C. c. Spooneri is a Chinese sub-species, introduced by E. H. Wilson in 1909. The 4-inch wide, white flowers with their four regular sepals are very shapely and appear in late May or early June. It is more vigorous and hardy than *C. chrysocoma* but has not such a long flowering season nor quite such a wealth of flowers.

C. c. S. var. *rosea* is a fine pink-flowered variety.

C. macropetala (A.G.M. 1934) is a graceful Chinese and Siberian species. Though described as long ago as 1829 it was first introduced by Purdom for Messrs. Veitch about 1911, and was again introduced four years later by Reginald Farrer. He wrote of it, "Clematis sp. belongs to the Altragene group and is of incomparable loveliness. I only know it in the Ghyll of Tien-Tang (10,000 feet elevation) where it rambles frailly through light bushes to a height of two or three feet and then cascades downwards in a fall of lovely great flowers of China-blue, so filled with petaloid processes that they seem as double as any production of the garden". There is almost a Dahlia-like look about the form of the flowers and the late Ernest Markham called it the "Downy Clematis" owing to the appearance of the young shoots. *C. macropetala* flowers in June and may well be grown in the manner suggested by Farrer's description. It is quite reasonably hardy.

A fine form raised by Ernest Markham is *C. m.* 'Markham's Pink', with slightly larger, mauve-pink flowers and stronger growth.

C. lanuginosa, *C. patens* and hybrids such as *C.* 'Miss Bateman' are also in flower in June. (See pages 173 and 265.)

The Clematis mentioned above all grow well on limy or acid soils and, like other members of the family, are best with their roots in the shade and their heads in the sun.

They may be propagated from seed, but the resulting seedlings are sometimes inferior to the elect seed parent. Layering is fairly successful but, on the whole, the propagation of these Clematis is best left to the specialist nurserymen who provide the amateur with a sturdy young pot-grown plant ready for planting out. Dogs, and especially puppies, are very liable to destroy Clematis unless the plants are safeguarded by strong wire-netting. Care must also be taken to protect the young plants from mice and slugs which have a fondness for the young growths whose safety is essential for the plant's establishment.

Clematis grow perfectly well if simply planted in shrub beds and allowed to ramble about over hardy hybrid Rhododendrons, etc. When treated in this way no pruning is needed.

When starting a young plant, the roots should be soaked and then gently disentangled if potbound and the shoots may have the first inch or two laid in a little channel formed in the soil to encourage them to form their own roots above the graft. Finally the upper stems are pruned off at a foot from the ground to induce bushiness at the start.

Occasionally a really valuable and lovely species or variety gets lost and goes out of cultivation. As stated previously a surprisingly common cause is simply a muddle over the name. This seems strange, but such are the casualties from various causes other than the weather, that unless a shrub is constantly asked for and planted in new gardens it soon becomes practically extinct. If the name is not known, the essential renewal does not take place and only a few survivors in old gardens may be preserved.

This happened to a certain very beautiful **Late-flowering Evergreen Azalea** usually known nowadays as "Azalea macrantha". According to the rules, the correct name of this plant is *Rhododendron indicum*, but a certain Chinese species, *R. Simsii*, the tender greenhouse Azalea, was known under that name, and, when planters who wanted the hardy Japanese species were sent the tender Chinese species instead, the plants died the first winter and thus demand ceased and the true plant almost died out.

As it happens, it is one of the finest and hardiest of this group of spectacularly beautiful Azaleas. E. H. Wilson reported it as "a prime favourite in Japanese gardens". George Forrest described it as "very beautiful by the sides of mountain streams in June with its large bright red flowers contrasted with *Iris Kæmpferi*". *R. indicum* was first described by Sweet in 1833 when it was introduced to a Chelsea nursery. After about 1850, as it would not "force", a fatal drawback in those days of innumerable hothouses, it was soon superseded by the tender Chinese species *R. Simsii* which is still the basis of the florists' potted Azalea. The true *R. indicum* persisted, however, in its double variety— var. *balsaminæflorum* ("Azalea rosæflora") which has always enjoyed considerable popularity owing to its very unusual, double, rose-like, salmon flowers (pale Vermilion H.C.C. 18/2). The best single-flowered form is, however, much superior for general planting, having large, full flowers 2¼ inches across and very freely borne with five broad, rounded lobes of a rich orange-pink (pale Scarlet H.C.C. 19/2) marked with Crimson on the upper lobe. In habit the shrub is low and mounded and a notably vivid evergreen, hence its popularity in Japanese gardens, and it bears clipping well. The lanceolate leaves are of a dark green with a faint reddish cast and the slender shoots are covered with appressed chestnut-brown hairs. In autumn many of the leaves turn crimson.

R. indicum is probably a degree hardier than most of the true "Kurumes", but is rated as about the same hardiness as *R. obtusum* forms "C". Thus we have a beautiful evergreen shrub of convenient size (usually a yard across and half as high ultimately) with notably large flowers of the most highly popular colouring. But this is not all, for in addition to these virtues the plant flowers after most other Azaleas are over—right in the "June gap" when most gardens are particularly ready to welcome a brilliantly coloured and beautiful flowering shrub.

R. indicum is not common in the wild, according to E. H. Wilson, who found it truly so only on Yaku-shima island. It is also, however, reported by others from Hondo and other localities. But in the Japanese gardens it is very commonly planted, nearly two hundred named forms being recognised and it is known there as "the June-flowering Azalea".

A further interesting note to add to the scanty records of this shrub is provided by Reginald Farrer. He imported plants from Japan and though he confused it, as was then customary, with the "Azalea indica" of the trade (*R. Simsii*) and therefore expected the early death of the consignment, he reported with delighted surprise† that over a period of five years these Azaleas never suffered and rarely failed to produce abundance of bloom. "And this", he continues, "though they are planted in merely ordinary garden soil, *permeated with lime*, and though quite unsheltered and unprotected." It will be remembered that his garden lay near Ingleborough in Yorkshire which is generally considered to be a distinctly cold district. The italics are mine.

The clones available here today are as follows:—

R. indicum macranthum ("Azalea macrantha orange"). This appears to be very near the "type" but as the wild plant is reported as variable in colour ("bright red to scarlet, sometimes rose red")‡ and this superlative orange-pink form is propagated as a clone, it is proper to give it varietal rank. This is the finest form I have seen with large orange-pink (H.C.C. 19/2) flowers as previously described. It is very free flowering; in June the tip of every branchlet ends in a flower, making a most lovely display of glorious colour. I would place it in the best

† "Alpines and Bog Plants", by Reginald Farrer, Edward Arnold, 1908, p. 29.
‡ "A Monograph of Azaleas", by Ernest Henry Wilson and Alfred Rehder, University Press, Cambridge, 1921, p. 24.

dozen first-class flowering shrubs for small gardens on lime-free soil with a favourable climate.†

R. i. 'Kokin Shita'. This is, in my opinion, either a variety of R. indicum or a hybrid. It is described in the *Rhododendron Handbook*, 1947, as a sub-variety of R. obtusum. 'Kokin Shita' is, at all events, distinctly inferior to the var. *macranthum*. The smaller and more thin and starry flowers are the same colour, but they quickly fade in the sun whereas those of the latter hold their colour comparatively well. The habit is weakly and dwarf, with narrower, thinner leaves. The flowering date is the same.

R. i. 'Satsuki'. This variety is sometimes grown under the name of R. *macrostemon*; that Azalea is, however, listed as a variety of R. *obtusum* in the *Rhododendron Handbook* and is obviously no connection, being described by E. H. Wilson as having "small flowers, minute calyx and long exserted stamens three times as long as the corolla".‡ In habit this variety or hybrid much resembles R. *indicum macranthum* and I find it almost impossible to distinguish them when out of flower, but the flowers are not quite so fine, being very slightly smaller, with narrower lobes and they are only a Crimson Pink (H.C.C. 22/2) in colour. I note that this form does not produce fertile seed, which *macranthum* does, so possibly it has some other species in its make-up as well as R. *indicum*. The flowering date is slightly earlier in its commencement than that of R. i. *macranthum* but owing to its peculiar successional habit of flowering it remains in bloom much later, being still effective in July. This quality places it in the noble company of the Camellias, Chænomeles, *Magnolia Sieboldii*, the H. T. Roses, the Spanish Broom, and the Hydrangeas, plants whose continuous succession of flowers over a long period make them invaluable for certain positions where this trait is necessary. When we have this quality coupled with great hardiness, a dense, bushy habit and evergreen foliage of singularly attractive appearance we recognise a great garden shrub (see illustration page 208).

No doubt breeders will one day give us an Azalea incorporating the best characteristics of 'Satsuki' and the fuller and more brilliantly coloured flowers of *macranthum*. In the meantime I raise my hat to R. i. 'Satsuki'. It is widely found in commerce and I have had it from half a dozen different nurseries, sometimes under the name of R. i. 'Pink'. A less attractive form with petaloid stamens also appears under the latter name which it may well retain. The flowers open all at once and it tends to fade in the sun. 'Satsuki', on the other hand, stands up

† See climatic zones, p. 25.
‡ "A Monograph of Azaleas", by Ernest Henry Wilson and Alfred Rehder, University Press, Cambridge, 1921, p. 24.

very well to full sun exposure. This Azalea is to be seen in most of the
great gardens where flowering shrubs are an important feature and, of
course, at the R.H.S. gardens at Wisley where, the Curator tells me,
it has signally distinguished itself. One of the objects of this book is to
bring such little-known but absolutely first-class shrubs to the notice
of gardeners. This group has great possibilities for the amateur breeder.

R. i. balsaminæflorum (Azalea rosæflora). This is the well-known
variety with double, salmon flowers shaped like miniature Roses. It is
more dwarf in habit than *macranthum* and in the south-east definitely
needs shade for free growth, and also to preserve the delicate colour of
the flowers. It is a pretty little thing, but of very artificial appearance,
suitable for one of those shady little courtyards attached to houses that,
if the proper soil is imported, can be made so delightful with Ferns,
Camellias, *Hydrangea serrata* and other shade-lovers.

R. i. ' Bungo-nishiki ', orange red flowers, petaloid centres.

R. i. 'Midsummer Beauty', large shapely vermilion flowers, vigorous.

R. i. ' Misomogiri ' appears to be almost identical to ' Bungo-nishiki'.

R. i. var. *crispiflorum* has pink flowers with petaloid centres.

R. i. var. ' Hakatashiro ' has sparse large pure white flowers.

R. i. var. ' Tanimanoyouki ' (' Coral Ivory ') is described as having
salmon flowers with a white zone on the petals.

' Vida Brown ' (*R. i.* × *obtusum* var. *Caldwellii*), a new hybrid, was
shown at R.H.S. Chelsea Show in May 1948 by Messrs. D. Stewart of
Ferndown, Dorset, and received an A.M. in 1960. Each inflorescence
consists of two large flowers 2 inches across or more, one inside the
other. The colour is a crimson-pink and the plants shown were very
free-flowering. On small bushes the flowers appear almost too large
but on more mature specimens they should be highly effective.

' General Wavell ' a hybrid with huge flowers 3¼ inches across of a
pleasing carmine-pink (*indicum* × *Simsii* × *indicum*) is a superb new
variety of compact low habit (A.M. 1959). When this becomes commercially available it will be a great acquisition.

R. i. lasciniatum has, according to E. H. Wilson, a deeply lascinate
corolla.

R. i. variegatum is described as a variety with white and red striped
and spotted flowers, blooming irregularly the year round.

An old Dutch Azalea variety, listed by Messrs. Marchant of Wimborne and others as *illuminata* or *optima*, with large, double, salmon-red
flowers and notably shortened anthers, has a strong look of *R. indicum*
and may, as I suspect, be found to be a hybrid of this species. It flowers
at about the same time as the earliest flowers of the variety *R. i.* ' Satsuki '
but blossoms all at once.

I have no information regarding the large number of garden varieties of *R. indicum* cultivated in Japanese gardens. Even without taking into consideration the Japanese garden varieties of *Hydrangea serrata*, *Pæonia suffruticosa* and other species, there is obviously a very rich unexplored field for the plant hunter waiting there, even now.

As regards cultivation "Azalea macrantha" as it is still known in the nursery trade, seems to have no special fads, beyond a cool root-run, rich in humus, and the usual Evergreen Azalea requirements. My plants grow well on a very high and exposed slope with no protection from the wind or sun other than the usual pegging-down when first planted and the provision of a mulch of bracken. These precautions are, however, essential to protect the younger stems from early autumn frosts, where these occur, as this is the one weakness of this species.

Another fine late-flowering Azalea is *R. Kœmpferi* var. 'Mikado'. This Azalea opens its pale salmon (Azalea Pink H.C.C. 618/1), wavy-edged flowers at about the same time as *R. indicum*. Another variety of *R. Kœmpferi*, named var. 'Daimio', has brighter and larger flowers (pale Fire Red H.C.C. 15/3) which open much later, after *R. indicum* 'Pink', and it, also, appears to be scarce in commerce.

These varieties came originally from Messrs. Veitch's nurseries in Exeter and are extremely valuable for their hardiness and beauty of flower late in the season after the others are over. 'Mikado' and 'Daimio' are perhaps best grown in the shade of distant trees as their delicate flower colours bleach somewhat in the hot midsummer sun, though less so than those of most other varieties of *R. Kœmpferi*. This limits their use a little, but *Cornus Kousa*, with its large white-bracted flowers, *Abutilon vitifolium* with pale Cobalt Violet flowers, and *Sophora viciifolia* with its bluish pea-flowers can offer both the necessary shade and timely complementary colourings.

One of the best arrangements that I have had was when these little Azaleas grew in the shade of one of those late-flowering and unusually blue-toned plants of *Rhododendron ponticum* that was my reward for combing a whole hillside in Surrey covered with feral Rhododendrons. The *ponticum* was eventually pruned and trained into tree form, this being an excellent way of dealing with large specimens of this species. Among the beauties of the new gardens in Windsor Great Park not least are the massive evergreen trees, of perfect garden size, obtained by skilful pruning of the old original woodland specimens of this humble Rhododendron. A good coloured *ponticum* "colour-charts" at about Imperial Purple, but exceptional specimens will be found of slightly bluer tone and they are worth looking out for.

Another variety or hybrid of the hardy, free-growing, wind-resisting, sun-enduring, "fly-proof" *R. ponticum* provides us with one of the loveliest and most unsung of Rhododendrons. There are, it appears, several forms of white-flowered *R. ponticum*, collectively named var. *album*, but this variety, propagated as a clone, is of quite outstanding beauty. I can trace no name for this particular hybrid form (believed to be *R. ponticum* × *brachycarpum*) and, as it is highly valuable in my opinion, venture to propose for it the name of 'Tondelayo', the neglected jungle beauty. 'Tondelayo', then, resembles *R. ponticum* closely in habit and general appearance but the leaves are notably longer, slightly downy at first, narrower and more pointed and of a deeper, less shining green. The flowers open from faintly pink-flushed buds, forming a remarkably fine, open truss about 6 inches high and about 7 inches in diameter composed of about eighteen flowers each perfectly poised on a flower-stalk about 2 inches long. The especially valuable distinction of possessing a "top flower" which fills and crowns the centre of the truss is notable. Each flower stands out separately from its neighbour providing a perfect presentation. The individual corollas are deeply divided into five lobes, the lower ones long and narrow and the upper lobe broader and shorter. The colour is an unusually pure and flawless white with, upon the upper lobe, a feathered flare of brilliant Geranium Lake slightly suffused with gold in the centre. The flowering time is appreciably later than that of typical *R. ponticum* which is usually going over as 'Tondelayo' opens. (See illustration, p. 161.)

Thus it will be seen that we have here a shrub with all the well-recognised advantages of *R. ponticum* but without the disadvantage of the purplish-pink flower colour. It is, in fact, a beautiful hardy, evergreen flowering shrub which the nurseryman can sell with confidence for planting in any garden whose soil is not limy, anywhere in the British Isles. Without an effective name this lovely, orchidaceous flower would merely continue to languish unasked for.

The acid-soiled garden has had plenty of lovely plants to choose from in the preceding pages. It is time to consider some lime-tolerant species flowering in June.

Kolkwitzia amabilis, known in America as the "Beauty Bush", is a twiggy Chinese shrub introduced by E. H. Wilson for Messrs. Veitch in 1901. At its best, which is generally after a hot summer followed by a mild winter, it is very attractive when seen near at hand. It forms a cloud of tiny purplish-pink foxgloves on a bush perhaps 7 or 8 feet high. At a distance it is not very effective, as the colour is just that pale, commonplace purplish-pink that one has more than enough of already —so regrettably ubiquitous is this tint in every hedgerow. But the

freedom of flower can be such, and the form of the little corollas is so
dainty, that it must be rated high as a personality in any garden. Its
flowering in early June is a valuable trait; if it came out in the middle of
May we should not give it such a warm welcome. Being Chinese it will
endure a limy soil and, indeed, is not particular in this respect. It is
perfectly hardy and will even flourish in Denmark.

As regards cultivation, as it is found "among rocks at 10,000 feet
elevation", a situation not liable to cause excessive dryness at the root,
yet with full sun, seems to be indicated, and it certainly grows well
under such conditions and appears to be quite hardy. On the other
hand it is a shrub which takes some time to mature sufficiently to flower
really freely. The fruits are not commonly borne except in very hot
summers, so the best means of increase is by means of fairly soft
cuttings in a sand frame with bottom heat in late summer, but firmer
cuttings will sometimes root in the sand-box.

Few of the **Honeysuckles** are very effective in the garden, seldom
surpassing our own wild species in beauty. The wild Honeysuckle is a
sinister plant, deceiving us with its pretty flowers, whose juices no
Honey bee can ever suck. The innocent Ivy is blamed for throttling
trees, though any careful observer can see that it never constricts limb
or branch, merely running lightly up and along. With the Honeysuckle
it is another story; its steely stems, immensely strong and absolutely
unyielding, disdain the well fortified, mature tree but twine round a
sapling's trunk. When the poor thing tries to grow, the Honeysuckle
refuses to relax its grip by even a fraction of an inch. Thus the victim
can only swell unevenly in a spiral bulge, and, with its growth checked,
the Honeysuckle easily overtops and smothers it, often fatally unless it
can support life by some subsidiary stem. So let there be no question
of allowing Honeysuckles to scramble up choice flowering shrubs or
trees.

A short selection follows:—

Lonicera japonica (A.G.M. 1950) is a very fragrant, almost evergreen,
Japanese Honeysuckle, almost hardy and of great vigour climbing up
to twenty feet or more. The flowers are a pale yellow, opening almost
white, and appear from June onwards over a long season.

L. etrusca, a Mediterranean species with almost evergreen foliage,
and a succession of dense spikes of fragrant yellowish-white, purple-
tinted flowers throughout summer, is one of the best of the more
ordinary sorts. *L. e. superba* is a particularly fine form.

L. americana is a fine hybrid of this crossed with *L. Caprifolium*.

L. tragophylla (A.G.M. 1928), is a Chinese Honeysuckle introduced from Hupeh in 1900 by E. H. Wilson. It has large, yellow, scentless flowers in late May and is one of the most effective and reasonably hardy.

L. sempervirens, the Trumpet Honeysuckle, is an American species and more or less evergreen, with unscented orange-scarlet flowers. Although quite hardy in America (Zone III Rehder, includes New-foundland!), Bean recorded it as not hardy enough for any but specially favoured gardens in the south and west of this country. This is particularly regrettable in the case of *L. s. superba*, a beautiful variety with bright scarlet flowers. Perhaps the form available here is a tender one from the South and a new importation would prove quite hardy.

Certain hybrid forms are hardier.

L. Tellmanniana, a cross between the two previous species, has deep orange-yellow, tubular flowers in clusters in June. It is not fragrant but is quite hardy.

L. Heckrottii is another hybrid, with rich pink flowers, yellow inside, in June. It is quite hardy and a good grower.

L. Brownii fuchsioides has fine scarlet flowers, and this hybrid, (*L. sempervirens* × *hirsuta*) though not as hardy as the last named, is reasonably so in any but a very cold spot. In my view it is the hand-somest of all Honeysuckles and is superb on a whitewashed wall or scrambling up some tall shrub of little value.

L. ciliosa, the western Trumpet Honeysuckle, is quite hardy, growing as far north as British Columbia. The "type" has yellow flowers, sometimes tinged with purple, and the var. *occidentalis* is described as having larger and brighter flowers.

These climbers may be grown with Roses and Clematis on the trellis so useful in small gardens to provide ornamental screens, dividing up the various sections of kitchen garden, playground, fowl-run, etc. in an attractive way. The Honeysuckles are not very particular as to soil, but like a fairly moist root-run. Aphis attack often occurs, and unless the plants are well sprayed with a suitable insecticide growth is liable to be spoiled.

Propagation may be effected by seeds, and cuttings of practically ripe young shoots may be rooted in August under a bell-cloche.

Apart from the great families with numerous related species there are genera which offer only one or two species suitable for the garden.

Raphiolepis umbellata (*R. japonica*), is an evergreen shrub of the Rose family from Japan. It has leathery oval leaves and is of good, compact habit and is said to reach 10 feet in height though usually seen about half that size. In June the fragrant white flowers open in dense panicles on the ends of the shoots. They are five-petalled, upright but Cherry-like and, about ¾-inch across. This Raphiolepis is quite reasonably hardy and will grow well in limy or acid soil in full sun with wall shelter from cold winds. It may be propagated from seeds or by cuttings, if half-ripe shoots are placed under a bell-glass in July.

R. u. var. *ovata* has more rounded leaves.

A tender hybrid form with rose-pink flowers is 'Coates Crimson'.

Penstemon Scouleri is one of the few shrubby members of a large American family, comprised mostly of herbs. Opening in June, the slaty-blue, foxglove-like flowers are about an inch across and 1½ inches long. *P. Scouleri* is a native of Western North America and seldom exceeds 1 foot 6 inches in height. Thus it takes a useful place among the many dwarf shrubs that may be associated so effectively and conveniently in the small garden. It contrasts well with the pale yellow Helianthemums and the similarly coloured Potentillas and the white Cistus that also enjoy the sunny places on freely drained soils, whether limy or acid, that suit the little Penstemon so well.

It is easily increased by July cuttings and, though shortlived, grows and flowers cheerfully enough in all but our coldest and dampest summers. In mild winters the leaves remain but turn purplish.

P. heterophyllus (A.G.M. 1929), with Flax Blue flowers, is also shrub-like and fairly hardy and *P. cordifolius*, a Californian with a looser, more straggling habit, atoned for by scarlet flowers in late summer, is less hardy, but possibly worthy of a position at the foot of a south wall in a mild garden with a limy soil which precludes the planting of the full selection of flowering shrubs available.

P. Menziesii is a prostrate, creeping species with tiny evergreen leaves and blue-violet flowers, 1½ inches long, in June. A white form, var. *albus*, also occurs.

All the Penstemons are easy-going as regards soil so long as their position is warm and well drained and they can be grown from cuttings or seeds in the usual manner.

In freedom of flowering only the Evergreen Azaleas equal *Cornus Kousa*, most spectacular, in our climate, of a large family whose members are mostly somewhat dull shrubs from the gardener's point of view. (A.M. 1958.)

C. Kousa, from Japan, forms an unusually picturesque tree about 20 feet high, with tiered branches that bend gracefully down at their ends when loaded with the massed white flowers in June. These flowers are composed of a central green button which is actually a group of true functional flowers, surrounded by four large white petaloid bracts. In good forms they appear to be broad, shapely, waxy, pure-white petals, sometimes with a pink tip; in bad ones they are more bract-like, thin, coarse-textured, twisted, narrow and stained. Seedlings vary greatly and, in addition, individual plants even vary the shape of their flowers a little from year to year according to the rainfall and the feeding they receive. In the form of the flower and its spacing on the branches there is a wide range in quality, so that named, clonal forms of shapely flowered individuals are much to be desired. Unfortunately, apart from seed-raising, it is rather a difficult plant to propagate.

It is also a shrub that needs some care, and a well-enriched soil, acid and carrying plenty of humus. Furthermore a young plant can be killed by the jobbing, self-styled gardener with a couple of ill-timed snips with his shears. I once heard an old legend to the effect that the Persimmon, *Diospyros Khaki*, was at once killed if cut with the knife. Curious, I therefore secured a healthy specimen and, as soon as it was well established, cut it down with my big Saynor. For some years the plant apparently revelled in this unusual treatment annually and I then let it grow in peace. Years later I absentmindedly snipped a few unwanted side branches off a seedling of *C. Kousa* and was surprised to see it die almost at once from the injury in the most unmistakable way. I had the legend wrong; it probably referred to *Cornus Kousa* and the K was about the only part that I had got right! I would therefore strongly advise anyone growing this lovely Cornel against pruning it in the younger stages. A knock with a motor mower or a wheelbarrow will also, I find, kill young plants more often than not. A wise precaution is to surround the sapling with a ring of wire netting, and an injunction against pruning may well also be attached on a conspicuous label.

C. Kousa flowers when about 6 feet high but needs a few more years of expansion to begin to make its real effect. The best position, I think, is as a lawn specimen, as the habit of the little tree is very attractive and both the red fruits and the rich autumn leaf colour are highly effective, additional features. Although the flowers are only white in colour, their delightful design and, literally astounding profusion, make it undoubtedly a first-class shrub and it has a spectacular beauty of form as a flowering tree of a high order. The effect is also one that lasts well, the bracts starting life in a greenish tint and slowly maturing to white as they enlarge. They remain in beauty for a long period and then, as with that other Japanese, bract-flowered beauty, *Hydrangea* 'Grayswood', begin to turn crimson.

C. Kousa var. *chinensis* is a Chinese form that is very similar in appearance. So similar indeed that I, for one, have great difficulty in distinguishing seedling forms. On the whole, according to Colonel F. C. Stern, V.M.H. (*R.H.S. Journal*, LXXII, Pt. 9, p. 371), the Chinese variety has broader leaves and bracts. But I must admit that the specimen with the broadest bracts that I have ever seen was a pure Japanese seedling. The weakness of the Chinese is, perhaps, that a large proportion of seedlings have flowers with coarse, ill-shaped, twisted bracts, though these are sometimes very large. This increase in the size of the individual flowers is very far from being an added beauty as it is their countless numbers, the exquisite finish of their form and their superb presentation that makes the densely packed great flat sprays so enchanting. On the other hand, the Chinese trait of lime tolerance is of the highest value, making it a "first-rate garden plant, perfectly hardy and easy to grow in any good soil with or without lime" (*loc. cit. sup.*).

For my part I would advise special care when planting these lovely Cornels. For lawn specimens we prepare, by bastard trenching, a circular bed 6 feet in diameter and add abundant humus which we mix thoroughly with the existing soil. This bed has to support the growth of the sapling to full treehood and, from then on, immense crops of flowers over a long period of years. After the bed is fully made, a part may be turfed over again, perhaps so as to leave only a well-mulched 3-foot-diameter bed for the little sapling at first. But the work will have been done before it is too late. I have observed fine trees, 20 feet high, going back badly and in a dry year producing immense crops of wretched, short-lived flowers, each only an inch across instead of nearly 4 inches. Much can be done by regular mulching and top-dressing, it is true, but it is never the equal of a bed really well made at the start which is also kept mulched and thus provides a large "sponge" affording a continuous supply of liquid nourishment, and even this should be reinforced by heavy watering in April and May.

As summer injury to the wood often causes at least the death of the branch, great care has to be used in staking and only a proper rubber-covered tie or a nylon stocking (page 29) should be used.

Few shrubs provide more beautiful or long-lasting sprays for house decoration, but the risks I have already mentioned should not be forgotten.

As regards their value in the garden scene I would go so far as to say that these Cornels are almost indispensable for the June flowering-shrub-garden. They lend themselves well, too, to delightful associations with other shrubs. In lime-free gardens "Azalea macrantha" (*R. indicum macranthum*), Azalea 'Daimio' (*R. Kæmpferi* var. 'Daimio') and the invaluable old Ghent Azalea 'Flamingo' will be found highly effective as companions, and perhaps, to intrigue the curious, *Hydrangea serrata* ' Grayswood ', whose floral bracts undergo the same curious colour changes, may occupy the shady side. In the warm gardens of coastal counties, *Leptospermum Nicholii*, with its clouds of little red flowers, may be risked, and, on chalky lands, *C. K.* var. *chinensis* may be neighboured, on the sunny side, by the pale cobalt-violet flowers of Sophora or Ceanothus.

The great Cistus family is composed of Cistus proper, white, and occasionally purplish-pink flowered, sun-loving evergreen shrubs from south Europe, and the yellow and red flowered Halimiums and Helianthemums. So far as my experience goes none of the Cistus are absolutely hardy, but most will usually survive for some years if planted in sunny, well-drained spots with the roots protected by a mulch of bracken in winter. They have the useful quality of growing well on lime.

Cistus laurifolius is probably the hardiest of all, but is also one of the least decorative in habit. As generally seen it is a gaunt, lanky evergreen about 6 feet high, with dark, often sooty-looking leaves.† The wild-rose-like white flowers typical of the family are produced from June onwards and are 2 or 3 inches across and, like those of most Cistus, usually drop their petals in the afternoon. It is one of those shrubs that need constant nipping and pegging down when young to induce a sturdy and bushy habit. When this is done a vastly improved appearance is attained. It is a good, hearty garden plant and easily increased by cuttings or seeds, and is really the only member of the family that could be called "reasonably hardy." It is, however, one of the least decorative.

C. ' Silver Pink ' (*C. laurifolius* × *villosus*) is about the best pink Cistus, having two-inch wide pale Tyrian Rose flowers, nicely presented and held until evening, on a sage-green bush about two-and-a-half feet in height.

C. *corbariensis* (*C. laurifolius* × *salvifolius*). This decorative hybrid with its dark leaves and profuse white flowers, gives us one week of intense display and is one of the hardiest.

C. *ladaniferus*. This has the noblest flower of all, owing to the massiveness of its fine golden central boss and the boldness of the great maroon brush-mark that decorates each petal. But there is only one almost four-inch-wide flower on the end of each twig and this

† The sooty mould is the most serious enemy of the Cistus. Spray at once with fungicide.

drops at noon, and its habit is straggly and its constitution weak. Thus the hybrids offer us better value in the garden.

C. cyprius (*C. laurifolius* × *ladaniferus*) is one of the best of the larger hybrids, being hardier than the noble *ladaniferus*, and holding its flowers longer. These are borne in clusters instead of singly, and are nearly 3¾ inches across, white with a lemon centre upon which is blazoned a big maroon blotch for each petal. This is a long-lived plant. Only a few years ago I noted that William Robinson's old plant at Gravetye, that I knew as a boy, was still in good health.

C. lustanicus decumbens (*C. ladaniferus* × *hirsutus*). This is probably the most effective of all Cistus for the garden and is a handsome, compact 3 ft. × 5 ft. evergreen bush with 2¾ in. white flowers with a small maroon blotch at the base of each petal, appearing continuously from midsummer to frost. (See illustration, p. 209.)

C. populifolius is a bushy shrub four or five feet high, with vivid green leaves and handsome white flowers. It is not one of the hardiest. An illustration of a particularly fine specimen occurs in "The Flowering Shrub Garden", by the writer (*Country Life*, 2nd ed., 1947).

C. aguilari maculatus (*C. populifolius lasiocalyx* × *ladaniferus*). This fine hybrid has 3¾ inch white flowers with a good maroon blotch and holds its flowers into the afternoon. A big bush of six feet or more is soon built up.

C. obtusifolius (*C. salvifolius* × *hirsutus*). This is the most free-flowering and compact of the Cistus with pure white flowers. It forms a low dense bush about two feet by four and flowers almost continuously. Indeed, it seems that *C. hirsutus*, an undistinguished but particularly hardy white-flowered species, bequeaths remarkable free-flowering qualities to its offspring.

C. verguinii (*C. ladaniferus* × *salvifolius*) is a hybrid with a more dwarf habit of growth and white flowers with a dark centre of maroon and yellow, but is not hardier than *C. ladaniferus*.

C. albidus is a particularly pretty Cistus with white-felted and white-edged leaves and pale purplish-pink flowers. There is also a white-flowered variety.

C. crispus has purplish-pink flowers and is of low habit.

C. crispal 'Anne Palmer' (*C. crispus* × *Palinhaii*) bred by Major Collingwood Ingram was awarded the Reginald Cory Memorial Cup for 1960. A greener, stouter bush than ' Silver Pink ' with shapely flowers of Tyrian Rose, this should prove a useful new hybrid when it becomes generally available.

C. monspeliensis is a dense, rounded bush, as hardy as any, with narrow leaves and white flowers in clusters which open over quite a long season. A hybrid, *C. florentinus*, lasts until evening.

C. villosus is a variable species, usually with purplish-pink flowers, and one of the least hardy, but the ease with which it grows from seed largely compensates for this weakness. *C. parviflorus* with grey leaves, a dense bushy habit and rather small pale pink flowers, has suddenly and surprisingly proved itself to be perfectly hardy in even the coldest gardens, being undamaged there in January 1963 or during the even more destructive winter of 1968/69.

C. 'Sunset' is reputed to have the warmest pink flowers of the family (they appear to be the same colour as those of *C. pulverulentus* but I have not checked this), and a dwarf and compact habit of growth. Its parentage is not known for certain, but by some it is thought to be a hybrid of *C. villosus*; others consider it merely a form of *C. crispus* in which they also include *C. pulverulentus*. The flowers last until sunset.

C. purpureus (*C. villosus* × *ladaniferus*) (A.G.M. 1927) forms an aromatic-leaved bush 3 or 4 feet high with purplish-pink (Fuschsia Purple, H.C.C. 28/1) flowers with a deeper blotch in the centre. These are borne in clusters and make quite a striking effect when seen close at hand, but the colour is not a very attractive one and the plant is not one of the hardiest.

C. Skanbergii has greyish-green foliage and inch-wide, pale rose-pink flowers and is quite attractive in a quiet way though not outstandingly hardy. It is a natural hybrid of *C. monspeliensis* and *C. parviflorus*, introduced in 1929 from Greece.

C. Palinhaii (A.M. 1944) is a newly introduced species from Portugal. It is a dense, low, spreading bush less than 2 feet high with thick, shining, very sticky leaves, and 4-inch-wide, solitary, terminal flowers with pure white crinkled petals and "a conspicuous corona of golden stamens".† Unfortunately it is not very hardy and is subject to sooty mould.

C. 'Elma' (A.M. 1949) is a fine white (*C. Palinhaii* × *laurifolius*).

C. 'Paladin' (*C. Palinhaii* × *ladaniferus*, A.M. 1946) is even more beautiful with profuse and shapely white flowers with maroon and yellow centres produced in one burst of flowering, otherwise it might even surpass the more robust *C. lusitanicus*.

As regards the cultivation needs of the Cistus, the open, well-drained, sunny position required has already been indicated, but pruning and pegging-down at the start are helpful to induce a busy habit which helps to protect the stems and prevents wind-rocking. Cuttings and seeds are ready methods of increase and few insects seem to trouble the family. Thus their white flowers, shining from dry banks, may

† *R.H.S. Journal*, LXIX, p. 311.

economically complement the more troublesome and exacting Roses, or temporarily drape a verge which the lower branches of a nearby permanent evergreen will one day cover. The Cistus do not move well and so are best planted out from small pots directly into their garden positions, preferably in spring after the time of frosts is past.

The great asset of the Cistus is their ability to make quick and abundant flowering growth on hot, bare, poor-soiled, dry places which few other shrubs would enjoy. They will even grow under Pines so long as the sun can reach them. The white or purplish-pink flowers are valuable because they appear after the spring beauties are over, but, being so fleeting, they are not to be recommended to those who enjoy their gardens chiefly in the afternoons or evenings.

For the rapid furnishing of new gardens, the temporary filling of spaces between permanent shrubs, and for that fascinating new development—the shrub-rock-garden—they are admirable, but no reliance, of course, should be placed on their permanence. As an example, when our old shrub garden was first installed, on a virgin site, almost all kinds of Cistus were planted. Twelve years later the permanent shrubs had filled their spaces nicely and the specimen flowering trees were grown nearly to perfection, but all Cistus, except the indomitable *C. laurifolius*, had succumbed, and the permanent shrubs had spread their green skirts over the vacant ground, as planned.

Thus in the making of new gardens such transient beauties as Cistus, Brooms of the *C. scoparius* section and Tree Lupins have their essential part. They act as temporary tenants or caretakers of the ground, helping to keep it decorated, clothed and fertile until it can be taken over by the permanent ornaments.

Fuller information regarding this family may be found in "A preliminary Study of the Genus Cistus", by Sir Oscar Warburg, M.A., *R.H.S. Journal*, LV, Pt. 1 and "Cistus Hybrids", by the same author, *R.H.S. Journal*, LVI, p. 217.

The **Halimiocistus** are interesting examples of healthy hybrids between two closely related genera. They are only to be recommended for warm sandy or limy gardens but in such places they are so free-flowering and attractive that they are worthy of mention here.

Halimiocistus Revolii (*Cistus salvifolius* × *Halimium alyssoides*) is a rare and very dainty little natural hybrid from the south of France with a continuous succession of exquisite little white flowers stained with yellow at the centre. It holds its flowers until late evening and is the most effective of all these hybrids, but sadly tender.

H. Sahucii (*Cistus salvifolius* × *Halimium umbellatum*) is a low, rather sprawling evergreen with relatively large, shapely, white flowers. It is quite effective among the hot colours of the garden Helianthemums but it has not the persistence in flower of the last or its charming bushy habit, at its best in a Close Boskage bed where it seems quite hardy.

H. wintonensis (*Cistus salvifolius* × *Halimium lasianthum*) has very striking, tricolour flowers, 2 inches across, with the white petals blotched with maroon and having a yellow base, sadly tender.

This group consists of delicate and charming little evergreen shrubs for warm perches among rocks. A hard winter often kills them and they are, anyhow, seldom very long-lived, but they are among the most interesting furnishings for suitable parts of a new garden where more-permanent and slower-growing shrubs will eventually need their space.

A delightful family of evergreen shrublets flowering in the June gap is that of the **Helianthemums** (A.G.M. 1926) and their close relatives the Halimiums. Although ubiquitous they are seldom given the serious attention that, in my opinion, they deserve. To the plantsman, the garden varieties are too mongrelised to be interesting botanically, perhaps, but for the shrub gardener who believes that the garden as a whole must come first, they are highly important. For we have here a range of dwarf evergreen shrubs of excellent habit, reasonable hardiness, very wide soil tolerance and varied and brilliant flower colouring, making their effect just at the moment when many gardens are duller than in the depths of winter. After all, even in the British climate, fine days when the garden should be enjoyable are more likely to occur in June than in December!

The progenitors of the garden varieties are *Helianthemum glaucum* from Southern Europe and *H. appenninum* and *H. nummularium* (*H. vulgare*) natives of Britain, with white and yellow flowers. The garden varieties differ in habit from small-growing types with brilliant, shining green leaves to larger and more straggling growers with grey, downy leaves. The typical specimen forms an evergreen cushion over a foot across and with care will more than double that size.

There are a large number of varieties† and among the best are:—

'Apricot', bold orange flowers.

'Ben Affleck', large orange flowers with a deeper centre.

'Ben Attow', large primrose-yellow flowers with a deeper centre.

'Ben Fhada', vivid yellow.

'Wisley Pink', good grower.

'Ben Ledi', crimson-maroon flowers.

'Ben Mare', orange flowers with a red centre and good foliage.

† See *R.H.S. Journal*, 1926, pp. 119-123 and 1927, p. 84. Also the standard work, Sweet's *Cistineæ*, 1825-1830.

'Ben Vane', terracotta-orange flowers.
'Ben Venue', vivid red flowers.
cupreum, flowers of a coppery tone.
'Magnificence', Geranium Lake.
'Miss Mould', fringed vermilion.
rhodanthe carneum, flesh pink flowers.
'Supreme', intense crimson, early.
'The Bride', white flowers and grey foliage.
'Wisley Primrose', soft yellow.
'Highdown Apricot', pale but lovely.
'Highdown Red', small but vivid
'Arpeggio', pink with a red eye..

There are also a number with doubled flowers as follows:—
'Alice Howarth', deep pink.
'Rose of Leeswood', rose.
'Snowball', white.
'Jubilee', pale yellow.
'Fireball', red.
'Mrs. C. W. Earle', crimson.
'Golden Ball', rich yellow.
tigrinum plenum, orange.

In addition to the above garden hybrids, there are a number of species of Helianthemum and the closely related Halimium well worth growing in warm dry gardens where their timely flowering may succeed the bulk of the spring flowerers and complement the shade-loving, late-flowering kinds from sunny knolls nearby.

Helianthemum canum (*H. vineale*) is a tiny native shrublet, forming a little mound a few inches high with bright yellow flowers. It is quite hardy but so small that it needs looking after carefully.

H. glaucum is a Southern European species with yellow flowers and greyish leaves. From this many of the glaucous-leaved garden varieties are probably derived.

H. lunulatum is a charming, fragile little evergreen, often shaped rather like the glass dome of an old-fashioned clock, with intense Canary Yellow flowers with an orange spot at the base on little stalks in June and sometimes into July. A flower rises and opens daily for each little cluster until all are gone. It comes from the mountains of Italy.

The **Halimiums** are a very valuable but little-known family containing many first-class shrubs for the garden.

Halimium ocymoides (*Helianthemum algarvense*) (A.G.M. 1932) is a delightful Portuguese shrub of dense bushy habit usually about 1 foot

6 inches or 2 feet high. The delicately formed flowers, in separate, erect panicles, are rich yellow with a very dark purplish central blotch and over an inch across, and the leaves are silvered with a white fur, giving a grey-green effect to the bush. It is not very hardy but a plant of charming personality, especially valuable for gardens with limy soils where dwarf flowering evergreens are scarce.

H. halimifolium. This species is rather similar but is a taller and more slender grower, with bright canary yellow flowers with a small chocolate blotch at the base of each petal. On the whole, while both species are attractive, *H. ocymoides* is the finer of the two, making a more compact grey bushlet in the winter. It is reasonably hardy but succumbs sometimes, when old, in a hard winter.

H. lasianthum (*Helianthemum formosum*) is an outstandingly fine species from Portugal, forming a low shrub with horizontal branches. The flowers, which open in succession, are 1½ inches across and bright canary yellow with a chocolate blotch at the base of the petals. The leaves are silvery on the under side. It is the hardiest and most long-lived of this group and makes a shrub of good but rather open habit, about 2 or 3 feet high and more in width, maintaining its evergreen foliage well in winter. Its brilliant flowers are effective on June and July mornings.

H. alyssoides has pure yellow, cupped flowers and greyish leaves. The habit is dense and cushiony, but rather coarse, forming a mound about 1 foot 6 inches high and 3 feet across. It flowers over a long period from early June onwards, but presents its flowers less gracefully than the preceding.

H. × 'Farall', (*lasianthum* × *atriplicifolium*) has more massive, greyer foliage and larger, unmarked yellow flowers on a four-foot bush.

H. umbellatum is an evergreen of erect, rosemary-like habit with white yellow-centred flowers among reddish young growths. It is not very hardy and requires a warm spot.

The Halimiums, Helianthemums and Halimiocistus are ideal shrubs for planting among dwarf Brooms in the hotter parts of rocky slopes where moister and more sheltered parts may be planted with evergreen Azaleas, Lithospermum and alpine Rhododendrons. While maintaining the character of the planting they provide a succession of flower of brighter colouring than that of the Heaths, enabling us to cut out those dingy magenta pinks that quarrel with all pure and vivid flower colours.

They will grow on limy soils; indeed, many are found on limestone formations, but they grow perfectly well in fairly acid soil so long as the position is sunny, well drained and elevated. The great drawback of the genus is that the plants often drop the petals of their flowers as soon as they are pollinated. Opinions differ as to the advisability of pruning and shearing back after flowering to aid compactness. Some species seem at times to suffer from this treatment. Pegging-down, on the other hand does, I think, achieve the object even better and can never do any harm. Cuttings of most kinds strike fairly readily, and seeds, even of the garden Helianthemum varieties, are quite a good method. In the latter case the particular variety will not come true, of course, but the plants obtained are often very attractive.

The **Weigelas** are not of very great value as regards their effectiveness for the small garden, but they flower in June and July and as they will grow in alkaline conditions, are therefore of some interest for gardens with limy soils whose owners do not wish to be troubled with more exacting plants. The true species of Weigelas are generally less effective than the garden hybrids and, even with these, the tubular flowers are too sparse and do not last very long, and the colouring is not really brilliant enough for a coarse shrub often 6 to 8 feet high and of equal width.

The following is a selection of garden varieties and hybrids :—

W. ' Abel Carrière ' (A.G.M. 1931) has large pink flowers.
W. ' Bristol Ruby ' (A.M. 1954) is a very good red.
W. ' Conquête ' has deeper purplish-pink flowers, 2 inches across.
W. ' Espérance ' has pale pink flowers of a warmer tone than most.
W. ' Eva Rathke ' is not so vigorous in growth and has dull, deep crimson flowers. Unlike the others, it does not do well on limy soils.
W. ' Le Printemps ' has large, pale crimson-pink flowers.
W. ' Newport Red ' has deep crimson flowers on a more dwarf-growing plant than most.
W. ' Mont Blanc ' has large, creamy-white flowers.
W. ' Variegata ' has pretty variegated leaves, fls. pink.

The chief merit of the Weigelas is that they will put up with poor conditions and neglect better than many choicer shrubs and at least provide some colour in June.

They will, mostly, grow on limy or acid soils in sun or shade with equal cheerfulness. Pruning is not necessary, but the oldest branches may be removed after flowering occasionally, so as to keep the shrub on fairly young wood. Cuttings may be struck in the sand-box in late summer.

Very different in character and as rare as the Weigelas are common, *Zenobia pulverulenta*, from the S.E. United States is a curious peat shrub of irregular, thin, arching growth with strange and rather lovely flowers. It was introduced long ago and has been an inhabitant of a few gardens for forty years or more. The leaves and young shoots have a curious blue-white bloom and this contrasts pleasingly with the white flowers, like very large Lilies-of-the-valley, in late June. They make no great display but the plants are very attractive individually.

Z. p. var. nuda has leaves of ordinary green and smaller flowers.

Z. pulverulenta needs a peaty soil and may be increased by July cuttings, or even seeds sown as described for dwarf Rhododendrons.

Another solitary member of a small family flowers in June, *Abutilon vitifolium.* This Chilean shrub, introduced in 1836, is unfortunately rather tender and so only to be recommended for the coastal counties and the south and west. In such places, in a sheltered spot shaded by distant trees, it is often very beautiful, growing, in time, from 6 to 15 feet or more in height. The wood is soft, and among the large, downy, greyish-green, vine-like leaves the Mallow-like, pale cobalt-violet flowers appear in groups on the ends of the twigs in late June. There is also a white-flowered variety which contrasts well with the pale violet " type ", (A.M. 1961).

It is easily increased from seeds of which a good crop is generally produced. It will grow in either limy or acid soils equally well and though beautiful in flower, has little decorative value at other times. In sunny and draughty situations the Mallow Bush, as it is sometimes called, often drops its flower-buds unopened. It is not a long-lived shrub, even in its native home, and is a miff, being apt to die suddenly when least expected.

The great race of Philadelphus, now included with Deutzia in the family of Hydrangeceæ, with deliciously perfumed, but merely white, flowers hovers on the borderline of the first-class category. The greatest asset of the "Syringa", if I may use for it this charming old name unfortunately belonging, in fact, to the Lilac, is its blossoming time of late June when, so often, it alone provides the flowers of the roadside garden shrubberies. Many of the varieties are somewhat ugly in habit, or have a poor flower presentation that is not decorative, but some are lovely in all respects, except that of winter furniture. The species vary in height from 2 to 15 feet.

According to Mr. H. G. Hillier, a leading authority on the genus (Tree and Shrub Conference 1938), there are about forty species known.

but, owing to hybridisation, their exact identification is often a very difficult matter.

Philadelphus coronarius, the common south European species, with small creamy-white, very fragrant flowers, is notable for having a yellow-leaved garden variety—var. *foliis aureis*, which can be highly decorative when grouped among other shrubs with unusually coloured foliage.

P. Delavayi is an "umbrella name" under which shelter a great number of forms, many of which, I know to my cost, are of no value whatever. But there are also some really good forms and among these *P. D.* var. *nymansi* appears to me a particularly fine Philadelphus. Flowering in early June, the inch-wide, cup-shaped flowers, in racemes of about eight, appear among the large, furry leaves that are covered with a glaucous bloom. More desirable still, in my opinion, is another form, 6 feet or more in height, also raised at Nymans, which flowers in late July with a great profusion of fragrant flowers. It was described and figured in *The Flowering Shrub Garden*, 1st edition 1938, by the writer, but is not in commerce. *P. insignis* is probably the best available substitute.

P. pubescens (*P. latifolius*), from the S.E. United States, is the finest of the species in flower in late June and is commonly found as a big shrub often 15 feet high in old gardens. The white flowers are not so powerfully fragrant as those of *P. coronarius*, but carry sufficient perfume to be highly agreeable. It is an admirable shrub for large gardens or wherever there is plenty of room for it to be allowed to grow freely. In the small gardens the choicer hybrid varieties give a much better return.

P. incanus is a useful Chinese species owing to its late flowering, being usually at its best in late July. It has hoary leaves and fragrant cup-shaped flowers in clusters of half-a-dozen or more.

P. microphyllus is of dwarf, dense habit with solitary, fragrant flowers, an inch across, in June. It is often very disappointing as to freedom of flower.

P. argyrocalyx, an attractive species from New Mexico, possibly a sub-species of the preceding, was first introduced only in 1922, and has fragrant, usually solitary, white flowers $1\frac{1}{4}$ inches across. It is less tall than many, attaining about 6 feet at most. In habit it is singularly graceful, the arching shoots of the previous year being set with rows of the large and handsome flowers.

P. pekinensis var. *brachybotrys* was the label attached to a fine, but regrettably almost scentless, new Philadelphus with enormous round flowers exhibited in 1948 by Colonel F. C. Stern of Highdown. The wild species is said to be small-flowered and of no great beauty, so this variety is exceptional.

P. grandiflorus (A.G.M. 1923) is the scentless North American species with 2-inch-wide rather narrow-petalled flowers singly or in threes on the ends of the branchlets which has produced many hybrids in which traces of these characteristics appear. It seems to me to lack the most valuable quality of its genus, and, like so many of the Philadelphus species, is hardly good enough as a flowering shrub for the small garden.

There are a number of superior hybrid varieties such as 'Coupe d'Argent', 'Voie Lactée', 'Norma', 'Atlas', 'Conquête' and 'Rosace', with large single flowers, sometimes 3 inches across, usually only slight fragrance, and, often, a somewhat gawky habit. They are all useful shrubs for planting in odd corners to add fragrance to the garden air, but a bed planted up solely with them is a winter eyesore that their summer flowers cannot redeem.

P. insignis (*P. pubescens* × *californicus*) is a fine hybrid of the larger kind, making a graceful bush perhaps 10 feet by 10 feet. The fragrant, single, cup-shaped flowers, with overlapping petals and handsome centre of golden anthers, are borne in panicles in July. Thus the succession of fragrance can be kept going very pleasantly if one has the old *P. coronarius* to start it, P. 'Belle Étoile' to follow and *P. insignis* and *P. incanus* to end up with.

P. Lemoinei erectus is a graceful, small-leaved, and small-flowered variety of twiggy, upright, but bushy habit about 6 feet high. The cloud of little fragrant flowers is very attractive. Curiously enough, if seedlings of almost any Philadelphus are grown they will often be found to be of this type though not quite so fine. The great French firm of Messrs. Lemoine of Nancy who have produced so many splendid varieties of Lilacs, Peonies, Hydrangeas and other plants, were also responsible for the first hybridisations in the Philadelphus family. This produced a whole new race of charming garden shrubs of which the above is an example.

Another group of Philadelphus is that of the purple-centred varieties. Among these P. 'Beauclerk', with small leaves and large, broad-petalled flowers with yellow stamens, and 'Sybille', with orange-scented, purple-centred flowers, are outstanding, but the most beautiful of all Philadelphus, in my opinion, is the variety 'Belle Étoile'. (Illstn. p. 145). This forms a graceful, twiggy bush about 5 feet high of unusually good habit for a member of this genus, with large, rather square, fringed, white flowers with a purplish centre and a delicious fragrance. They are carried with an unusual grace which makes 'Belle Étoile' a first-class flowering shrub for late June and remarkably fine as a lawn specimen.

Among the double-flowered forms the well-known and strong-growing 'Virginale' (A.G.M. 1926), whose buxom appearance suggests a rather fuller life than the French adjective conveys, is outstanding. The habit, with unwise and niggling pruning, can be downright ugly, but when left to its own devices, or when entire branches only are occasionally cut right down, this can be quite passable and the flowers are so large and handsome that it is quite a fine sight in the more highly gardened parts of the grounds. Its appearance, however, does not consort well with more natural plantings, where it looks as jarringly out of place as Hortensias in a wood or Calceolarias on an alpine precipice. Such garden-type, artificial-looking varieties at once make the surroundings look merely unkempt, rather than natural and wild.

'Bouquet Blanc', about 3 feet high, has smaller double flowers in clusters and is very sweetly scented. Having a compact bushy habit it largely avoids the artificial appearance of 'Virginale' and looks well anywhere where double flowers are acceptable.

'Girandole', 'Albâtre', 'Glacier' and 'Enchantment' are other double-flowered varieties, the last-named being one of the latest to bloom, with dense, crowded spikes of small flowers. 'Manteau d'Hermine', with cream-coloured, fragrant, double flowers, is notable for a dwarf habit of growth that makes it one of the most suitable for cramped places.

As regards their placing in the garden, the poor winter landscape appearance of the Philadelphus makes their use in quantity in prominent positions inadvisable. Apart from the virtues of 'Belle Étoile' as a specimen, they are best in odd corners where they may scent the air and complement neighbouring plantings of more colourful shrubs.

Their quality of indifference to soil conditions makes them particularly useful in limy gardens and their virtual indestructibility makes them suitable for places where more vulnerable treasures would not be safe.

They may be propagated by seed, which usually gives a small-flowered progeny, or by cuttings of hard wood in the sand-frame in February or, best of all perhaps, by layers.

A June flowerer that is much more exacting as to soil requirements is *Kalmia latifolia*, the Mountain Laurel or Calico Bush, an evergreen from the United States. In its native land it is reported sometimes to reach 30 feet in height but mature specimens are usually only about 8 feet high in this country. In the open the bush is fairly dense and rounded in form and in June appear the clusters of frilled, cup-shaped, crimson-pink, speckled flowers three-quarters of an inch across. In this country, unless the shrub is in full sun, it is seldom as free-flowering as could be desired and the habit is rather loose. On the other hand when fully exposed, it is often very beautiful near at hand, though in most forms the colouring is so weak that it plays no great part in the summer garden landscape.

K. latifolia requires an acid soil with plenty of leaf-mould to grow well and, in my view, full sun to flower well. It is perfectly hardy, making a fine display at the Arnold Arboretum which has a much colder winter climate than any part of Britain. If crowded in among other bushes it is often lacking in symmetry and shy of flower, the best position being as a lawn specimen or among dwarf shrubs. Seed is the easiest method of increase.

K. l. myrtifolia is, I think, a far finer form for the small garden than the " type " and a mature specimen in full sun forms a superb 3-foot dome of pale crimson in late June, when it is most appreciated. It is quite first class and a notable treasure for the lime-free garden.

K. l. ' Clementine Churchill ', (A.M. 1952) is the crimsonest Kalmia I have ever seen and was the result of seed-raising from the deepest coloured plants for a number of years. Unfortunately the difficulties of propagation restrict the distribution of this fine variety. Of late years Kalmias have lacked the moisture at the roots that they must have in the growing season.

The propagation of the Kalmias from cuttings is difficult. Even when assisted by hormone treatment they are very slow to form roots, although a fair percentage will do so eventually with this aid. Layers are more certain for the amateur, but they are also often very slow to root. Seeds, on the other hand, are quite an easy method, following the procedure recommended for dwarf Rhododendrons on page 90, but one cannot be certain of reproducing either an extra rich-coloured form of the common species or the superlative variety *myrtifolia* by this means. The flower colour, being a pale tint of crimson, is what is often called peach pink and this varies in depth though not often in hue. Seeds should be taken from the deepest coloured form available, otherwise most of the seedlings will be found to have flowers of a very pale colouring.

The deepest ordinary form is sometimes distinguished as *K. l.* var. *rubra* (see illustration opposite) and the palest, having flowers that are almost white, as *K. l. alba*. Alfred Reeder described another variety, *obtusata*, as being of compact habit and slow growth, but it does not appear to be in cultivation in this country.

Requiring similar soil conditions, *Bruckenthalia spiculifolia*, a small heathlike evergreen from the mountains of S.E. Europe, 6 inches or a foot high with rosy, open-mouthed, pitcher-shaped flowers in June, joins up the low-toned, pinkish sequence of flower of the Heaths. It is

Potentilla Farreri

Kalmia latifolia rubra

Styrax japonica

Hydrangea macrophylla 'Vulcain'

a pleasantly bright and vivid green in winter and may be increased by seeds, carefully sown as advised for dwarf Rhododendrons (page 90). Cuttings, as for Heaths, can also be grown.

From these minor treasures we turn now to one of the greatest, yet one of the most exasperating of garden shrubs; a plant having the very highest qualities but also the most regrettable defects—the **Rose.**

The finest Roses for appraisal as flowering shrubs for the garden include many garden hybrids the details of whose original ancestry are lost in the mists of antiquity. The most important of these ancestors, whose "blood" must be in every good garden Rose because it alone carried the genes of perpetual flowering, is a certain red Chinese Rose.†

Now the Roses, like the Camellias, the Tree Peonies, the Hydrangeas and now, alas, even the Rhododendrons, have been bred for a different purpose to that for which we shrub-gardeners wish to use the plants. They have been bred primarily for appraisal as cut flowers. Efficiency, of course, demands specialisation and the greater the efficiency for the one purpose the less for another entirely opposed. Consequently it is not among the winners of prizes for cut blooms that we may expect to find flowering shrubs of beauty as such. Quite a different specification is required when we want to see the Rose as a lovely growing bush, densely aglow with flowers at intervals from midsummer to first frost. There are, of course, some Roses ostensibly bred "for garden decoration", but unfortunately the majority of these fail lamentably for one reason or another to measure up to our particular requirements.

It is not everyone that finds altogether beautiful the peculiar shape invented for the very double exhibition Rose, with its high centre and very thick stalk to ensure that the monstrous bloom is seen in profile as it stares up at the sky. In any event, it is too artificial in appearance to consort with more natural-looking shrubs, and the earthy, rectangular mess, set with snags and stumps, that so often constitutes the "Rosebed" is a six months' eyesore that cannot possibly be tolerated, even behind the dense Yew hedge generally used to screen its ugliness from our sight.

Can Roses be grown effectively as flowering shrubs without concentration-camp treatment in these awful beds? This is the question the artist-gardener asks. The only authoritative answer is that of the plants themselves and it will be found that all those that are really good,

† "Notes on the Origin and Evolution of our Garden Roses", by C. C. Hurst, Sc.D., Ph.D., F.L.S., *R.H.S. Journal*, LXVI, p. 242. See also *Hortus Sempervirens* by J. S. Kerner, t. 114, Vol. X (1804) for a fine coloured illustration of this historic plant.

Q   E.F.S.

healthful garden plants will, as might be expected, grow to perfection, so long as their pest-control requirements are attended to, in the verges and bays of beds of other flowering shrubs or as lawn specimens.

A plant can only produce so much petal material, so we must decide whether we want this in the form of a reduced number of flowers, each having a lot of petals, or in the form of a greater number of flowers, each having only the minimum effective number of petals. For the decorative *shrub*, I think we want the greater number of "single" or "semi-single" flowers. Fortunately, there is a fine selection of these available in all the usual Rose colours.

Now as to the habit of the shrub, must we suffer the almost herbaceous, snaggy-looking, "leggy" plants which are put up with, as a matter of course, in the "Rose-bed"? The answer is that provided we do not insist upon the individual flowers reaching the maximum size for the variety, and provided that we feed and protect the plants with the assiduity essential to grow any Rose well, many varieties will make large, healthy, shapely bushes with an almost permanent framework that will last for years. Eventually, perhaps, they carry too much old wood and if they are then cut right down to the ground, will reform themselves nicely in a couple of seasons, given a little thoughtful pinching and tying-out to ensure a well-spaced foundation framework.

Good cultivation is admittedly the keynote in forming fine shrubs from garden Roses, and good results cannot be expected unless this matter is carefully attended to. A widespread misconception is that Roses prefer a clayey and even a limy soil. Actually they do not, they become martyrs to "Black Spot"; what they like about the chalklands is the free drainage always given by a subsoil of this nature, not the alkalinity.

According to one of our most successful exhibitors and breeders of Roses[†] an acid soil, about pH 6 and very rich in humus, is the ideal. I find that Roses that are kept heavily mulched with fallen leaves grow quite well enough in a very sandy soil as acid as pH 5·50, a figure which I like to aim at, as it pleases the Rhododendrons that precede the Roses and ensures blue flowers on the Hydrangeas whose duty it is to complement them and to succeed them when their first flush of bloom is over. A turf-loam, made simply by rotting down turves until the grass and weeds in them are dead, is, I think, a particularly favourable medium for Roses and the practice of burying turves well below the roots when planting is very effective. Our shrub-rose has to decorate the garden for many years with the minimum of fuss and bother and

† Bertram Park, "Some Modern Roses", *R.H.S. Journal*, LXXIII, Pt. 1, p. 18 *et seq.*

this precaution, and the addition of plenty of humus to the topsoil, will make certain that it can do so effectively.

Next we must consider the requirements of the Rose as to aspect. The plant is very definite in its preference here; the aspect must be fully exposed to sun and air, but very violent winds are, of course, harmful, as indeed they are to all shrubs that are expected to grow 4 or 5 feet high.

Thus the optimum conditions we have arrived at for our Roses have, we find with some surprise perhaps, a remarkable resemblance to those suitable for our hardy hybrid Rhododendrons and Azaleas and for our Hydrangeas. But the aspect requirement is slightly different; the Rhododendron likes the lightly dappled shade better than the full day's sun and is grateful for some tempering of the full blast of the wind. The Hydrangea does not mind the wind but its delicately tinted flowers are sometimes shrivelled by sun. Our beds, however, have usually a sunny and a more shaded side and this difference is just enough to please all three of these splendid garden shrubs, if they are given their preferred aspects.

What the Rhododendron family is in spring and the Hydrangea in late summer, so is the Rose in midsummer, the king. Difficult as it is to select the best from the hundreds that just fail to provide the perfect shrub for one reason or another, the immense variety makes them adequate collectively.

Already, I am sure, breeders seeking the mammoth prize bloom have put many a perfect shrub-rose on the bonfire. I would venture to give a tentative specification for such a variety in the hope that some breeder may give us shrub-gardeners a treat. Let them give us, then, a Rose capable of making a shapely, strong and healthy permanent bush 10 feet across like 'Felicia', an almost indestructible, single flower like that of 'Betty Prior', and a gloriously vivid colour combined with automatic self-dead-heading like 'Border King'. We need not worry about the defect of the over-thick flower stalk, as this will be corrected by the "large bush" method of growing. Needless to say we do not want the flowers to face the sky—so that we only see their thin edges; we want them to look at *us*, so that we see them full-face. The outsides of the petals of Roses are naturally duller in colour and partly obscured by the calyx in the earlier stages.

Another point that will determine our choice of varieties for growing as flowering shrubs and to be viewed as such, is the system of flower production. Some varieties bloom mildly but continuously, others make a tremendous display and then take a short rest, and then repeat. I think the latter type is much the most effective for our particular purpose. This is quite another matter to the "Rose-bed" requirements, let us remember; we are giving first consideration, as always, to the garden scene as a whole. The spring effects are over—our Rose orchestra is tuning up and then, suddenly, it starts. To be as good as what has gone before, and what will follow later, it has got to be very good indeed and no " Ca' canny " policy can be good enough. The rest period will coincide with the full glory of the Hydrangea and Genista effect in July, so we shall not grudge the Roses their quiet time. They will then come again with greater vigour to take a full part in the grand finale in August.

There is an amazing difference in the beauty of flower of the different varieties in distant effect. Some appear as mere lumps of formless colour, and surprisingly weak colour at that, compared with many other flowering shrubs. Indeed, in general the Rose is not so very vivid in colour; it is really rather on the weak side. Some varieties, however, and ' Donald Prior ' is notable for this, have such a presentation as to give a lovely *flowery* effect at a distance. Much can be learnt by study of this important feature at nurseries and trial-grounds. I used to go to the National Rose Society's ground and, standing on the highest and most distant spot, direct an assistant to selected patches of effective mass display. Curiously enough it was for the shapely masses of its bloom on small plants, rather than for its superb deportment as a large shrub and wonderful sprays for cutting, that I first selected ' Felicia '.

As I have said, I do not know a perfect Shrub-Rose, but many varieties have one or other of the necessary qualities.

In recent years the rather sickly Hybrid Teas have moved towards rather less suitable types for growing as flowering shrubs and the Floribundas have tended to become almost herbaceous in appearance with crowded, flat, almost umbelliferous flower assemblages that are quite unsuitable for the shrub beds. Worse still from our point of view, the target of some breeders is to produce flowers of the artificial shape of the Hybrid Tea in multiple heads on the herbaceous-looking plants. Good sensible business men that they are, they are turning out what the Public thought it wanted. But the Public has already begun to discover that the big rose-beds planted with these things are not really any good at all. In June a good burst of flower starts and all seems well. But then the rotting flowers begin to outnumber the fresh ones; Mildew and Black Spot run like wildfire through these unhealthy concentrations, and ferociously armed briar suckers sprout everywhere, and the vision of a dream garden without toil fades tragically away.

Fortunately Nature, with her sportive and ambivalent character, has taken a hand in the breeding to give us shrub gardeners some very lovely little shrub Roses suitable for growing among other shrubs as well as the huge ramping six-footers that the breeders classify under this heading which are really more suitable for single specimen positions in rough places. Or is it, perhaps, as I suspect, that there are unsung poets among the raisers who dream that instead of the ugliest bush in the garden bearing the sweetest flowers, the Rose of tomorrow shall be a lovely verdant dome of green offsetting the sparkling colours of its flowers as a shrub of beauty in its own right? Anyhow, there are some lovely shrubs among the new Floribundas.

Each year I spend a day or so among these new productions and, as a result of study, try out a dozen or more of these varieties on the shrub garden. If they fail they are taken out. Some are sufficiently effective to have remained for a decade and are still playing a useful part in the decoration of the garden. The weakly Hybrid Teas are now best relegated to practical straight rows in the kitchen garden where the beautiful flowers can be conveniently cut off the ugly little plants and take their proper place in bowls in the house.

On the whole, the Floribundas are the best Roses for the shrub beds where singly interspersed among other shrubs of similar size and requirements I find that they do not need the perpetual spraying so necessary in those unhealthful rose-beds.

The following selection have proved their worth:—

' Allgold ', a very neat bush but a muddly flower.
' Anna Wheatcroft ', superb vermilion, single, good habit.
' Border King ', vivid cherry-red rosettes, self-cleaning.
' Dairy Maid ', yellow, single.
' Donald Prior ', still the most effective red, self-cleaning.
' Fashion ', orange-pink double, requires dead-heading.
' Firecracker ', carmine, single, requires dead-heading.
' Orangeade ', orange-red, showy.
' Paprika ', vivid red, bushy habit, free-flowering.
' Sunny Maid ', vivid yellow, single.
' United Nations ', warm, pink, semi-double.
' Vilia ', lovely orange-pink, single, neat bush.

These all have bright and attractive colours that play a fine part in the garden landscape. They are mostly about three feet and thus intersperse nicely among the Rhododendrons and Hydrangeas of the third rows.

There are a number of big bushes too large and rampant for the shrub beds that are admirable as single specimens set in the grass where they can be managed much more easily. Popular among these are those known as Hybrid Musks. In fact the foliage and habit show us clearly (and research bears this out) that, in reality, they shared the same ancestral species as the Polypoms—*Rosa multiflora*—a white-flowered oriental climber. They seem to have nothing whatever in common with *Rosa moschata* with its pale green stems, pale blue-green leaves and positively alarming vigour. Mine has enveloped a telegraph pole and looks as though it could easily engulf a pylon. Be this as it may, some of the old "musks" are still unbeaten and are included in the following section for specimen bushes. Here are a few that are outstanding for positions where there is not room for a 6 ft. × 8 ft. specimen but where a bush of a width of four feet would be right. (For other Roses species see p. 198.)

'Charming Maid', single, orange-pink.
'Cocktail', single, red, yellow centre, long-lasting.
'First choice', single, vermilion-scarlet.
'Golden Wings', shapeliest fragrant yellow single.

These can also go among the larger shrubs in the beds if desired as they are of neat habit. Then, for places where there is plenty of room for big bushes that can almost look after themselves, the following are worthy of note:—

'Aloha', (climber), double pink.
'Bonn', carmine, double.
'Felicia', shapely, fragrant double pink flowers.
'Firedance' (low climber), carmine-red, perpetual.
'Maigold' (low climber), orange-yellow, fragrant.
'Nevada', white, single.
'Penelope', single or semi-double, blush.
'Prestige', double red.
'Réveil Dijonnais', orange-carmine single, perpetual flowering.
'Scarlet Fire', red, single, an exquisite flower.

There are larger bushes and the new Kordesii "Parkroses" are highly interesting. Examples are:—'Parkdirektor Riggers', blood-red, semi-double, nice open centre, free and perpetual; 'Ritter von Baumstede', very deep pink, full flowers, in clusters; 'Zitronenfalter', vivid yellow. These all have extra healthful vigour and make stalwart bushes such as one longs to see forming a beautiful, life-saving barrier on the centre zones of dual carriageways where they could arrest runaway cars more safely than harder objects.

The above selection are perfectly suitable for growing interspersed with Hortensias in the verges and bays of beds whose evergreen centre planting is formed by Japanese Azaleas or hardy hybrid Rhododendrons or, in limy soils, other flowering evergreens of garden type. The more natural-looking single-flowered varieties consort best with the Lacecap Hydrangeas similarly backed by Evergreen Azaleas or by Rhododendrons of less pronounced garden type. Among the almond-

green young leaves of the Hydrangeas in spring the ruddy young growths
of the Roses are highly decorative against the background of the bright
Rhododendron flowers and their dark foliage. The stronger-growing
Roses may also be grown as large lawn specimen bushes with delightful
effect.

As regards colour schemes, the most effective that I know is when
the yellow, white and orange scheme is interlaced with the Cambridge
and the Royal blues of the Hydrangeas and the stronger yellows of
Genistas. When this comes off, the July effect is as vivid and lovely as
that of the Azaleas in May. In the first few years, in important places
near the house, the display may be reinforced with annual plants,
always the best temporary trimmings among shrubs. In sunny spots
deep purple small-flowered Petunias are also particularly effective and
the delightful combination remains gay and colourful until the first
hard frosts. Following the unusually mild winter of 1948, the Petunias
revealed their true character as tender flowering shrubs, by flowering
profusely from hard woody branches in 1949.

On limy soils we cannot have blue Hydrangeas, and then we may
intersperse the red and white varieties of these among the Roses and let
the late Ceanothus hybrids and Clematis ' Perle d'Azur ' provide the
blue among Genistas backed by Choisyas, evergreen Barberries and
Escallonias.

There is a prevalent idea that Roses require clay and that they
cannot be well grown in sandy soils. But I believe that it is simply
a question of supplying the plants with sufficent wholesome water
without waterlogging and so drowning the roots. On our sandy
slopes Roses grow perfectly under very wet conditions with water
running round them all the time but in the drier parts away from the
streams they are noticeably weak.

With ever increasing building and development the water-table is
continually lowered and the continuous destruction of trees throughout the country further reduces the supply of soil water. The usual
spring drought is no sooner well under way than the Local Authorities find it necessary to ban the use of water for garden purposes.
Thus our Roses suffer unless we have an old well that can be utilised
with an electric pump or have arranged storage of that best of all
types of water for plants—rain-water. The best way to do this is to
have cylindrical tanks on good foundations running right up to the
height of the gutters. We then have sufficient pressure, without the
cost of pumping, to supply the water by gravity wherever it is
wanted.

As to the vexed question of pruning, before I dare to speak I must
repeat that the shrub gardener's target is quite opposed to that of the

ordinary rose grower and my method would doubtless not suit his requirements at all.

What makes the rosebush, when pruned in the usual manner, unsightly to our eyes is the snaggy, bare base and, above all, the unnatural-looking angles of the pruned branches, with their new shoot duly sprouted from the outward bud below the cut. My method, which was suggested by the plants themselves and not by any human being, is never to cut a shoot anywhere but at the base and to do so only when that shoot appears to be too old to be useful. Flowering young shoots from the base are religiously *not cut at all* after flowering, only the seed heads are removed. The idea is *not to stimulate* a new shoot from a flowered stem. Good feeding and cultivation stimulate the Rose to grow and if it is not incited to make secondary new growth from a shortened stem it will often make it right from the base, and this is what we want it to do.

Much depends on the vigour of the basal "burl" and this is always treated with great respect, and surgical care is taken to keep it healthy and clean of all dead snags and exactly positioned just below ground-level. The worst of the Rose is that those horrible briar suckers from the stock so often cause the gardener dangerous and painful wounds. Thus there is no more valuable product of the home propagator than the trouble-free, wind-firm Roses, grown from cuttings, that no money can buy.

Not all Roses respond to this method, I admit, but quite a number do very well indeed and the principle at least secures the most comely and well-furnished shrub possible. Some kinds tend to make long growths, and these are gently arched over and tied down in a natural-looking curve to suit the furnishing of the bed.

Occasionally an old Rose may die when moved, but usually if the plant to be moved is then and there cut down to within a few inches of the stump or base and this is pared clean of all dead wood with surgical care and the patient is then at once very firmly planted with the burl just below ground-level, more often than not that Rose will make a fine new top and provide as good a display as any hard-pruned young plant in the garden. It is useless to move a Rose without cutting away the top. Few shrubs respond more spectacularly to a mulch of fallen leaves than Roses. Plants growing in almost pure white sand, kept mulched, are far more vigorous than unmulched plants growing in heavy loam.

Many of my buxom Roses, smiling in their beds among other shrubs, were old stumps that have been moved several times. The age of a Rose is simply the age of its oldest wood. If it gets worn out it means, I think, that either the variety or its cultivation is at fault.

In the critical first growing season of a Rose daily vigilance is needed to protect the vital new shoots from pests. One or two concealed caterpillars or a few bunches of aphis can be fatal, and with a delicate patient I prefer the finger and thumb to any chemical insecticide.

For the house walls the great **Climbing H.T. Roses** are unbeatable. The reason for the wretched performance of the usual wall Rose is almost invariably that the unfortunate plant has been merely half buried, with its roots still twisted up in a bunch, in the appalling rubbish filled in around the foundations by the builders, when the house was built. It is remarkable that such plants survive at all. It would be much better to install one climber properly, by excavating and carting away the rubbish and replacing it with a couple of barrowloads of turf loam, than six, merely stuck into the existing, impossible, growing medium. Properly planted,† fed and tied-in, almost any of the climbing H.T.'s will cover the front of a post-war-sized house in a reasonably short time and produce the effect of a vertical bed of Roses that will be a sight really worth seeing.

Ramblers, that is to say varieties of *R. wichuraiana* parentage, are not suitable for walls. They need the air blowing through them.

I do not find there is so very much difference, of effect on the Rose, in the various aspects of walls. The main point is to choose a flower colour which will best suit the tone of the building material. At the worst, it is not difficult nor, moreover, very expensive, to alter the colour of—say—a repulsively red wall, to a reasonably quiet grey by the mere application of a single coat of tinted cement-and-sand slurry put on with a whitewash brush in dry weather.

As for the method of tying and training, there is nothing better than inch-square oak trellis or wiring the wall completely with vine-eyes (iron driving pegs with a hole for the wire) strung with strong wire in such a manner as to form 2-foot squares. With this support the Roses can almost be left to their own devices, once the initial tying-out in fan formation is achieved. Another good method is to fix a big staple firmly in the wall a foot above the plant and then fix a row of them into the wall-plate blow the guttering. When all are connected to the bottom staple a ready-made fan is formed.

Among a wide selection of climbing Roses available today may be mentioned the following:—

'Golden Showers', clear vivid yellow, perpetual.
Clg. 'Comtesse Vandal', magnificent warm pink.
Clg. 'Etoile de Hollande', dusky red, vigorous.
Clg. 'Lady Hillingdon', buff yellow, one fine showing, warm wall.

† See Installation, p. 27.

Clg. ' Mme E. Herriot ', orange-pink, black spot addict.

Clg. ' Mrs. Sam McGredy ', salmon-pink, two displays.

Clg. ' Ophelia ', pale blush pink, vigorous.

Clg. ' Peace ' (Mme A. Meilland), superb after three years.

Clg. ' Picture ', shapely pink; one-and-a-half displays.

Clg. ' Shot Silk ', orange-pink; one-and-a-half displays.

' Danse du Feu ', vivid red, perpetual, slow starter.

' Lady Waterlow ' rose pink, fragrant, perpetual.

' Lawrence Johnston ', semi-double, straw yellow, warm wall.

' Réveil Dijonnais ', carmine and aureolin yellow, perpetual.

Some of the **Rambler** section are so attractive that an opportunity to grow them on fences, or the trellis screens so useful as divisions in the small garden, should not be missed. Such a screen can produce a wall of flowers that can hardly be equalled by any other kind of shrub. The " Barbier " types have all the charm, and none of the disadvantages, of the " old Roses ", in my opinion. They should therefore be especially sought for by those to whom such Roses appeal. On the other hand, they are less effective for brilliant colour at a distance and where such an effect is required the stronger coloured modern varieties should be chosen although they may lack the dainty form and fragrance of the " Barbiers " and, unlike them, must be pruned and retied every year.

The following is a short selection of the choicer Rambler Roses suitable for trellis screens:—

' Albertine ', orange-pink, fragrant, semi-double and superb. Barbier type.

' Aloha ', over-double pink, perpetual and free-flowering.

Clg. ' Goldilocks ', yellow, perpetual, flowers fade untidily.

' Crimson Conquest ', velvety intense red, very showy, one display.

' Easlea's Golden Rambler ', yellow, handsome large flowers.

' Elegance ', clear yellow, large, full flowers, vigorous.

' Emily Gray ', buff yellow, fragrant, good foliage.

' Evangeline ', pink, single, fragrant, July-flowering.

' François Juranville ', warm pink, fragrant, fine foliage and a rapid grower. Barbier type.

' Léontine Gervais ', orange-pink, fragrant, fine foliage. Barbier type.

' Maigold ', orange-yellow, fragrant.

' Meg ', orange-yellow, fragrant, perpetual.

' Mermaid ', pale yellow, poor shape, spottily perpetual with never enough flowers open to make a real display.

'New Dawn', pale pink, perpetual flowering.
'Soldier Boy', scarlet, single, perpetual.

The *wichuraiana* Ramblers flower later, in late June or more often in July. It is best if the flowered stems are removed each autumn. Among the best are:—

'Dorothy Perkins', pink, *wichuraiana* type.
'Evangeline', pink, single, fragrant.
'Excelsa', bright crimson, *wichuraiana* type.
'Félicité et Perpétue', off-white rosettes, almost evergreen.
'Lady Gay', rich rose pink, *wichuraiana* type.
'Lady Godiva', flesh-coloured sport of 'Dorothy Perkins'.
'Mary Wallace', rose pink, semi-double.
'Sander's White', very fragrant.
'Veilchenblau', purple, vigorous.
'White Dorothy', a white-flowered sport of 'Dorothy Perkins'.

All the types of roses mentioned have their place in the good shrub garden. Some of the least prepossessing as to the individual flower such as, say, 'Dorothy Perkins', have the virtue, rare among roses, of making an effective display of closely massed flowers for a fortnight —and this in July when so many gardens, particularly those that are cold and limy, are desperately short of colour.

These Ramblers repay careful pruning, training, spraying and feeding when they show signs of needing it. The difference between well-cared-for plants and those that are neglected is immense. In the small garden the essential screens are ideally provided by inch-square oak trellis, or easily formed of interlaced bamboos, or bought ready-made and at once treated with Cuprinol green-colouring preservative. The usual tiresome erection of larch poles does not really suit these Roses at all as it does not provide a sufficiently spacious support on which to train the growths out fanwise; even tall chestnut fencing or wire netting is better.

Another delightful way of growing the "Barbiers" is over the trees of a derelict orchard. Once well established and trained to the top of the trees, they will cascade down in flowery waterfalls, making a most delightful picture. There is also the system of budding Roses of this type on the top of strong Briar poles so as to form the well-known "Weeping Standards". These are seldom effective unless a vast iron stake is used to support the arrangement and then the whole thing is apt to look too artificial. Compared with those seen in sunnier climates, even the properly built, classic-columned pergola often looks forlorn and out of place in England. One feels that the vast expense incurred would have given a better return even if only half of it had been used to purchase really choice shrubs and flowering trees.

The "Old Roses" have many admirers but I must confess to never having succeeded in getting them to grow with the healthful vigour and freedom of flower characteristic of the more modern hybrids, although the Hybrid Teas in the same beds may have made shoots a yard high crowned with a veritable umbrella of flower buds.

An exception has been the thornless ' Zéphyrine Drouhin ', an old " Bourbon " hybrid with reddish leaves and very fragrant double flowers of a rather regrettable Rose Madder, that too commonplace " cake pink ", so hard to place, which unfortunately colours many otherwise charming flowers. Zéphyrine makes fine specimen bushes and strikes easily from cuttings which are just stuck into the bed, wherever a plant is required, and left there. Actually the tone of pink of ' Zéphyrine ' harmonises quite happily with pale blue Hydrangeas. An extraordinarily cheap bed that I once planted simply by sticking in shoots of both these easily " struck " shrubs made a very fine effect a few years later. ' Kathleen Harrop ' is a pale pink sport.

There are, however, a number of outstanding old Roses that are particularly worthy of note. As one usually sees them, diseased, gaunt, pest-ridden, almost flowerless, and herded into depressing collections, they are not very decorative. Some hold, however, that with care and pruning at the right time, which is, with most, immediately the flowers are over and not in spring, they can, with the frequent sprayings necessary to keep any Rose clean and thriving, be grown so as to be quite attractive as flowering shrubs.†

For the red and white-splashed *Rosa gallica versicolor* I can raise little enthusiasm, but the habit is good and there are, fortunately, self-coloured varieties.

The Damask Rose, 'Madame Hardy', is a beautiful old white-flowered variety with very shapely flowers, symmetrical, double, and opening flat to show the golden stamens, and is generally acclaimed as one of the most beautiful of all the old-fashioned sorts.

' Queen of Denmark', a fine pink Rose with grey foliage and delicious fragrance, is another notable old variety.

'Tour de Malakoff', with large, typically "cabbagey" flowers of cerise, carmine and purple, is probably the finest of the survivors of the *Rosa centifolia* race, making a strong but "leggy" bush that should

† "Shrub Roses for the Modern Garden", by G. S. Thomas, *R.H.S. Journal*, LXXII, Pt. 6, p. 170 and illustrations.

surely be pegged-down rather than tied up to a stake like a Delphinium, as shown in an illustration accompanying the article cited above.

The "Mosses", cousins of *R. centifolia*, have their followers, and nine or ten varieties are still listed by nurserymen, but they are too vulnerable to mildew for the shrub garden.

In the notes mentioned above it is pleasing to find a word of praise for the curious old Rose 'de la Grifferaie', often found in ancient gardens as the surviving rootstock of a long defunct 'Maréchal Niel'. Its masses of ultra-fragrant cerise flowers, that quickly fade to pale purple, are often very decorative. But, in my opinion, the charm of the old sorts is very perfectly exemplified in the lovely, trouble-free, healthful climbers of the "Barbier" strain such as 'Léontine Gervais' and 'François Juranville' which are described in the section devoted to climbers.

Mention of these climbers reminds us that several members of the **Clematis** family are in bloom in June. Owing to the fact that the most effective Clematis are hybrids of mixed parentage whose peak flowering time generally comes in July, they are grouped together, in a section dealing with their parent species also, in the chapter devoted to that month. (See pages 263–267.)

Another gorgeous climber having a variety that flowers earlier than the normal, in June, is *Campsis radicans*. This variety, *præcox*, and its parent species will be found described on page 320.

But now we must leave the environs of the house where the more sophisticated garden varieties, needing frequent care and attention, are planted. The wilder parts of the garden, where less-domesticated species provide less spectacular and lasting effects with but a tenth part of the work must not be forgotten. Here June flowers should be as plentiful as they were in spring and, for that matter, as they will be in late summer also.

Fabiana imbricata, an erect, rather Heath-like, evergreen shrub from Chile, which really belongs to the Nightshade family (Solanaceæ), is seldom seen. About 6 feet or more across and high, the bush has long, downy, tapering branches evenly set in June with short, slender twigs each terminating in a narrow, white trumpet-flower about ¾ inch long. Unfortunately *F. imbricata* is rather tender and can only be recommended for a sunny position in an elevated garden with a well-drained soil, either acid or limy, in the southern and western counties. It has been well illustrated (Fig. 20, Jan. 31, 1948) in *The Gardeners' Chronicle*.

F. i. prostrata is a dwarf form with smaller leaves and pale mauve flowers, rather hardier than the "type".

F. i. violacea, recently introduced (1925-27) from the Andes by H. F. Comber, is hardier than *F. imbricata* and has pale mauvish flowers and shorter leaves. The habit is more lax and spreading and it makes a wider bush.

Late summer cuttings of side-shoots may be struck under a bell-glass. It is best, however, to lift these when rooted and winter them under glass for planting out in spring.

Chionanthus retusus, the Chinese Fringe Tree, is a deciduous member of the Olive family like the Ash, the Lilac, the Privet and the evergreen *Siphonosmanthus Delavayi*. This species forms a shrub or small tree usually about 10 feet high in this country. In late June the feathery masses of snow-white, very narrow-petalled flowers, in upright panicles on shoots of the current year, cover the tree in quite a spectacular manner in a warm season, much less so if it has been cold and wet. It was introduced from China by Robert Fortune in the middle of the last century, but few plants were seen until about 1880 when it was reintroduced by Charles Maries. It is beautiful as a lawn specimen, in flower at a time when there are not many flowering trees in bloom.

C. virginica, the American Fringe Tree, is very similar, but the slightly fragrant white flowers are borne on hanging panicles densely packed like a fringe beneath the branches.

Both species are better when propagated from layers, as budded or grafted trees are weakly and of poor habit. A good rich loamy soil is required, but no objection is made if this is slightly limy. The Chionanthus move well, like Cherries, and, on their own roots, grow quickly in any sunny spot and are quite hardy.

The midsummer garden has few more spectacularly beautiful decorations than *Genista tenera* (formerly *G. virgata*) and particularly, its near relative *G. cinerea*.

G. tenera (A.G.M. 1923) came from Madeira whence it was introduced to Kew by Francis Masson in 1777. It is a tall shrub, branching low and rising to 9 or 10 feet as a rule, though, by frequent shearing of the young wood when young and after flowering, it can be made to form a dense low bush. Though resembling *G. cinerea* in general appearance, the softer, more numerous, larger, broader, silkier leaves, with a silver edge, the more evenly distributed racemes of flowers, and the abundant seed that is set, usually serve to distinguish it. Young plants of this species are noticeably much more lush and leafy.

In late June or early July the Madeira Genista covers itself with fragrant little yellow pea-flowers, delightful in effect from near or far. Indifferent to soil and asking only for a reasonably sunny spot, it is one of the indispensables of the shrub garden. When out of flower, though deciduous, the mass of green twigs makes young specimens appear as mounds of vivid pale verdure most attractive in the garden landscape. Few young shrubs achieve a more rapid rate of growth and G. tenera is thus particularly valuable in new gardens.

Easily raised from seeds sown as soon as ripe in small pots in the greenhouse, or in spring in the cold-frame, the amateur can soon raise a good stock. The seedlings must be planted out before they become potbound or they will fail to anchor themselves properly. In cold districts plants that are kept sheared back so as to shelter the stems by their own twigginess are safest, and this is also helpful to avoid wind damage which often kills top-heavy young plants. But anywhere in the south G. tenera is hardy enough for any position and Mr. Bean recorded that it had almost naturalised itself in the Kew woods.

Genista cinerea (A.G.M. 1933) comes from South Europe, particularly Southern Spain, and is a lean, tall shrub usually rising on several stems from near ground-level to 8 feet or more. The fine specimen, however, in Cambridge Botanic Garden is, after thirty-seven years, 18 feet high and 25 feet through according to Mr. F. G. Preston of Cambridge. The leaves are small, very narrow, firm and pointed and the racemes of highly fragrant little Aureolin Yellow pea-flowers hang grouped in bunches in amazing profusion in late June or early July. The flowering-time is usually a little later than that of the preceding and the bunched racemes, the small stalkless, narrow, pointed leaves, the thinner habit and the fact that this species rarely or never produces seed in this country, serve to distinguish it from G. tenera which, though probably only a geographical form of G. cinerea, is distinct from the garden viewpoint, but the specific position is obscure.

G. cinerea is one of the most spectacularly beautiful of all summer flowering shrubs and as it will grow equally well on limy or acid soils, should be in every garden. Unfortunately it is still extremely rare owing to difficulties in propagation.

As this leguminous shrub, like others of its kind, does not draw its nitrogen from the soil, it is particularly valuable for giving light shade to Rhododendrons, Azaleas and blue Hydrangeas, where it is desirable

to have the shade-providers growing in the same beds as the bene-
ficiaries. This Genista can sometimes be propagated from cuttings taken
with a "heel" and put under a cloche in July, but I have not been very
successful, nor have many of my nurserymen friends. Seed, which
provides the strongest plants, is rarely formed or ripened here, so supplies of fresh seed from Spain would be exceedingly welcome. By this
means this absolutely first-class flowering shrub could be propagated
in such quantity as to make it an effective feature in every good garden.

G. cinerea is usually just too early in flowering to complement the
blue Hortensias for long, but flaunts its glorious mantle of flower
among the Roses, the reddening, but slowly shrivelling bracts of
Cornus Kousa, the lively masses of crimson-pink of *Rhododendron
indicum* 'Satsuki' and the white avalanches of Philadelphus.

A light, warm, well-drained soil is the most favourable for both these
Genistas, but either acid or limy conditions suit them almost equally
well. Their one weakness is their failure to withstand strong winds unless
planted out from pots before the tap root has become bent. Even then
the young plants should be repeatedly pinched back or a sudden gust
may twist and destroy the tap root. I have lost many fine specimens
from this cause.

On the whole, *G. cinerea* is the more decorative and fragrant of the
two species as it displays its flowers to greater advantage with a better
presentation. In the young stages *G. virgata* looks more attractive, but
as the plants reach maturity the European species indubitably proclaims
its superiority. At the same time, *G. virgata* is so much more easily
propagated that it can be used much more freely as a Wild Garden
plant wherever it can be protected from rabbits.

Much better known, but of more questionable value is *Carpenteria
californica* (A.G.M. 1935), an evergreen shrub of the Saxifrage family
from California, of doubtful constitution and hardiness in this country.
Most specimens have a shabby look owing to winter damage. Miss
Jekyll first flowered this species in 1885 at her famous garden at Mun-
stead Wood near Godalming in Surrey. The fragrant flowers are white,
about 3 inches across, and appear in clusters in late June and the
yellow anthers make an attractive centre. On the whole it is too tender
to be a really reliable investment for the small garden, but good specimens are sometimes to be seen even in the midlands.

A warm sunny spot at the foot of a south wall, with well-drained,
but moist soil, which may be limy, neutral or acid, is the best place for
this species. The plant suffers particularly from the effects of fog which
prevents its being a success near London and other large towns. It may

Genista cinerea

Rhododendron Kæmpferi 'Daimio'

Hydrangea Serrata ' Grayswood '

Hoheria glabrata

be raised from seeds but forms vary widely in the substance and beauty
of their flowers, so that plants raised from cuttings of the best form are
more desirable.

Another shrub that can only be recommended for warm gardens is
Convolvulus Cneorum. It is a beautiful silvery, blue-green, leafy evergreen a foot high and 3 feet across, with fragile, blushed flowers of the
typical shape of its genus, opening successively over a very long period.
Unfortunately it is only hardy enough for the South and West and
needs a warm sunny bank, but it is so decorative in the garden landscape and grows so easily from cuttings struck in the greenhouse, that
I include it here. In warm gardens, whether limy or acid, it is indispensable for foliage effect alone but proper contrast with darker and
warmer coloured bushes, such as *Erica vagans*, Azalea 'Tyrian Rose',
Cistus, clipped common Brooms, *Berberis Thunbergii*, etc., is necessary
to get the full value of the effect. It is often killed by mice.

In association we may plant another silvery-leaved shrub having
rather similar requirements. *Phlomis fruticosa* (A.G.M. 1929), the
Jerusalem Sage, belongs to the Mint family and was introduced from
the Mediterranean in the sixteenth century. In June the small, dense
clusters of yellow flowers appear in the axils of the leaves but they are
not particularly effective. Like *Senecio laxifolius*, this Sage is grown
more for its silvery-grey foliage effects, so attractive in the composition
of the all-the-year-round garden. Unfortunately it is scarcely hardier
than the Senecio or *Convolvulus Cneorum*.

The Jerusalem Sage will grow on limy or acid soils equally well but
requires a warm, sunny position. Cuttings can be struck under a bell-
glass or polythene cover in July.

The **Escallonias** are a race of South American evergreen shrubs of
rather doubtful hardiness. They are, however, invaluable for seaside or
warm gardens on chalky soils, as, except for *E. virgata*, they will support
almost any kind of soil conditions quite well. The flowers are small,
and somewhat coarsely formed and seldom colour the bush solidly,
and the hue is, unfortunately, often of a weak purplish-pink. Thus few
Escallonias really measure up to the specification laid down for inclusion in the first-class category for the small inland garden. The
hardiness of the species is also, with the exception of *E. virgata*, barely
up to the "reasonably hardy" standard according to my tests, many

plants having been killed-back severely by the cold war winters whilst those I list in the "reasonably hardy" category, growing nearby, were practically undamaged. Furthermore, inland, instead of growing more beautiful with age like other flowering evergreens, the Escallonias gradually become shabby and ugly so that they stand out as eyesores in old gardens among shrubs of other species that have reached the full glories of maturity.

None the less, for the benefit of seaside gardens, I list the more effective below, due warning having been given.

Escallonia macrantha, a denser evergreen than most, is useful for seaside hedges. It has rather sparse, crimson-pink flowers throughout the whole late summer period.

E. montevidensis is a tall species that requires the protection of a south wall in most places. The white flowers, $\frac{3}{4}$ inch across, in panicles about 6 inches or more in length have a faint, unpleasant smell, when closely sniffed. It is often at its best in late August and good even in September.

E. punctata is probably the best of the crimson-pink-flowered species and grows fairly rapidly to a height of nearly 15 feet. The habit is loose and the panicles of flowers appear from June onwards.

E. rubra pygmæa (*E. r. uniflora*) forms a compact bush about 3 feet high, as a rule, with small, dull crimson flowers in late summer; it is a "witches' broom" form of *E. rubra.*

E. virgata (*E. Philippiana*) is a "reasonably hardy" member of the family, but not evergreen like the others. It is a rather open-habited shrub about 7 or 8 feet high, with arching branches well covered with the small white flowers in short racemes on the ends of the branchlets in late June.

The hybrid varieties are more effective, on the whole, and somewhat hardier than the species; the following is a selection:—

E. 'Pride of Donard' is surely the finest of all, a handsome compact evergreen bush of 7 feet with profuse bold crimson flowers making an effective display.

E. 'Apple Blossom' is a similar sturdy handsome evergreen bush with large pink flowers, very different to the thin, sprawling habit of the older sorts.

E. 'Donard Brilliance' is a 7-foot variety with larger (up to an inch across), but sparser, crimson flowers with golden stamens. The foliage is bright green and abundant and the habit is elegant.

E. 'Donard Seedling' has pinkish buds, opening white, in June.

E. edinensis (*E. virgata* × *punctata*) is one of the hardiest sorts, with pale crimson-pink flowers opening from crimson buds. 'Slieve Donard' is very similar.

E. 'C. F. Ball', raised by the late C. F. Ball at Glasnevin in 1911, is a taller variety with fairly large crimson flowers.

E. exoniensis (*E. pterocladon* × *rubra*) was bred by Messrs. Veitch of Exeter and is a tall shrub sometimes 15 to 20 feet high, worth consideration as an informal windbreak or hedge. It bears blush-white flowers.

E. 'Crimson Spire' is a new hedging variety of slender upright habit with small crimson flowers.

E. Iveyi chance-bred at Caerhays, Cornwall, is thought to be a hybrid of *E. montevidensis* and *exoniensis*. It is a tall evergreen with large white flowers and very handsome, but a really hard winter usually damages it.

E. langleyensis (A.G.M. 1926), (*E. virgata* × *punctata*?) is another variety bred by Messrs. Veitch of Exeter in 1897. The crimson-pink flowers, on short sprigs all along the arching branches, appear from June onwards. It is one of the finest of the older varieties and hardier than many. If cut back by frost in winter, it often breaks from the base in spring again, and against a wall it is fairly safe.

These hybrid Escallonias will put up with careless planting in unimproved, poor, rough soils, polluted with builders' rubbish, in the most creditable manner. They survive where most shrubs would perish. As the average person who is not much interested in gardening will rarely take the trouble to install a flowering shrub properly at the start, this is a very valuable quality. The nurseryman can sell the plant with less than the usual, all too well-founded, misgivings as to its fate at the hands of the purchaser. The little bush struggles along and usually manages to establish itself in time. For the rougher parts of limy-soiled gardens in coastal districts the Escallonias are in their element; wind does not worry them much, and, though rather thin, they are at least evergreen and so give some shelter to other plants.

Most kinds can be easily struck from cuttings of half ripe shoots in the sand-frame, or even against a north wall.

Pruning-back in spring is helpful to encourage the production of young flowering wood, and as an aid to compactness. Old plants in neglected gardens are usually a sorry sight in contrast to the healthful maturity of other flowering evergreens. Thus, in gardens able to grow better things, their use will be chiefly as temporary fillers whose space will be required by more permanent plants later on.

Caesalpinia japonica is an 8-foot deciduous shrub of great qualities and grave defects. The doubly pinnate (twice divided) ferny foliage and foot-long racemes of canary yellow, red-marked flowers, each nearly

1½ inches across in June and July, are certainly very beautiful. But it is not hardy, it bears the most ferocious thorns and its habit of growth is very straggling. Thus it can only be recommended for a warm corner, preferably against a wall, in a fairly extensive garden. It has no objection to limy soil.

C. Gilliesii, a South American counterpart, is more tender, though it will grow quite well against a wall in the south. The racemes are upright and more compact and the flowers have conspicuous protruding scarlet stamens.

Pterostyrax hispida, the Epaulette Tree, deserves to be better known. It is hardy and reaches thirty feet with large vivid green leaves growing rapidly and soon producing masses of small fragrant white flowers hanging in panicles about six inches long; in June. Von Siebold first described this species, introduced in 1875.

Seeds are the best means of increase and a rich light soil and sunny position suits this species best.

So we have shown, I think that this month offers us abundant material for the decoration of our gardens with fine flowering shrubs. Yet when June ends the wise gardener can feel that he may look forward to an equally fine display of flower later. All this time the July and August flowerers have been perfecting their young shoots of the year that will bear the succeeding flowers. It is just this happy circumstance of growth that provides us with such a full and satisfying succession. There need be no repine for past glories, an equally fine display is yet to come.

It should be pointed out that many of the hybrid varieties of Clematis described in the succeeding chapter are in flower in June. *Potentilla fruticosa* will also have commenced flowering though usually its best display comes later. The unusually early-flowering variety of the American Trumpet Vine, *Campsis radicans* var. *præcox*, described in the next chapter, will also be in flower this month.

CHAPTER VI

JULY AND AUGUST

*Means that the plant tolerates limy soil.

JULY AND AUGUST

THIS period covers the later summer from July right up to the first frosts. Fortunately there is a wide selection of good shrubs available though, possibly, the effectiveness of the flowering during this period is more dependent than any other on a favourable garden climate and a neutral, or, preferably, acid soil. Gardens with such fortunate conditions show at this time massed flower displays every bit as spectacular as those of May. Hydrangeas, Eucryphias, Spanish Brooms, Genistas and Fuchsias carry the garden and on warm walls the splendour of the scarlet Trumpet Vines eclipses all that has gone before.

The elimination of blue Hydrangeas, Heaths and Eucryphias is rather a severe handicap for limy gardens, and of Spartium, Senecio, Ceanothus, Hoherias and Fuchsias for very cold ones. Roses, Hibiscus, Genistas, Clematis, Potentillas, Hypericums, Buddleias and Hydrangea species and those hybrids of crimson and other colourings must therefore receive the more attention and, fortunately, they can provide superb flower effects. A greater difficulty is the dearth of good flowering evergreens for such places. As a result, if the winter scene is to be really good, it may be necessary to use some non-flowering evergreens and this inevitably robs the flower effects of some of their wholeheartedness.

Among shrubs with really large and gorgeous flowers the **Clematis** takes a high place. It is so beautiful as to be desirable for all gardens, but its value is even higher for those having a limy soil which are consequently denied the beautiful blues of Lithospermum and the hardy Hydrangeas. On such soils it is a shrub of the very first importance.

The wild species are, on the whole, less spectacular than the garden hybrids. Among the more important parents are the following:—

Clematis lanuginosa was originally introduced from China by Robert Fortune about 1850. It has very woolly leaves, and large white, or pale lilac flowers nearly 6 inches across in early June and has a somewhat dwarf habit of growth, reaching only to about 6 to 8 feet.

C. florida is a rather fragile Japanese and Chinese species with longer and more wiry stems, smaller, creamy-white or violet flowers in June and July, and glossy, dark green leaves

263

A Japanese garden variety of this species, *C. florida bicolor*, flowers earlier, in June, but is mentioned at this stage for convenience. The stamens are transformed into petal-like organs forming a central rosette of a purple colour which contrasts well with the white petal-like sepals surrounding it. The flowers are about 3 inches across and borne with great profusion. It was a favourite of the late Miss Wilmott of Warley. Var. *flore pleno* is similar, but all white in colour.

C. patens is a Japanese species, introduced by von Siebold in 1836, with pale violet flowers 6 inches across, in May and June. With its hybrids, it is dealt with earlier in the work.

C. Viticella is a free-flowering, 20-foot, south European species with 2- to 3-inch violet or blue flowers and divided leaves, dying back in winter nearly to the ground. The late Ernest Markham, an authority on this genus, estimated that a plant of his that had scaled a holly hedge, bore five thousand fully open flowers at one time. *C. V. alba luxurians* (A.G.M. 1930) is a fine white-flowered variety.

These were the wild species from which among others the following garden hybrids were evolved:—

C. Jackmani (A.G.M. 1930) is one of the commonest and most hardy and handsome of the hybrid Clematis. It was raised in 1860 by Messrs. Jackman of Woking and is said to be a hybrid of *C. lanuginosa* and *C. Viticella*. Identical plants have, however, been long grown in Japanese gardens. The well-known, deep violet flowers are highly decorative, but the foliage turns black and remains on the stems in a very unsightly way in winter. Consequently some study has to be given to the placing of the varieties of this type, so that their unattractive appearance in the dead season will not be too prominently displayed. If grown for the decoration of house walls, the provision of a host-shrub, such as the charming and ultra-hardy *Euonymus Fortunei gracilis* (*E. radicans foliis variegatis*) with its brilliant winter foliage, helps to preserve the Clematis growth and hides many of the blackened leaves. On the whole, in the open garden, the Clematis is best grown and trained up some unimportant tree or bush or so as to decorate a trellis screen in company with climbing Roses of almost any type but the Wichuraiana Ramblers, whose pruning would be dangerously untimely for the Clematis. I once had the most delightful summer effects with this Clematis simply grown on tripods of Bamboo canes in the beds, but the winter effect was unsightly unless the plants were cut down in late autumn instead of spring, and the tripods were removed. Though it is said to be better to prune them in spring the plants usually survived this treatment. Like the others of this section, this Clematis has curious flowers in that they have no petals, the petal-like sections being really sepals, but the design of the flower is none the less exquisite and traditional. As pruning depends upon the group to which the hybrid belongs (see p. 266) the name of the group is mentioned with each variety.

C. J. alba is a white-flowered form, otherwise similar.

C. J. rubra has brownish-crimson flowers.

'Beauty of Richmond' is a fine mauve-flowered variety of the *C. lanuginosa* group.

'Comtesse de Bouchaud' is not a strong grower and has 6-inch, pale purplish-pink flowers over a long season in summer. Jackmani group.

'Ernest Markham' has crimson-purple flowers and is probably the finest of its colour. It is a hybrid of *C. Viticella* parentage.

'Lady Betty Balfour' has flowers, often 8½ inches across, of a deep violet-purple with yellowish-white stamens and is one of the finest varieties for the later part of the season. Viticella group.

'Lady Northcliffe' has deep violet-blue flowers with pale yellow centres in May and June and is one of the finest of all of the *C. lanuginosa* group.

'Huldine' is a very strong grower of *C. Viticella* parentage, blooming rather late in the season, with white, translucent flowers barred and flushed with lavender-pink on the outside, produced in charming sprays with great freedom. Ernest Markham, who bred this Clematis and was in charge of William Robinson's superb garden at Gravetye Manor, East Grinstead, Sussex, always reckoned this the finest as a cut flower for table decoration.

'King George V' is a newer variety with flesh-coloured flowers barred with pink. Lanuginosa group.

'Marie Boisselot' is a very lovely white-flowered variety of the Lanuginosa group with a broad-sepalled, full flower of beautiful form.

'Mme E. Desfosse' has very large violet flowers, sometimes 10 inches across, and is of moderate growth, blooming fairly early in the season.

'Mme Van Houtte' has beautifully formed, white flowers equally large and is also a moderate grower of the Lanuginosa group.

'Miss Bateman' is an early flowerer with white flowers with brown anthers and is a member of the Patens group.

'Perle d'Azur', of the Lanuginosa section, is an excellent August-flowering pale blue, especially recommended for its informal growth and freedom of bloom among shrubs.

'Pourpre Mat' is valuable for being the last to open, deferring its flowering usually until late August. The flowers are a glowing crimson purple and very freely borne. The growth is very vigorous indeed. It is a member of the Viticella group.

'Royal Velours' has deep purple flowers freely produced on a vigorous plant. Viticella group.

'Ville de Lyon' flowers early and also late and is a very free flowering and vigorous variety. The flowers are crimson and particularly effective against light coloured walls. It is rather prone to mildew attack which requires spraying with one of the copper fungicidal sprays or dusting with green sulphur dust when the foliage is moist. Viticella group.

C. 'W. E. Gladstone' has extra fine, large flowers of a blue-lavender shade, with deckle-edged sepals, and belongs to the Lanuginosa group.

The above selection will cover the long flowering season of these glorious-flowered climbers from June or July to frost and the spring-flowering kinds, such as C. *montana*, C. *patens*, etc. combine to cover the greater part of the garden year when flowers are enjoyable.

The Clematis of the groups dealt with here grow best, like most climbers, when their roots are in the shade and the upper part of the plant can emerge into the sun. They do quite well in neutral or acid soils provided that the situation is well drained, and grow excellently in limy soils. Most authorities hold that the Clematis is one of the few shrubs benefited by added lime and they are certainly among the most beautifully flowered shrubs that can be grown in the limy garden. In an article in the *R.H.S. Journal*† Mr. Jackman recommends that the soil should be rich, open, stony and well drained and kept moist by a mulch and that, under very acid conditions, some old mortar rubble may be added with advantage. I prefer, however, not to add any lime. If too much is given Clematis becomes unable to assimilate the necessary mineral trace elements.

Few climbers are more beautiful and effective for the decoration of the trellis, so useful for screening and background purposes. The chief drawback is the constant attention required to train the young growths out in spring, fanwise, for if this is not regularly attended to the plant often gets into a hopeless tangle and wastes its energy in unprofitable growth. When some unimportant shrub or tree is used as a host for the Clematis and there is no question of covering a definite area with decorative growth they can be left largely to themselves once they have been guided up the hosts's trunk or branches. At Gravetye, previously mentioned, they were very lovely grown in this way. At Kew a fine collection is grown up untrimmed oak branches formed into rough tripods by fastening them together at the top.

As regards pruning, all types are best shortened back when they are first planted. The Jackmanii type are best looked over in spring and any dead stems removed, then one or two of the shoots may be cut off about a foot from the ground so that new growth may clothe the base, as

† "The Clematis as a Garden Plant", by Rowland Jackman, *R.H.S. Journal*, LXXI, Pt. 12, p. 349 *et seq.*

otherwise this gets somewhat bare in time. Young plants of all varieties are best cut back to two feet from the ground in their first spring. Varieties which flower on the old wood such as the Patens group (for most of these see under late May, p. 173) and the Lanuginosa group, obviously need little pruning, otherwise the flowering wood is removed. On the other hand, those that flower on the young shoots of the year, like the Viticella group, can do with quite severe cutting-back to encourage new growth. Ernest Markham recommended shortening all growths by half in February, but they grow well enough without.

Mice and slugs are two pests which are so troublesome as almost to debar the large-flowered Clematis from the more outlying and wooded parts of the garden. Breakback traps, set under large inverted flower pots to save the birds, and Meta slugicides are the best remedies.

Propagation, for the amateur, may readily be effected by layering low shoots into plunged pots. The "serpentine" method by which the selected branch is alternately buried and brought out into the air all along its length, is not always successful by any means, but very rewarding when it comes off. The practised seed grower may also sow the seeds and raise interesting young plants, but these cannot be expected quite to equal the glories of the seed parent, which was probably the finest seedling out of many hundreds raised. On the other hand, their health and vigour is better than that of grafted plants.

When installing a young Clematis the precaution of firmly fixing a strong piece of protective wire netting round the lower part of the stems should always be taken. Otherwise the first puppy, or indeed, any dog short of tooth exercise, will inevitably chew them up and destroy the plant.

Provided that the plants are in the fully dormant state the roots may be gently uncurled and spread out when planting. When installing a Clematis against a wall the best plan is to set the young plant carefully and firmly in the ground at the correct depth and about 2 feet away from the wall. Then the lower part of the stems may be gently bent over into a shallow trench formed in the direction of the wall and lightly covered with loose soil. The true variety will then probably form its own roots on the buried portion. Where slugs are to be feared a final spadeful of weathered and sifted coke ashes may be spread round the stems. The mortality among newly planted Clematis is very high but if these measures are taken there is little risk of loss.

The Potentillas or Cinquefoils are admirable garden shrubs for any type of soil, except perhaps a badly drained clay.

Potentilla fruticosa is a small, untidy, deciduous bush widely found in nature in the northern hemisphere, even in England near the High Force of Teesdale. The leaves are divided into about five leaflets and the yellow or white, strawberry-like flowers are an inch or more across. Potentillas start flowering in May, in June, or early July, and they often continue to open a few flowers until summer ends. They seldom have sufficient flowers out at one time to make a really whole-hearted display but are nearly always able to show a fair number. In height they are usually about 2 or 3 feet but the varieties differ greatly in size and flower colour and there are over twenty of them. All are greatly superior to our wild form as garden plants.

Among the more distinct and valuable are the following:—

P. f. 'Elizabeth' is a bold 3-foot bush with the stems and shoots covered with bronzy hairs and clear yellow flowers $1\frac{1}{2}$ inches across. A fine, continuously flowering variety.

P. f. Beesii is similar to *nana argentea* described later, but bolder and slightly larger. (A.G.M. 1957.)

P. f. dahurica is a compact dwarf suitable for rock garden use with inch-wide, pure white flowers.

P. f. Farreri is one of the most brilliant and effective varieties, with vivid Buttercup-yellow flowers, but it does not make such a large and shapely bush as *Friedrichsenii* or 'Katherine Dykes', being rather thin in habit.

P. f. Forrestii is of stout habit and has pale yellow flowers.

P. f. Friedrichsenii is a cross between the "type" and var. *dahurica*, and is an unusually tall vigorous bush up to 6 feet high with dark green leaves and large pale yellow flowers.

P. f. grandiflora. The leaves and flowers are larger than the "type", the latter being yellow and $1\frac{1}{4}$ inches across.

P. f. 'Katherine Dykes'. This is thought to be a cross between *P. fruticosa* and *P. f.* var. *Friedrichsenii*. The flowers are about an inch across and of a soft Canary yellow and open rather earlier than those of most varieties. 'Katherine Dykes' makes a fine large, shapely bush and is one of the finest of all as a garden shrub.

P. f. mandschurica has creamy-white flowers and leaves silvered with dense, whitish silky hairs. It is a dwarf shrub seldom exceeding 1 foot in height.

P. f. nana argentea is a dwarf variety with silvery leaves and small yellow flowers.

P. f. obtusifolia is a free-flowering 2-foot bush with small clear yellow flowers.

P. f. ochroleuca has large pale sulphur-yellow flowers on a sturdy, upright 3-foot bush.

P. f. Purdomii is a late variety about 2 feet 6 inches high with large pale yellow flowers. It was found in Tibet.

P. f. 'Tangerine'. A fine new variety with orange flowers giving best colour in light shade.

P. f. Veitchii. The leaves are a silvery grey-green, and silky haired; the large flowers are pure white; a fine 3-foot Chinese form, particularly notable and opening very early—in May.

P. f. Vilmoriniana (A.G.M. 1926). A fine Potentilla growing up to 4 feet in height with intensely silvered velvety leaves and large creamy-white flowers. A very beautiful variety.

The Cinquefoil is perfectly hardy and, given proper drainage, will grow on any, even on limy, soil; thus it is surprising that it is not more commonly seen. It is a fairly attractive shrub provided that it receives occasional "manicuring" to remove old seed pods and dead leaves, which is essential if it is not to look very shabby in winter. Whilst not really spectacular, it is valuable as a constant bloomer late in the season and always gay and charming except in winter, when its appearance is deplorable. Propagation can be done by seeds, or in the case of special varieties required true to type, by cuttings of fairly ripe side shoots in late summer. If taken with a "heel" of older wood these root very readily. The Potentillas are not particular either as to soil or position but do best in a fairly sunny and well-drained spot.

It is most regrettable that such a beautiful foliage shrub as *Senecio laxifolius* (A.G.M. 1936) is barely hardy enough for any but southern or coastal gardens. A shrubby member of the Composite, or Daisy, family from New Zealand, it makes a spreading four-foot bush of silver grey with the shapely leaves very gracefully presented so that it is always most attractive to the eye while it is in good health. In early July heads of bright yellow daisy-flowers appear but they are of no great ornamental value. Indeed, I soon cut them hard back so as to get more of the young leafy shoots, It is then contrasted with dark-foliaged shrubs or rusty-coloured shrubs such as *Erica vagans*, or when complementing the orange-red of autumnal leaves that this beautifully drawn, silvery shrub makes it best effect. To do this really well, an odd plant or two is quite insufficient—a dozen are needed in the picture, planted singly and generously interspersed, so that the whole foliage effect of the garden landscape is lighted up by the contrasting silveriness boldly interlaced among the deeper tones. It will grow equally well in limy or acid soils and, apart from frost damage, is a good, rapid-growing, healthy garden plant. Fortunately it strikes easily from July cuttings placed under a bell-glass or in pots of sandy soil in the greenhouse and thus, even if a hard

winter kills it, its retention is a practical proposition. Certaintly few
shrubs are more worthy of this trouble, for this Senecio is of the highest
year-round effectiveness in the garden landscape. It requires a sunny,
well-drained, open position; in shady places it grows soft and sprawling.
Rabbits destroy it in winter if they get the chance, so it is not to be
recommended for the Wild Garden, or unprotected places.

Other members of this family, *S. cineraria* with pinnate leaves, and
rotundifolius, a noble, rounded bush of 7 or 8 feet, though both too
tender for most inland gardens, are superb in the sea-wind along the
warmer parts of the coastline.

Santolina Chamæcyparissus, the "Lavender Cotton" is another silvery
bush. It is a shrub of the Daisy family with curious qualities and
curious drawbacks. A well-grown and regularly trimmed plant provides
a plumy mound of silvery-white persistent foliage that is very effective
in the composition when well contrasted with shrubs of suitably varied
foliage tints. The yellow flowers, in July, themselves also contrast
attractively and there is a form with flowers of a much paler yellow
which I have seen in Cornwall which adds greatly to this effect when
associated with the "type". Hardier than *Senecio laxifolius, Convolvulus Cneorum* and *Phlomis fruticosa*, it provides gardeners in colder
districts with a more reliable grey-leaved shrub.

The Lavender Cotton can be divided or struck from cuttings placed
under a bell-glass in July, provided the weather is warm, otherwise
heat is necessary. It is not particular as to soil, growing quite well in
limy soils, but is best in a sunny, open position. After a time the plants
get untidy in habit unless regularly pinched, pegged down, trimmed
and layered. Indeed, it is one of the few shrubs that I would recommend
cutting hard back to the stump every spring if one has not the time to
attend to it constantly.

The common **Lavender**, *Lavandula officinalis* (*L. Spica*) though dear
to us for its pleasant associations and the scent of its flowers and, to a
less degree, of its leaves is, by nature, of rather an ungainly habit.
Clipping every spring keeps it to a reasonably compact form but, all
too soon, it gets shabby and must be started all over again from cuttings.
It is therefore a matter for rejoicing that a compact and naturally
shapely variety of this plant should recently have come to light. This is
L. o. nana atropurpurea or 'Hidcote variety'. It forms a shapely, dense
mound covered with the flowers on their long stalks in July and August.
In colour these are a notably deeper and of a more vivid purple than

those of the old favourite. In other respects it resembles the common Lavender and similarly responds best to a warm light soil.

Among late flowering plants for a wall or bank we may consider *Berberidopsis corallina,* an uncommon, rather tender, evergreen sprawler, or climber. It was introduced from the forests of Valdivia in 1862. The racemes of red, globose flowers hanging from stalks that are also red are produced from the axils of the uppermost leaves and form a fine picture, where conditions are sufficiently mild, from July to frost. A shaded wall, protected from the bite of the north wind by fairly distant trees appears to be the best site. Leaf-mould should be added when planting and an acid or at least neutral soil is necessary. Propagation may be effected by layering or by cuttings of half-ripe short shoots placed under a bell-glass or polythene cover in July.

Feijoa Sellowiana is a difficult, curious, and spectacular member of the Myrtle family from South America. An evergreen with glossy green silvery-backed leaves growing up to 18 feet high, it does not get enough sun heat to flower freely in mild south-western gardens, and in places where winters are colder it seldom lives long enough to give a good account of itself. The solid, waxy, solitary flowers in July are, however, highly attractive. They are 1½ inches across and white with crimson centres and showy red protruding stamens. The Feijoa needs a really warm south wall and a moist, light acid soil, and even then it is a chancy proposition, but when it succeeds it is a magnificent sight.

Seeds from the edible fruits which are only produced in very hot summers may be sown in a greenhouse or cuttings of half-ripe shoots may be struck there in a propagating box in July.

Among the indispensables is *Spartium junceum* (A.G.M. 1923), the **Spanish Broom,** an absolutely first-class garden plant rewarding the industrious gardener with a dense bushy shrub continuously and spectacularly in flower from June to frost. On the other hand it reacts immediately to ill-considered positioning and neglect by making a gaunt, twisted leg from which straggle many dead, and a few live, rush-like stems only spasmodically bedecked with the large, honey-scented Aureolin Yellow (H.C.C. 3/1) pea-flowers whose standards are a full inch across. The Spanish Broom has been with us for several centuries, but well-grown specimens are not common, as its natural habit in the wild is to creep up among spiny "maquis" shrubs and then burst into a cloud of stems safely out of reach of the goats that usually infest its native regions along the shores and among the islands of the Mediterranean. Hence the clippers, or better, the razor blade must be constantly at work to induce branching and keep down the height, and the position must be sunny, fully exposed and, preferably, isolated. On hot, dry banks, in either limy or acid soils, this great Broom is particularly at home and its extraordinarily long season of bloom makes it a most valuable garden decorator as, if it is prevented from seeding, it outlasts the glorious but fleeting Genistas with an almost continuous late summer display. It is very easily grown from seeds sown in small pots, from which the young plants should immediately be planted out into their permanent positions. Once the tap-root has become frustrated and curled around the inside of the pot the plant cannot hold itself firmly in the ground and will blow over just when it appears to be reaching perfection.

Two varieties are recorded, but not seen by me—an old double form —var. *plenum*, still grown at Kew, and a whitish-yellow-flowered one— var. *ochroleucum*, which sounds much more attractive.

On the whole the Hydrangeas are the best associates as their long season of flower parallels that of the Broom. On a slightly limy soil the many white-flowered Hydrangeas complemented by the rich red varieties that show their best colour only under these circumstances, will make an interesting combination. On an acid soil the blues and whites will group superbly with the Aureolin Yellow of *S. junceum* and the Lemon Yellow of *Hypericum* 'Hidcote'. All that is lacking is a really good orange-flowered shrub to complete the picture, although Poly-antha Roses such as 'Paul Crampel' will be found to provide that telling spice to the composition in a reasonably satisfactory way.

The **Stewartias,** which rather remind one of deciduous Camellias, qualify very doubtfully for inclusion here as really effective shrubs. Making quite large trees, up to 30 feet high, they bear their fine white flowers in June and July, when they are welcome enough. Their presentation, however, is so singularly bad that they make no distant effect, and every plant photographer knows how difficult it is to find even one small branch bearing flowers well enough displayed to make a passable picture.

None the less, flowering trees are such an essential part of the shrub garden at all times that we must take a lenient view of the short-comings of any species kind enough to flower in late summer. We have to provide the shade which reduces the labour of weeding and improves the growth and beauty of the majority of the finer shrubs, and the trees also give us additional flower effects at a greater height than the shrubs can attain.

Stewartia koreana, a tree up to 50 feet high in its native Korea, flowers in late June or early July and is one of the more decorative species. The wild-rose-like white flowers, 2 or 3 inches across, appear singly or in pairs in the leaf axils, facing in all directions. Introduced to America by E. H. Wilson in 1918, it is a more beautiful tree than the more commonly seen *S. Pseudo-camellia*, and the foliage colours attractively in autumn. In habit it is stiffer and more upright than the others and when fully established flowers more freely. As a partly fastigiate (like a Lombardy Poplar) hardy tree of decorative flowering and autumn foliage effect this species might be considered suitable for seed propagation in quantity for street and park planting in the future.

S. Malacodendron is a shrubby American species introduced as long ago as the early part of the eighteenth century. It is not often seen, however, owing probably to its miffy temperament and awkwardly placed flowers. These are on the verge of being very beautiful, being about 3 inches across with somewhat thin white petals and a bold and arresting centre of black-purple stamens and anthers. Unfortunately the texture of the petals is so papery that they do not hold their form but flop about almost at once, and furthermore the flowers face all ways and so do not complement one another so as to achieve a pleasing group effect.

S. monadelpha, recently imported, is said to reach fifty feet in Southern Japan and to have small white flowers with violet anthers. It has been undamanged by frost, but is shy-flowering.

S. serrata is an uncommon Japanese species with small, cup-shaped white flowers, stained with red outside, about 2½ inches across, with an attractive centre of yellow anthers. They are very freely borne but in the usual awkward manner of the genus. It appears to be reasonably hardy, but is not commonly obtainable in nurseries. The autumn colouring of the leaves is often particularly vivid.

S. sinensis is a Chinese species with brightly coloured bark introduced by E. H. Wilson in 1900, making a small tree up to 38 feet high. The small white flowers are about 2 inches across and fragrant. The autumn colouring of the leaves is very good and this species is listed by several nurseries.

S. ovata (*S. pentagyna*) is a smaller species, up to 15 feet high, native of the southern United States and introduced over a hundred years ago. The flowers borne, in late June or early July, singly in the leaf-axils as usual, have creamy-white petals attractively waved, and conspicuous yellow anthers. Unfortunately the symmetry of the flowers is often spoiled by deformed petals and other irregularities.

S. ovata grandiflora is a finer form with purple stamens and larger

S

flowers, 4 inches across. It is now somewhat rare in commerce, which is to be regretted as this is about the finest of all the Stewartias.

S. Pseudo-camellia. This common Japanese species introduced towards the end of the nineteenth century by Messrs. Veitch of Exeter is rather disappointing. It grows easily enough, but makes but little show, so hidden are the flowers among the foliage and branches. They are white and slightly cupped, with a central boss of golden stamens. The autumn foliage sometimes colours quite attractively.

As regards the placing of the Stewartias they may be planted to provide, ultimately, the shade trees for beds of flowering shrubs such as Azaleas and Hydrangeas. It is, however, doubtful if they are sufficiently effective to take the place of the Cherries, Crabs, Peaches, Magnolias, Robinias, Laburnums, Cornus, Kœlreuterias and others that so admirably carry out the double function of providing both valuable shade and spectacularly decorative flower effects.

The cultivation required is the provision of a fertile acid soil enriched with leaf-mould and kept mulched with fallen leaves to prevent both drying out in summer and excessive frost penetration in winter.

Seeds are the best means of propagation, mature trees, especially those of *S. Pseudo-camellia*, ripening large crops of seed in favourable seasons. Cuttings can sometimes be struck of fairly well ripened wood taken in August and placed under a bell-glass.

Cotinus Coggygria is the new name of our old friend *Rhus Cotinus*, the **Venetian Sumac,** a member of the Cashew family from south Europe. In the "type" form, the handsome, spreading 12-foot bush has roundish green leaves and plumy masses of feathery purplish-crimson inflorescence that almost cover the plant in early July. In autumn the leaves turn a fine yellow. Winter pruning improves the foliage.

The variety *C. C.* var. *purpureus* (A.G.M. 1930) has beautiful foliage, opening a rich crimson and turning purple, and similar curious flowering to the "type".

C. C. var. *purpureus* "Nottcutts variety" is even deeper and more vivid in its autumn colouring. 'Royal Purple' is purpler but dull in autumn.

The "Smoke Plant", as it is also called, is one of those shrubs that flower better in a poor soil, either limy or acid. It may be increased by cuttings of half-ripe shoots placed beneath a bell-glass in July. The red-leaved varieties are among the most brilliant of foliage shrubs, but like all those with such colouring, some care has to be taken in their placing so that the unusual tone does not make too sudden a contrast with normal coloured leaves. Among other shrubs of unusual foliage colour, or in autumn, these Sumacs are superb.

Cotinus americanus (*Rhus cotinoides*) is a rare shrub of no floral beauty but of such flaming vividness of autumn leaf colour as to be almost unsurpassed in this respect. Like *Berberis Thunbergii* and *Acer* 'Osaka Suki' its solo display is so spectacular that all the surrounding leaf tints of autumn are shown up to advantage, reflecting its intensity in quieter tones.

An acid turf-loam and an open position seem to be necessary to get the best effect and a year or two must pass before a specimen will show its true quality. The leaf-colouring is varied as well as vivid: orange, scarlet, purple, yellow and green being often shown on one plant. Layers are probably the best method of increase but it is not a very rapid one.

One of the most lovely of white-flowered deciduous shrubs, *Hoheria glabrata* (*Plagianthus Lyalli* var. *glabrata* A.G.M. 1926) flowers in July. The name has been much argued over but a seldom mentioned but important point for the gardener is that there are two horticulturally distinct **Hoherias** in cultivation in this country. *H. glabrata* (the word means "nearly not hairy") forms a shapely shrub with bright, pale green, faintly lime-like leaves, and the white, honey-scented, Cherry-like flowers, 1½ inches across, are waxy yet translucent and cover the bush in a spectacularly beautiful manner provided that the soil is not very rich, in which case overleafiness may hide many of the flowers. The largest specimen that I knew was at Grayswood Hill, Haslemere, and I estimate its spread as being nearly 20 feet with a height of about 8 feet. I have seldom observed this species to set good seed and it flowers towards the end of July. It is rather tender.

Hoheria Lyalli is more treelike in habit, with duller, greyer green, more markedly serrated leaves and more numerous but slightly smaller and thinner-textured flowers. It is, I think, equally beautiful and flowers regularly about a fortnight before *H. glabrata* and usually sets good seed if the season is propitious. Seedlings grow very rapidly indeed and provide most effective shade trees growing among Rhododendrons which protect the trunks of the Hoherias from excessive winter frost and are in their turn benefited by the overhead canopy provided. Seedlings of *H. Lyalli*, although planted many years after a large group of *H. glabrata* grown from layers, have easily outstripped them in height, being over 10 feet tall. The fragrance appears to be similar, but, when young, the seedlings have a curious juvenile foliage much waved and serrated at the margins. It seems to be desirable to have both species, as the presence of the two kinds provides a succession of bloom. The finest form of *H. Lyalli* that I have seen (at Nymans, Handcross,

Sussex) is *H. L.* var. *grandiflora*, which has superbly presented medium-sized flowers with dark anthers. Mr. James Comber informed me that this lovely variety was sent out by Messrs. Le Chenault of Orleans, but, alas, it is now apparently extinct.

These Hoherias are among the few shrubs from the Southern Hemisphere which avoid the queer and incongruous appearance which so many of these have for eyes accustomed to the northern flora.

In very hard winters Hoherias are sometimes reported to be killed to ground-level, though *H. Lyallii* passed through the severe temperatures of January 1963 quite unharmed. The trunks of many specimens are partly protected by other shrubs and possibly this is a desirable precaution. Where this is not possible it is probably a good plan to prune young plants so as to induce the formation of several stems from the ground-level so that, should the trunks be killed, shoots will the more readily spring from the base again.

These Hoherias come from New Zealand where they are known as "Mountain Ribbonwood". They are first-class shrubs that should be grown in all gardens in the southern counties. They will grow in a limy soil and, under such circumstances, should be one of the first choices for a warm spot. Curiously enough they are quite rare in gardens, although many equally tender species such as Ceanothus and Escallonia are very commonly grown.

As regards cultivation, the usual precautions to prepare the site with humus and a good and well-worked but not over-rich soil are advisable in view of the fact that the shrub can be expected to produce huge crops of blossom for many years. Both species can easily be grown from seed and they soon make bushes of flowering size. Seed is more often set by *H. Lyalli* but a warm summer will usually enable *H. glabrata* to ripen a few pods. So strong and numerous are the seedlings that these fine shrubs will undoubtedly become available at very reasonable prices. Thus one may hope to see them ere long decorating hundreds of gardens in coastal and southern districts. To these, such beautiful July-flowering trees will be a great acquisition and be yet another reminder of the debt we owe to the good people of New Zealand.

Another species of Hoheria, *H. populnea lanceolata* (*H. sexstylosa*) is a small, willowy, white-flowered evergreen tree that, unfortunately, is insufficiently hardy for any but specially favoured south-west or coastal gardens. It was discovered in New Zealand in 1825 by a Mr. C. Fraser and inhabits both the north and south islands. Flowering in August, the thinner and more starry white flowers show up well against the rather dark green, lance-shaped shining leaves. Thus, where conditions allow, the gardener should take advantage of his good fortune and plant this lovely species. Mine is over 20 feet high.

The late-summer-flowering section of the **Ceanothus** family provides us with several attractive blue-flowered shrubs. They are, if anything, slightly less hardy than the Hydrangeas which easily provide superb blues in acid soils, so their chief value will be for warm gardens whose soil is too alkaline (limy) for these to give blue flowers. The best garden shrubs of the family are of very mixed hybrid origin containing the "blood" of the tender *C. cæruleus* (*C. mexicanus*) and of the hardier *C. americanus*. The late Alfred Rehder, whose "Manual of Cultivated Trees and Shrubs" is followed in the nomenclature used in this book named this section × *C. Delilianus*. Few Ceanothus are really quite up to the "reasonably hardy" standard, almost all having succumbed during severe winters which failed to kill plants which I have considered fully entitled to be placed in this category.

One of the toughest and best known is *Ceanothus Delilianus* 'Gloire de Versailles' (A.G.M. 1925). It is a somewhat rambling, 10-foot shrub, making strong soft shoots in all directions, with panicles of pale Lobelia Blue flowers from July onwards. Though partly evergreen in mild climates, it usually loses its foliage and looks very battered in winter. It is one of the hardiest of the section. 'Topaze' is similar but less vigorous, though brighter in colour.

C. D. 'Indigo' has flowers of a fine deep blue colour but is markedly less hardy, barely surviving in any but favoured gardens.

C. D. 'Henri Desfosse' is one of the brightest blues; 'Marie Simon' has pink flowers; 'Ceres', a strong grower, has pinkish-mauve flowers; 'Georges Simon' is one of the hardier sorts with pink flowers; 'Gloire de Plantières' is rather dwarf and has deep blue flowers.

There is also *C. D.* 'Charles de Trichet' (*C. Albertii*). This variety, introduced in 1878, is described as having flowers "of a clear, soft blue, most admirable planted near water in shade".† This recommendation no doubt applies to the mild Irish climate. In England autumn and spring frosts might be too severe in such a situation. At any rate this variety is proving hardier than most and is being again propagated. All Ceanothus were killed here in West Sussex in 1963.

C. Burkwoodii (*C. D.* 'Indigo' × *floribundus*) (Cory Cup 1930) is a hybrid between the summer-flowering and the spring-flowering sections and is one of the better sorts. It is a fast-growing shrub of good bushy habit with shining, oval, evergreen leaves about an inch long and $\frac{1}{2}$ inch wide. The flowers are a good bright blue for a Ceanothus, with cheerful yellow anthers, and are borne in panicles 1 or 2 inches long from July onwards. 'Autumnal Blue' is similar, with larger flower trusses of a slightly softer blue and is one of the hardiest of the race, often the only survivor of 1963.

† Sir Frederick Moore, R.H.S. Shrub Conference, 1938.

Although they will grow under limy conditions, these Ceanothus are best on a deep, warm, well-drained soil and in a hot, sunny position. Pruning, for this section, is done in late March to encourage the production of flowering shoots; it is really best restricted to the removal of weak or damaged branches. Cuttings can be rooted fairly easily, though often rather slowly, in the sand-frame.

The splendid family of the **Brooms** continue their summer-long service of providing us with a sequence of fine yellow-flowered shrubs highly decorative in the garden.

Genista æthnensis (A.G.M. 1923) is a 10- or 15-foot, thin-habited, almost leafless shrub ablaze with sprigs of little yellow pea-flowers, individually very similar to those of *G. cinerea*, in July. It comes from Sardinia, Sicily and the slopes of Mount Etna whence it takes its name. It is perfectly "reasonably hardy" in these islands in any sunny spot with free drainage, and is a shrub that should decorate every garden, as it will grow on almost all types of soils. The thin shade it provides is very helpful to many other shrubs and never too dense, while its roots do not rob the soil. It is long-lived, for the family, and very aged specimens nearly 20 feet high are sometimes seen in old gardens, precariously propped up, and, perhaps, sporting but one little tuffet of flowering growth on the topmost twigs. Sometimes it is grown by skilful cultivators as a naturally weeping standard tree when it is spectacularly beautiful, particularly as a lawn specimen. The decision as to whether it is to be allowed to grow naturally, as it wills, or to assume the standard-tree shape must be taken immediately it is planted. If the latter is required it must be kept to one stem and carefully tied up to a stake, all other growth being pinched off when young, until the required height is reached.

G. tinctoria. The "Dyers' Greenweed" is too coarse to be a first-class shrub, but it flowers late into autumn and is a useful temporary caretaker for odd corners. It is a native weed in many parts of this country. The most effective form is probably the variety *flore pleno* which forms a dense bushlet often only 8 inches or so in height, densely covered with bright yellow but shapeless little flowers in July and August. Unless a watchful eye is kept, it easily becomes a martyr to a purplish aphis which is such a persistent infestor that frequent sprayings are necessary. 'Elatior' is an ugly variety of tall growth.

Cytisus nigricans, a bushy shrub about 3 feet high, comes from Central and S.E. Europe and was introduced long ago, in 1730. The yellow flowers are borne in spire-like racemes in July and August. Like

some other members of this family it is one of the few flowering shrubs
that actually *require* pruning. This takes the form of removing the flower
spikes, when over, to save the plant's energies in seed production, and
also, to induce a compact and bushy habit, cutting back any straggling
shoots before growth commences in spring. *C. nigricans* is an attractive
and effective Broom very decorative in the late summer garden and
really more valuable that most of the various-coloured, spring-flowering
garden hybrids which flower at a time when there are so many other
colourful shrubs in bloom.

A sunny, well-drained position suits it and seeds are the best means of
increase. Like most other Brooms it requires to be protected from
rabbits.

Indigofera Gerardiana is a very late-leafing shrub, allied to the
Brooms, with arching slender shoots, attractive, lush, pinnate leaves
and racemes of small, purplish-pink pea-flowers in July. It is not really
very effective but has a possible use for screening some plant which
becomes dull and unattractive in late summer when its flowering is over.
A white variety, var. *alba*, is now seldom seen.

I. decora is a pretty dwarf species from China with pink and white
flowers freely borne in late summer. There is also a white form.

I. hebepetala, a Himalayan like *I. Gerardiana*, has crimson and rose-
coloured pea-flowers, much more pleasing in colour than those of that
species.

I. Potaninii is a somewhat hardier Western Chinese species with
racemes of pink flowers over a long period from June onwards. It is
rather loose in habit unless attended to.

Most of the Indigoferas require a sunny position. They can be
increased readily from seed and are not particular about soil.

An attractive complementary display to the charms of the Genistas,
and other pea-flowers, is provided by some of the latest flowering
Philadelphus. As a family they interbreed so readily that seedlings of
many varied types and flowering dates appear. The late-flowering ones
are worthy of care as they add fragrance to the garden in late summer
when scented flowers are scarce.

One of the finest late-flowering sorts is a form of *Philadelphus
Delavayi*, raised at Nymans, Handcross, Sussex.

P. incanus is a Chinese species flowering in later July. Both these are
more fully described with the other members of the family in the June
section on page 236.

A family whose flowering time centres about July is that of the **Abelias.**

Abelia floribunda is an evergreen shrub from the high mountains of Mexico, with small ovate leaves and rosy-purple jasmine-like flowers in June. It is slender in habit and usually about 4 feet high. It is rather tender and is most likely to succeed against a wall facing south.

A. uniflora, an evergreen Chinese species introduced by Robert Fortune, is the finest member of the family, being "reasonably hardy" and having blush-white flowers, orange tinted at the throat, an inch long and as wide at the mouth. It is free-flowering and from June onwards makes quite a fine display. Unfortunately it is very scarce.

A. grandiflora, an evergreen hybrid of the above, is much more commonly seen. The flowers, of similar colouring, are actually smaller, but it is a more vigorous plant. Its great quality is the persistence of its flowering from July right into autumn. Although attractive on close inspection, it makes no display for distant effect.

A. Schumannii is a deciduous species introduced from China by E. H. Wilson, with purplish-pink flowers abundantly produced singly from the leaf axils of the shoots over a long period. It is not very hardy but even if cut back in a hard winter, usually shoots up again in spring. But for the singularly poor colour of the flowers it would be a most attractive little thing.

Though not first class, the Abelias are useful for their late flowering and their ability to grow in limy soils. With the exception, perhaps, of *A. uniflora*, they make no great display. All like warm, well-drained positions and most can be increased by cuttings of half-ripened branchlets in the sand-frame.

In gardens favoured with neutral or acid soils a number of **Rhododendron hybrids,** having in their ancestry the August-flowering *R. auriculatum* "B" ***, the blazing scarlet-flowered but tender *R. Elliottii* and *R. eriogynum* "D" ****, the dwarf, deep plum-coloured *R. didymum* "B" ** or the large-leaved, hardy, fragrant lily-flowered *R. discolor* "B" ***, may play a fine part in late summer decoration.

Though hardy, *R. auriculatum* is too difficult a plant for the average garden. Even in our favoured wood the large and fragrant white flowers are often spoiled by adjacent scorched leaves, and plants in Cornish gardens seem little better. The hybrids are an improvement, it is true, but seldom sufficiently so to qualify them as really good garden plants according to our definition, but we hybridists are ever at work and no doubt ere long such plants will be available. Forerunners are 'Polar Bear' (*R. diaprepes* × *auriculatum*) with very large fragrant white flowers in August and 'Farall Target' with red flowers.

R. eriogynum "D" ****, a splendid species from open thickets in Yunnan, is unfortunately only hardy enough for very favourable gardens in the southern and western counties. It has superb, vivid red flowers in late June and 'Grand Finale', its hybrid with 'Doncaster' is one of the most effective late hardy sorts.

R. 'Redcap' (*eriogynum* × *didymum*), and R. 'Nutmeg' (*didymum* × *griersonianum*) which is hardier and more resistant to dry conditions, are among the best late Rhododendrons, having deep red flowers on bushy plants 2½ ft. high with 'Damozel' a long-lasting, taller growing red, and 'Romany Chal' "C" *** (R. 'Moser's Maroon' × *eriogynum*).

R. discolor "B" *** is a fine, ultra hardy, late-flowering Chinese species. The huge pale-coloured flowers are fragrant and beautiful but unfortunately of such a thin and papery texture that they are all too vulnerable to battering by wind.

R. 'Azor' has large rose-pink flowers and is a hybrid with R. *Griersonianum* to which that brilliant creature, as usual, has not, unfortunately, bequeathed its rich colouring.

'Flameheart' ('Azor' × *auriculatum*) with huge carmine flowers with a red centre is a noble sight in the woodland and quite hardy. I self-pollinated this and have now flowered a large number of the F2 generation. Few breeders have been privileged to see the results of their own F2 crosses, for thirty years' work is entailed. The target was a red-flowered hardy Rhododendron opening in late July, and this has been duly attained. Indeed, I am convinced that the future of Rhododendron breeding lies in the production of F2 generations of the best hybrids, for the genes regroup into all sorts of fascinating new combinations. The different seedlings varied in flowering time from late June to mid-October; in colour from pure white to pinks of all shades, to crimson and to scarlet, but leaf characters varied much less.

Propagation from cuttings has not succeeded so we must now wait for grafted plants to mature. 'Farall Target'—late July red is already registered.

R. Ungernii "A" **, is a hardy species from the Caucasus, but its little pinkish-white trusses, borne in July, are not very showy, being somewhat buried among the leaves.

Whilst we are considering this family we may mention two attractive Azaleas that also flower late.

R. viscosum "A" *** (A.G.M. 1937), is an American Azalea species growing up to about 6 feet high with sticky white, or pale purplish-pink, fragrant flowers in July. It was introduced here early in the eighteenth century. The clove-like fragrance is very agreeable but the flowers are too small and concealed to make it a first-class shrub.

R. arborescens "A" ** is greatly superior to the preceding, with larger white flowers, with purplish filaments, better presented and with a more pleasing and powerful scent. It comes from the Appalachian Mountains, where it grows up to 20 feet high by the banks of streams. It is rather scarce in commerce although *R. viscosum* is quite a common shrub. *R. arborescens* was introduced in 1818 but has never "taken on" for some reason. While it is not very showy it has a refinement of drawing that the previous species lacks and should adorn every lime-free garden because of its delicious heliotrope fragrance which per-fumes the summer evenings in the most delightful manner. It flowers a fortnight or so earlier than *R. viscosum*.

Some interesting varieties have been described in America. They sound highly attractive and desirable and are as follows:—

R. a. flavescens having pale yellow flowers with a deeper blotch on the upper lobe.

R. a. rubescens which has rose or purple flowers with some yellow on the upper lobe.

Both the above Azalea species are perfectly hardy and grow well in any lime-free soil which is reasonably moist. They may be propagated by seed or layers.

The Azalea 'Farall Flamingo', as registered, it now transpires, is a species coming true from seed. Flowering very freely, with rather small, soft orange flowers in late June or early July and having a fine autumn leaf colour of a deep beetroot hue, it is a very useful variety described on page 214.

R. amagianum is an interesting and rare Azalea from Mt. Amagi, Japan. It was first exhibited by Lord Aberconway on July 6, 1948 at the R.H.S. meeting. The flowers, in trusses of two or three only, though larger and more solid and fleshy, rather resemble those of a good form of *R. Kæmpferi*, but the foliage and habit are totally different. The leathery, round, but pointed leaves, in threes at the ends of the branch-lets, have a remarkable resemblance to those of *Gaultheria Shallon* in texture and surface veining, but they are not evergreen. Early July is the natural flowering time, I now find, and therefore this species is at once one of great interest. A flower of a soft and lovely orange pink at such a moment of the garden year, borne on a shrub of natural appearance would fill a gap that many would like filled.

There are other lovely late-flowering Azaleas, but unfortunately they are scarce and difficult to get.

R. cumberlandense from Kentucky, flowering after *R. calendulaceum*

(p. 214), has exquisite orange, scarlet or blood-red flowers and grows about 7 feet in height. It should be perfectly hardy in the British climate. 'Flamingo' is possibly a form of this.

R. prunifolium, from Georgia, U.S., is, even in its wild form, probably the finest of all the deciduous Azaleas. Flowering in the latter part of July with scarlet or orange-red flowers of unusually large size it is a strong and vigorous grower making a bush about 8 feet high. It is quite hardy, withstanding sub-zero temperatures without harm and is "easily and fairly quickly raised from seed".† Unfortunately not in commerce.

In addition, *Viburnum tomentosum* 'Rowallane' and *Leptospermum Rodwayanum*, mentioned in our June section, will also be in flower in July and the latter will last into August.

A type of Rose of considerable value as a flowering shrub is the Polyantha Pompon. In fact I am not sure that these are not the most indispensable of all for the shrub gardener who is determined to keep up the sequence of flower right through from spring to autumn. The typical pompon forms a small neat bush about eighteen inches high and wide, and quietly builds up a mass of buds while the Floribundas are wasting their strength by vainly tying to compete with the overwhelming flower-power of the late Azaleas in June. Thus, in July, the Pompons are ready to make a dramatic showing of vivid colour. There are so many good orange-scarlets that it is hard to decide between the merits of 'Golden Salmon Supérieure', 'Hurst Gem', 'Paul Crampel' or 'Gloire du Midi'. They should, of course, be properly interspersed with other shrubs, and they diversify the yellow of *Senecio laxifolius* of *Cytisus nigricans* very pleasantly. The pale salmon-flowered sorts, such as 'Coral Cluster' and 'Little Dorrit' also look well near them and cool the scarlets charmingly. All other Roses of attractive warm flower colour inherit this from the lovely but Black-Spot ridden 'Austrian Copper'. These being branch-sports from a pink Rose, avoid this tainted ancestry.

In late summer the sequence of flowering trees continues, though the choice becomes rather more limited. Particularly welcome are the charms of *Koelreuteria paniculata*, the China Tree. This interesting Chinese and Japanese tree has never become common, although it was introduced in the eighteenth century, is reasonably hardy and produces deep yellow flowers well massed in July, when such rich colour

† "Deciduous Rhododendrons at Gladwyne, Pennsylvania", by Mrs. Norman Henry, *The Rhododendron Year-Book*, 1946, R.H.S.

is particularly welcome. Perhaps the reason for its neglect is that it needs warm sunny weather to appear at its best. The habit, when young, is rather gaunt and the pinnate (or ash-like) leaves are at first reddish-green. The pyramidal panicles of small yellow flowers are produced on the ends of the branches and are followed by bladder-like fruits, and the leaves colour early in autumn to a fine yellow. *K. paniculata* was named for Professor Koelreuter of Karlsrühe.

The China Tree is very well worth planting for its excellent contribution to late summer decoration and is of help in balancing the garden effects, so that spring does not have an excessive preponderance of colour. It might well be tried out as a street tree as it is quite hardy and though not very long-lived, grows well in towns, eventually making a compact tree about 30 feet high.

K. p. fastigiata is a narrow-columnar form.

K. p. apiculata was introduced in 1900 by E. H. Wilson from Szechwan and is a good hardy form with smaller and more numerous leaflets and flowers and fruits particularly freely when young. It is one of the most desirable trees for the garden and quite undeservedly neglected.

In hot summers *K. paniculata* sometimes sets seed which may be sown in pans in the frame and the resultant seedlings grown on. It may also be propagated by root cuttings but this is rather a complicated matter for the amateur. It is not particular as to soil but needs a warm, sunny position. It is sometimes attacked by borer beetles.

The genus **Veronica** is a large one containing an enormous number of rather tender species of which only a few members of the more woody section, now placed under **Hebe**, are of value as outdoor flowering shrubs for favourable gardens.

Hebe Traversii (*Veronica Traversii*). In my opinion, this is one of the finest of the family as an outdoor shrub, even in Cornwall where many of the more tender species flourish. There are a number of flowering shrubs that demand single specimen positions and *H. Traversii* is certainly one of these. In a bed, mixed up with other bushes, its curious extending method of growth makes it a shabby and lopsided mess just when it should be at its best. Isolated plants, on the other hand, often form noble rounded specimens 6 feet high and 8 feet across. The small evergreen leaves are almost hidden by the 2-inch long racemes, packed with the little white flowers with their purplish anthers, from July onwards. 'White Gem' is a hybrid of smaller and more compact growth.

H. cupressoides is another species hardy enough to be worth planting in warm seaside gardens. It has a curious cypress-like appearance, forming a slender bush about 4 feet high, with pale bluish-green, needle-like leaves and pale blue flowers in clusters from late June onwards. To preserve the attractively bushy, rounded habit, which is its chief charm, it should be given an open position on a sunny slope.

H. Hectori is a smaller, rather Juniper-like species of similar type with white or pink flowers in small heads rather sparsely produced.

H. pimeloides is a dwarf species making a nice dense little bush with spikes of purplish-blue flowers in late June, July and into August, and rounded, glaucous leaves. A variety, *glauco-cærulea*, is more vigorous and pronouncedly bluish, with darker purple flowers.

The three most effective flowering shrubs of the older bush "Veronicas" are very distinct. 'Blue Gem', a comely evergreen hybrid with blunt thick spikes of bright Veronica Violet flowers is, alas, too tender for any but gardens with good air drainage or situated close to the sea; 'Autumn Glory' is more sprawling unless clipped back after flowering; the leaves are smaller and darker, and so are the flowers. 'Violet Snow' is a *salicifolia* hybrid with big pale violet spikes about five inches long and an inch thick, that fade to white. It is the hardiest of all and perpetual flowering.

Of the new sorts, 'Fragrant Jewel' has deliciously scented blue flowers on a dense evergreen 4-foot bush; 'Great Orme' is more slender with vivid pure pink flowers; 'Carl Teschner' is a moleheap-sized evergreen with blue flowers.

Of the large-flowered half-hardy *speciosa* hybrids, so useful for warm coastal gardens, 'Alicia Amherst' with Oxford Blue flowers and empurpled foliage is one of the most effective.

A perfectly hardy foliage plant with silvery evergreen leaves is *H.* 'Pagei'. It forms a cushion six inches high and perhaps three feet across. The white flowers in spring are not remarkable. The origin of this plant is a mystery. (A.M. 1958.)

H. hulkeana is a big sprawling, rather tender species with spectacular panicles of innumerable small lilac flowers and serrated oval evergreen leaves.

H. macrantha has unusually large white flowers but a leggy habit.

The larger Hebes, as one should now call these shrubby Veronicas, will also grow on chalky soils and are thus particularly valuable for such districts along the coastline where, with Fuchsias, *Senecio laxifolius, Hydrangea maritima, Spartium junceum,* Rosemary, Escallonias, *Phlomis fruticosa, Abutilon vitifolium, coronilla glauca,* Olearias, Hoherias, Tamarisks and other maritime shrubs they revel in the moist and salty winds.

Half-ripe shoots will strike fairly readily if placed under a bell-glass or in the warm sand-frame in July. They sow themselves freely.

With some plants it is not easy to decide whether they should be considered as herbs or shrubs.

Romneya Coulteri the **Californian Bush Poppy** (A.G.M. 1929), is, in this country, almost herbaceous in habit, making soft shoots from the ground with divided green leaves, and the well-known, huge, golden-centred, fragrant, papery, white poppy-flowers are aglow from July onwards. It is a charming plant for the foot of a south wall with a deep rich soil in which the roots will wander and send up shoots as often as not on the far side of the wall.

R. trichocalyx is a closely related sort with blue-green leaves, a less finely formed but firmer flower and a slightly hardier constitution.

In place of the circlet of rich golden-yellow fluff from which a dark-based, slender cone emerges, *R. trichocalyx* has merely a pompon or button of stamens in the centre of the flower and the more separated petals are stiffer, lacking the crinkled perfection of *R. Coulteri*. Yet at a distance it is the more decorative shrub, for the firmer "drawing" of the flowers shows up most attractively, while those of *R. Coulteri* appear merely as a series of formless blobs. But, alas, instead of the delightful fruity scent, likened to the bouquet of a fine old Hock,† which charms us in *R. Coulteri*, *R. trichocalyx* can only offer us a rather nasty daisy-like smell.

For perfection we need both kinds perhaps, and, in the warmer gardens, a group planted against a dark evergreen background will present a particularly lovely sight when well established. The best form is the hybrid between the two. It makes a stouter and more compact bush with equally fine flowers rather better presented. The blue-green foliage, more closely massed, is also much more decorative. In warm gardens, particularly on limy soils, the Romneyas are most valuable for late summer display and they are not expensive to buy. Their habit is dashing, but untidy, and a position sheltered from strong winds and a little training, and even light staking of the young growths, is helpful to good deportment.

In the colder districts the plants should be cut to the ground in late autumn and have a thick mulch of braken placed over the roots.

The Romneyas do not object to a limy soil so long as it is well enriched and reasonably deep. Root cuttings with an "eye", taken from short pieces of surface roots, just buried in sandy soil and put in gentle heat will usually send up shoots and thus form new plants. It

†"Romneyas", by C. T. Musgrave, V.M.H., *R.H.S. Journal*, LXIV, Pt. 12, p. 353.

is not, however, an easy method for the amateur. Young plants must be carefully potted-on until set out in their permanent positions, as these Romneyas do not move safely, being very sensitive to any interference with their root-system.

It is possible, in a good warm summer, to get fertile seed if *R. Coulteri* is hand-pollinated with pollen from *R. trichocalyx* (*loc. cit.*). When ripe, the seeds should be sown, preferebly in thumb pots, as otherwise many plants die in pricking off.

A Holly-like evergreen South American shrub is *Desfontainia spinosa*, introduced by William Lobb for Messrs. Veitch of Exeter, where it first flowered in 1853. Its hardiness is really only sufficient for gardens in the coastal counties along the English Channel and the Irish Sea. The leaves are opposite instead of alternate, otherwise most would take the plant for a small Holly, but the 1½ inch long, tubular, red and yellow flowers are highly unusual. Unfortunately they are too narrow, being usually less than ½ inch across at the mouth, and they droop among the leaves so as to be rather poorly presented. Their best point is that they are borne in July when such rich colouring is not common. If grown in the shade the plant grows well enough but is rather shy-flowering; in full sun it is apt to be damaged by the sun shining on the frozen leaves in the mornings. On the west coast of Scotland very large and healthy plants are to be found and I am always surprised not to see well-grown specimens more commonly in Cornish gardens where one would expect this plant to make a fine display. In the average garden it is a disappointing shrub and I would only recommend it for the west coast.

D. spinosa requires an acid soil well enriched with leaf-mould, and above all, a moist atmosphere, and can be struck from cuttings in the sand-frame fairly easily. In warm years it sets seed and can then be propagated in this way also.

The shrubby St. John's Wort, or **Hypericum** genus provides several good species for the garden; the Lemon or Buttercup-yellow flowers are both gay and superbly shapely, and, furthermore, borne with remarkable freedom late in the season.

Among the most important is *Hypericum patulum*, yet the original Japanese form of this shrub is of no great account, being somewhat tender and short-lived. The following forms, however, are good garden shrubs:—

H. p. var. *Forrestii* (A.G.M. 1924) is a more or less evergreen shrub of good bushy habit about 4 or 5 feet high and as broad. From July or early August onwards, the Buttercup-yellow, saucer-shaped, five-petalled flowers, 2 inches across, appear, making a charming picture among the red-barked branchlets and bright green, tongue-shaped leaves. No shrub in my garden seeds itself as freely as this, old plants being soon surrounded by innumerable true seedlings. This useful quality enables us to use the plant freely as a "filler" but care should be taken to cut off the seed pods before their contents ripen or the good work may even be overdone. Some of the leaves colour superbly in autumn if the weather is favourable. *H. p. Forrestii* was collected by G. Forrest in the Lichiang Range in Yunnan.

H. p. var. *Henryi* is another superior form from China, introduced by Professor Augustine Henry at the close of the last century. The flowers are slightly smaller than those of the var. *Forrestii*.

H. p. 'Hidcote variety' is the finest of all the Hypericums that I have seen. Its habit is very bushy and compact; the unusually large flowers do not fade so quickly in the sun and are freely borne over a very long season. The orange stamens of the central tuft contrast pleasantly with the vivid fresh yellow of the petals. It sets no seed.

H. Hookerianum. This species was originally introduced from Assam by Thomas Lobb. On the whole it is a better garden shrub than the original type form of *H. patulum* but less effective than its variety *Forrestii*. It is said to be distinguishable by the fact that its branchlets are round in section while those of the latter are two-edged. *H. Hookerianum* is, however, thinner and more lanky in habit and the leaves are rounder, rather than tongue-shaped like those of *H. patulum* var. *Forrestii*.

H. Moserianum is a hybrid between *H. patulum* and *H. calycinum*. It only grows about 1 foot 6 inches tall and is unfortunately rather tender. The top growth is often killed back in winter but it usually shoots again in late spring. The flowers are large for the size of the plant and open one at a time from the usual cluster formation. It does not creep at the root like the following species.

H. calycinum, the " Rose of Sharon ", is a low shrub about a foot or 1 foot 6 inches high, very useful as a carpeter in rough places. It is hardly up to garden standards although the Lemon Yellow flowers are very large, being about 3 inches or more across with a conspicuous brush of stamens in the centre. It is quite hardy and grows well on chalky banks. It is easily increased from pieces of the creeping rootstock.

H. Leschenaultii is a Malayan and Javanese species less effective than *H. patulum* var. *Forrestii*. It gets badly cut back in winters that leave the latter species unhurt, and in the wet and sunless summers all too common in England, it often does not flower until September is well advanced. Even grown to perfection, as in 1949, it is a disappointing species except, perhaps, in a few very favourable localities.

H. 'Rowallane Hybrid', raised by Mr. Armytage Moore by crossing *H. Leschenaultii* and *H. Rogersii*, is a shrub reaching 5 or 6 feet with bowl-shaped Buttercup-yellow flowers (H.C.C. 5) 3 inches across. In my experience unless planted deep enough to keep the roots unfrozen and given a warm spot it grows weakly and starts to flower too late.

The shrubby Hypericums are very valuable in the late summer shrub garden in association with the blue Hydrangeas, thus providing a delightful blue and yellow effect. On limy soils they grow well in the more moist positions, with added leaf-mould.

Light shade and a well-drained position with a moist subsoil are preferred. They are often attacked by small grey insects which eat away the surface of the leaves, making the plants dirty looking and unthrifty. When this occurs the pocket dust-gun provides a convenient remedy. Some authorities recommend cutting back *H. p. Forrestii* nearly to the old wood in April but all such cutting interferes with the natural symmetry of the growth to suit its position. With me this species is of fine, dense, twiggy habit when old, and has gracefully arching sprays when young. I have not seen the need for the secateurs on any of the considerable number of plants grown, except to remove over-abundant seed pods.

These Hypericums are an easily propagated group, division and cuttings placed under a bell-glass offering ready means of increase.

Ceratostigma Willmottianum (A.G.M. 1928) is a slender little shrub found in China by E. H. Wilson in 1908 and the great Miss Willmott was the only person who raised plants from seeds he sent back. She thus, most deservedly, gave the plant its name. *C. Willmottianum* grows about 2 feet high with many thin stems from the base, terminating in a cluster of bright blue flowers in July in which only one or two are open at one time. The succession is therefore good but the distant effect rather weak. Its hardiness is just up to the "reasonably hardy" category. The summer growth usually dies down in winter and in early spring the plant often looks as though dead. A light scattering of bracken over the roots, however, preserves it and the little shrub has time to grow enough new wood to make its contribution in late summer.

C. plumbaginoides is a foot-high semi-shrubby plant with fine blue flowers very like those of the preceding but produced later in the season, lasting into October. The leaves then turn a bronzy red so that it is well worth having as an addition to the dwarf carpeting shrubs. It is

T   E.F.S.

hardy enough to make a fine showing in the open in north Lincolnshire
so can be more widely planted than the other.

Perowskia atriplicifolia, the Afghan Sage, qualifies doubtfully for
inclusion, but its fine hybrid 'Blue Spire' is certainly a very notable
improvement. The long upright silvery-white shoots are set with slender
branchlets bearing little whorls of the tiny, labiate, brilliant violet-blue
flowers. In certain lights and certain positions these can be very decorative but for most positions the habit of the shrub is almost too gawky
to be bearable. It is a sun-loving plant from the hot and arid parts of the
Himalayas, forming a large part of the almost invisible vegetation which
shimmers in the heat haze among the blazing rocks of the N.W. frontier
of India. Pruning to the base every spring is recommended but new
spindly shoots, 3 feet or more long, merely emerge and on these the
flowers appear in due course. Possibly incessant nipping might make a
more compact and comely shrub of it but the best course is probably
to plant it in a small group so that the evening sun illumines the slender
silvery spikes against a shadowed background.

It is not particular as to soil, growing even in limy soils, so long as it
gets the sun. Cuttings are reported to root under a bell-glass in July,
but I have had few successes by this method.

Easier to grow than most but less decorative in flower, *Polygonum
baldschuanicum* is a rampant climber really too obstreperous for the
small garden. Given an eyesore to cover as quickly as possible at all
costs, it has its uses. The feathery sprays of tiny white flowers backed by
bright green foliage are quite pleasing in August. It is not self-support-
ing, so requires wires, or a length of wire netting fixed to the wall, to
twine into or the whole thing may come adrift in a high wind. It is not
particular as to soil and may be propagated from cuttings taken with a
heel, the end being just trimmed smooth with a sharp blade before
insertion in sandy soil under a shaded bell-cloche in a warm spot.

In August, flowering trees continue to offer their sequence of flowers
and the **Catalpas** are particularly valuable at this time when much tree
foliage has begun to assume a dull tone.

Catalpa bignonoides is a beautiful late-flowering tree introduced in
1726 from the eastern United States. It has large leaves of a fresh
yellowish-green and Horse Chestnut-like panicles of white flowers,
striped inside with yellow and spotted with brownish-purple, in early

August. It is a very bushy-headed tree and withstands wind surprisingly well. There are also a number of oriental species and hybrids some of which are equally effective. The Catalpas will, no doubt, be grown more widely now that planters are beginning to take more interest in the later summer flowers.

C. b. aurea is a variety with rich yellow-green leaves making quite a striking mass of colour. It is notable for park plantings where copper Beeches, blue Cedars, Negundas, Silver Poplars and other trees of unusual leaf colourings are used for massive effects.

C. b. Koehnei has yellowish centres and yellow margins to the leaves.

C. b. nana is a dwarf, bushy form which very seldom flowers. Grafted standard-high it provides the mop shape which is thought desirable for certain formal situations.

C. b. pulverulenta, with white-spotted leaves and *C. b. variegata* with leaves blotched with yellowish-white are not particularly ornamental.

C. ovata, a Chinese species cultivated in Japan, forming a tree about 30 feet high with white, yellow-stained and pink-spotted smaller flowers is not commonly seen or offered by nurseries.

C. o. flavescens is described as having flowers suffused with yellow but even smaller than those of the "type".

C. hybrida (*C. Teasiana*) is an American-raised hybrid flowering in July and of great vigour in the hotter summers of the United States. In Britain it is reported to be less effective than *C. bignonoides*.

C. h. japonica, also thought to be a hybrid between the preceding species was introduced from Japan about 1886. The flower-head is more pyramidal in shape and the flowers are of a purer white than those of *C. ovata*, and dotted with violet. They are notable for being fragrant. This is a strong and quick-growing form, but unfortunately now scarce.

C. h. erubescens, another hybrid, has small but very numerous fragrant flowers of a more purplish cast, as is also the foliage. As described by Mr. F. G. Preston,† a tree 30 feet high in the University Botanic Gardens, Cambridge, is a conspicuous sight when in bloom in August.

C. speciosa, a southern United States species, is a fine timber tree in its native forests, sometimes 100 feet in height and the wood has extraordinary durability. The flowers are sparser but individually larger. It is not so well suited to our climate as *C. bignonoides*.

C. Fargesii is a western Chinese species with pale purplish-pink flowers spotted with brownish-red and stained with yellow.

† "The Gardeners' Chronicle", Jan. 15, 1949, p. 22.

C. F. Duclouxii is a particularly fine form described by Mr. J. S. L. Gilmour† as "up to 65 feet in height with pink-dotted, pale pink or white flowers with yellow-banded throats". The best clonal variety of this fine Catalpa is generally considered to be 'Borde Hill', with lilac-pink flowers in dense clusters.

C. Bungei is a bushy-habited small tree of 30 feet reported to be shy-flowering in this country.

The Catalpas are attractive trees for gardens where a tropical-looking atmosphere is sought. A garden, I think, should always look more fertile than the surrounding land; there should be something of the oasis about it. Such large-leaved species as these and the Bamboos, Mahonias, Fatsia, Yuccas, large-leaved Rhododendrons, etc. have a great effect in achieving this object.

The Catalpa is best as a lawn specimen tree; cramped up with other growth its natural symmetry is lost.

The species are not very particular as to soil but do best, like all trees, when this is enriched by the addition of a mulch of leaves or bracken.

With *C. bignonoides*, if the tree form is desired, young specimens require care in encouraging a definite leader by cutting back competitive shoots, otherwise this Catalpa grows as a large bush.

Seeds produce the best trees, but cuttings of the hybrids and special forms may be struck, if bottom-heat is available.

Though a member of a family mostly known as flowering trees, *Æsculus parviflora*, the "Dwarf Buckeye" is a deciduous, bushy shrub about 8 feet high, like a miniature white Horse Chestnut, flowering in July or August. It is hardy and vigorous and it is a pity that the beautiful red or yellow flower colour worn by some of the other Buckeyes is not present in this sturdy species.

It forms quite an attractive lawn specimen and like all the members of this family submits well to moving, responds quickly to good cultivation and has no rigid soil requirements.

Seeds, sown as soon as they fall, are the best means of increase but unfortunately they are only ripened in quite exceptional seasons. Rooted pieces may sometimes be detached and grown-on to form new plants.

Mere rarity is seldom a virtue but there are times when we seek a plant that is new and strange to our eyes. There are, curiously enough,

† *R.H.S. Journal,* LXII, Pt. 3, p. 139.

many old established occupants of our gardens that have, for one reason or another, never become widely known.

Wisteria japonica is an uncommon member of its family flowering in July and August, introduced in 1878 by Charles Maries for Messrs. Veitch of Exeter, that great nursery of the past to whom we owe so many fine trees and shrubs.

The flowers, a pale yellowish-white and in racemes up to a foot long, are individually rather small but so numerous as to make a charming effect when this climber is grown up some unimportant tree or suchlike support. Forming an attractive feature of a distinct type in the August garden landscape this Wisteria is worthy of more attention than it has received. It takes time to reach effective size but grows steadily and will finally envelop a small tree in a most remarkably picturesque manner.

Like the other members of the family a moist rich soil is preferred and it may be increased by layers. Scarce in commerce.

The greater convenience and clarity gained by splitting up unwieldy genera containing species of widely differing types has already been acclaimed in the Apple, Pear, Whitebeam and other families. The Spiræas also benefit. The fluffy-spired herbs are now Astilbes, only the typical Bridal Wreaths now remaining as Spiræas. Most flower earlier but some species retard their flowering until late summer.

Spiræa bullata is a pretty little dwarf shrub from Japan, compact and rounded and about 1 foot 6 inches high with rosy-pink flowers in dense corymbs in July. At that time it forms a dome of colour that is quite acceptable, providing a succession of flower with the evergreen Azaleas, Helianthemums, dwarf Brooms and Heaths that are so attractive for those low effects of flowery carpeting which it is one of the objects of this book to recommend.

S. densiflora is a hardy, 2-foot deciduous American shrublet with domed pink corymbs an inch or more across in late summer.

S. japonica, in its typical form is almost a weed, with its magenta-pink flowers and rank growth, coming up from self-sown seedlings in every likely spot. It is quite useful for rough places where its flower colour is not objected to.

S. Bumalda 'Anthony Waterer', a hybrid of the above, has brighter and deeper coloured flowers in July and a more dwarf and compact habit of growth, making a shrub of 3 or 4 feet each way. This is quite a useful thing for rough, unimproved soils.

These Spiræas will grow quite well in moderately limy soils, though more vigorously in acid soils. Where it is desired to keep the plants to a small space the shoots of the previous year may be cut back to the older wood in spring, but such pruning is to be avoided if possible. Bushes thus treated have an ugly, snaggy appearance that is markedly less attractive to the eye in winter than a bush of natural branching. With some kinds flowering is slightly improved, it is true, but it is at the expense of attractive and natural-looking form in the winter landscape. Cuttings root freely in the sand-box or under polythene in late summer.

Sorbaria Aitchisonii and *Holodiscus discolor*, formerly considered as Spiræas, may be taken together. They are tall, 10-foot, rather tropical-looking shrubs with feathery plumes of white flowers that make a short but impressive display in late July or early August. They are at their best on the flanks of some noble, semi-woodland glade, perhaps in the background of Hydrangea groups where their graceful arching habit may be well displayed. *H. discolor* is, I think, the more decorative of the two and may well be used in a corner of quite a small garden with advantage. The name change from the familiar Spiræa is to be welcomed as, from the gardener's viewpoint, these shrubs seemed to have little in common with the other members of that family.

Both shrubs are hardy and not particular as to soil. They may be increased by seeds, though hybrid offspring may result, or by detaching rooted pieces. Some thinning out of the growths is desirable when these get too crowded to flower well.

Two valuable members of the great **Magnolia** family flower in the late summer.

Magnolia virginiana (*M. glauca*) the "Swamp Bay" of the south-eastern United States is a charming little tree usually about 12 to 15 feet high. The waxy-white flowers, about $2\frac{1}{2}$ inches across, are endowed with one of the most delicious of flower scents but last for only a few hours in perfection. The leaves are glaucous beneath, that is to say, covered with bluish-white bloom, and the whole appearance of the little tree is delicate and charming. It does best in a moist, rich soil, such as regular mulching soon provides, with its head in the sun to encourage freedom of flowering. It is now scarce.

M. grandiflora, the "Bull Bay", is the most beautiful of full-sized evergreen flowering trees in its native home in the southern United States, where, alas, it is all too often destroyed wholesale by the Negroes without a thought. I have seen specimens 100 feet in height in some of the Florida backwoods and, especially where the scarlet Bignonias decorate the trunks, the sight is one of the most splendid I have known. For garden purposes there are two forms that are so greatly superior to the others that care should be taken to secure them. One of these is the variety 'Exmouth' which has large, rather pale green, shiny leaves, foxy-red beneath, and grows very quickly, flowering when quite young and, indeed, at all times with remarkable freedom. In my old garden a plant of 'Exmouth' had grown to 20 feet and produced hundreds of flowers before a seedling form of the common type planted near had grown above 6 feet or ever produced a flower. 'Exmouth' also appears to be hardier. The other variety, *gloriosa* (or 'Goliath'), is also preferable to the common type; it has larger flowers and broader leaves rounded at the ends and green beneath and is a less upright grower. The south walls of all sizable mansions should, I think, be decorated by these superb and lovely evergreens. In the open, when grown as a tree, gales and snow often break down the branches and these may be braced with steel cables and eyebolts bolted through the trunk with advantage. As is now generally recognised, a small bolt passing completely through a limb, or the trunk, does much less damage to the tree than any form of band around the bark. The bark, and more particularly the cambium layer just beneath, are the actively living portions of the stems; the centre wood is more structural than vital.

As regards cultivation, a good turf-loam enriched with a leaf mulch grows these Magnolias as well as any soil that I know. Propagation is difficult for the amateur, and even layering *M. grandiflora* is by no means always quickly accomplished. Well-damped, half-rotted Pine sawdust is said to tempt rootage better than anything else. Increase is always worth trying with such an expensive subject and particular care should be taken to bend the young branch up *abruptly* and to fix the base of the bend very firmly in position.

The **Tamarisk** family are mostly thin-habited, maritime, or sand loving shrubs very valuable for exposed, sandy, seaside gardens.

Tamarix pentandra (*T. hispida œstivalis*) is one of the most beautiful. It is a deciduous species with racemes of pink flowers covering the ends of the current year's shoots in plumy masses. Sternly cut back each year it produces these the more freely and is a fine sight in August and September and the spicy scent, which has been compared to gingerbread, is not unattractive. The variety 'Rubra' is much superior.

T. tetrandra, the spring-flowering Tamarisk, *T. juniperina* with very decorative summer foliage, and *T. anglica* the evergreen English Tamarisk that flowers in late summer are all worth growing, close to the sea.

They are easily propagated from cuttings put in the ground in early winter, as for Roses. By the sea the natural, sandy, salty soil suits them perfectly but inland they will be found to require a good moist loam.

Like the Camellias, the **Hydrangeas** have for long borne a largely undeserved reputation for tenderness owing to misunderstandings as to their positioning, pruning and cultivation. In general it may be said that in the British Isles it is only cold gardens that are situated in frost-holes or low-lying situations subject to frequent severe spring and autumn frosts, that cannot grow the more suitable varieties quite successfully out of doors.

Like the Rose and the Tree Peony, the Hydrangea is over-sanguine and starts making growth too early and continues too late in the season for safety in low-lying places. When travelling through the countryside of Britain the observer will note superb plants in the cottage gardens on all the hills and few or none in the closed valley bottoms where the cold airs collect in late spring or early autumn. Even in such places as these, however, certain varieties and species of the Hydrangeas can often be grown quite successfully provided that they are planted in full sun and exposure with a thick mulch of bracken kept over the roots in winter and that they are carefully pruned in spring and have controlled liquid feeding in early summer.

A bar to their planting by gardeners has been the misconception that there is only one variety, called "the common Hydrangea", which is of service only as an indoor pot-plant. There is, of course, no such thing; one might as well call any ubiquitous garden Rose variety "the common Rose" when, of course, all these varieties are selected seedlings propagated as clones just as the garden Hydrangea varieties are. Many of these are "reasonably hardy" in the British Isles. The important point is to select those hybrid varieties which flower freely from side shoots if the terminal bud is winter-killed. The names of these are singularly important as they also vary widely in effectiveness and in hardiness as outdoor plants, see listings overleaf.

Hydrangea macrophylla (*H. hortensis*, *H. opuloides*, etc.) is a hybrid race containing the "blood" of both the maritime and the woodland species and may be divided into two separate sections—the Lacecaps, or flat-headed forms with an inflorescence similar to that of the wild prototypes, composed of a central area filled with small fertile flowers surrounded by an outer ring of large and showy sterile ray-flowers, and the Hortensias, which were mostly bred on the Continent and in which the flower-head is globose in form and composed almost entirely of the large sterile flowers.

Taking the Hortensias first, a Chinese garden form of *Hydrangea maritima* first reached this country when imported from China through the agency of the great Sir Joseph Banks in 1739. This original variety, of Hortensia type, is still to be found in old gardens. It is a large, coarse-growing plant for which the varietal name 'Joseph Banks' has been proposed.† Usually bearing very large, lumpish heads of pale purplish-pink flowers, it is actually one of the least attractive as a garden shrub, although very fine almost anywhere *close to the sea*. Inland it is much less effective than others as it does not flower from side shoots if the terminal bud is killed by frost.

Following on the importation of the Japanese hybrid Hortensia clones 'Otaksa' and *rosea*, from about 1907 onwards extensive breeding of the Hortensias took place in France and, to a slightly lesser extent, in Germany and Holland. In the course of time hundreds of varieties have been produced for use as pot plants. By chance some of these inherit hardiness, freedom of flower, resistance to sun and wind and vigour of constitution. Others, though perhaps good for pot work, are not suitable for outdoor growing.

For growing as open-air shrubs in the garden, certain varieties are pre-eminent; others fade or burn and are insufficiently hardy and free-flowering for outdoor life. But which to choose out of these depends largely upon whether the soil of the garden is alkaline or acid. In the first instance the flowers will be pink or red, in the latter, blue or purple. The reason for this is that limy conditions make the plant unable to assimilate the necessary aluminium and other mineral trace elements. It is the aluminium, not iron, as formerly believed,‡ that causes the crimson pigment in the sepals to turn blue. Consequently the gardener whose soil is limy will be well advised to grow the warm pinks, carmine-crimsons and whites rather than spend endless labour on feeding aluminium to obtain, with difficulty, a few blue flowers. On a neutral soil it is worth growing a few good blues carefully fed with extra aluminium.

If the soil is very limy, so as to make the plants chlorotic (yellow-leaved and unthrifty), feeding with ½oz Murphy Foliar Feed dissolved in a gallon of water will usually cure the trouble. The alkalinity of the soil also locks up the available natural iron so essential to the Hydrangea and indeed, though to a lesser degree, to other plants, so that even fruit trees have to be dosed with iron pills inserted in their trunks when grown on very limy soils. Sunlight usually enhances rather than fades the red flower-colouring.

† *The Hydrangeas*, by Michael Haworth-Booth, Constable & Co. (1950).
‡ R. C. Allen, *Contributions to the Boyce Thompson Institute*, Vol. XIII, pp. 221-242.

The following is a selection of Hortensias for limy soils:—

'Mme Mouillère' has white, serrated sepals and is early flowering. It is a very beautiful variety, particularly against a north wall.

'Heinrich Seidel' is a fine deep cherry red with serrated sepals and a moderate to tall grower. It is remarkably fine when well established but requires a favourable climate.

'Westfalen' is vivid Crimson, similar to 'Vulcain' but stronger in growth, with very shapely flowers. It sends up flowering shoots from the base like an herbaceous plant if well fed. It has the most intense colouring of all the Hydrangeas. (See illustration facing p. 304.) The best red. (A.M. 1958.)

'Preziosa' (A.M.). A new hybrid with evident *H. Thunbergii* characteristics. Flowers greenish white, turning red in sunlight, and reddish foliage. Extra hardy, but a weak grower outdoors with me.

'Violetta'. A medium-sized bush with neat red or violet flowers of unusually vivid colour.

'Pia'. A 6-inch dwarf bushlet with deep pink flowers; probably a branch sport.

'Harry's Red'. The best of the new continentals tested for outdoor planting.

Many Hortensia varieties are branch-sports and these sometimes revert to the original which is often completely different. Alas, the lovely dwarf orange-red 'Vulcain', for example, seems to have permanently reverted to a medium-sized shy-flowering variety with undistinguished deep pink flowers.

I have tried out new red-flowered varieties offered on the continent but none are as hardy and free-flowering outdoors as 'Westfalen'. But 'Westfalen' was quickly discarded by the trade because it is useless under glass owing to its susceptibility to botrytis. It needs a sunny, windy place to grow well.

The blue varieties that give a Cambridge blue in acid soils are best avoided in limy districts as their pale pinks are colder in tone, and less attractive than those mentioned.

On the other hand, on an acid soil of pH 5·50 or lower, the best Hortensias for the purpose will become blue- or violet-flowered naturally, in time. In any event they are easily assisted in such soils, to attain a beautiful pure colour by feeding with aluminium sulphate, a quarter ounce to a gallon of water or, though this is rather risky, by adding from one to seven pounds of the same to the surrounding soil in Autumn, depending upon the size of the plant from 5-inch pot size to that of a 3-foot established bush. As with those recommended for a limy soil, iron should be given in the same way if a plant shows yellowish foliage at any time. When they are grown blue-flowered, light shade helps to preserve the flowers.

The following are specially desirable Hortensia varieties for an acid soil.

'Vibraye' ('Générale Vicomtesse de Vibraye'). This hardy old variety is still valuable owing to its ability to flower from side-shoots, should the terminal bud be killed, and its very marked readiness to give a pure Spectrum Blue flower. It is a tall grower with rather slender shoots and mid-season flowering. The best blue.

'Mousseline'. This early variety has better formed, less crowded flowers and more shapely heads than the preceding but does not "blue" so readily. Once settled, it is very good indeed. It is a strong grower, with almost unspotted green stems and flowers both very early and very late. The autumn colouring is particularly good and it is notably hardy.

'Holstein' is a sky blue with serrated sepals and is rather a weak grower, flowering early and very freely.

'Hamburg' is a good deep blue in acid soil and of strong growth; in neutral soil it comes a bright rosy-pink and the flowers always last well turning a beautiful deep red in autumn. It requires shade and a favourable climate but the huge fringed flowers are superb.

'Maréchal Foch' is one of the best dark blues for distant effect and quite remarkably free-flowering.

'Goliath' is a tall grower with fairly small heads of large mauve-blue flowers at mid-season. It is remarkably fine near the sea.

'Domotoi' is an old Japanese variety with picturesque pink or blue-lilac, strangely doubled flowers. It is a vigorous but medium-sized plant making a good display late in the season. It is not a very ready bluer but has a quaint charm of its own.

'Gentian Dome' is a new deep blue that seems very promising, if a little shy. The flowers last well.

'Mme A. Riverain' is like 'Mousseline' but distinguishable by the coloured leaf stalks and less shapely flowers.

'Niedersachsen' is a splendid late pale blue, rather tender.

'Kluis Superba' is a splendid dark blue of compact free-flowering habit but fades in full sun.

'Europa' like 'Altona' but a less compact corymb more purely blue and with a paler green, shinier leaf.

'Altona' is a magnificent blue for those who like very large flower heads. It is a stout grower and one of the finest as a specimen plant in a tub or for exhibition, but not very hardy. The flowers last for months and turn scarlet in autumn. (A.M. 1957.)

'Ami Pasquier' is, in acid soil, one of the best rich purple-flowered
varieties, the colouring being exceptionally vivid. It is a moderate
grower, up to 3 feet high, and has the shapely individual flowers
characteristic of the best varieties. The leaves turn a fine red in
autumn.

'Amethyst'. This is the latest of all to flower, being at its best in
September; thus it is only suitable for the more frost-free gardens.
The colour is violet-blue and the doubled sepals are attractively
serrated. Growth is very stout and the leaves are of an unusually deep green.

'Westfalen' and 'Vulcain' have intense violet or deep blue flowers
in acid soils, depending on the degree of acidity. In three or
four years they build up into dense low bushes, only a foot or
so in height, ideal for the small garden. (See illustrations facing
pp. 241 and 304.)

As to the garden use of the Hortensias, I think that the rather artificial
appearance of the flower-heads makes them unsuitable for naturalistic
or woodland planting. They demand the more formal beds near the house
where they associate most delightfully with the H.T. Roses, the hardy
hybrid Rhododendrons and other "garden variety" types of flowers.
There are no more delightful furnishings, if *Camellia japonica* varieties
are also added for spring effect, for the entrance courtyard, front
garden, or porch. I give these descriptions because the principle of
decorating this important part of the garden effectively, right at the
start, is, in my view, equally essential for Castle, Manor or Cottage.

For woodland and naturalistic plantings, rather than the Hortensias,
we should plant the informal Lacecaps, described later, which resemble
the wild species in the form of their flowers and are perfect for this
purpose.

Few plants are more effective when grown in tubs than the Hortensias,
as the soil can be controlled exactly to suit the flower colouring required
of each variety. In a very acid-soiled district the gardener may grow
the red varieties in neutralised soil with the extra iron so easily fed to
the plants in such containers and in a limy district he may rejoice in the
purest blues and richest purples grown in specially prepared acid soil
watered only with soft rain water.

The hardiness of certain varieties of the Hortensias is much greater
than is generally supposed. In gardens where spring and autumn frosts
are rife they are sometimes killed nearly to the ground and though
the roots of established plants always survive and send up fresh shoots,
the flowering is spoiled for the earlier part of the season. Some varieties
of this hybrid race have tender species in their ancestry and are thus

unsatisfactory outdoors. The planting of tender varieties grown "soft" for use as pot plants has given the Hortensias a largely undeserved reputation for tenderness; established old plants of the hardier sorts have withstood the severest cold probable in these islands with impunity. They are ideal for house foundation planting.

There are fine bushes over a hundred years old in gardens in good positions in some parts of this country. An interesting example is that of Bingham's Melcombe, Dorset, where an old picture by Joseph Nash drawn over a century ago showed a number of strong Hydrangea bushes in front of the house. A *Country Life* photograph taken recently showed them to be still there and in superb health, and the late owner, Lady Grogan, wrote to me and confirmed that they were the original plants.

As regards cultivation, the Hortensia enjoys most an acid turf-loam —about pH 5·50—fairly rich in humus and having plenty of moisture such as a stony clay subsoil often provides. In short, any soil that suits Rhododendrons should suit blue Hydrangeas. Rainwater is deficient in mineral compared with soil-water. Thus when the leaves are continually wetted while the soil remains rather dry, chlorosis often occurs. This is curable by a good soaking of the soil with water enriched with Maxicrop Plus or by Foliar Feeding.

In soils of an acidity of pH 5·50 and more, the flowers of suitable kinds are naturally blue and the leaves a healthy deep green, as such conditions make the natural aluminium and iron freely available to plants. Lime locks up plant foods of this kind making them insoluble and unavailable to the plant and itself burns up the humus so that its valuable water-retaining qualities no longer come into play. By mulching and adding humus and feeding the Hortensia with Murphy Foliar Feed containing sulphate of iron, the plant is able to grow quite happily in fairly alkaline soil. The aluminium, on the other hand, has only slight beneficial effect, other than making the flowers blue by chemical action on the crimson pigment in the sepals, but such feeding is only readily feasible on neutral or acid soils. On limy soils it is best to go in for the red or white varieties.

As regards pruning, the object for outdoor shrubs is to obtain a large number of small heads well distributed rather than a few, top-heavy, monstrous blooms that will look out of proportion and possibly flop at the first heavy shower. To encourage this, some growers pinch out the top buds of strong shoots, in early spring. The two buds immediately below them plump up, and both flower in the same or the following year.

This type of pruning may be done but it is not essential. What is absolutely essential is the thinning out of over-numerous shoots when the old top growth has been destroyed by an unusually severe winter.

The young shoots which emerge in a dense sheaf must be thinned out until each has plenty of light and air all along its length. Otherwise the overcrowded growths do not ripen fully or flower and are sure to be killed the following winter. Dead wood must be removed promptly.

It is a mistake ever to cut down a Hydrangea bush. If the plant is too large for its position, move it, complete with a ball of soil like a Rhododendron. Then replant a variety of the correct size on the old site. The varieties range from 1 foot in height, like 'Vulcain', to 5 feet, like 'Vibraye' and there are all sizes in between.

When starting young plants it is best to let them grow for a couple of seasons before giving aluminium, as it tends to check growth if they are forced to produce blue flowers before they are well established.

The next section of the varieties of *H. macrophylla* is that of the **Lacecaps.** These are, in my opinion, even more beautiful as flowering shrubs whose natural grace makes them ideal subjects for informal planting and, owing to the form of the head, even as cut flowers for appraisal in the hand or the vase, but they do not give quite such solid masses of rich colour as are attainable with the Hortensias.

The flower-head follows the pattern of the wild species,† being a flat corymb composed of a central mass of the true fertile flowers, whose shape somewhat recalls those of the common yellow Stonecrop. They are surrounded by a ring of the large, sterile ray-flowers which are similar to those of which the Hortensia flower-head is composed but much larger in size. The shape of these ray-flowers is often enchanting, the sepals being exquisitely formed with wavy and serrated edges of delightful pattern.

The artist, who often turns sadly away from the somewhat shapeless corymbs of too carefully fattened exhibition Hortensias, finds in the Lacecaps a new flower-shape of classic perfection that has already, as I ventured to prophesy, taken its place in floral designs.

The difference in the flowering times and hardiness of the various Lacecaps is so marked that careful attention has to be given to this point, or planned effects will fail from lack of synchronisation. As this section, which comprises the finest of all the Hydrangeas for growing outdoors in the naturalistic shrub-garden, has been but little studied and recorded, I give fuller particulars below than are given for the better-known Hortensia types.

Most of the Hortensias are scentless, but the Lacecaps have the added charm of fragrance. The scent is not of the very highest quality, it is true—rather reminding one of that of the wild Meadow Sweet—

---

†All varieties and species of Hydrangea are described in a recent monograph by the writer, *The Hydrangeas* (Constable & Co. Ltd., 1950).

but it makes a pleasant contribution to the atmosphere of the late-summer garden, adding "body" to the tang of the Roses and the sweetness of the Spanish Brooms and late Azaleas.

What we lack are Lacecap varieties of the really vivid colours of such Hortensias as 'Westfalen', 'Ami Pasquier' and 'President Doumer'. Since the richest-coloured Lacecap, 'Bluewave', was the result of a chance shot in 1904, it should not be beyond the powers of future breeders to give us this alliance of lovely flower form and really rich colouring. All the following varieties may be grown in moderately limy soils with the special feeding necessary which is described in the Hortensia section.

H. m. ' Lanarth White '. (A.M. 1949.) This Hydrangea was first observed in the famous garden of Mr. Michael Williams of Lanarth, and there, to this day, are to be seen the most glorious great ancient bushes of this beautiful shrub. The numerous ray-flowers are a singularly pure white and have four or five somewhat irregular-sized, sharply pointed sepals, and a few sterile flowers are also sometimes produced among the bright blue central fertile flowers. The pointed leaves are usually rather a yellowish-green unless the plant is iron-fed. ' Lanarth White ' is one of the earliest of the Lacecaps to flower, being often inbloom when July begins. Its unusually irregular flower shape does not lend itself to cultivation for increased size and it is therefore best in an exposed sunny position in fairly poor soil where it will produce a larger number of smaller and shapelier flowers on a very dense and decorative bush about 2 feet high. It is one of the most free-flowering of all Hydrangeas.

H. m. Veitchii is the next to flower and is one of the finest of the white-flowered Lacecaps for a shady position. This hybrid forms a tall, rather slender-branched bush with broad, bullate and notably acuminate leaves. The large ray-flowers have usually three entire, or slightly notched, sepals of large size fairly regularly formed, but, like all Hydrangeas, it reacts so readily to rainfall and position that there is much variation.

H. m. Mariesii (A.G.M. 1938) is a fine Japanese variety and one of the oldest in cultivation, having been introduced from Japan by Charles Maries in 1880. The inflorescence is bunshaped and, in form, midway between that of the Hortensias and the Lacecaps. Sterile ray-flowers of various shapes and sizes appear mixed with the central fertile flowers and the larger ray-flowers of the outer ring have usually four entire, rounded sepals pale pink in colour—only bluish under very highly aluminous conditions. This variety responds well to good cultivation, such as a moist soil and generous feeding afford. In a neutral turf-loam the pink colouring, though pale, is warm and attractive and the shapely flowers are large and beautiful. In time it forms a graceful bush 6 feet high. The true variety is rather scarce.

H. m. 'Bluewave' is probably the commonest and most spectacular of the Lacecaps and, owing to its great hardiness, one of the most valuable of all Hydrangeas as an outdoor flowering shrub for gardens enjoying an acid soil. (A.M. 1956. F.C.C. 1965.)

This Hydrangea was bred by Messrs. V. Lemoine of Nancy and introduced in 1904. It is not described by E. H. Wilson or other authors so far as I can discover, but fortunately the plant can speak for itself, being greatly appreciated in the many gardens all over the country that it decorates so well.

'Bluewave' forms a large, strong, dense, permanent bush usually 5 or 6 feet high and even wider across, though by pruning it can be kept to 4 feet if absolutely necessary. Its hardiness is exceptional and, once well away, it rarely suffers winter damage but strong direct sunlight sometimes scorches the foliage. The flower-heads are flat and strongly supported on the stout branches. The ray-flowers, typically, are large and beautifully shaped with a delightful waved pattern of symmetrical serrations. The centre part is paler but the four sepals are a tint of Gentian Blue (H.C.C. 42/3) in acid conditions and some shade of pink or lilac depending exactly on the degree of alkalinity, in a neutral or limy soil. It does not "blue" as readily as many Hydrangeas, but once well fed and settled does not often throw odd pinkish flowers and better repays the trouble of aluminium feeding to give a pure blue than almost any other variety. It is a common shrub in old gardens, surviving neglect and the bitter winters of nearly half a century with ease. In full sun, in an unusually hot summer, the leaves scorch and the flowers bleach to a purplish tinge and thus the shade of a wall or distant trees and a little seasonal feeding with aluminium are needed for this glorious flowering shrub to show at its best. (See illustration facing p. 305.)

A curious feature is the very late flowering-time of this Hydrangea; it is rarely fully out until August is well on, when it associates superbly with the Ecuryphias, the Hypericums and also many of its own kindred whose phenomenally long flowering season keeps them still in bloom. It is common in Cornwall and the West and, indeed, all the southern counties of England.

H. m. 'Whitewave', (A.M. 1949) is a superb variety found in a number of old gardens. It is a sister seedling to 'Bluewave' and was brought out by Messrs. V. Lemoine in 1904. We received plants from Messrs. Smith of Guernsey before the war. It is a strong grower rather resembling 'Bluewave' but easily distinguished by the concave, spoon-shaped leaves and the huge, white or faintly flushed, ray-flowers which have the same delightfully waved edges.

Hydrangea macrophylla 'Westfalen'

Hydrangea macrophylla 'Veitchii'

Hydrangea macrophylla 'Bluewave'

Campsis Tagliabuana 'Mme. Galen'

It flowers about mid-season, with *Mariesii*, and is best in full sun in an open position in rich, well-mulched soil. It is one of the finest of all Hydrangeas, the inflorescence being about 8½ inches across with numerous beautifully shaped ray-flowers each often 3 inches across. It lasts in beauty for many weeks and is one of the most striking of white-flowered shrubs.

H. m. lilacina is an attractive hybrid variety. Messrs. V. Lemoine of Nancy also raised this interesting Hydrangea from naturally pollinated seed of *H. m. Mariesii*. This variety has a strong look of *H. serrata* in the matt, acuminate leaves and reddish shoots. A chocolate-brown line around the edge of the young leaves is characteristically very distinct. The ray-flowers are markedly serrated and rather thin in texture and small in proportion to the size of the plant. In a limy soil they are pink, ranging to quite a clear blue in highly acid soil.

H. m. 'Tricolor' is an old variety with brilliantly variegated foliage of three colours, sea-green, pale yellow and deep olive green; 'Quadricolor' is even brighter coloured, adding vivid yellow. Although somewhat prejudiced against such leaf-colourings I must admit that the fine qualities of this variety have made it one of my favourites, as the corymbs are very attractive and very freely borne over a remarkably long period and the healthful-looking and vigorous foliage is very decorative indeed. With aluminium feeding the flowers are a pale blue and the plant is then one of the handsomest of this artificial type, and looks particularly fine in a tub or large pot.

The Lacecaps have an advantage over most of the Hortensias in that wind and rain do not bow the flowers to the ground, but they remain erect and comely upon the bushes, indifferent to the blast. Both kinds associate particularly charmingly with yellow Roses, the Hortensias among the double garden sorts in the more formal parts, and the Lacecaps among the "singles" in more naturalistic plantings. The kitchen-garden appearance of the Rose-bed is thus, at a stroke, happily abolished and the flowery display of late summer rivals, and often indeed eclipses, thanks to safer weather, the glories of spring.

My earlier attempts to grow the Lacecap varieties of *H. macrophylla* in the wood-garden failed at first owing to the fact that insufficiently large individual beds for the specimens were made, too dry positions were selected and mineral feeding was not given to plants on steep slopes where such nutrients had been for centuries leached away from the leaf-mould and peat by heavy rains; also no slug poison was applied to check these destructive pests. When care is taken to avoid these mistakes the Lacecaps will be found to be amazingly effective in bringing late summer beauty to woodland glades glorified by Azaleas and Rhododendrons in spring and early summer.

U   E.F.S.

Few shrubs are more easily propagated than these Hydrangeas. Short July cuttings of side-shoots with four leaves left, root almost invariably in the simplest glass-covered sand-box or even in sandy soil against a north wall. Damping-off is the one danger in frames, and fungicidal sulphur dusts have enabled even this trouble to be obviated.

H. serrata is a Japanese hybrid race containing a preponderance of the "blood" of *H. acuminata, H. Thunbergii* and *H. japonica* which are woodland rather than maritime species. Unlike the varieties of *H. macrophylla,* the *serrata* varieties were mostly bred in Japan. The first crossings between the various woodland species were made centuries ago and I know of no new varieties that have been produced of recent years.

H. serrata varieties really require shade and a moist rich soil to look their best. They are, however, somewhat hardier than the varieties of *H. macrophylla,* and flower particularly freely from side-shoots. Slugs seldom eat their young shoots.

The parental species of the woodland hybrid race are attractive garden plants in themselves. Among these are the following:—

H. Thunbergii is a charming miniature Hydrangea usually 1 or 2 feet high, but attaining 3 feet under good conditions, with a ring of rounded, almost orbicular, three-sepalled ray-flowers, of quite a rich crimson-pink surrounding the central fertile flowers. The shoots are slender and crimson in colour when young, later turning brown, and the puckered, acuminate leaves are also reddish with a greyish bloom. It is commonly available in commerce.

H. acuminata is a very beautiful and distinct Hydrangea for a moist, shady situation on an acid soil, as the ray-flowers which have four large, entire, even-sized, ovate sepals, are very numerous and take on a brilliant blue colour under such conditions. The shrub is remarkably floriferous and of dense and bushy habit. It is rare in commerce, though stocks are now being built up. This species was first described by Von Siebold and is well figured in Siebold and Zuccarini's "Flora Japonica". According to several authorities it is common in Japanese gardens. The leaves are dull surfaced, slightly puckered, and often reddish or purplish when exposed to the sun. They end suddenly in a sharp point, being what is termed acuminate, though no more markedly than those of many of its kindred. Its wild habitat is Japan and Korea.

H. acuminata var. 'Bluebird'. This is a fine selected form with flowers of a slightly more vivid blue and larger size. Unlike *H. macrophylla,* all these woodland species require light shade except in the west, and the blue colouring of the flowers of this variety is particularly readily faded by the sun. (A.M. 1960.)

H. acuminata 'Diadem' (A.M. 1963). This superior clone was selected from a large number of seedlings. It forms a compact 2½-foot bush with purple-red foliage, if in sunlight, and delightful pale blue flowers that often open as early as June. Hardier than most Hydrangeas, it is a most attractive small shrub for the garden.

H. japonica. The wild form is absolutely hardy, a slender bush with narrow leaves of remarkable freedom of flower. Indeed every joint normally carries flowers very like those of 'Grayswood' but only a quarter of the size.

H. japonica var. *macrosepala.* This is an old Japanese variety of Von Siebold's species *H. japonica.* This lovely Hydrangea was beautifully figured by Regel in his "Gartenflora" (1866 15 t. 520) and I think we may assume that he got the plant from his friend Maximowicz, gardener to the Czar of Russia, who brought back a large consignment of Hydrangeas from Japan in 1864. Forming a 5-foot, densely twiggy bush with long slender deep green leaves, *macrosepala* flowers with amazing freedom in July. The corymbs have usually only four or five unusually large white ray-flowers with boldly serrated sepals and the fertile flowers are a blushed white. Thus the lacelike effect of the plant in full bloom is singularly beautiful; indeed even finer, in my opinion, than that of *Viburnum tomentosum Mariesii.*

The garden varieties of the *H. serrata* group are becoming increasingly popular, as they grow well in shady places where Rhododendrons provide the spring and early summer flowers. Succeeding them in bloom they give the wood-garden an all-summer display which adds greatly to its interest and beauty.

H. serrata var. *intermedia.* This clonal variety is of such an indestructible and easily propagated nature that it is very commonly seen. It is a coarse, strong-growing shrub over 6 feet high in acid soil and shade. The foliage is intermediate between that of *H. Thunbergii* and *H. japonica* and so are the flowers. The ray-flowers are three-sepalled and deeply and regularly serrated, usually hollowed in the centre. In neutral or alkaline soils the fertile central flowers are pink, in acid soils blue, but the ray-flowers open white and gradually turn crimson whatever the soil. Owing to its objectionable habit of twisting its few ray-flowers over to face the ground, its decorative value is not great.

H. s. var. *rosalba.* This clone bears some resemblance to the preceding, but is much superior as a garden shrub. The ray-flowers are usually four-sepalled and turn a brighter crimson and do not twist so soon; furthermore the inflorescence has usually from five to seven of the showy ray-flowers instead of the meagre three or four of *H. s. intermedia.* The foliage has a characteristically pale, bloomy look which makes it easily distinguishable even out of flower. It is common in commerce, but the preceding variety is often mistakenly sent out instead.

H. s. var. 'Grayswood' is one of the finest of all the clonal varieties of *H. serrata* that I have seen. It forms a tall, slender-branched shrub 5 feet high or more. The leaves are at first markedly concave and matt, yellowish-green and reddish-brown and acuminate. The flowers are as beautiful as those of the Lacecap varieties of *H. macrophylla* and almost as large. I would place it absolutely in the front rank of first-class late-flowering shrubs for a shady position. The large ray-flowers are particularly numerous, there being usually seven or nine surrounding the inflorescence; they have four beautifully serrated sepals, the lower one being characteristically elongated which gives the flower a distinctive and singularly attractive shape. In colour they are at first white, then they gradually turn to an even brighter and more intense crimson than those of the variety *rosalba.* They last long in this condition and though they finally twist to face the ground the effect of the shrub is often highly decorative until hard frost comes, owing to the fact that the under-surface of the sterile flowers becomes brightly coloured by exposure to light. Thus, unlike most Hydrangea flowers, those of 'Grayswood' instead of fading, get more brilliant in colour as they age. (See illustration facing p. 257.) (A.M. 1948.)

H. serrata var. *stellata* (*H. s. prolifera*) is an extraordinary variety with attractive doubled flowers. It may turn up in some old garden but I am afraid that it is apparently extinct in this country. Indeed, all the plants in cultivation in Europe were propagated from one surviving plant brought home by Maximowicz. The foliage is rather similar to that of the variety *intermedia* though this form has not the remarkable vigour of that plant.

The garden value of the Japanese woodland species and hybrids is high. The finest forms, such as *H. s.* var. 'Grayswood', *H. japonica macrosepala* and *H. acuminata* 'Bluebird', are ideal late summer shrubs. A degree hardier than *H. macrophylla,* they grow with equal ease from cuttings and, preferably in rich acid soil and light shade, can be grown anywhere in these islands. If the terminal bud is killed by an unusually severe winter they will flower cheerfully enough from side shoots formed along the surviving stems.

Although, in favourable soils these Hydrangeas can make a plant almost as large as the average run of *H. macrophylla* varieties they are usually smaller and more slender-branched and can be kept to a height of 2 feet or so with pruning, if necessary.

A rich, deep, acid soil containing plenty of humus seems to suit this type of Hydrangea best and, though it will survive in full sun, the finest plants are always to be found enjoying the shade of distant tall trees. In Cornwall, on the other hand, I have seen superb plants growing in full exposure in cottage gardens, but the grey skies and frequent showers, together with the moist maritime atmosphere, make a different climate from the plant's point of view.

Unlike the Hortensias, with their typical "garden variety" look, the Hydrangeas of this section have the delicate refinement of wild species and are thus ideal to enliven, in late summer, the wilder woodland sections too often entirely monopolised by Rhododendrons. There is no reason why such spots should be flowerless from July onwards, except perhaps for the somewhat fugacious blossoming of *Rhododendron auriculatum*. Azalea 'Daimio', *Rosa Moyesii, Rhododendron amagianum, R. indicum macranthum, Genista virgata, G. cinerea, G. æthnensis, G. tinctoria, Hoheria glabrata* and *Cytisus nigricans* all help the continuity of flower; but the woodland Hydrangeas in their various forms are outstanding for this purpose and can "take over" the decoration of the wood-garden in late summer with surprising effectiveness.

There are a great number of other species of Hydrangea, but not many that are really sufficiently decorative to require mention in this work, devoted only to outstandingly effective garden plants available in this country.

Hydrangea Sargentiana, a tall grower with massive foliage, perhaps over-large and bold for the flowers, can hardly be considered as quite up to the decorative standard demanded by the small garden. Though quite pleasing in the shady woodland, it is outclassed in flower effect by the finer forms already mentioned, even in Cornwall. Shade is essential for it.

H. arborescens, an American species, has the merit of great hardiness to recommend it. In the variety *grandiflora* the flower-head is globose and almost entirely composed of sterile flowers, like that of the Hortensias, but the colour is only a yellowish-white and the habit is often so weak that the flowers flop over on to the ground. At Grayswood Hill colonies have practically died out whereas *H. macrophylla* and *H. serrata*, alongside, have made huge permanent bushes. With regular feeding and no pruning, however, the plant can be built up to form a stronger and more decorative shrub than those usually seen. Thus grown it is useful for cold gardens where *H. macrophylla* will not thrive, but it is curiously fastidious regarding soil conditions.

H. quercifolia, the Oak-leaved Hydrangea, comes from the S.E. United States and is a handsomer shrub, but owing to frost damage the white-flowered panicles are seldom sufficiently numerous for the framework, and thus it requires a favourable garden climate to show its true beauty. The autumn leaf tints are notable.

H. paniculata, a bone-hardy Japanese, Chinese and Saghalien Island species is best known in the old variety 'Grandiflora', with large, rather shapeless panicles of congested sterile flowers too heavy for their stalks, in August.

H. p. 'Floribunda', a Japanese garden variety is a far lovelier garden shrub bearing boldly erect shapelier panicles of mixed fertile and sterile flowers in late July. Unpruned it makes a handsome nine foot bush. (A.M. 1953.)

H. p. 'Praecox' is equally superior as a garden shrub. Opening its fragrant panicles of large creamy stars in early July in the greatest profusion on a shapely stalwart bush of eight feet, it complements red Roses in the most delightful way. (A.M. 1956, A.G.M. 1960.)

H. heteromalla, a Chinese species, is hardy and vigorous, making quite a large and sturdy bush about 8 feet high. The flat corymbs, 6 inches across, are composed of creamy white flowers. It is quite an attractive shrub for an odd corner, but not effective for so long a time as the garden sorts. In woodland it makes a pleasing small tree.

H. involucrata, a dwarf Japanese species with decorative white ray-flowers and blue fertile flowers, is one of the most attractive. It has a curious whorl of bracts at the base of the flower-head and is almost sub-shrubby in habit. It is just "reasonably hardy" but dies back somewhat in winter. It flowers very late, often not opening fully until August or even September. There is a valuable Japanese garden form with pink doubled flowers *H. i.* var. *hortensis*. This is hardier and has a stronger constitution besides being more effective. (A.M. 1956.)

H. strigosa, a Chinese species, has a superior form usually known as *H. aspera macrophylla*, but, according to Alfred Rehder, correctly named *H. strigosa macrophylla*. This has large leaves sometimes nearly a foot long and flat flower-heads 8 inches across of a pale purple. It forms a vigorous, upright shrub up to 8 feet high and the flowers remain decorative far into autumn. It is, I think more decorative than *H. Sargentiana*, and somewhat hardier, though often killed back to the ground in hard winters in all but the southern and coastal counties.

H. aspera is a closely allied species, not very hardy in its common Himalayan form; it has downy leaves and purplish ray-flowers. The upright habit of the flowering shoots distinguishes it from *H. villosa*.

H. villosa. This fine species, introduced by E. H. Wilson from Western Szechwan, China, in 1908 has superlative forms of special merit. The finest I have seen is a superb specimen 8 feet high and across in the late Sir Frederick Stern's famous garden on the chalk at Highdown, near Worthing. It grows admirably in this soil and, in spite of the limy conditions, its flowers are a beautiful pale violet-blue, and these are qualities of the very highest value. In mid-August the flat corymbs about 6 inches across and of charming form and excellent presentation covered the great bush with a lacy mantle of colour.

Another form in commerce here and also ascribed to this species has serrated edges to the sepals of the sterile flowers and a less compact inflorescence with small ancillary heads alongside the main corymbs. This is similar to that described by Mr. W. J. Bean as having first flowered at Kew in 1915.†

H. villosa is readily grown from seed and slightly different colour forms are found mostly with pale violet flowers. It is one of the finest of the species for general garden use, forming a fairly large shrub about 8 feet high, with deep sage-green leaves, golden and furry on the underside. It must have moist soil in the growing season.

The Hydrangeas of these hairy-leaved Asiatic types occur in scattered habitats over a vast range of country across China to the Himalayas and the sorting out of allied species and forms is a complicated business. Many species of great beauty and probably hardiness remain to be imported.‡ There is no doubt that when the best and hardiest forms are generally available, clonally propagated from cuttings, we shall have a very valuable addition to late-flowering shrubs capable of being grown in either limy- or acid-soiled gardens.

Most of the species need a moist soil and light shade, and can be propagated from half-ripe side shoots in the sand-box or under polythene in July. As with most Hydrangeas the critical time is the young plant's first winter and therefore it is best either to plant them from pots in early autumn so that they have time to get established before severe frosts come or to set them out in spring after frosts are over. Those who have a greenhouse may grow most of the species from seed. This is ripe about December and may be at once sown thinly in *well-firmed* sifted sand and leaf-mould, much in the manner described for Alpine Rhododendrons, p. 90.

But, in our sequence of flowering bushes, we have lingered too long in cool and bosky places. It is time to consider what may be afoot on sunbaked hillsides where the garden climate is the very opposite. In such spots the **Yuccas** are at home. They are an extraordinary genus of tropical-looking plants from the southern United States and central America. Why the Yuccas should be hardy it is not easy to understand,

---

† "Trees and Shrubs Hardy in the British Isles", Vol. III, p. 188.
‡ For a description of all the known species see *The Hydrangeas*, by Michael Haworth-Booth, Constable & Co. (1950).

but they are. To my eye they always appear out of place grouped near more typical plants, shrubs and trees of the northern hemisphere. On the other hand in courtyards near modern garden-houses or loggias where a rather tropical atmosphere is often highly pleasing or, again, on hot sandy slopes, where other southern plants affect the landscape, they are superb. They need, I think, as careful placing as the hardy Palm, the Canna, Phormium tenax or the Mahonias and Fatsia that, in association, so readily provide the sub-tropical décor fitting and enjoyable in certain places.

Yucca filamentosa, with low tufts of the pointed blade-like evergreen leaves and profuse panicles of loose yellowish-white flowers; *Y. glauca* of more formal outline, with narrow glaucous green leaves and erect spires of greenish-white flowers; *Y. gloriosa*, the most striking of all with huge erect panicles of superb, drooping, creamy-white flowers above the clusters of stiff, straight, spine-tipped leaves, are all effective for the purposes described, and, when matured, flower in July and August.

When the plants get too leggy, the tops can be cut off and rooted in a pot of sandy soil in the greenhouse. They can also be propagated from rhizomes detached from the plants and potted off in heat. A warm, light soil suits the Yuccas best but they are not very particular.

The **Buddleias** are a popular family owing largely to their vigorous and indestructible nature and the fact that their flowers attract butter-flies. Their habit of growth and general appearance when out of flower, and too often actually when in flower as well, is, however, hardly that required for year-round beauty in the garden landscape.

Buddleia Davidii (*B. variabilis*) (A.G.M. 1941), the common Buddleia, is too well known to need description. The purple flowers turn brown so readily that it is almost impossible to find a perfect spike unspoiled by such decay. The habit is coarse and the growth so naturally successive that the pruning-away of the older wood is desirable to ensure the larger spikes produced on the young stems. Thus age, instead of bringing picturesqueness of form, leads only to a more unnaturally disjointed framework, possessing neither the advantage of the permanent shrub nor the winter-disappearing herb.

In its favour it may be said that the common form of this Buddleia is virtually indestructible and propagates itself freely both by seed and trodden-in shoot. The hearts even of those who do not care for it in the garden are warmed by its cheerful colonisation of blitzed ruins and such-like waste places.

The variety 'Isle de France' is unusually vivid in colour and massive in spike and, of late, breeders have produced a number of other varieties which also excel in this respect. 'Royal Red' with foot-long Imperial Purple spikes, 'Fascinating' with even longer pink ones, Royal Purple, violet, and 'White Profusion', a pure white, are notable.

There are two interesting new dwarf forms of the excellent 'Royal Red'. Both have variegated foliage. 'Royal Red Variegated' is a fairly vigorous grower but sometimes reverts to the green-leaved form. 'Harlequin', a smaller and weaker plant, is more stable and is valuable for the small garden.

'Border Beauty' is a newcomer, a compact six-footer with slightly bluer purple flowers than 'Royal Red'.

B. globosa has, if anything, a more gaunt, coarse and ungainly habit than the previous species described. The flower-head is a panicle of eight or more ¾-inch, ball-shaped clusters of Tangerine Orange fragrant flowers. Unfortunately the shrub is so large that they are too small to be proportionately effective.

B. Weyeriana (*B. Davidii* var. *magnifica* × *globosa*) is an interesting hybrid with the ball-like flower clusters of *B. globosa*. In colour these are a combination, being yellowish-orange suffused with mauve. The brightest variety commonly obtainable is var. 'Golden Glow', 'Moonlight', with pale, creamy flowers with an orange eye, is another. Breeding continues and no doubt varieties with brighter coloured flowers will appear.

B. Fallowiana, from Yunnan, China, is a vigorous shrub of 6 feet or more with the leaves and young shoots partly covered with whitish fur and dense spikes of fragrant mauve flowers† in late summer. It is only hardy enough for favourably situated gardens. Hardier, bluer-flowered and more silvery-leaved is the splendid new 'Lochinch' for which a rosy future seems assured. The flower spikes do not brown prematurely.

There is a white-flowered form—var. *alba*—with orange centres to the flowers, which is more attractive than the mauve-flowered "type" and one of the finest of all the Buddleias.

Like the other members of its family *B. Fallowiana* is readily increased from July cuttings placed under a bell-glass or in the sand-box.

Nandina domestica is a curious Bamboo-like Chinese evergreen shrub of the Berberis family. It is much prized in Japanese gardens but is barely able to show its full beauties in any but the warmer parts of this country. The stems are erect and unbranched, reaching 6 feet or more in height. The much divided leaves are very decorative, being a foot or so in length and usually bright red when young and again, though often

† *R.H.S. Journal*, Vol. LXIV, Pt. 11, p. 544.

more purplish, in autumn and early winter. The flowers, in foot-long white plumes at the top of the bush in late summer, are not particularly decorative but the large panicles of red berries that follow them are vivid and well presented. Furthermore the "Heavenly Bamboo", as Reginald Farrer called it, is one of the precious band of shrubs giving us a really lasting leaf colour whose display carries on sometimes right up to Christmas, instead of leaving us with bare stems after only a few days of autumn colouring.

N. d. var. *atropurpurea* is a variety with bright purple leaves.

As regards soil, a moist and acid one is preferred and a sheltered position in full sun suits the Nandina, as I may call it, being the only species of its genus. In Japan it is usually grown in some courtyard near the house and indeed it looks best as a specimen in such a position rather than closely associated with other plants.

Propagation is easiest from seeds, cuttings being slow to root, or grow.

Fragrant evergreen flowering climbers are rare and we therefore especially value the **Trachelospermum** genus. They are allied to the Periwinkles and come from Japan and China.

Trachelospermum asiaticum (*T. divaricatum*) is a "reasonably hardy" species from Korea and Japan with leathery, ova leaves, an inch or so in length, and abundant pale orange, fragrant, inch-wide periwinkle-like flowers in slender, terminal cymes during July and August. A vigorous twiner, it will reach 15 feet or more and cover quite a large area. A fine specimen at Kew showed, according to W. J. Bean, no signs of injury from frost over a period of thirty years. This is a charming climber in a quiet way and its delightful fragrance is notable.

T. jasminoides, a Chinese species introduced by Robert Fortune in 1844, is less vigorous and good forms have larger and more pointed leaves and larger and more fragrant, pure white flowers. It has generally been found to be much less hardy than *T. asiaticum*.

A variegated form, *T. j.* var. *variegatum*, has the leaves blotched and bordered with creamy white in quite an attractive manner but it is very shy-flowering. Var. *Wilsonii* has narrower leaves which often turn crimson in autumn.

A form common in southern Europe, sometimes distinguished as var. *japonicum*, is hardier and more vigorous, with broader leaves which often turn to attractive crimson and bronze tints in winter.

T. jasminoides likes a warm wall and a light sandy and peaty soil. *T. asiaticum* is less particular and grows and flowers beautifully for many years in ordinary soil on a south wall in our Demonstration

Garden on the east slope of Black Down Hill, West Sussex. Increase may be made by July cuttings placed under polythene.

Passiflora cærulea the **"Passion Flower"** of Brazil really needs a warm wall in a mild district. The strange design of the large and handsome bluish, five-petalled and five-sepalled flowers is thought to have a religious significance—there is no question of the fruits having any amatory consequences. Orange-coloured and egg-shaped, they are rarely ripened here and, anyway, unless grown in a warmer climate, are too full of troublesome seeds. From these, however, young plants are very easily raised, but cuttings are equally effective. Perhaps more curious than really beautiful, the flowers open, as a rule, in small batches from June to September without ever making a real display. To get real freedom of flower a restricted root-run or a really poor soil is necessary and the growths require shortening back to half their length in early spring. With this treatment this old climber, which has been with us for well over two hundred years, will give a fairly good account of itself and may be expected to make quite a good showing in July. In mild winters the hand-like leaves are often evergreen and the strong tendrils readily attach themselves to any convenient support but, without a sunny wall behind, the flowers are seldom abundant, even when the other precautions mentioned are taken.

P. c. 'Constance Elliott' is a variety with white flowers.

The **Clethras** are a family of, mostly, rather dull shrubs with small white flowers in dense spikes late in summer. Far the most beautiful species, *Clethra arborea*, the Lily-of-the-Valley Tree, is an exquisite flowering evergreen but is, unfortunately, too tender for Britain proper, though it grows well enough in the Channel Islands, on the south coast of Ireland and even in a few favoured Cornish gardens.

Clethra Delavayi, a deciduous species from Yunnan, has dense racemes of downward-pointing white cups in July. It is the most attractive of the Chinese species, but needs a moist, acid soil with shelter from wind and a mild climate. It is said to reach 40 feet in height.

C. monostachya, also a deciduous Chinese species, was introduced by E. H. Wilson and has solitary spikes of fragrant flowers. This is a hardier plant, but grows to only about half the height of the preceding.

C. Fargesii, another Chinese species introduced by E. H. Wilson, has densely flowered, slender, 6-inch racemes in terminal clusters. It requires a mild climate and moist peaty soil.

The common hardy American species *C. alnifolia* has, in the best form, sometimes distinguished as var. *paniculata*, terminal panicles of small fragrant white flowers in August. It is an easily grown shrub in moist soil, reaching to about 8 feet high.

Clethra barbinervis is a Chinese and Japanese species with small white flowers in compact, downy panicles five inches or so in length. It is not quite as hardy as *C. alnifolia*, being caught sometimes by late spring frosts, but it is rather better looking.

The Clethras may be propagated by seeds, cuttings and layers. Their late flowering qualities are their best recommendation and they may play a useful part in woodland gardens in association with other shrubs that succeed the Rhododendrons in bloom. A soil free from excess lime, what is known as acid, is required. An acid soil may often be recognised by *Rhododendron ponticum* growing almost wild where it occurs. The presence of Heather or Heath is another certain guide.

Kadsura japonica is an uncommon evergreen twiner from Japan allied to the Magnolia family. The small, fleshy, solitary, cream-coloured flowers, in July, make no great display, but the leaves turn to rich red and purple tints in autumn and in favourable seasons this effect, which lasts well in favourable weather, is intensified by the addition of round clusters of scarlet fruits. In a courtyard, against a grey or whitewashed wall facing south, it can be quite attractive. The Kadsura prefers an acid soil enriched with leaf-mould and can be struck from cuttings placed under a bell-glass in July. There is a variety, var. *variegata*, with leaves broadly margined with white.

The Mutisias, a race of South American Gazania-flowered, climbing Daisies, are, like so many plants from that region, very exacting in their requirements and thus have a name for being tender and difficult. Even when cultural success is attained I am not at all sure that the result is really beautiful, even without taking into consideration the naturally untidy habit of the plants. Possibly this is just another example of a personal opinion that the flora from south of the equator very seldom looks right mingled with the northern flora. When one has ranged across the northern hemisphere, with eyes constantly alert for plants, the northern flora comes to form a harmonious picture in one's mind. The southerners seem to introduce a bizarre and jarring note that is slightly irritating. Be this as it may, I have come to the conclusion that the Mutisias are too miffy and demanding to repay the amount of attention required to keep them alive.

Mitraria coccinea. This Chilean evergreen has one-inch long mitre shaped flowers of the purest glowing scarlet in summer. It can cover a six-foot wide and high wall space or run up a tree, and roots freely around. Like most South Americans it needs acid soil and plenty of moisture. The common form is rather shy-flowering except when it climbs up a shrub into the sunlight, but a superior form collected in Chile and introduced to the famous gardens at Borde Hill, Haywards Heath, Sussex by Mr. Desmond Clarke seems to have the added merit of being hardier as well as being more floriferous. As it layers readily, cuttings should not be difficult. It is at its best in west coast gardens.

Aralia elata. This is a most unusual-looking but quite effective flowering tree, sometimes called the Angelica Tree. Covered with sharp thorns it has large Hemlock-like leaves and large umbels of small white flowers in panicles in late summer. It seems to be perfectly hardy, there being fine trees in the north midlands. It can reach 30 feet if suckers are cut off and it is carefully trained up into a tree.

Phormium tenax. A plant of high ornamental value is not often equally valuable for purely utilitarian reasons but the Phormium, besides being one of the most decorative of all foliage plants, with quite a handsome red flower, provides the gardener with excellent string of any required thickness and great strength, or even an effective tree-tie, down in the garden right where he wants it. It is in winter that foliage plants play their part and at that time the Phormium's sword-like 3-foot unbreakable leaves, alternating silvery green and olive green, stand out superbly gracefully in the garden landscape. Though a New Zealander, it survives any but very exceptional winters.

Pileostegia viburnoides is an evergreen climber that flowers very late, often in September, with milky white panicles of small long-stamened flowers that show up well against the dark green leafage. A self-clinger and quite hardy, it is surprising that it has not become commoner, especially as it strikes from cuttings. It has a wide range, being found in India, China and Formosa.

Mention of the cool greenhouse reminds me of that modern equivalent of the old Conservatory—the Sunroom. There, one of the most cherished autumnal performers is *Camellia sasanqua* 'Crimson King'. Growing in acid soil in a large pot, this slender evergreen is in flower from October to January with a continuous succession of its shapely red five-petalled flowers decorated with a nice central boss of rich yellow stamens. In my experience Sasanquas are not satisfactory outdoors even against a warm wall in Sussex, but the extra warmth of Sunroom conditions enables them to flower most delightfully.

Lapageria rosea is another beautiful late-flowering South American climber that is really just too tender and too vulnerable to slugs to be reliable outdoors. I flowered it well for some years, outside, on a north wall, in black woodsy soil; but unavoidable neglect regarding protection from slugs and the cold winters of the war period proved fatal. The heavy, solid, waxy, pink bell-flowers are very beautiful but usually open rather too late in such a position. In a cool greenhouse, or even an unheated greenhouse, it is much more satisfactory, for this evergreen twiner can be trained along the rafters so that the flowers hang down most decoratively.

Some love **Ivies** and others dislike them. For my part, I like Ivy on a strong tree such as an Oak. Everyone who has used his eyes carefully, and pondered the matter in an open-minded way, knows perfectly well that this climber does no harm whatsoever to such a host. Unlike the deadly Honeysuckle, it exerts no pressure whatsoever upon the trunk or limbs neither does it work its way outside the leafage of the Oak and so cut off its light, nor, even, does it compete with the deep roots of its host, benign and wholesome in death, as in life. I have in years past regaled my farm beasts, sharp-set in a hard winter, with its palatable foliage. I deplore the foolish who cut it down, preening themselves on a noble act, and I condemn utterly the false wiseacres who instruct the young to do the same, acting on a false premise. It is only in those very rare cases where an Ivy has found and run up a very young sapling that any harm is done. Of the innumerable fancy sorts I commend *Hedera Helix* var. *aureo-variegata* (*H. H.* var. *chrysophylla aurea variegata*) with large handsome leaves boldly blotched with gold.

In smoky towns where bare walls abound and few plants flourish, the Ivies provide pleasant greenery, so long as the dirt is frequently hosed off their leaves and they are occasionally rejuvenated by the addition of clean fresh soil. Almonds, Robinias, Catalpas, Cherries, Pyracanthas, Hydrangeas, Figs and *Magnolia Soulangeana* are also notable for surviving a smoky atmosphere with great fortitude. H.T. Roses of the varieties having shiny leaves are, by the way, notably more soot-resistant than the matt-leaved sort and should therefore be chosen in preference to others by the town gardener.

The **Eucryphias**, a southern-hemisphere family with exquisite, fragrant, four-petalled white flowers, bloom in August. They have, unfortunately, a grave defect from the garden point of view for, although few flowering trees are more beautiful when in flower, their display is sometimes short-lived. In addition, many of the hybrid seedling forms take many years to grow to flowering size. On the other hand many are beautiful, merely as evergreens, for favoured gardens.

Eucryphia glutinosa (A.G.M. 1935) is a beautiful little flowering tree, introduced from Chile by Messrs. Veitch in 1859. The largest specimen I know is about 15 feet high and much wider, as it has layered itself in many places where low branches have touched the ground. The branches are upright but pliant, bending over to the ground beneath the weight of the massed, 3-inch-wide, white, four-petalled flowers with their ample tassel of stamens whose form recalls those of *Hypericum calycinum*, the "Rose of Sharon". The divided rose-like leaves have almost an evergreen look and turn to vivid orange-red colourings in autumn and they hang on so long that this Eucryphia is one of the finest of all shrubs for early winter colours. The flowering time is early August, and for a day or two this Eucryphia is one of the most beautiful of white-flowered shrubs. All too soon the petals fall, or brown, and all is disarray. Grown from seed, a large proportion of the young plants will be found to have ugly little double flowers. They may often, but not always, be detected before flowering by their bushier habit. To grow *E. glutinosa* well, a rich acid soil is needed and, duly fed, mulched and attended to, the young trees grow fast and flower when about chest-high. In poor soils, unmulched and with meagre care, they are slow and loath to flower. Were it not for the extra boon of fine autumn and winter leaf tints I would almost hesitate to include this charming species among effective flowering trees and shrubs, so short-lived is the flower effect. During its splendour, however, it is of the first class and that moment is as fortunately timed as the autumn leaf display which outlasts all but that of the Evergreen Azaleas.

E. lucida is a Tasmanian tree up to 60 feet high in its native island. The exquisite almond-scented, white flowers, though much smaller, being but an inch across, are even more beautifully formed, and the red-tipped stamens filling the centre are beautifully drawn. It has a delicate charm of a high order and the small, divided, evergreen leaves and slender, strong, ascending branches make it decorative at all times. Layers sometimes flower at 6 feet high, but seedlings are often very slow to flower, in my experience. The flowers last well.

E. cordifolia, a stouter, even later-flowering Chilean evergreen tree of great beauty is, alas, too tender for any but warm coastal gardens or those sufficiently elevated to avoid untimely frost.

E. nymansensis, a hybrid (*E. glutinosa* × *cordifolia*) is probably the most effective, reasonably hardy member of the family. It forms, eventually, a sturdy tower perhaps 20 feet high covered in August with a profusion of lovely waxy, white, four-petalled flowers, honey-scented and always abuzz with bees. An awkward winter will destroy the evergreen leaves and spoil the flowering for the season but it makes up for these defects when all goes well. It is definitely a long-term investment, being very slow to flower, but a good one for a reasonably favourable place. (See illustration facing p. 321.)

Thanks to its parentage including the lime-tolerating *E. cordifolia*, it can even be grown on a chalky soil, but regular feeding is needed to keep it growing strongly under such conditions.

E. intermedia is a hybrid between *E. glutinosa* and *E. lucida*. In its best forms it is a delightful little tree, but seedlings are often a long time growing before they flower freely and the variety 'Rostrevor' is of this type. Particularly fine forms, flowering freely when young, have been bred at Grayswood Hill, Haslemere; they have not yet been named.

The Eucryphias practically require a garden free from excessive frosts owing to relative elevation, and they prefer an acid soil well enriched with humus. Seeds and layers are the easiest means of propagation. I have even obtained fine young plants by breaking low branches half through and then burying that point carefully in good turf-loam. Cuttings can also be struck beneath a bell-glass but are often rather slow to root.

In late summer bloom some of the most gorgeous of known climbers that will grow in our climate. They provide a soft rich scarlet flower-colouring of the utmost brilliance complementary to the splendid flowers of the later-opening pale blue-violet Clematis. Yet how seldom does one see the great Trumpet Vine of China, *Campsis grandiflora*, in even the most celebrated gardens. More often the ultra-hardy American species *C. radicans* may be found rioting on cottage walls, but the invaluable hybrid *C. Tagliabuana* is so rare that I know of but one mature specimen in this country.

The banal Ceanothus and the ubiquitous Firethorn or Escallonia are really no more hardy than these more naturally scandent wall adornments, the **Campsis, Tecomas,** or **Bignonias** (as they have been variously named) true climbers that will hold their places with but small attention once the early training and tying are accomplished.

Campsis grandiflora is a Chinese climber long cultivated in Japan. The twining stems are set with divided leaves and on the ends of the season's shoots in August the long open panicles of large orange-scarlet trumpets, 3 inches across at the mouth, are borne. On a sunny wall this most gorgeous of all climbers is

Clematis 'Lady Northcliffe'

Eucryphia nymansensis

Rose 'Réveil Dijonnais'

"reasonably hardy". Layers and hard-wood cuttings are possible methods of propagation but few nurseries have parent plants. Very late in starting growth outdoors, *C. grandiflora* is really better suited to conservatory or sun-room culture. Once grown and trained so as to fill the available space, the young growths may be spurred back to the old wood as is done with vines. *C. grandiflora* flowers when young so is an excellent investment for a sun-room. It is never over-rampant and always free-flowering by nature, although in a very cold, short and wet summer it may fail to open its flower buds in time outdoors.

C. radicans is an American species and, surviving the destruction of the forests, has even become a weed in that country "taking to fence-rails like a song-sparrow". It is hardier, but more rampant and with smaller, more tubular and much less vividly coloured trumpet-flowers. This climber was brought back to this country early in the seventeenth century and is absolutely hardy. Unlike *C. grandiflora*, *C. radicans* attaches itself by aerial roots quite efficiently when the support is a tree stump or cliff. On a house-wall wires or nails are desirable as well, or it may be wrecked by a storm, but it is really not good enough for such a position. On a tree in the wood-garden it is highly decorative.

C. r. prœcox is an early-flowering variety blooming in June.

C. r. flava has dull orange-red flowers.

C. r. speciosa is a shrubby form making annual shoots 2 feet long from the framework of old wood. The flowers are less vivid in colour than those of a good form of the "type".

C. Tagliabuana 'Mme Galen' (A.M. 1959) is a hybrid combining all the virtues of the two preceding species. The foliage is intermediate and the flowers, in shorter and more crowded panicles, are deeply-coloured but as vivid as those of *C. grandiflora* and almost as large. (See illustration facing p. 305.) This superb, perfectly hardy climber should be, I think, our first choice for a south wall, being capable of the most gorgeous effects. Unless spurred back like a Vine, it is not quite so free flowering as *C. grandiflora* when young. At the same time the flowers open earlier than those of *grandiflora* so that it is certain to be effective, even in a bad summer when the still unopened buds of that species are finally destroyed by September frosts. This most desirable hybrid is at last obtainable in this country, so we may look forward to seeing it decorating south walls in many parts of Britain in future.

C. T. Thunbergii is another hybrid variety with flowers having a shorter tube and the lobes turned back.

The origin of these hybrids is not known. There is a fascinating account† of how Mr. W. T. Smith, the curator of the Washington Botanic Gardens, noticed that both the American and the Chinese

† Bulletin, Arnold Arboretum, Series 4, Vol. I, p. 1.

species of Trumpet Vine were in flower at the same time on the walls of the buildings. Now the natural pollinators of these long-tubed flowers are the humming birds. Indeed, these flowers, like most berries too, owe their scarlet colouring to the fact that that hue is the one that most attracts birds; it is not attractive to bees. The humming birds were flying from one species of Campsis to the other, busily sipping the nectar provided and incidentally interchanging the pollen adhering to their burnished feathers. Mr. Smith, observing this, carefully saved the seeds, which produced evident hybrids of the two species. The origin of the hybrid race is not known, and it is to his sowings of these that we owe our knowledge of the hybridity of this race. They were named many years previously, in 1859, when Roberto de Visiani applied the term *Tagliabuana* in honour of two famous Italian gardeners—the brothers Tagliabue. The variety 'Mme Galen' is far the finest of these Campsis and provides a good example of the indubitable value of successful hybridisation. 'Mme Galen' combines the beauty of flower of *C. grandiflora* with the vigorous constitution and great hardiness of *C. radicans*. (A.M. 1959.)

Bignonia capreolata is another most beautiful species of Trumpet Vine. Like many of the finest of the American Azaleas, this glorious climber is, in its best *red-flowered* form (Lake Iamonia, Tallahassee, Florida), almost non-existent in this country.

There is a plant at Shrewsbury and a layer from it at Reading, but so far as I know the other plants in this country are all of an inferior form with ragged, dull yellow and brownish-red flowers. This Bignonia is one of the most lovely of all climbers, even out of flower, the lanceolate evergreen leaves, one above another, covering the ascending stems that form aerial roots like Ivy. In the best forms the gentian-shaped flowers are a rich, pure red, making quite a cloud of brilliant colour amid the tree tops of its native Florida forests. On a house-wall its deportment is admirable and two large plants on the south wall in my old garden were quite unharmed by the severe winters of the war period, though *Ceanothus Veitchii* and other plants of uncertain hardiness succumbed, alongside. (A.M. 1958.)

The Campsis and the Bignonia require a warm wall where they can get well roasted in summer and also a well-dug loamy soil to secure good, but not excessively soft, growth. The Campsis are best secured to a light wooden trellis fixed to the wall, but the Bignonia can attach itself to rough stone or brick, although it is safer to nail the wall and tie it in occasionally. For an attractive contrast one may grow nearby the huge blue Convolvulus flowers of the 'Morning Glory' (*Ipomœa cærulea*) or the wide violet stars of the great garden Clematis. All these are plants of the first class, repaying the care of the keen amateur in no uncertain manner. For propagation, layers are an easy method for the Bignonia. Cuttings of the Campsis of ripe short dormant shoots, taken in winter and carefully trimmed at the "heel" will root under a bell-glass, but even more readily with bottom heat in the propagating-house.

Tropæolum speciosum, the Flame Flower, is another vivid late-flowering climber. It is less woody, often disappearing almost to ground-level in winter, and, unlike the others mentioned above, is really best either on a shaded wall where it may scramble up another wall shrub, or in a bed of tall flowering shrubs among which it can climb at will. The rich green, hand-shaped leaves are always attractive and the delightful flower buds, poised and shaped like a flight of minnows, even more so, but the pure carmine flowers, of an exquisite crimped and tailed shape that is all their own, are unique. I have seen the Flame Flower doing wonders on a Yew hedge in the bleakest part of the Midlands, so no qualms need be felt at trying it anywhere.

A cool, leafy, shaded soil is advisable with good drainage and above all no hoeing, "digging over", or other destructive interference. To complete the intriguing personality of this fascinating plant it produces azure-blue peppercorns as seeds and from these, or pieces of the white root thongs, it may be propagated in well-shaded, woodsy soil. An unproved theory of mine is that the morale and vigour of a small emerging shoot of this plant is greatly helped by the immediate pro-vision of a tempting, twiggy support. The top of a cane of *Arundinaria nitida*, with its many slender branchlets, is just the thing for the purpose.

While the Campsis and Bignonia set aflame the hotter walls the Flame Flower may perform this service for the shadier ones. This charming little plant is also an essential late summer adornment for the Rhododendron groups and has often delighted me among the white-flowered Lacecap Hydrangeas.

Few members of the **Fuchsia** family qualify for our "reasonably hardy" category, although many of the large-flowered garden forms can be grown in warm gardens near the sea-coast or indeed any garden enjoying good katabatics (see p. 25) and well-drained soil.

There is a wide choice of such varieties suitable for outdoor culture and it is best to select those with the more boldly presented and vivid flowers. Many kinds recommended as hardy are more quaint than effective. On the other hand ' Margaret ', a splendid vigorous, erect variety with large red sepals and purple petals, 'Mme Cornelisen', an unusually hardy vivid red with a pure white skirt, 'Rose of Castile', violet and cream, and 'Mrs. Rundle' and 'Aurora Superba', with carmine and orange flowers, are good examples of the showier kinds. In a well-drained sandy soil, kept well mulched with a thick layer of dead leaves to protect the roots in winter, such plants have flourished outdoors for over a decade in many gardens, to my knowledge. For drooping over a retaining wall the all-red 'Marinka' is very effective if deeply planted, as all Fuchsias should be at the start.

Fuchsia magellanica var. *riccartonii* is an unusually hardy and free-growing, but less spectacular, member of the family, effective as an outdoor shrub in districts having too cold a soil for the large-flowered varieties. Making free, sturdy growth it is notably more decorative than the equally hardy *F. gracilis* which has more slender stems and less vivid and boldly presented flowers.

The intense Turkey Red of the buds and calyx lobes of the Fuchsias is a most welcome colour in the late summer shrub-garden. The Fuchsia is so readily struck from cuttings that it is one of the most convenient shrubs to use to fill up any vacant spaces in the beds, and we can seldom go wrong by using such late-flowers for this purpose. In hard winters the upper growth of even *riccartonii* is killed back, but the root system of most varieties almost always survives if given a forkful of litter or suchlike protection, and sends up a strong sheaf of flowering shoots that provide one of the brightest patches of colour in the following August. In favourably situated gardens *riccartonii* and *gracilis* often retain their permanent framework over winter but are then seldom so free-flowering as plants that have been cut back.

A warm position where the soil does not get too dry suits the Fuchsias best but they are not particular so long as the soil is not cold and ill-drained. Being easily propagated and inexpensive plants it is worth risking them outdoors in all gardens in the south and west. When planting, it is a good plan to place a shovelful of rotted bracken deep down below the roots. Such is the avidity of Fuschia roots for this material that they will seek it out and colonise it intensively at such a depth as to make their safety from winter frosts a certainty. For the same reason bracken is not a good surface mulch for Fuchsias as they then make yard-long surface roots which will be too much exposed to winter frost. A living Heath is really the best root protector.

The later-flowering **Heaths** are the most valuable members of their genus for the garden, to my mind, but the family weakness in colour unfortunately persists. Muddy and dull purplish-pinks are to be avoided at all costs, for not only are they unattractive in themselves but they spoil all the beautiful pure colours by their presence. But if one wishes to convert the untidiness born of unavoidable neglect into a picturesque and attractive natural wildness, the Heaths, particularly *E. cinerea,* will be found to achieve this in an almost magical manner if planted as informal edgings.

Erica cinerea, the **Scots Heath,** or "Bell Heather", is the most vividly coloured of the hardy species. The wild "type" has flowers of an intense Orchid Purple (H.C.C. 31/1) and in poor acid soil in an open position grows very quickly to an effective flowering size. The wiry stems, clothed with the short, evergreen, needle-like leaves, end in a raceme from 4 to 6 inches long clustered with the urn-shaped flowers, in groups of seven or eight on small branchlets. In my experience an acid soil is particularly necessary for this Heath and the poorer the better, as in a good loam it grows so rank and soft as to be much less decorative than when kept somewhat starved, when the shorter and firmer racemes remain upright and unharmed by any frost.

The best garden varieties have flowers of more attractive colourings than the "type" but are more expensive and often less vigorous in growth. The following is a selection:—

E. c. var. *coccinea* is a dwarf variety, only about 6 inches high, with vivid, deep-crimson flowers borne rather earlier in the season. It is probably the reddest of the crimsons.

E. c. atrorubens is a vigorous purplish-crimson-flowered variety.

E. c. atropurpurea has brighter purple flowers than the wild form.

E. c. 'Lady Skelton' is a glorious new red.

E. c. atrosanguinea ("Reuthe's variety") is similar to *E. c. coccinea* but stronger and later-flowering. "Smith's variety" is rather brighter in colour in the mass. Both are sadly scarce.

E. c. 'Frances' is more of a cerise red and an attractive variety of good habit.

E. c. 'Golden Hue' is valuable for its golden foliage, which, turning red in winter, enlivens the deeper tones of the other Heaths.

E. c. 'Golden Drop' has coppery foliage also turning red in winter and 'John Eason' has similar foliage to 'Golden Hue' and deep pink flowers.

E. c. 'Domino' is a fine white with black sepals and flower-stalks and is of dwarf habit.

E. c. alba has white flowers.

E. c. 'P. S. Patrick' is a strong grower with long spikes of vivid purple flowers over a long period. One of the finest varieties for garden decoration when interspersed with the "type" and other sorts.

E. c. lilacina has paler green leaves and spikes of lilac flowers.

E. c. 'C. D. Eason', one of the most attractive of the many pink-flowered varieties, has deep green foliage and a good habit. Others are *carnea*, 'C. G. Best', 'Eden Valley', 'Knap Hill', 'Rose Queen', 'Apple Blossom' and *rosea* (A.G.M. 1928).

E. c. pygmæa is a dwarf form with pink flowers; others, similar, are 'Startler' and 'Mrs. Dill'.

The Scots Heaths are among the most effective of all carpeters for lime-free soils, covering the ground with an attractive and labour-saving green and russet mat and enlivening the later summer garden with their massed flowers whose purplish tones harmonise quite well with the pure deep blues of certain Hydrangeas.

In their cultivation the labour of weeding is minimised and the decorative value of the Heaths is improved if the soil conditions are made rather extreme. The poorest and most acid and firm soil suits them well and does not give weeds much chance to become troublesome. Full exposure is desirable also to keep the plants compact and free-flowering. Pruning, which takes the form of shearing off flowered shoots in early spring, is very helpful and the product will be found a useful addition to the mulch around larger flowering shrubs.

These Heaths may be propagated by layers, scooping out a little hole in peaty, sandy soil and bending a shoot into it and out again so that an elbow-bend is formed, made as acute as possible without breaking the shoot. The abrupt bend checks the sap-flow, and roots are usually made quite quickly. For cuttings, bottom heat and a propagating house are really necessary for a good "take", but success is often achieved under bell-glasses when conditions happen to come right. The little side shoots, about an inch long, are pulled off with a "heel" and this is trimmed with a razor blade, then the lower leaves are carefully cut off so as not to tear the stem. Then the little cuttings are half buried in pots of peat and sand, particular care being taken to make the base of each quite firm with the dibber. Finally, the pots are stood in a trough of water until the earth is well saturated and then sunk to the brim in the soil and the bell-glass is firmly put over all with a piece of light hessian tied to the knob to keep off direct sunlight. These Heaths transplant quite easily providing that care is taken to preserve the fine roots within a ball of soil.

Erica vagans, the **Cornish Heath**, is another valuable species for the shrub gardener. It is a dense, bushy Heath of excellent habit and fine winter appearance and a good variety will have flowers of a pale Crimson tint (H.C.C. 22/3). Unfortunately, adjacent browned corollas infuse a muddy tone into the bush, so that we do not get the value of this beautiful clean "peach pink" for very long. The short blunt spikes carry whorls of rich green leaves below and the bush may attain a height of about 2½ feet and a spread of 4 feet.

E. v. 'Mrs. D. F. Maxwell' is one of the finest of all the Heaths, with flowers of a Crimson pink (H.C.C. 22/2).

E. v. 'Lyonesse' is a splendid white-flowered variety with glossy, rich green foliage and fine large spikes.

E. v. 'St. Keverne' (A.G.M. 1937) has rose-pink flowers.

E. v. nana is a dwarf with creamy-white flowers and chocolate anthers.

E. v. rubra has flowers of a crimson pink.

The Cornish Heath is, I find, assisted both in compactness and vigour by a little spreading out of the branches with a trowelful of tempting peaty soil added to hold them in position. A poor, but moist peaty, sandy soil and free drainage in an open position suits this species best and shearing back of straggling shoots and old flower heads helps the appearance of the bushes. Propagation may be effected as described for *E. cinerea*, but more moisture is needed for this species which cannot resist dry conditions so well as many others.

E. ciliaris, the **Dorset Heath,** has a more rambling habit with small greyish, oval leaves set closely in threes on the stems. The flowers, narrowly pitcher-shaped and also in threes, form short upright racemes on the ends of the shoots. The wild type has unpleasantly coloured purplish-pink (H.C.C. Cyclamen Purple 30/2) flowers but several of the varieties improve on this.

E. c. Maweana is a stronger grower with larger flowers, from Portugal.

E. c. 'Mrs. C. H. Gill' has purplish-crimson flowers and dark green foliage.

E. c. 'Stoborough' has large white globular flowers superior to the old white form *alba*.

The Dorset Heath will thrive in richer ground than most of the other species and can be similarly propagated.

The **Irish Heath** is a notably beautiful and easy-going species of dense and compact habit and having a remarkably long flowering season. It needs little attention beyond an occasional top-dressing with peat and cutting back the flower shoots in winter. Often opening in June, this Heath continues in flower almost until winter begins. *Dabœcia cantabrica*, (*D. polifolia*) (A.G.M. 1930), is a bold and handsome species about 2 feet high, with large, egg-shaped, Cyclamen Purple flowers borne in upright racemes over a long period.

D. c. alba is a white-flowered variety of great charm and vigour.

D. c. atropurpurea has more vividly coloured flowers than the "type".

D. c. Prægeræ is a remarkable form with crimson flowers that was found on Connemara Heath, hardy and vigorous but sprawling.

D. c. bicolor has mixed white, pink and purple flowers.

D. azorica is a closely allied species from the Azores. It has an attractive low, dense habit, forming a mound about 6 inches high with erect racemes and Fuchsia Purple flowers of similar shape to those of *D. cantabrica*. It is rather tender.

Erica Tetralix, the common Heath, is, in comparison, hardly sufficiently decorative in habit to be effective in the garden, and browned corollas spoil the small clusters of very pale purplish-pink flowers.

Erica terminalis, the **Corsican Heath,** is notable as one of the few late-summer-flowering species that will grow well in a limy soil. The form commonly obtainable has rather dull purplish pink flowers but, in the wild, I have seen what appear to be forms with purple, pale pink and vivid pink flowers which seem to be a definite improvement. If starved in an open situation this Heath remains comparatively dwarf and compact but if well fed it may go up to eight feet or more.

Calluna vulgaris, the **Heather,** is less vivid in colour than most of the Heaths, being only the palest tint of Petunia Purple (H.C.C. 32/3) and its little flowers are so much more widely spaced on the stems that its effect is less vivid at a distance than that of many Heaths of the same flower-colouring. On the other hand, it grows more vigorously than the Scots Heath and self-sown seedlings appear more freely. In sandy soils free from lime it is a useful "filler" between growing shrubs eventually needing the space, as single plants are so easily pulled up when no longer required. Some improved varieties are listed below.

C. v. 'H. E. Beale' (A.G.M. 1942) is a pale purplish-pink double-flowered form found in the New Forest. The variety 'County Wicklow' is similar, but prostrate. 'Peter Sparkes' is an improved 'H. E. Beale' with more and slightly brighter pink flowers.

C. v. 'J. H. Hamilton' is a pretty little Heather of dwarf growth, with pink, double flowers forming attractive little rosettes. (A.M. 1960.)

C. v. 'Camla' has double pink flowers on short, upright stems.

C. v. Serlei is a fine white-flowered form with a handsome habit and bright green foliage.

C. v. S. aurea has bright golden foliage all the year round and white flowers, one of the best.

C. v. Hammondii is a strong-growing white-flowered variety.

C. v. H. auræfolia has similar flowers but the young growths are golden-coloured.

C. v. H. rubrafolia has the new growth bright red and the flowers purple.

C. v. alba plena is a fine double-flowered white variety that originated in Germany; it is one of the finest of all the varieties of Heather. (A.M. 1960.)

C. v. 'August Beauty' has white flowers on drooping spikes.

C. v. Alportii has deep green foliage and dark, dull purplish-crimson flowers on a somewhat stiff and upright plant.

C. v. 'C. W. Nix' is similar but brighter in colour and later in flowering.

C. v. 'E. Hoare' is deeper still in colour than *Alportii*.

C. v. coccinea has flowers of a brighter crimson and pale greyish, downy foliage.

C. v. 'David Eason' is another crimson and has a more dwarf and spreading habit and blooms later.

C. v. 'Goldsworth Crimson' is a later-flowering variety with long spikes of deep crimson flowers.

C. v. 'Tib' is a variety with double, purplish-crimson flowers that was found in the Pentland hills. (A.M. 1960.)

C. v. alba aurea has golden foliage and white flowers.

C. v. aurea has golden foliage turning red in winter and pale purple flowers, like the wild type.

C. v. cuprea has coppery foliage turning red in winter.

C. v. 'Multicolor' and 'Prairie Fire' have scarlet late winter foliage growths that are very effective. The flowers are ordinary.

'Gold Haze' has vivid yellow foliage and white flowers.

'Orange Queen' has orange foliage and purple flowers.

'Golden Feather' is aptly named, turning orange in winter.

These coloured foliage varieties are most valuable in the lime-free garden, lighting up the Close Boskage plantings in both winter and spring in the most attractive manner. As the flowers are not wanted the bushes may be topiarised to form beautiful domes of colour.

C. v. 'Tom Thumb' is compact and fairly dwarf, with pink flowers.

C. v. 'Mrs. Ronald Gray' is a prostrate variety with reddish-purple flowers.

C. v. minima ('Smith's variety') is very minute, forming tiny cushions that turn red in winter.

C. v. 'Silver Queen' has silvery hairs on the foliage giving a grey effect.

These Heathers are of reasonably compact growth and, as late-flowering evergreens, have their value as labour-saving carpeters for peaty, sloping gardens. Although the flower-colouring is weak, it comes, at least, at a time when most shrubs are going over and turning their leaves to their autumnal tints rather than competing with more vivid flowers. Plenty of white is needed to relieve the sombre purplish-pinks and to lead up to the occasional splashes of yellow provided by some of the Legumes.

A poor, sandy soil, which must be free from lime, suits the Callunas best; on strong loams the plants soon become too rank and leggy.

Propagation of the named varieties may be effected by layering and the wild type may be grown from seed. Clipping off the old, flowered stems in early spring, before growth begins, improves compactness.

Some of the larger shrubs including the **Clerodendrons** defer their flowering until late in the season. *Clerodendron trichotomum* is a tall, rather coarse, Chinese shrub of the Verbena family, usually about 10 feet high with 6-inch-long, oval leaves and starry white, fragrant flowers about an inch across, with a red calyx. These are very freely borne and are followed by blue fruits. It is no more than just "reasonably hardy", the downy young shoots being often cut back by frost in late autumn. Blooming in August, this is a handsome shrub for large, warm gardens, especially if it can be viewed from higher ground, in colder places it is less effective. It will grow in a limy soil. Seeds and suckers enable it to be readily propagated.

C. t. Fargesii is rather similar, but the calyx is green instead of red and the fruits are a brighter blue. It is slightly hardier, but seldom quite so effective in bloom. It was introduced from China by Père Farges in 1898.

Both these Clerodendrons require an open, sunny but sheltered spot and free drainage. Mixed up in a "shrubbery" with other large shrubs they are not attractive but a specimen rising from a carpet of dwarf-growing, low shrubs makes quite a fine late summer picture.

Among the medium-sized shrubs flowering at this time is a beautiful **Caryopteris**, *C. clandonensis* (A.G.M. 1942). This hybrid, raised by Mr. A. Simmonds in his garden at Clandon near Guildford about 1931, is superior to its parents (*C. incana* and *C. mongholica*) as a garden shrub. The Aster Violet flowers, in trusses in the leaf axils of the outer ends of the shoots of the year, appear in late summer when it can provide a pleasing mass of soft colour. To attain this it should be pruned annually in spring, each shoot of the previous year's growth being cut back to two pairs of eyes. With this treatment the bush assumes a reasonably compact form, about 4 feet high. 'Ferndown' and 'Kew Blue' are new varieties slightly bluer in flower colour. Caryopteris should be struck from cuttings of the best forms which is quite an easy matter. Seedlings vary greatly and, though possibly an even finer form might turn up, they usually vary for the worse. A sunny position is desirable, but the plant seems to have no particular preference as to type of soil and is therefore of special value for alkaline districts.

Whilst the hybrids surpass *C. incana* (*C. Mastacanthus*) and *C. mongholica*, there is another species that is very well worth growing, particularly on limy soils where the Hydrangeas cannot provide late-summer blue. This is *C. tangutica*, discovered long before, but only introduced from Khansu, China, by Reginald Farrer in 1915.† It is of denser and more bushy habit than *C. mongholica* and is also hardier. The flowers open at the end of July covering the bush in a haze of violet-blue. The leaves are a more attractive, deeper green than other kinds and in cultivation *C. tangutica* will reach a height of 5 feet by 8 feet in diameter. Unfortunately it is now rather rare in nurseries.

Skimmia japonica. To call this an effective flowering shrub is rather stretching the point but the foliage is so attractive, with the fragrant white flowers and persistent vivid red berries in the winter, that the bush qualifies as a decorative object. Furthermore the Skimmias grow well under quite dense trees. The bushes are either male or female, so to get berries both sexes must be associated. The variety 'Rubella' with prettier and more fragrant flowers is a male and the allied Chinese species *S. Reevesiana* and its hybrid 'Foremanii' are bisexual but have not such vividly coloured fruits. Unless bees are kept the best displays of red berries are got by assisting pollination with a rabbit's tail tied on the end of a cane.

The Skimmias grow best in acid soil but are not very fastidious. They are very easily propagated from either seeds or cuttings and are particularly useful as ground cover under the larger tree Magnolias, where they protect the tender root systems of these trees from trampling and hoeing.

There are shrubs that are all-the-year-round decorative pieces of garden furniture. Others are frankly ugly in their winter dress of bare

† "The Plant Introductions of Reginald Farrer", by E. H. M. Cox, p. 33.

branches. When this characteristic is coupled with an unusually late-leafing habit we must insist on quite an outstanding flower display to compensate for these defects. Even then, we must plan the position of such a plant with extra care so that the long period of ugliness is not too obtrusive, yet the moment of glory is well displayed. William Robinson and other good judges have condemned the **Hibiscus** as making an insufficient return in flower for its seven months of drabness. Yet a big bush of a good variety in full bloom will demand recognition as one of the great flowering shrubs.

Hibiscus syriacus, the Bush Mallow, is a very old inhabitant of our gardens yet, although perfectly hardy, it is very rarely seen. The bush grows slowly to about 10 feet in height, with upright, twiggy branches and somewhat oak-like leaves. The flowers, Magenta in the wild form and shaped like those of the Mallow to whose family it belongs, are about 3 or 4 inches across, usually with a darker eye and an attractive column of yellow stamens in the centre.

There are many varieties and the following is a short selection of the best:—

H. s. *cælestis* has flowers of a violet blue with a darker eye.

H. s. 'Bluebird' has better blue flowers and more of them.

H. s. 'Red Heart' has huge white flowers with a red heart.

H. s. 'Hamabo' has blush-pink flowers with a large crimson blotch at the base and flowers rather late. It is one of the loveliest varieties and came from Japan.

H. s. 'Woodbridge' has vinous-red (H.C.C. Magenta 27/2) flowers very boldly displayed. The true variety has very large, wide-open flowers.

H. s. 'Rev. W. Smith' has pure paper-white flowers of good open shape.

H. s. *monstrosus* has white flowers with a dark eye.

H. s. *totus albus* has creamy-white flowers.

A Chinese sub-species *H. sino-syriacus* has broader leaves and is slightly less hardy but has rather larger flowers of less open shape and similar colours.

In a cold, wet autumn the Hibiscus drops many of its flower-buds unopened but in a warm September it can be highly decorative. At other times it is rather a bare and ugly bush so care should be taken not to give it too prominent a position.

This shrub seems to have no special preference as to soil but needs a warm, sunny wall to flower freely. Cuttings will often root under a bell-glass but the resulting plants are unusually slow to get going and though the usual grafted plants are by no means quick growers they are so much better than cuttings in this respect that they are preferable. The Hibiscus does not always transplant successfully, so care should be taken to get the bushes into their permanent positions at an early age.

Quite the opposite of the Hibiscus in its qualities is *Fatsia japonica* (*Aralia Sieboldii*). This noble evergreen shrub is best known as an indoor pot-plant but is really quite "reasonably hardy" outdoors in the southern counties. The huge, nine-lobed leaves are very handsome and in late autumn the panicles of ball-shaped heads of white flowers appear. It is a common inhabitant of Japanese gardens and is very decorative near formal masonry or wherever a somewhat bold and tropical evergreen effect is required. A plant of this member of the Ivy family reached 9 feet in height and became one of the most effective features of the terrace in my old garden. In spring the unfolding, hand-like, young leaves assume a charming attitude and are covered with a soft red fur on a silver ground. In courtyards, near loggias and arising from paved areas there are few better shrubs of architectural form and it has been undeservedly neglected for this purpose. The designer seeking plants of tropical character to give the desired atmosphere to the surroundings of a modern outdoor garden-room will find in this plant one of the answers to his quest.

Any good soil that is not excessively limy seems to suit the Fatsia, and, though it can be propagated from cuttings of half-ripe shoots under a cloche in a warm summer, this is somewhat chancy, and it is probably best to buy young plants in pots and put them out in spring after frosts are over. Pruning is not necessary but a stem may be cut out at ground-level before growth starts in spring if the plant gets too leggy. New shoots will then spring from the base and clothe it effectively. On the other hand it is singularly effective when grown in tree form with a single clean stem.

Another fine evergreen is *Mahonia lomariifolia*, a handsome new Mahonia from Yunnan, China, with huge spiny leaves divided into about thirty leaflets rather similar in character to *M. japonica* (see p. 46). The cluster of numerous short, upright, yellow flower-spikes opens in late October or November and thus one or other member of this family covers the season from early winter to spring. With its whorls of fierce tropical-looking leaves it is an impressive plant for a snug courtyard position where its appearance is more telling than when it is secluded in a woodland dell.

A new hybrid, 'Charity' is somewhat hardier and equally decorative but a position sheltered from the north-east is necessary to ensure its growing well. Any good deep soil, whether slightly limy or not, suits this Mahonia. Propagation is not easy for the amateur. In a favourable season seed may be ripened and this should be carefully sown, if possible in thumb pots plunged in a box of sand and peat mixture so that the risky business of transplanting these difficult movers may be made safer.

Another late flowerer that is almost too late is *M. Fortunei*. Even when a propitious warm autumn gives it every encouragement its October flowers have a rather thin unhappy look and its architecture lacks the bold design of that of 'Charity'.

The **Lespedezas,** leguminous, clover-like, Japanese and Chinese sub-shrubs with rosy-purple pea-flowers at the end of summer are hardly effective enough for general planting.

Lespedeza Thunbergii is much the best of them. Its growth is luxuriant and attractive or it would not be so highly valued in Japanese gardens; but it starts its growth so late that it is unsightly among the spring-flowering shrubs and a cool spell in early September will often spoil its display just as it begins. In a favourable season its pendulous branchlets terminate in large panicles of flower in impressive profusion.

Viburnum Tinus, the common **Laurustinus,** is an admirable winter flowerer beginning often in November and, wisely dodging the worst weather, it is often still in bloom in April. Its good qualities have, however, been its downfall for it has become so common that few bother to plant it when planning new groupings. It requires a sunny position to flower really freely, and, above all, to enable it to assume the pleasingly dense and rounded form proper to the bush.

V. T. var. *hirtum* is hairy and has larger leaves but is less hardy.

V. T. var. 'Eve Price' (A.M. 1961) has carmine-pink flowers.

V. T. var. *lucidum* is less compact in habit, if larger flowered, and, again, less hardy.

Cuttings may be rooted beneath a bell-glass from July shoots in the usual manner and this Viburnum is not particular as to soil.

Now, at the end of this period comes the unexpectedly beautiful moment when, though flowers are over, the colouring of the leaves gives the well-planned naturalistic shrub garden a new pattern in soft and rich tones, even more closely in harmony with the surrounding landscape than that which has gone before. The beauty of subtly contrasting forms and foliages, without the distracting flowers, shows up the more clearly and often surprises us with its loveliness. The dark blue-greens, pale yellowish-greens, sea-greens and black-greens of Rhododendron, Evergreen Azalea, Alpine Rhododendron, Camellia and Holly show up the bright almond-greens of Hydrangea foliage, contrasted with their autumn-reddened flowers, the red-greens of Roses and the silver-greens of Senecio and Santolina. The Brooms, solid cushions of velvet (thanks to the ever-busy shears!) complement the silvery yellow-green, plumy mounds of the Genistas or the stern, spiky architecture of the Mahonias.

Already the Japanese Maples are aflame to add that vivid red that every picture craves—like Turner's floating carrots in the storm. *Viburnum Mariesii*, Sargent's Cherry, *Berberis Thunbergii*, *Koelreuteria paniculata* and certain Hydrangeas give other early leaf colour effects that hint of more to follow. Their show is brief but bright and in the end it will be the turn of the evergreens to carry the garden all winter till the new leaves come again. If there are not enough of such plants to do so effectively, the remedy is simple; there are plenty awaiting our call, for these Islands have that essential characteristic of a great gardening country, they suit the beautiful broad-leaved flowering evergreens that are the backbone of all enduring beauty in the garden landscape and are denied to so many other places.

CHAPTER VII
AUTUMN AND WINTER

NOW that our long succession of flowers is finished let us examine the autumn and winter scene as it should appear in the garden laid out primarily for the sequence of early and late spring, midsummer and late-summer flower effects. Provided that the principle of giving preference to flowering shrubs that also offer year-round beauty has been adhered to, it will be found that a very satisfactory autumn and winter picture is achieved.

It will have been noted that evergreen flowering shrubs are the most strongly recommended for the main masses of the plantings. Furthermore, neatness and compactness of habit have been particularly insisted upon and species of a size small enough to be in the right scale for the smaller gardens of today have been especially commended. Without the evergreens, the garden landscape has no real winter composition and, equally regrettable, the autumn leaf colours are quite ineffective in the landscape. They require the contrast and background of vivid deep green to show their full beauty, apart from the fact that they must also have the shelter from wind that evergreens best provide if the display is to last for a reasonably long period.

Many deciduous shrubs that are first class in flower are also outstanding for autumn leaf colour and this quality has been duly mentioned in their description. In fact, I know only a very few species, among the shrubs whose sole merit is their autumn leaf colour, that can surpass them. In this short list I would place the following:—

Berberis Thunbergii, a lush and comely green in summer and always aflame with orange leafage and red berries in autumn, this easy-going species gives us a fine red bush that is highly decorative in the garden landscape for many weeks on end.

Cotinus americanus (*Rhus cotinoides*), planted in poorish soil in a sunny but wind-sheltered spot, this rare plant flames in autumn with the vividness of an Azalea in spring.

Acer 'Osaka Suki', this Japanese Maple, bred especially for the purpose, is unfailingly scarlet all over in autumn and the pattern of the leaves is a delight of which one never tires.

Betula pendula, the true Silver Birch, is a glory of white and gold that nò exotic that I have seen can surpass. It should be noted that the commoner downy Birch (*B. pubescens*) is not attractive, while the Silver is always beautiful.

These, I would say, should be added to the flowering kinds in the furnishing of the perfect garden. There are hosts of other autumn-colouring species that are often highly praised but I do not think that they really pay for themselves except in very extensive gardens.

If the composition were carried out with pure greens and autumnal foliages alone it would lack both subtlety and variety. The bronzes, silvers, red-tipped greens, blue-greens and grey-greens cannot be left out without serious loss. Fortunately many shrubs of great beauty of flower provide winter foliage of just these colourings. Few of the grey-greens are absolutely hardy but the effect of *Senecio laxifolius*, *Halimium ocymoides*, Santolina, etc. is so telling both in lighting up dark corners and in intensifying the brightness of sunny places that they are invaluable. The evergreen Azaleas are unique in providing bronze and red-tipped green foliage in winter but unfortunately they can only be grown in acid soils.

The semi-evergreens are of quite outstanding value in the early winter scene. They retain many brilliantly coloured leaves for as many months as the autumn-tinted deciduous sorts offer us days. Outstanding among these are *Eucryphia glutinosa*, Azalea 'Hinodegiri', Azalea 'Tyrian Rose', good forms of *Rhododendron Kæmpferi*, *Mahonia Aquifolium* and its fine variety *Moseri*, *Berberis Veitchii*, *Hypericum patulum Forrestii* and *Stranvæsia Davidiana*. In a different way, the Hydrangeas join this precious company by decorating the early winter garden with their persisting flower-heads, at first vividly tinted with green or red, later turning to a clear buff colour. By liberal use of plants of these kinds the gardener may be certain of surprisingly beautiful effects during the earlier part of winter.

Now as to form as distinct from colour. This is perhaps even more important and more exacting in its requirements. It is also more difficult to secure in perfection. The difficulties are twofold. We require, above all, neatness and a certain massive compactness, in scale with the size of our picture. Again, we require a certain homogeneity, or evenness in the texture of the plant material. It was, surely, a seeking after this quality that impelled our grandfathers to plant those great Yew hedges that so effectively dominated the composition of so many old gardens. But nowadays we like to grow a comparatively immense selection of different species almost all of which were denied to our forefathers. People of taste in other fields complain that all artistry in our gardens is swamped by mere horticulture. Yet these conflicting claims can be satisfactorily met by compromise and ingenuity, provided that we are sufficiently wholehearted in our determination to achieve all-summer bloom combined with winter landscape.

Of the berry-bearing shrubs there are few whose advantages outweigh their summer dullness. The following short list is selected from the many hundreds of kinds available:—

Cotoneaster frigida. This tree species has both superb and worthless forms; *Watereri*, 'St. Monica' and 'Cornubia' are fine varieties. Skilful pruning is often called for to grow a shapely and free-bearing tree.

C. Wardii, a graceful, spraying bush of good-natured vigour, is another outstanding member of the family.

C. Dammeri, a well-behaved little carpeter, is neat in habit and singularly free with its red fruits.

Ilex Aquifolium, the English Holly, in the form of a female tree of the wild species rather than one of the named varieties which seldom fruit so freely, cannot be excelled by any exotic.

Sorbus Esserteauiana, a Chinese Mountain Ash, with apparently indestructible scarlet berries, and a very vigorous constitution, is the most spectacular of its family.

Stranvæsia Davidiana, already mentioned for its retention of scarlet leaves for a long period, also excels by the freedom of its long-lasting red berries.

Pyracantha coccinea Lalandii, grown as an open-ground bush—not as a wall shrub whose flowering wood has often to be cut away—can hold its own against any competition in early winter. Later *P. atalantioides* follows with an even more vivid display lasting until spring comes.

Pernettya mucronata, a South American prickly evergreen of the Heath family with white, pink, purple or crimson berries in astounding profusion and apparently unpalatable to birds, is remarkably effective on acid soils so long as both sexes are present.

If a place can be found for these one may be certain of having included some of the finest species grown for their decorative fruits.

"Overcoat plants" whose flowers open in the bitter winter weather give me more pain than pleasure, but, for the enthusiast *Camellia Williamsii*, *Hamamelis mollis*, *Chimonanthus praecox*, *Erica Carnea* and the old yellow Jasmine are the most generally effective.

Thus, with the addition of only a few species of outstanding winter decorative value the shrub garden can delight us through the dead season until the spring flowers open again.

INDEX

341